Steam, STEEL & Statutes

TRUE TALES FROM COLORADO LEGAL HISTORY

A Compilation of Historical Perspectives Articles
from *The Colorado Lawyer*, 2002–2010

by

FRANK GIBBARD

and featuring

TOM I. ROMERO, II
JEFFREY P. KELSON
BILL C. BERGER
ROBERT M. LINZ
CLAIRE E. MUNGER

Steam, STEEL & Statutes
TRUE TALES FROM COLORADO LEGAL HISTORY

ISBN: 978-1-930993-78-5

Published by:
CONTINUING LEGAL EDUCATION IN COLORADO, INC.
1900 Grant Street, Suite 300
Denver, Colorado 80203-4301

Phone: (303) 860-0608
Fax: (303) 860-0624
Website: www.cobar.org/cle

Toll free: (888) 860-2531
E-mail: clebooks@cobar.org

Dawn M. McKnight, Esq.
Assistant Executive Director
Colorado Bar Association CLE

Darlene Johnson
Managing Editor
Colorado Bar Association CLE

Lisa Travis Fischer, J.D.
Acquisitions Editor/Manager
Colorado Bar Association CLE

Trish Wilkinson
Cover Design/Desktop Publisher

Cover photos:

Top: Antique steam locomotive in the American West by Fredrik Arnell/istock photo.com. Bottom (from left): Alma Temple in Denver (courtesy Darlene Johnson); Marlon Dewitt Green (courtesy Flint Whitlock); Josie Bassett Morris cabin (courtesy National Park Service).

COLORADO BAR ASSOCIATION, CLE
CLE in Colorado, Inc. is the nonprofit educational arm of the
Colorado Bar Association and the Denver Bar Association

To my grandmother,
Veva Gibbard,
a fellow lover of history

ABOUT THE AUTHOR

Frank Gibbard was born in Oklahoma and grew up in Southern Illinois. He has lived in Colorado since 1983, when he married his college sweetheart Christine and moved to her hometown of Fort Collins. He has two children, one of whom is a sophomore at the University of Colorado and the other a high school junior. Frank is a 1990 graduate of the University of Wyoming College of Law, where he was awarded the Order of the Coif and served as Justice (president) of Phi Alpha Delta law fraternity. After a clerkship with Justice G. Joseph Cardine of the Wyoming Supreme Court, he worked in private practice in Cheyenne before assuming his present position as a staff attorney at the Tenth Circuit Court of Appeals in Denver in 1995. Since 2003 he has also served as Secretary of the Tenth Circuit Historical Society.

Frank's ancestors were already living in Oklahoma before statehood. As a child, his great-grandmother, born in 1892, fascinated him with tales of her childhood picking cotton in Alabama. His grandmothers also regaled him with stories of their ancestors in Oklahoma and Texas, who traded with the Indians, made fortunes in the oil business, stole horses, preached to the drunks on skid row, and sometimes drank to excess themselves. His great-aunt Helen Gibbard Hall wrote a number of books on North Texas history, and two of his relatives are honored with busts in the Cowboy Hall of Fame.

PREFACE

The History of "Historical Perspectives"

H istorical Perspectives" first appeared in *The Colorado Lawyer* in July 2002. "Raging Waters at Cub Creek: A Homesteader Confronts Prior Appropriation" was written by Tom Romero, Legal Studies Fellow at the Center of the American West at the University of Colorado-Boulder. In one thirteen-line paragraph, Romero discussed a 1914 water law case involving Josie Bassett Morris and her livestock's right to access Cub Creek. Who would imagine a water rights case could be summarized in thirteen lines?

The Colorado Lawyer Board considered several history-related proposals to determine the suitability of this type of information in the Colorado Bar Association's official publication. For the Board's consideration were historical vignettes, such as "Thirty Years Ago Today in Colorado Legal History"; brief narratives on the history of various areas of law; and abbreviated presentations on the history of the public trustee system.* The Board ultimately agreed to publish short accounts of Colorado legal history only as space permitted — and not to exceed one page in print.

The first indication that Historical Perspectives would find a home in *The Colorado Lawyer* was its placement on the Table of Contents.

---

* In February 2002, *The Colorado Lawyer* published "A Brief History of Colorado's Public Trustee System (1894–2002)" by Willis Carpenter.

This occurred in September 2002. Tom Romero continued to contribute bi-monthly articles through 2003.

In March 2004, Frank Gibbard, a staff attorney with the Tenth Circuit Court of Appeals and Secretary of the newly formed Tenth Circuit Historical Society, submitted his first Historical Perspectives article for publication. He has been the primary contributor since 2004.

On the heels of that first half-page article and during the eight years since its publication, Historical Perspectives has blossomed into a quarterly column in *The Colorado Lawyer* and its suitability is without question. The articles have generated enormous reader interest and support and, along the way, others — Jeffrey P. Kelson, Bill C. Berger, and Robert B. Linz and Claire E. Munger — have been inspired to contribute history-related articles of their own. Readers have always been encouraged to submit manuscripts for our publishing consideration.

With this compilation of Historical Perspectives articles, CBA–CLE has opened the doors to Colorado's colorful legal history. The staff of *The Colorado Lawyer* is grateful to Tom Romero for laying the groundwork to a fine tradition, and to Jeffrey P. Kelson, Bill C. Berger, Robert B. Linz, and Claire E. Munger for their worthy contributions.

Frank Gibbard's love of history and penchant for writing shine in every article he has submitted; each one is a joy to read. It has been a privilege and pleasure to publish Historical Perspectives in *The Colorado Lawyer.*

Leona Martínez
Managing Editor, *The Colorado Lawyer*

PUBLISHER'S ACKNOWLEDGMENTS

We are grateful to Managing Editor Leona Martínez of *The Colorado Lawyer* for allowing us to publish this interesting and entertaining collection of articles from the Historical Perspectives column, and to Frank Gibbard for his tremendous help in putting the book together. Not only did he write many of the articles herein, he also suggested the organization of the book and wrote the section introductions, each of which is a colorful and informative "mini" history lesson about Colorado. We also appreciate the fine work of the other authors whose articles appear here — Tom I. Romero, II (the original author of the Historical Perspectives pieces), Jeffrey P. Kelson, Bill C. Berger, Robert M. Linz, and Claire E. Munger — who showed the unique ability to take little-known or forgotten cases and bring them to life in a vital and fascinating way.

Illustrating this book on a tight time schedule was both fun and challenging. Fortunately, we received submissions and permissions from willing and capable individuals: Colorado Supreme Court Justice Greg Hobbs; CBA Historian David Erickson; historian/author Flint Whitlock; Captain Chris Weldon of the Delta County Sheriff's Office; photographer Nancy Garman; Colorado Supreme Court Librarian Dan Cordova; and CBA-CLE staff members Gary Abrams, Ellen Buckley, and Katherine Haas. We also appreciate the entities that provided timely permissions and access to historical photographs and sites: Denver Public Library Western History Collection; Colorado Historical

Society; University of Colorado at Boulder, University Archives; Tenth Circuit Library; Forney Transportation Museum; National Park Service; and Denver Water.

Finally, we thank book designer and desktop publisher Trish Wilkinson, who took a vague design concept and turned it into a stylish, attractive publication that genuinely reflects the topics and time period covered.

Darlene M. Johnson
Managing Editor
Colorado Bar Association CLE

Dawn M. McKnight
Assistant Executive Director
Colorado Bar Association CLE

FROM THE AUTHOR

This book has been a long time in coming, and I have many people to acknowledge for what I hope will be its success. Its roots lie in 2003, when Tenth Circuit Judge Robert Henry recruited me to assist him, Judge David Ebel, and Judge James Logan in forming a historical society for the Tenth Circuit. In the fall of 2003, the Tenth Circuit Historical Society was born.

Around the same time, Tom Romero, who had been doing a bang-up job writing a Historical Perspectives column for *The Colorado Lawyer*, left his job as a professor at the University of Colorado to pursue a teaching opportunity in another state. Arlene Abady, who edited *The Colorado Lawyer* at that time, needed someone to replace Tom in writing the columns. She turned to Robert Harry, the Tenth Circuit Historical Society's courtly and energetic President (and a well-known lawyer emeritus at Davis Graham & Stubbs). Bob and I worked on the first few columns together as a Society project — a fun experience for me, as Bob is fantastic to work with on just about anything. Around the middle of 2004, Bob cut me loose to fly solo on future columns. The rest, as they say, was history.

For background research for the columns, I turned to Dan Cordova, then a research librarian at the Tenth Circuit Law Library. I was not disappointed. Dan is an A-list researcher who brings every bit of professionalism and tenacity to his role as historical researcher that he did to his previous job as Army intelligence officer. After Dan left the Tenth Circuit library to head the Colorado Supreme Court Law Library, he continued to provide me invaluable assistance with my columns. He also recruited research librarian Lynn Christian, who has taken over much of the responsibility for the day-to-day research I need to keep the ink flowing. Thanks, Dan and Lynn, for your excellent help, always impressive and often provided to me on very short notice.

I have also benefitted from the excellent assistance of two *Colorado Lawyer* editors, Arlene Abady and Leona Martínez. Their suggestions and encouragement have helped me immeasurably to improve the columns over the years. I would particularly like to thank Leona for believing in me enough to expand the column from a one-page feature to a department of the magazine, and most recently, to a column. She also believed strongly in this book project, and encouraged me to contact the editors at Colorado Bar Association CLE to get the ball rolling.

Thanks are also due to the people who have read and provided feedback on my columns over the years. In this category are Bob Harry, Judge Ebel, Cathy Eason, Andy Lester, Elaine Howe, my grandmother, Veva Gibbard — to whom this book is dedicated — and others whose interest is appreciated but whom I may have momentarily forgotten. Thank you also to the guest columnists who have contributed articles and to the readers of *The Colorado Lawyer* who have taken the time to write me letters and e-mails over the years concerning the column. I truly enjoy the feedback.

I would also like to thank Assistant Executive Director and Publications Director Dawn McKnight and Managing Editor Darlene Johnson of Colorado Bar Association CLE, publisher of this volume. I worked on a daily basis with Darlene as this book was being finalized, and I found her assistance to be highly professional at every step of the process.

Finally, thanks are due to my wife, Chris, and my daughters, Ariana and Ericka, for their encouragement and enthusiasm for this project and their patience with the time I spent working on it during our nights and weekends.

Frank Gibbard
October 2010

FOREWORD

S even years ago, Frank Gibbard asked me to help him find "some Colorado legal history" for an article he was writing. The article was to appear in *The Colorado Lawyer*, and if it was good enough, he thought he might be asked to write more in the future, a tantalizing prospect. As a reference librarian for the U.S. Courts Library in Denver, I had worked with Frank on a few court-related projects, which had gone well, so I promised best efforts and mapped out a research strategy. Upon delivery of the raw research, Frank began to write. Little did we know at the time, but the wit and wordsmithing in that article would help Frank become a regular columnist for *The Colorado Lawyer*, a well-deserved post indeed. For Frank is not only a keen thinker and a gifted writer, but also a generous person. I thank him here, as I have many times in person, for including me (and others) in his work as well as the kind attribution in his byline. Also noteworthy is the faith and patience of Leona Martínez and *The Colorado Lawyer* editorial staff. Over the years, they were asked, more than once, to extend a deadline because the researcher needed more time, and approval was given every time. The quality of the work before you now reflects their trust in the authors, and their attention to detail when faced with short publication deadlines.

The Colorado Lawyer is the official publication of the Colorado Bar Association. Not surprisingly, it is an excellent publication. Like many others, I look forward to every issue. Just as it is topical and interesting, it is also an historical record. The Historical Perspectives column reminds us of that fact. It is a point of personal pride to be connected with these articles and authors, and I look forward to our continuing association.

Dan Cordova
Colorado Supreme Court Librarian

CONTENTS

III: "THAT OLD TIME RELIGION"

IV: MURDER MOST FOUL

V: OUR FELLOW CREATURES

X: NIGHTMARES AND TRAGEDIES

XI: THE BUSINESS OF NEWS

XII: DISORDER IN THE COURTS

I

HOW IT ALL BEGAN

INTRODUCTION

L ife on the American frontier could be ugly, short, and lawless. Something about the grand hopes created by vast horizons coupled with the harsh conditions of the mountains and plains seemed to bring out the worst in people, from claim-jumpers and horse thieves to card sharps and cold-blooded killers. The territory that eventually became the State of Colorado was no exception to this Western antinomianism. Though the Colorado territory was in theory part of the United States, which had a sophisticated system of federal, state, and local courts, attempts at imposing that system onto frontier life got off to a very rocky start indeed.

Official, "top down" efforts at creating a judicial system for pre-statehood Colorado foundered on conflicting jurisdiction, dubious authority, and abortive organizational schemes. Meanwhile, crime and controversy continued to prey on the territory's inhabitants. Into this judicial void stepped "bottom-up" courts, formed on an ad hoc and local basis. In the absence of official authority, ordinary citizens created "people's courts" and "miners' courts" that possessed acceptable levels of legitimacy while dispensing a crude form of frontier justice. Though they were not destined to last, the miners' courts in particular played a vital role in deterring lawlessness on the Colorado frontier.

THE "TOP DOWN" JUDICIARY

The initially disorganized, hit-and-miss efforts at imposing judicial order on the territory reflect the state's anarchic early settlement and development. Administratively, "Colorado" was subject to a long period of divided sovereignty after the land was acquired from France and Mexico during the first half of the 19th Century. During the period 1854 to 1861, the territory that would later become Colorado was split into areas claimed by no less than four territorial governments: those of Kansas, Nebraska, Utah, and New Mexico. These territorial governments, which were in many cases just getting organized themselves, did not generally have the resources or the incentive to establish institutions for an outlying and sparsely populated territory of mountain and plain.

Even if they had, there was little demand at the outset for a sophisticated court system in Colorado. The prospectors, mountain men, adventurers, dreamers, and schemers who filtered into the territory in the early days had little use for formal judicial institutions. If they wanted anything, it was a basic form of justice that would punish lawbreakers and protect their property rights. Only with a gradual increase in the state's commercial and professional population, and a better-established constituency for traditional judicial institutions, would the third branch of government assume a more settled and organized form in Colorado.

An early and premature attempt at organizing a "top-down" judiciary for Colorado occurred in 1855. In that year, the Kansas territorial legislature created "Arapahoe County," an entity located within Kansas Territory. This political subdivision included all of Kansas Territory west of the 103rd Meridian, comprising much of what is now southeastern Colorado and the eastern portion of the Colorado Rockies. Its county seat was Mountain City (today part of Central City, Colorado).

With grand intentions, the territorial legislature vested Arapahoe County with a court system and even appointed a judge for it, a man named Allen P. Tibbetts. Because there was no demand for his services among the Native Americans and mountain men within his territory, however, Judge Tibbetts never heard a single case. In fact, there is no evidence he even set foot in Arapahoe County. He thus earned the dubious honor of being the first early Colorado judge who exercised (or more precisely, failed to exercise) his duties entirely in absentia. He would not be the last.

In 1859, the Kansas territorial legislature subdivided Arapahoe County into six counties by carving out five new mountain counties. This grand gesture likely had little immediate effect in promoting civilized living on the frontier. The immediate future of Colorado government lay more with islands of local and municipal civilization that had begun to dot the mountains and plains than with large-scale territorial structures created by legislative fiat.

One such island of civilization arose on the high plains when the City of Denver and its sister city Auraria were organized in November 1858. Not long afterwards, lawyers began arriving in town, migrating across the plains in their covered wagons, hornbooks in hand. These pioneer lawyers would later play key roles in the development of an organized bench and bar.

In the meantime, ineffectual attempts at imposing judicial order continued. By March 1859, the reorganizers of Arapahoe County, still part of Kansas Territory, optimistically invested various officials, including a county probate judge and justices of the peace, with judicial authority. In typical early Colorado fashion, however, the jurisdiction of the probate judge, Seymour W. Wagoner, remained in serious doubt because he was never formally approved by the Kansas territorial legislature. He served for only a short time, in fact, before his authority became fatally undermined by a new set of territorial courts, those of so-called Jefferson Territory. These courts, as will be seen, would themselves, in turn, suffer a crisis of legitimacy.

The strange and short-lived history of the Territory of Jefferson begins in October 1859. In that month, backers of an independent territory in the Pikes Peak region, employing the spurious reasoning that land in that region remained in Native American hands and was therefore available for creation of a new territory, voted Jefferson Territory into existence. Jefferson's legislature went to work creating a "top down" judiciary with a vengeance. Within a short time they had drafted a constitution for the territory and appointed a Supreme Court, consisting of a chief justice and two associate justices. A civil and criminal code, adopted wholesale from those of the eastern states, quickly followed, as did an elaborate court structure consisting not only of the aforementioned supreme court, but also district, county, and justice of the peace courts. The only problem was that in the considered opinion of many residents of the territory, Jefferson and its courts had no legal authority whatsoever. They reasoned, not without some force, that since they were technically still part of Kansas Territory, the self-proclaimed Jefferson Territory was a nullity.

The many blooming flowers of judicial authority now began to choke each other out. At one point, a litigant in Denver wishing to bring a civil action had his choice of no less than four conflicting venues with varying degrees of legitimacy: the Jefferson Territorial courts; a Court of Common Pleas organized by the City of Denver; the Arapahoe County, Kansas courts; and a glorified miners' court operated by something called the "Arapahoe County Claim Club." In a sense, the problem was not too little justice, but too much.

Two years later, however, in February 1861, Congress finally settled the mess by officially creating the Colorado Territory. In connection with establishment of the Territory, it created a set of unitary judicial institutions that would finally "stick." This is not to say that all was smooth sailing from that point on. Administrative problems continued both in the executive and judicial branches of government.

Colorado Territory's first governor, appointed by President Lincoln, was William Gilpin, a man who faced many challenges, including Confederate sympathies within his territory. Apparently, he was not up to the task of resolving them. Historians regard Governor Gilpin, whom Lincoln replaced fairly quickly, as either lackluster or downright incompetent.

Under the territorial system of justice, the 100,000-square-mile Colorado Territory was divided into three judicial districts: the first headquartered in Denver, covering the area east of the mountains; the second in Central City, covering the mountainous areas to the northwest; and the third in Canon City, covering the southwestern portion acquired from Mexico. If appellate review of district court decisions was needed, the three territorial judges would sit together as the Colorado Territorial Supreme Court. This peculiar form of organization required the Supreme Court justices to review their own decisions reached as district court judges. Decision-making in such cases must have required a high level of diplomatic finesse.

While Chief Justice Benjamin F. Hall did an excellent job organizing the first judicial district in Denver, his cohorts performed in a less praiseworthy manner. The judge assigned to the third district did not arrive and hold court until months after his court session was scheduled to begin. The judge assigned to the second district never showed up at all. It was an inauspicious start for the Colorado courts.

COURTS CREATED BY POPULAR EFFORT

Into the judicial void of the late 1850s stepped two forms of popular justice. For criminal cases, there were the so-called "people's courts." When required, an assembly of local citizens formed to try malefactors and to dispense punishments. The people's court would generally choose one of their number to serve as judge.

The punishments imposed included hanging, flogging, banishment, and fines. Justice in the people's courts was swift, brutal, and generally unencumbered by lawyerly concerns about substance and procedure. Surprisingly, however, the results were not predetermined, in the sense of a "fair trial with a hangin' to follow." Popular courts actually acquitted some defendants. Others escaped from custody, avoiding the ultimate penalty in a less formal fashion.

Other forms of civil and criminal justice grew out of the "miner's courts" established in mountain areas. Lawyers were prohibited in these courts. The laws they applied were written in a simple, easy-to-understand format. A dissatisfied litigant could appeal their verdicts to an assembly of all the men in the district.

The miners' courts played an important role in establishing natural resource and property law in Colorado territory. In recognition of this role, the territorial legislature that met in 1861 would confirm the judgments of the miners' courts and adopt many of their codes into official mining law for the territory. They are a textbook example of an informal authority stepping into a void created by a lack of effective official institutions.

FOR FURTHER READING

David L. Erickson, *Early Justice and the Formation of the Colorado Bar* (Denver, CO: CLE in Colorado, Inc. 2008).

Jeannie Towle Mellinger & Molly Wingate, *The Colorado Court of Appeals: History of Colorado's Intermediate Appellate Court* (Denver, CO: CLE in Colorado, Inc. 2008).

Stephen J. Leonard, *Lynching in Colorado 1859–1919* (Boulder, CO: Univ. Press of Colorado 2002).

Hon. James K. Logan, ed., *The Federal Courts of the Tenth Circuit: A History* (Denver, CO: U.S. Gov't Printing Office 1992).

George E. Lewis & D.F. Stackelbeck, *Bench & Bar of Colorado* (Denver, CO: Bench & Bar Publishing Co. 1917).

A Diamond Anniversary
Tenth Circuit Formed and Robert E. Lewis Becomes First Chief Judge

BY FRANK GIBBARD

This year marks the seventy-fifth anniversary of the federal Tenth Circuit. A visitor to the second floor of the Byron White U.S. Courthouse in downtown Denver can view the official portraits of the judges who have served the Court of Appeals for the Tenth Circuit during its seventy-five years. The last portrait, at the end of the long, sunlit hallway, is that of the Circuit's first chief judge, Colorado jurist Robert E. Lewis (1857–1944).

Judge Lewis was a natural choice to head the fledgling Circuit. With his precisely-trimmed moustache and firmly set jaw, he looked almost archetypically judicial. By all accounts, his demeanor matched his appearance. "Judge Lewis was described by contemporaries as of very stern and severe mien, and no frivolity was allowed in his courtroom. Young attorneys tended to feel in awe of him."[1]

Judge Lewis's history reads like a Western novel. His father, Colonel Warner Lewis, served as a Confederate soldier and was the sole survivor of an Indian massacre in Coffeyville, Kansas. Robert Lewis learned the law in his spare time while working as a schoolteacher. After his health was ruined during arduous political campaigning in Missouri, he sought refuge (like his contemporary, gunfighter "Doc" Holliday) in

Hon. Robert E. Lewis, the first
Chief Judge of the Tenth Circuit
Court of Appeals
Courtesy Tenth Circuit Library

Colorado's dry and temperate climate. He soon was elected to the Colorado district court bench.

In 1906, Lewis began his nearly forty-year tenure on the federal bench by becoming Colorado's second federal district court judge in an era when American legal culture was becoming increasingly professionalized and standardized.[2] Lewis exemplified judicial formalism and conservatism. He opposed the moralizing tendencies of the Progressive Era and, later, Roosevelt's New Deal legislation.

In 1918, Lewis received an unusual commission: to preside over the third murder trial of Robert F. Stroud, the famous "Birdman of Alcatraz." Stroud was accused of killing a prison guard at Leavenworth. The federal judges in Kansas had all recused themselves. On the first day of trial, Lewis was furious to discover that the impoverished Stroud's attorneys had abandoned him to conduct a paying trial in another state. Lewis appointed new attorneys. Stroud was convicted, and Lewis sentenced him to death. Stroud's sentence was later commuted to life imprisonment.

Lewis remained a federal district court judge until 1921, when he was appointed to the Court of Appeals for the Eighth Circuit. On February 28, 1929, President Calvin Coolidge signed the bill creating the federal Tenth Judicial Circuit. The new Circuit, headquartered in Denver, was created by splitting the former Eighth Circuit roughly in half along a north/south axis. Judge Lewis, who served as chief with three other judges, was largely responsible for organizing the new Tenth Circuit Court of Appeals, which heard appeals from federal courts and administrative agencies in the states of Colorado, Kansas, New Mexico, Oklahoma, Utah, and Wyoming.

An examination of the Circuit's published cases from its first year of existence reminds us of a time capsule from the end of the Roaring Twenties. The court faced cases involving moonshiners and revenue agents;[3] automobile/railroad accidents;[4] and claims by World War I veterans.[5]

Judge Lewis remained an active member of the court until 1940 and heard cases until his death in 1944 at age 87. Sixty years later, the roster of the Circuit has grown to include twelve active judges and five senior judges, more than half of all the judges who have ever served on the court. Federal jurisprudence in Colorado owes a great debt to the Colorado judge who lent his extraordinary talents to the Tenth Circuit at its inception.

Original printing: *The Colorado Lawyer*, June 2004. A judicial biography of Judge Lewis can be found in Logan, ed., *The Federal Courts of the Tenth Circuit: A History* 50-54 (U.S. GPO, 1992). A shorter biography also is available in Eason and Hemming, *United States Court of Appeals, Tenth Circuit 60th Anniversary: A Commemorative Booklet* (1989) at 9. A good account of Lewis's role in the Robert F. Stroud case can be found in Gaddis, *Birdman of Alcatraz: The Story of Robert Stroud* 41-59 (Mattituck, NY: Aenoian Press (reprint), 1976). The Congressional Act creating the Tenth Circuit is the Act of Feb. 28, 1929, ch. 363, § 1, 45 Stat. 1346. For a helpful discussion of the early years of the Tenth Circuit, including the American socio-political climate in 1929, see Stanley and Russell, "The Political and Administrative History of the United States Court of Appeals for the Tenth Circuit," 60 *Den. L.J.* 119 (1983).

NOTES

1. *The Federal Courts of the Tenth Circuit: A History* (Denver: U.S. GPO 1992) at 54.

2. *See generally* Hall, *The Magic Mirror: Law in American History* 211-25 (Oxford Univ. Press, 1989).

3. *Bogileno v. U.S.*, 38 F.2d 584 (10th Cir. 1930); *Bergedorff v. U.S.*, 37 F.2d 248 (10th Cir. 1929).

4. *Chicago R.I. & P. R. Co. v. Fanning*, 42 F.2d 799 (10th Cir. 1930).

5. *Long v. U.S.*, 45 F.2d 590 (10th Cir. 1930).

A Herculean Task

Benjamin F. Hall Organizes the Colorado Territorial Courts

BY FRANK GIBBARD

The Central Overland Express stagecoach rolled into Denver late on the night of July 7, 1861, carrying four passengers. One of the four received a special welcome in the next day's *Rocky Mountain News.* His name was Benjamin Franklin Hall, and Coloradans had anxiously awaited his arrival for months.

Legislator, author, and historian, Hall was a New York native who had made a name for himself "back East" in Republican politics. President Abraham Lincoln had just appointed him Chief Justice of the Supreme Court for the Colorado Territory. The position paid only $1,800 per year, a pittance in Denver's gold rush economy. Hall would later complain that the salary only defrayed his personal expenses, leaving him to work essentially for nothing.

Hall faced a Herculean task. Not only must he serve as both a trial and appellate judge, not only would he be called on to try both state and federal cases, but he would be responsible for organizing the Bench and Bar for the entire huge territory.

Perhaps, on his way to his lodgings that night, Hall passed by the courtroom set aside for him on Denver's Fifth Street, near the *Rocky*

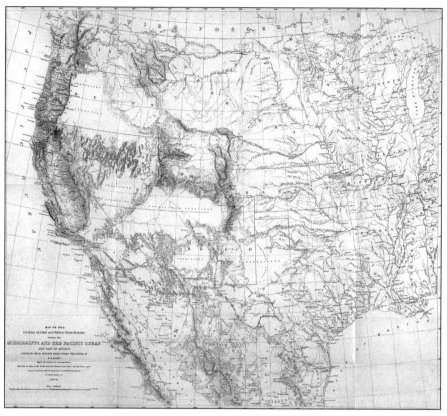

Map of "The United States and Their Territories," 1857–58
Greg Hobbs collection

Mountain Herald office. It was better than that provided for most territorial judges, who often met in improvised bars or dining rooms.

Despite the low pay and the heavy responsibilities, or perhaps because of them, Hall hit the ground running. Within four days of his arrival, he had taken his oath of office, convened the district court, announced rules of practice, appointed a commission to examine candidates for the Bar, and sworn in twenty-seven attorneys. One of these was Moses Hallett, who would himself later serve a long term as territorial justice and as a federal district judge.[1]

Hall had been provided little in the way of a law library, but this was to be expected at a time when the largest law library in Denver boasted a magisterial fourteen volumes. He also received little help from his two new colleagues on the Bench. S. Newton Pettis of Pennsylvania, who had arrived before Hall, spent some time fishing in Colorado, then left the territory a month after taking his oath, becoming the only Colorado territorial justice never to hear a case. Charles Lee Armour of Maryland would not arrive in Denver until late October, and he delayed his departure from Denver to his post in Central City until the following February.

When the system was working, the territory's three judges served as both district court judges and as part of a three-judge appellate panel. A litigant who appealed would have his or her case heard by the very judge who had denied the claim at the trial level, together with two of that judge's colleagues. Surprisingly, during its fifteen-year history, the Colorado Territorial Supreme Court reversed nearly 50 percent of the reported appeals presented to it.[2] Perhaps, as one commentator has suggested, when two justices prepared to reverse their "learned" colleague's decision, they sent him out for a drink, an amenity offered all too frequently to the judges in those days.[3]

When Hall took office, the firing on Fort Sumter had just signaled the beginning of the Civil War. Hall made no secret of his sentiments: he opened the September 1861 term of court with "a patriotic pep talk . . . warning against treason."[4] His talk created a firestorm of controversy among Coloradans, many of whom had Confederate sympathies. Hall later achieved notoriety by denying a writ of *habeas corpus* to Confederate sympathizer Captain Joel McKee.[5]

Hall continued as a Colorado territorial judge until 1863, when he resigned in dismay over his low salary and returned to Auburn, New York. He practiced law there until his death in 1891, and is buried in Auburn's Fort Hill Cemetery.

Original printing: *The Colorado Lawyer*, November 2004. The researcher may find useful a brief article by Fred Y. Holland entitled "Benjamin Franklin Hall, First Chief Justice, Territory of Colorado," 9 *Dicta* 48 (Dec. 1931). Hall himself authored a number of books on history, politics, and religious topics, some of which are available on microfiche through the Denver Public Library, along with portions of his correspondence. Also, several daily editions of the Rocky Mountain News during the month of July 1861 describe the organization of the Territorial Courts.

NOTES

1. Guice, "Colorado's Territorial Courts," 45 *Colorado Magazine* 204, 207, 216 (1968).

2. *See* chart in Guice, *The Rocky Mountain Bench: The Territorial Supreme Courts of Colorado, Montana, & Wyoming,* 13 (New Haven, CT: Yale Univ. Press, 1972).

3. *Id.* at 12.

4. Guice, "Colorado's Territorial Courts," *supra*, note 1 at 211.

5. *See The Privilege of the Writ of Habeas Corpus Under the Constitution,* No. 31, Folio 60 (D.Colo. Oct. 14, 1861).

The Early History of the Colorado Court of Appeals

BY ROBERT M. LINZ AND CLAIRE E. MUNGER

> The history of courts is more or less a history of their judges, for
> courts are very much what the judges make them.
> —Judge Wilbur F. Stone, *History of the*
> *Appellate Courts of Colorado*[1]

I n 1969, the Colorado General Assembly enacted legislation to create
the Colorado Court of Appeals.[2] In 1970, the court held its first session. It immediately began to alleviate the overcrowded docket of the
Supreme Court as an intermediate appellate court. However, this was
not the first time Colorado was served by a court of appeals; in fact, it
was the third time.

In 1891 and again in 1911, the Colorado General Assembly created
a court of appeals for the same reason it did in 1969 — to relieve the
Supreme Court of the burden of overcrowded dockets. Unlike today's
court, however, the earlier appellate courts struggled with their authority and acceptance.

Although the concept of an intermediate court of appeals is now
well settled, the earlier courts were uncertain about the place of an intermediate appellate court in the Colorado judicial system. The early
history of the Colorado Court of Appeals reflects this struggle to define
a judicial solution to providing efficient and effective appellate review.

THE ORIGINAL COURT:
1891–1905

In the second half of the 19th Century, settlers from the East were staking their claims for Colorado's land and minerals. The economic growth resulted in increased litigation for a court system still in its infancy. In the years when Colorado still was part of Kansas Territory, citizens organized various people's courts to administer justice.[3] When the Territory of Colorado was established in 1861, it provided for a judicial system comprising a Supreme Court, three district courts, and various other courts.[4] Each district court was composed of one judge. The three judges would sit as justices on the Supreme Court to review the decisions of the district courts—decisions they had rendered.[5] Naturally, this would require them to rule on one another's decisions. Justice Stone reported that the Chief Justice would:

> request one of his associates to retire while the two conspired to reverse the absent member, and thereafter the two associates politely hint that the Chief Justice should step out—to see a man—one at the bar, for example—while the two associate conspirators got even by taking the Chief down a peg in the reversal of his proudest decision.[6]

As the territory was transformed into the state of Colorado in 1876, the judicial system expanded. Even so, the Supreme Court still comprised only three justices.[7]

The Need for a Court

By the mid-1880s, the continued growth of Colorado resulted in an overburdened Supreme Court docket. It could take as long as three to five years for the Court to review a case.[8] This delay was a cause of great concern for the Bench and Bar alike, because neither counsel nor the Court wanted the overcrowded docket to delay resolution of legal matters, thus forcing unfavorable settlements.

Many solutions were presented to solve the crowded docket problem; however, the two solutions that gained most favor were: (1) create an additional appellate court, or (2) create a commission that would aid the Supreme Court in the review of cases. These two solutions were introduced as separate pieces of legislation in the 1887 session of the Colorado General Assembly.

Senate Bill (S.B.) 76. S.B. 76 was entitled "a bill for an act to create a court of appeals, [to] provide for the appointment of justices thereof, and to regulate the practice therein."[9] The bill was referred to the legislature's Committee on Judiciary. Judiciary committee members were concerned that the bill might not be constitutional, so they asked the Colorado Supreme Court to issue an opinion on the constitutionality of the bill.[10] The Supreme Court declared the bill unconstitutional, because it provided "that the decisions and opinions of the 'court of appeals' . . . shall have the same force and effect as the decisions of the supreme court."[11] The Supreme Court expected that the proposed court of appeals would serve as an equal court, with like appellate jurisdiction and power, which violated section 28, article 6, of the Colorado Constitution.[12] Given this report of the Supreme Court, the judiciary committee voted to indefinitely postpone the legislation.[13]

S.B. 86. Contrary to S.B. 76, this act to create a Supreme Court Commission met with success.[14] S.B. 86 established the Supreme Court Commission (Commission), which comprised three commissioners who would review cases assigned to them by the Court. The Commission would submit a written report to the Supreme Court's Chief Justice to include the facts of the case, the opinion of the Commission, and the authority.[15] The Court then could adopt the recommendation or prepare an opinion in the usual manner.[16] Importantly, the Commission would exist only for two years, "unless their services shall sooner be dispensed with by law."[17] The Commission was a failure, because its work lacked independence and finality; the Supreme Court was spending about as much time reviewing the work of the Commission as if it simply had reviewed the case from the start.[18]

The Court Created

With the failure of the Supreme Court Commission, a court of appeals once again was considered as a solution to the Court's overcrowded docket. In 1891, the General Assembly passed S.B. 98, an act "in relation to courts of review."[19] In this Act, the legislature created a court consisting of three judges with the same qualifications as the Supreme Court justices, appointed by the Governor and with the consent of the Senate.[20] This Act further established that the court "shall have appellate jurisdiction only" in civil and criminal cases, not capital cases, and that such jurisdiction would be final where the amount in controversy was less than $2,500. However, its jurisdiction was not final

> in cases where the controversy involves a franchise or freehold, or where the construction of a provision of the constitution of the state, or of the United States, is necessary to the decision of the case, also in criminal cases, or upon writs of error to the judgments of county courts.[21]

In addition to addressing various housekeeping matters regarding the court's organization, the Act also provided that the Supreme Court was to transfer cases to the new court of appeals.[22]

THE COURT'S
AUTHORITY CHALLENGED

The constitutionality of S.B. 98 was challenged almost immediately. In *People v. Richmond*,[23] the Supreme Court was required to consider: (1) what authority the legislature had to create an intermediate appellate court, and in so doing, (2) whether the legislature violated the constitutional guarantee of the supremacy of the Supreme Court in the state's judicial system.

In answer to the first issue, the Court cited Colorado Constitution, Article 6, § 1, which states that the legislature has the power to create courts in addition to those established in the Constitution.[24] As for the second issue, the Court stated that the Supreme Court's supremacy in the judicial system is not to be found in the extent of its jurisdiction but in the authority of its decisions and its place at the head of the judicial branch.[25] There is no language in the S.B. 98 to undermine this status. Furthermore, citizens possess "no natural or inalienable right" to a hearing in the Supreme Court and, as such, the legislature may reasonably vary the jurisdiction of the courts as public welfare may require.[26]

In its opinion, the Court also declared the "open secret" that it had been unable to timely process the number of appeals brought before it and that such delay had amounted to a denial of justice in many instances.[27] The Supreme Court upheld the constitutionality of the statute and the court of appeals commenced work on the backlog of appeals. Apparently, the legislature corrected the defects in the 1887 bill.

THE COURT DISSOLVED

Despite the Court's approval of creating the court of appeals and granting jurisdiction to the appellate court, many members of the Bar questioned the validity of the court of appeals. At the June 1900 Colorado Bar Association (CBA) annual meeting, the CBA's Committee on Law Reform (CBA Committee) proposed that the court of appeals be abolished. The CBA Committee urged that legislation be introduced at the next session of the legislature that would increase the number of justices on the Supreme Court from three to five or seven, abolish the court of appeals, and transfer that court's pending cases to the Supreme Court for disposition.[28] The supporters of the proposed legislation hoped that these changes would simplify legal proceedings, minimize the delay in processing appeals, and reduce the cost of litigation.[29]

Many members of the Bar supported this proposed legislation because they favored having a single appellate court. In an interview of Bar members about this pending legislation, one lawyer was quoted as saying that he could "see no advantage of having two appellate courts"; another lawyer thought the idea of having two appellate courts was "all nonsense."[30] It appeared that lawyers were concerned about the lack of uniformity in the law. One attorney thought that elimination of the court of appeals would be a "good thing to prevent any probable clashing in the matter of decisions between the two courts."[31] Another attorney favored eliminating the court because too often "the court of appeals overrule[d] the supreme court."[32]

Some support for these points of view may have derived from the 1899 case of *Mullen v. Western Union Beef Co.*[33] The appellate court's decision in *Mullen* was appealed directly to the U.S. Supreme Court, bypassing the Colorado Supreme Court. The U.S. Supreme Court ruled that when a matter is appealable to the state Supreme Court, the parties first must take their matter to the state's highest court before seeking relief from the federal courts. Therefore, the parties were required first to appeal to the Colorado Supreme Court.

Despite the support for the legislation among members of the Bar, the measure was not adopted by the Thirteenth General Assembly.[34] Judge Moses Hallett,[35] speaking as CBA President, stated: "Dual courts of review have not been satisfactory in any of the States and it is not probable that they can be made so in this jurisdiction."[36]

The CBA Committee returned to the legislature in 1903 and succeeded in getting a constitutional amendment placed on the 1904 ballot.[37] The proposed amendment would increase the number of judges on the Supreme Court from three to seven, terminate the court of appeals in April 1905, and enable two of the existing court of appeals judges to be appointed to the Supreme Court.[38] The amendment was approved by the voters. The legislature passed two additional acts in 1905 to provide for the transfer of cases from the court of appeals to the Supreme Court[39] and to transfer the property of the court of appeals to the Supreme Court.[40]

On April 4, 1905, members of the CBA, the Denver Bar Association, and other invited guests attended the last session of the court of appeals. Judge Charles D. Hayt presented a history of the court of appeals, in which he noted that "the object and purpose for which the court was created has been realized."[41] In his comments, T. J. O'Donnell, a prominent Denver attorney, noted that the court of appeals was:

Charles D. Hayt
Courtesy Denver Bar Association

an experiment feared by many and doubted by more, its very right to
a habitation and a name challenged, its usefulness for many years ham-
pered by the fact that its judgments were persuasive rather than conclusive[; even so, its opinions] secured an authority not given them by
statute.[42]

After these remarks, Chief Judge Charles I. Thomson, in somber
tones, thanked the assembled guests and requested that the baliff announce "the adjournment of this court *sine die.*"[43]
On April 5, 1905, the new Supreme Court was installed

in a bower of feminine and floral beauty, with the legal lights of the
Colorado bench and bar . . . [such that] the enlarged supreme court
burst into existence . . . in a mental and physical blaze of glory.[44]

During the ceremony, Colorado Court of Appeals Judges Julius C.
Gunter and John M. Maxwell were installed as justices of the Colorado
Supreme Court.

Julius C. Gunter
Courtesy Colorado Historical Society -
#10038690

John M. Maxwell
Courtesy Colorado Historical Society -
#10038691

THE COURT RECONSTITUTED: 1911–15

When the court of appeals was abolished in 1905, the opponents of an intermediate appellate court could celebrate their victory; their goal had been accomplished. However, it soon became apparent that the underlying docket problems at the Supreme Court remained unsolved. In fact, the docket problems were exacerbated by the 1904 Constitutional Amendment in which cases pending before the court of appeals were transferred to the newly formed Supreme Court for resolution.

Docket Problem Continues

As early as 1908, jurists raised the docket issue, noting the negative affects that the three-to-five year delay in processing appeals had on the practicing Bar, on business interests in the state, and on aggrieved citizens.[45] At the CBA's 1908 annual meeting held in Fort Collins, Judge Charles D. Hayt addressed these concerns to the assembled body.[46] He suggested that either the court of appeals or even the Supreme Court Commission be re-instituted as possible solutions, but that the CBA form a committee to study the problem.[47] Other members suggested the legislature modify or even eliminate the right of appeal in certain cases.[48] Although there was some disagreement about the number of backlogged cases on the docket and the time in which they could be disposed, the membership approved the formation of the committee.

In January 1909, the special committee reported to the CBA the following statistics:

1. When the Court of Appeals was abolished in 1905, it transferred 637 cases onto the docket of the Supreme Court, giving that court a total of 933 cases to decide, including its own cases.

2. By January 1909, the number of cases had been reduced to 777.[49]

Given this progress, the special committee recommended that legislative action be postponed until the 1911 legislative session, giving the court more time to reduce the backlog of cases.[50] In September 1909, however, the special committee reported that the number of cases on the docket actually had increased since January to 792 and was likely to increase further.[51]

In his report of the special committee's work, Hayt set forth the remedies devised by the special committee:

- First, the committee suggested that appeals could be limited by raising the amount in controversy requirement. However, Chief Justice Robert W. Steele[52] informed the committee that this solution was not likely to help, because when it had been done previously, it did not result in the reduction of any cases.[53]

- Second, the committee suggested that the Supreme Court need not file a written opinion when affirming the judgments of the lower courts. The committee believed that the Court already had this authority, but that members of the Bar would not favor this solution.[54]

- Third, it was suggested that the court of appeals be recreated. Because the court was abolished by constitutional amendment in 1904, the committee was concerned that the legislature now lacked the authority to create this court.[55]

- Fourth, the committee suggested the Supreme Court should increase the number of justices on the Court. However, the committee felt that this proposal would gain little support, because the CBA had just succeeded in securing the increase to seven members without correcting the overcrowded dockets problem.[56]

- Finally, the committee suggested that a commission be appointed to assist the Court. This commission would function in a similar capacity as the previous Supreme Court Commission of the late 1880s. However, the special committee acknowledged the objections to this proposal, given the history of the early Commission, the fact that the Commission lacked judicial power, and the fact that it could not enter a final judgment.[57] CBA members noted that Governor John F. Shafroth intended to call a special session of the legislature and that he was on record in favor of limiting appeals. Nonetheless, the CBA decided to postpone action until the 1911 legislative session and authorized the special committee to continue its work for another year.

A Consensus Emerges and a Legislative Solution Succeeds

In 1910, the docket problem worsened. By July 1910, the number of pending appeals increased to 825 cases.[58] Given the growing problem, the special committee proposed a two-pronged solution. It recommended that legislation be drafted that would create a new court of appeals. If that legislation failed, it would introduce legislation to create a commission to assist the Supreme Court with its backlog of cases.[59]

This report was discussed at length by the membership at its annual meeting held in Colorado Springs in July 1910. The main concern expressed with the creation of the court of appeals was whether such legislation would be constitutional in light of the 1904 Amendment abolishing the court of appeals.[60] The question was not answered by the body; it was deferred to review by the Supreme Court. Other members queried whether this new court of appeals would serve as an intermediate court or resemble the former court.[61] Still other members asked whether existing cases on the Supreme Court's docket could be legally transferred to the court of appeals.[62] Most important, members were concerned about the impact on the stability of the law when the Supreme Court overrules a decision of the court of appeals.[63] At this meeting, members raised other solutions, including abolishing the statute that required the Court to issue written opinions,[64] expanding the number of justices on the court,[65] and limiting the right to appeal.[66] Ultimately, these alternative solutions gave way to the approval of the special committee's report, with instructions to the committee to draft the two pieces of legislation for submission into 1911 legislative session.

Despite the misgivings of the committee, the legislation to create a new court of appeals met with resounding success in the legislature.[67] In eleven sections, the Act of June 5, 1911 gave the court of appeals structure and addressed the jurisdictional issues raised by having two appellate courts in Colorado. The Act creating the second Colorado Court of Appeals provided that the "court shall consist of five judges who shall possess the same qualifications required of judges of the Supreme Court, and shall receive like compensation."[68] The Act gave the Colorado Governor authority to appoint judges to the new court "with the advice and consent of the Senate" and provided that "no such appointment shall take effect until a confirmation thereof by the Senate."[69]

More important, the Act addressed the jurisdiction issues between the two appellate courts. The Act granted the court of appeals broad jurisdiction "to review and determine all judgments in civil cases now pending upon the docket of the Supreme Court" or to arise during the existence of the court of appeals.[70] Furthermore, Section 4 of the Act repealed all "statutes granting and regulating appeals from the district and county courts to the Supreme Court"[71] and provided that most[72] cases now pending on the docket of the Supreme Court be transferred to the court of appeals.[73] For its part, the Supreme Court retained jurisdiction to review decisions of the court of appeals that fell within certain classes of cases. These classes were: (1) decisions involving construction of a provision of the federal or state constitution; (2) those relating to a franchise or freehold; and (3) judgments for more than $5,000, exclusive of costs.[74] With these exceptions, however, the decision of the court of appeals in all remaining matters was final and conclusive.[75]

Finally, the Act provided that the Colorado Court of Appeals would "terminate and cease to exist at the end of four years" after the Act took effect.[76] With the passage of this Act, the combined appellate courts could begin to reduce the backlogged docket.

The Constitutionality of the Court Challenged

In August 1911, Governor Shafroth appointed the five judges to sit on the new court of appeals. These appointments included Tully Scott as Chief Judge; Alfred R. King; Stuart D. Walling; Edwin W. Hurlbut; and Louis W. Cunningham. However, the appointments were not effective until October 1, in part to give time to these lawyers to conclude their private practices, as well as to await for the new session of the Colorado Supreme Court in which it would transfer cases to the new Colorado Court of Appeals.

Governor Shafroth was moved by one other consideration, namely, that the law required the state Senate to confirm the appointments. Some lawyers argued that the appointments would be invalid until confirmed by the Senate, which would not be in session in the later half of 1911. Governor Shafroth, however, read the law to enable the Governor to appoint and swear into office the judges within three months of the next regular session of the legislature, at which time the Senate could confirm the appointments.[77]

On October 2, 1911, the five judges of the new appellate court took office. Soon thereafter, a lawsuit was filed by the CBA against these judges, challenging th e constitutionality of the court.[78] This lawsuit may have been a strategic move on the part of the CBA. In the opinion, there is reference to a statement made at oral argument by the CBA president "that the object of this action was to set at rest some doubt that had existed in the minds of the some of the profession relative to the legality of the new court."[79] In the discussion at the CBA annual meeting, when discussing the constitutionality of the court of appeals, the membership decided to leave that issue to a review by the Supreme Court.[80] Perhaps this lawsuit was that review.

The litigants raised two issues on appeal. First, they asserted the Act was unconstitutional because it limited the jurisdiction of the Supreme Court. Second, they asserted that even if the Act was constitutional, the manner in which the Governor appointed the initial panel of judges violated the provisions of the Act, and therefore was invalid.

Justice Musser, writing for the Court, answered the first issue by stating the Act simply regulated "the quantity of business before the court for a limited period."[81] He further contended that as the right of appeal was established by statute, it too could be altered or even eliminated by the legislature by statute.[82] Furthermore, the legislature was vested with a constitutional power to create "such other courts as may be provided by law."[83] Because the Act did not alter the Supreme Court's role as the head of the judicial branch, both the Act and the court of appeals were constitutional.[84]

For the second issue, Justice Musser engaged in a somewhat creative analysis of the Act to reach the conclusion that the actions of the Governor in appointing the judges were properly done. Although a plain reading of the Act indicated that the appointments to the court must be confirmed by the Senate prior to their taking office, he supported this position primarily by resorting to the absurdity of the result of the court of appeals lacking judges while awaiting confirmation by a session of the Senate not to take place some months later. The court of appeals would be created on the Act taking effect, and cases transferred to that court from the Supreme Court; even so, the court of appeals would lack judges to decide those cases.[85] He also cited the grave need for the court of appeals to relieve the congested docket of the Supreme Court.[86]

Justice Gabbert, who concurred in upholding the constitutionality of the Act, disagreed with the Court's analysis of the appointments issue.[87] Relying on the plain language of the statute to infer legislative intent, Justice Gabbert concluded that the appointees could not take office until confirmed by the Senate, regardless of the merit of the policy arguments set forth by the majority.[88] Interestingly, during discussion of the bill, an amendment to the Act was proposed in the Senate to remove the language of requiring "confirmation thereof by the Senate"; however, the amendment failed.[89] The *Griffith v. Scott*[90] decision was handed down on December 19, 1911, proving that the Court did not require three to five years to decide at least one type of case on its overburdened docket.

Expiration of the Second Court of Appeals

In April 1915, the court of appeals was scheduled for termination. Section 9 of the Act creating the court provided that the court would "terminate and cease to exist at the end of four years" of the effective date of the Act.[91] The termination was premature. Chief Justice Musser appealed to the legislature for it to continue the court of appeals for another two years. He reported that the number of cases on the docket was significantly reduced in the past three years — from 917 in 1911 to 446 as of December 1914. He further noted that the court of appeals was not able to transact much business until 1912, pending the outcome of the Griffith case.[92]

The legislature agreed with the Chief Justice and appropriated funds to continue the operation of the appellate court. Governor George Alford Carlson, however, did not share the legislature's view and vetoed the appropriation.[93] On August 4, 1915, the court of appeals held its last session. The five judges and seven court employees were thanked for their contribution, and the court was dismissed.[94]

CONCLUSION

When the second Colorado Court of Appeals disbanded in 1915, the state would not again enjoy the services of an intermediate appellate court until 1970, decades after the controversy and debate about authority and jurisdiction of the first two intermediate appellate courts had subsided. In the eighteen years that the early Court of Appeals existed, the court issued 2,325 opinions, filling the first twenty-seven volumes of the *Colorado Court of Appeals Reports*.[95] If the history of the courts is a history of the judges who occupy them, then those twenty-seven volumes are the history books of those judges' efforts to provide to the citizens of the growing state of Colorado a fair and efficient administration of justice. Our current appellate courts no longer conflict on matters of authority and jurisdiction; however, their history is the continuation of the hard work of these early settlers of the Colorado judicial landscape.

Original printing: *The Colorado Lawyer*, November 2008.

NOTES

1. Stone, "History of the Appellate Courts of Colorado," 8 Rpt. Colo. Bar Assoc. (CBA Rpt.) 15, 16 (1905). Wilbur F. Stone served as justice on the Colorado Supreme Court from 1877 to 1886. For a profile of Stone, *see* Bohning, "Six of the Greatest: Wilbur Fisk Stone," 31 *The Colorado Lawyer* 23 (July 2002).

2. Act of May 31, 1969, ch. 106, 1969 Colo. Sess. Laws 265 (an act to create a court of appeals and provide for the jurisdiction thereof).

3. Holland, "Early Colorado Courts and Judges," 9 *Dicta* 22 (1931–32). *See also* Bintliff, "A Jurisdictional History of the Colorado Courts," 65 *U. Colo. L.Rev.* 577 (1993–94).

4. Act of Feb. 28, 1861, ch. 59, § 9, 12 Stat. 172, 174 (1859–63) (an act to provide a temporary government for the Territory of Colorado).

5. *Id.*

6. Stone, *supra* note 1.

7. Colo. Const. art. VI, § 5 (1876).

8. Letter to the Editor, "A Bad Law," *The Daily News* (Denver) 2 (Sept. 3, 1885).

9. *Senate Journal of the General Assembly of the State of Colorado* at 242-43 (1887).

10. *Id.* at 255.

11. *In re Constitutionality of Senate Bill No. 76*, 21 P. 471 (Colo. 1886).

12. *Id.* at 472.

13. *Senate Journal, supra* note 9 at 282.

14. Act of March 7, 1887, 1887 Colo. Sess. Laws 428 (an act to regulate the practice in the Supreme Court by appointing commissioners).

15. *Id.* at 429, § 2.

16. *Id.* at 429, § 3.

17. *Id.* at 428, § 1.

18. Stone, *supra* note 1 at 19.

19. Act of April 6, 1891, 1891 Colo. Sess. Laws 118 (an act in relation to courts of review creating the court of appeals).

20. *Id.* at 119, § 2.

21. *Id.* at 119, § 4.

22. *Id.* at 120, § 5.

23. *People v. Richmond*, 26 P. 929 (Colo. 1891).

24. *Id.* at 930.

25. *Id.* at 931.

26. *Id.*

27. *Id.* at 933, 934.

28. "Bills Suggested by the Committee on Law Reform," 3 CBA Rpt. 149 (1900).

29. "Changes in the Judiciary," *The Denver Times* 4 (June 25, 1900).

30. "The Court of Appeals: Will it be Abolished and the Supreme Court Enlarged?" *The Denver Times* 2 (June 25, 1900).

31. *Id.*

32. *Id.*

33. *Mullen v. Western Union Beef Co.*, 173 U.S. 119 (1899).

34. "Address of Moses Hallett, CBA President," 4 CBA Rpt. 81 (1901).

35. Judge Moses Hallett served as Chief Justice of the Territorial Supreme Court from 1866 to 1876 and also as judge for the U.S. District Court. For a profile of Moses Hallett, *see* Kane, Jr., "Five of the Greatest: Moses Hallett," 27 *The Colorado Lawyer* 17 (July 1998).

36. "Address of Moses Hallett, CBA President" *supra* note 34 at 82.

37. "Report on the Committee on Law Reform," 6 CBA Rpt. 145 (1903).

38. Act of April 6, 1903, ch. 73, 1903 Colo. Sess. Laws 148 (an act to submit a constitutional amendment to the voters to enlarge the Supreme Court and eliminate the court of appeals).

39. Act of April 5, 1905, ch. 90, 1905 Colo. Sess. Laws 177 (an act to transfer causes pending in the court of appeals to the Supreme Court).

40. Act of April 5, 1905, ch. 91, 1905 Colo. Sess. Laws 178 (an act to transfer records, books, papers and other property belonging to the court of appeals).

41. Hayt, "History of the Court of Appeals," 8 CBA Rpt. 5, 6 (1905).

42. "Address of T. J. O'Donnell," 8 CBA Rpt. 10 (1905).

43. "Address of Judge Charles I. Thomson," 8 CBA Rpt. 12, 13 (1905).

44. "New Supreme Court Installed," *Fort Collins Weekly Courier* 10 (April 12, 1905).

45. "Address of Charles D. Hayt," 11 CBA Rpt. 28, 31 (1908).

46. *Id.* at 28.

47. *Id.* at 30.

48. *Id.* at 33.

49. "Report of Special Committee of the CBA," 11 CBA Rpt. 236, 237 (1909).

50. *Id.*

51. "Report of Special Committee of the CBA," 12 CBA Rpt. 123, 124 (1909).

52. Robert W. Steele was a member of the Colorado Supreme Court from 1901 to 1910, serving as Chief Justice from 1907 to 1910. His son, Robert W. Steel, Jr., was also a long-time judge in Colorado. *See* Steele and O'Donnell, "Six of the Greatest: Robert W. Steele, Jr.," 20 *The Colorado Lawyer* 1349 (July 1991).

53. "Comments of Charles D. Hayt," 12 CBA Rpt. 10, 11 (1909).

54. *Id.* at 11.

55. *Id.*

56. *Id.* at 12.

57. *Id.*

58. "Report of Special Committee of the CBA," 13 CBA Rpt. 196 (1910).

59. *Id.* at 197.

60. "Comments of Luther M. Goddard," 13 CBA Rpt. 48 (1910).

61. "Comments of Charles D. Hayt," 13 CBA Rpt. 43, 44 (1910).

62. *Id.* at 45.

63. *Id.* at 53.

64. *Id.* at 47.

65. *Id.* at 45-46.

66. *Id.* at 49-52.

67. "Comments of D. F. Carpenter," 14 CBA Rpt. 31 (1911).

68. Act of June 5, 1911, ch. 107, 1911 Colo. Sess. Laws 266, 267 (an act in relation to courts of review).

69. *Id.* at 267.

70. *Id.*

71. *Id.* at 268.

72. Section 5 of the Act omitted writs of error to county courts, which the Supreme Court is constitutionally required to review.

73. Act of June 5, 1911, *supra* note 68 at 268.

74. *Id.* at 269, § 6.

75. *Id.* at 268, § 4.

76. *Id.* at 270, § 9.

77. "New Court of Appeals Appointed by Governor Shafroth Take Office Oct. 1," *The Denver Post* 9 (Aug. 7, 1911). For a short profile of Shafroth, *see* Shafroth, "Six of the Greatest: John Franklin Shafroth," 33 *The Colorado Lawyer* 15 (July 2004).

78. *Griffith v. Scott*, 120 P. 126 (Colo. 1911).

79. *Id.* at 135.

80. "Comments of Luther M. Goddard," 13 CBA Rpt. 48 (1910).

81. *Griffith, supra* note 78 at 128.

82. *Id.* at 129.

83. Colo. Const. art. VI, § 1 (1876).

84. *Griffith, supra* note 78 at 130.

85. *Id.* at 134.

86. *Id.* at 134-35.

87. *Id.* at 135.

88. *Id.* at 141.

89. *Senate Journal*, April 29, 1911 at 1257.

90. *Griffith, supra* note 78.

91. Act of June 5, 1911, *supra* note 68 at 270.

92. *Senate Journal*, 1915 at 70-71.

93. "Appeals Court Ends Existence," *Rocky Mountain News* 3 (Aug. 5, 1915).

94. *Id.*

95. Statistic derived by running a Westlaw search looking for all opinions published by the court of appeals prior to 1916.

From *Dyer's Case* to Hard Bargains

Six Centuries of Covenants Not to Compete

BY BILL C. BERGER

Judges and litigators bogged down in cases dealing with covenants not to compete might think they are victims of the modern age. Covenants have become common, especially in Colorado's technology industries; however, they are far from modern. Anglo-American courts have been wrestling with covenants for six centuries.[1]

The first American case dealing with covenants not to compete was reported in 1811,[2] and the first English case was decided four centuries earlier in 1414. That decision was titled simply *Dyer's Case*.[3] In *Dyer's Case*, the court announced that all restraints on a worker's trade are void.

For the next three centuries, with only a few exceptions, English courts followed *Dyer's Case*, rejecting almost all covenants.[4] In 1711, Chief Judge Parker, who later became the Earl of Macclesfield,[5] announced what became known as the "rule of reason." The rule of reason imposed a general standard of reasonableness for covenants not to compete.[6]

In 1831, Chief Judge Tindal articulated what has become the modern common law test in *Horner v. Graves*.[7] In this case, Tindal identified the major factors that courts still use for determining reasonableness. He wrote:

[T]he greater question is, whether this is a reasonable restraint of trade. And we do not see how a better test can be applied to the question whether reasonable or not, than by considering whether the restraint is such only as to afford a fair protection to the interests of the party in favour of whom it is given, and not so large as to interfere with the interests of the public. Whatever restraint is larger than the necessary protection of the party, can be of no benefit to either, it can only be oppressive; and if oppressive, it is, in the eye of the law, unreasonable. Whatever is injurious to the interests of the public is void, on the grounds of public policy.[8]

The final English case that often is cited as fundamental regarding covenants not to compete was decided in 1894.[9] There, Lord Macnaghten brought the courts back to *Dyer's Case* and reemphasized the general rule that covenants are void:

The public have an interest in every person's carrying on his trade freely: so has the individual. All interference with individual liberty of action in trading, and all restraints of trade of themselves, if there is nothing more, are contrary to the public policy and therefore void.[10]

These cases are of particular interest in Colorado. One need only read Colorado's statute[11] and case law[12] to recognize that Lord Parker's rule of reason is still alive here. This is no coincidence. The first reported Colorado case on covenants was decided in 1909 in *Freudenthal v. Espey*.[13] There, the Colorado Supreme Court reviewed many historical cases and relied on them as the basis for its decision.[14]

First Published Decision — Dyer's Case

The first published decision to address restraints on a worker's trade — *Dyer's Case* — held that such restraints are void. The individual was a dyer. His former employer sought to enforce a restraint that would have prohibited the worker from competing for only six months and, then, only within one village. Modern courts might have little or no problem enforcing such a restraint.

However, in 1414, even the concept of a restraint was so offensive that the judge threatened the former employer with prison. The decision was announced in archaic Norman French, which has given us many tongue-twisting maxims, such as: *"(P)er Dieu si le plaintiff fuit icy il irra al prison, tanque il ust fait fine an Roye."*[15] Translated into English, this reads: "By God, if the plaintiff were here, he should go to prison until he paid a fine to the King."[16]

Historical Context

To understand why a judge would be so shocked by a six-month restraint, one must recall what was happening in Europe at the time. *Dyer's Case* followed on the heels of the Black Death in 1348. The Black Death had decimated Europe's workforces and, in 1349, England criminalized voluntary unemployment by passing the Ordinance of Labourers.[17] The thought that private individuals might, by contract, eliminate even one able-bodied worker from one village's workforce for just six months was too much for the judge to bear.

THE RULE OF REASON

In 1563, the Statute of Apprentices was passed. It imposed a mandatory seven-year restraint, during which apprentices could not compete; some guilds added an eighth year or even more. To prevent further restraints, a law was passed, called the Act for Avoiding of Exactions Taken Upon Apprentices.

The law changed in 1711, when Chief Judge Parker announced in *Mitchel v. Reynolds*[18] what has become known as the rule of reason. By 1711, the extreme labor shortages following the Black Death had ended. As labor shortages eased, a system of guilds developed. Quickly, guild masters came to realize the value of preventing their apprentices from competing. Thus, by the time Chief Judge Parker heard *Mitchel v. Reynolds* in 1711, the guild system had established a system of restraints for its apprentices, very much like covenants not to compete.

Without the prior labor shortages and in light of the guild system's established restraints, the courts were free to take a fresh look at covenants not to compete. That is precisely what Chief Judge Parker did in *Mitchel v. Reynolds*. He announced covenants would be enforced if reasonable. The analysis by Judge Parker merits quoting at length. The archaic language and creative punctuation are intriguing, but the clarity of his analysis is startling — even three centuries later here in Colorado. *See* the box entitled "Reasonable Test" for Judge Parker's analysis in his own words.

Chief Judge Parker articulated four goals for this new reasonableness test:

1) preventing abuse ("mischief") that could harm both the individual and the public;

2) preventing monopolies;

3) protecting an employer's legitimate interests, while at the same time prohibiting overly broad restraints; and

4) protecting an employee's right to sell his or her ability to compete.

These same goals can be found in modern Colorado cases.[19]

REVISING OR "BLUE PENCILING" RESTRAINTS

Chesman v. Nainby,[20] decided in 1727, was the first case to rule that the courts had the authority to revise and rewrite a restraint to make it enforceable. In *Chesman*, the plaintiff was a "linen-draper" who lived on Drury Lane, and the defendant was her protégé. The linen-draper had agreed to take her protégé into the business, under a bond. The bond contained a covenant not to compete, which covered one-half mile around the linen-draper's home "situate in Drury-Lane, *or any other house that she the said Margery Nainby, her executors or administrators shall think proper to remove to*, in order to carry on the said trade of a linen-draper" (emphasis added). In exchange, the linen-draper promised that she would teach the protégé "the trade or mystery of a linen-draper."

The linen-draper learned that her protégé was instructing her husband at their home in the trade of being a linen-draper. The protégé and her husband lived within one-half mile of the linen-draper's house on Drury Lane. The linen-draper sued. The protégé defended, arguing that the covenant was overly broad in that it effectively "puts it in the power of the plaintiff to prevent the defendant from exercising the trade in any part of the kingdom," because the plaintiff could decide to move anywhere at any time.

The court found for the plaintiff. The court agreed the covenant was overly broad, but revised it to enforce it only "for so much of the restraint as the breach extends to" — one-half mile radius around the plaintiff's house on Drury Lane. The decision was issued *per curiam*,[21] so the court did not elaborate on its authority to revise the restraint.

Although authorized by *Chesman* to revise covenants, some courts, like some modern courts, were reluctant to exercise that authority.[22] For example, in *Allsopp v. Wheatcroft*,[23] the court refused to rewrite a covenant that contained no geographic scope. Counsel successfully argued against revising the restraint, as follows:

> Then it is said that this contract may be bad to some extent but good for the rest, but it does not admit of division. It is either bad or good in its entirety.[24]

HISTORICAL COVENANTS

Originally, restraints on a worker's trade were not drafted simply as "covenants." Other formats were used. For example, *Dyer's Case* involved an "indenture," which is one of the most common forms of covenant.[25] In an indenture, the worker promised to pay his employer a substantial amount of money; however, if he refrained from competing within a certain geographical area for a certain term, the document stated the indebtedness automatically would be forgiven. Under Colorado law, a similar covenant continues to be available to employers.[26]

Given the variety of formats used, the law historically has looked beyond simple covenants not to compete. All restraints on a worker's trade have been subject to scrutiny by the courts. The Apprentices Act of 1536 prohibited all such restraints, even when implemented "by cautil and subtil means."[27]

REASONABLENESS SCOPE

Just as modern courts continue to struggle with issues regarding geographic scope,[28] so did historical courts. Originally, the courts strictly required restraints to state a definite geographic scope.[29] Then, in *Horner*,[30] Judge Tindal shifted the focus to a fact-specific scrutiny of the covenantee's needs.

In *Horner*, a dental assistant promised not to compete within 100 miles of his employer's town for as long as the employer was practicing dentistry. Judge Tindal held that the covenant was overly broad. The employer-dentist was engaged in a personal service and could not have serviced a 100-mile radius.

By 1894, in *Nordenfelt v. Maxim Nordenfelt Guns & Ammunition Co.*,[31] Lord Macnaghten was faced with emergent technologies. It had become possible for employers to do business far beyond a 100-mile radius. Lord Macnaghten announced the rule that modern courts continue to follow.[32] The rule says that depending on the circumstances, it may be reasonable to have a restraint with virtually unlimited geographic scope.[33]

CONTINUED AT-WILL EMPLOYMENT AS CONSIDERATION

For centuries, the courts struggled with how much consideration was required to support a restraint. In 1837, *Hitchcock v. Coker*[34] ruled that courts would no longer look into "the quantum of consideration,"[35] so long as there existed "any valuable consideration, however small."[36] Once that rule was announced, there remained one issue the courts still address today:[37] Is continued at-will employment sufficient consideration to support a restraint? By and large, the courts held that it was.[38]

LIQUIDATED DAMAGES

Liquidated damages clauses in covenants are not a modern invention either. In fact, liquidated damages clauses have long been sizeable parts of these restraints. For example, in *Mumford v. Gethering*,[39] the worker agreed to liquidate damages in the amount of 50 pounds, which was the equivalent of one year's pay. In *Jacoby v. Whitmore*,[40] a "shopman" who worked for an "oil and colour and Italian warehouseman" earned 28 shillings per week, or just less than 73 pounds per year.[41] The court did not hesitate to enforce his covenant, despite a liquidated damages clause for 250 pounds, which equaled approximately three-and-a-half years' wages.

"HARD BARGAINS"

Historical courts heard cases brought against uneducated or illiterate workers with little if any legal savvy. Defense counsel argued against enforcement of such covenants, calling them "hard bargains." In 1878, the judge in *Jacoby v. Whitmore*[42] showed little mercy for an illiterate worker who, along with sixty other workers, had been hired to walk an area of eight miles "with wheelbarrows and cans of oils" to sell his master's "mineral and other oils." The judge enforced the covenant:

> I think there can be no doubt that what the plaintiff did was simply and merely for his own protection for the purpose of keeping on his trade, and was not done with any view to oppress or take an unfair advantage of the defendant.[43]

The court rejected the defendant's argument that the covenant was a "hard bargain":

> I think it is impossible to suppose that [the defendant and the 60 other] men did not, when they met together, have some discussion on the subject and arrange between themselves whether they would sign the agreement or leave the plaintiff's employment, for that, I have no doubt, would have been the option tendered to them at that time.[44]

ASSIGNABILITY

Historical courts also addressed questions of assignability:

- If an employee provides the employer with a covenant, and if the employer then sells the business, does the *buyer* enjoy the benefits of that covenant?

- Can the employee compete against the buyer?

- Like modern courts,[45] historical courts generally held that, just as the employee had the right to sell his or her ability to compete, so the employer had the right to sell his or her protection from competition.[46]

CONCLUSION

Reading historical covenant not to compete cases is a fascinating window into the industrial and social issues of the last six centuries. Holdings have changed; analyses have been refined. "The times change, and we change in them" — "*tempora mutantur, nos et mutamur in illis.*"[47] However, despite all that has changed, modern lawyers and judges can still hear the echoes of these decisions in today's courtrooms.

Original printing: *The Colorado Lawyer*, April 2007. The author thanks Diane L. Burkhardt, Faculty Liaison at the University of Denver Sturm College of Law, Westminster Law Library, for her invaluable assistance in locating many of the authorities needed for this article.

NOTES

1. Blake, "Employee Agreements Not To Compete," 73 *Harvard L.Rev.* 625 (1960); Gilson, "The Legal Infrastructure of High Technology Industrial Districts: Silicon Valley, Route 128, and Covenants Not To Compete," 74 *N.Y.U. L.Rev.* 575 (1999); Handler and Lazaroff, "Restraint Of Trade And *The Restatement (Second) Of Contracts*," 57 *N.Y.U. L.Rev.* 669 (1982); *Hess v. Gebhard & Co., Inc.*, 808 A.2d 912 (Penn. 2002).

2. *Pierce v. Fuller*, 8 Mass. 223 (1811). *See Hess, supra* note 1 at n. 2.

3. *Dyer's Case*, Y.B. 2 Hen. 5, 5 Mich. 26 (C.P. 1414).

4. *Mitchel v. Reynolds*, 1 P. Wms. 181, 24 *Eng. Rep.* 347 (Q.B. 1711).

5. He often is referred to by both titles, interchangeably. *E.g.*, Blake, *supra* note 1 at 629 (referring to him as "Parker, C.J." and "Lord Macclesfield" on the same page).

6. *See* Handler, *supra* note 1 at n. 262.

7. *Horner v. Graves*, 7 Bing. 735, 131 *Eng. Rep.* 284 (1831).

8. *Id.*at 743. The language in these historical cases often contains apparently spontaneous capitalization, punctuation, spelling, and grammar. This article preserves the original language, without repeated use of "*sic*."

9. *Nordenfelt v. Maxim Nordenfelt Guns & Ammunition Co.*, A.C. 535 (1894), *affirming* 1 Ch. 630 (C.A. 1892).

10. *Id.*

11. CRS § 8-2-113.

12. *Reed Mill & Lumber Co., Inc. v. Jensen*, 165 P.3d 733, 735-36 (Colo.App. 2006); *Mgmt. Recruiters of Boulder, Inc. v. Miller*, 762 P.2d 763, 766 (Colo.App. 1988); *Energex Enters., Inc. v. Anthony Doors, Inc.*, 250 F.Supp.2d 1278, 1283 (D.Colo. 2003).

13. *Freudenthal v. Espey*, 102 P. 280 (Colo. 1909).

14. *Id.* ("While the questions presented by this record are of first impression in this court they have long since had consideration by both English and American judicial tribunals.")

15. *See* Blake, *supra* note 1 at 633.

16. Gilson, *supra* note 1 at n. 88.

17. 23 Edw. 3 (1349). *See also* Handler, *supra* note 1 at 722; Gilson, *supra* note 1 at n. 88. *Note:* The Ordinance of Labourers, also known as the "Statute of Labourers," has been widely reprinted on the Internet. Interested readers can find copies simply using the search terms "labourers 1349."

18. *Mitchel, supra* note 4.

19. *See, e.g., Mgmt. Recruiters, supra* note 12; *Energex Enters., supra* note 12.

20. *Chesman v. Nainby*, 2 Str. 739, 93 *Eng. Rep.* 819 (K. B. 1727). *See* Handler, *supra* note 1 at n. 6.

21. "*Per curiam*" is a practice that continues today, in which an appellate court issues a quick decision, often with little analysis. Although these usually are decisions that are not especially controversial, *per curiam* decisions need not be unanimous and can be exceptionally controversial. *See, e.g., Bush v.*

Gore, 531 U.S. 98 (2000) (decided *per curiam* but with multiple opinions and various justices joining various parts of the opinions).

22. For a recent definition of the "blue pencil" doctrine, *see Derek J. Sharvelle, M.D., P.C. v. Magnante*, 836 N.E.2d 432, 439 (Ind.Ct.App. 2005):

> Under this process, known as "blue penciling," a court strikes unreason-
> able provisions from the covenant. When applying the blue pencil, a
> court must not add terms that were not originally part of the agreement.
> Rather, "unreasonable restraints are rendered reasonable by scratching
> out any offensive clauses to give effect to the parties' intentions." (cita-
> tions omitted).

For examples of decisions recognizing a court's authority to blue-pencil a covenant's scope, *see Whittenberg v. Williams*, 135 P.2d 228, 229 (Colo. 1943) (noting it is not only within the court's authority to do so, but a court should do so because a covenantor — whether the seller of a business or, as in *Whittenberg*, an employee — who has "accept[ed] a full consideration" in exchange for his covenant and then breaches that covenant "is so lost to a sense of moral obligation" that the "courts should certainly not hunt for legal excuse to uphold him in such moral delinquency"); *Doubleclick, Inc. v. Paikin*, 402 F.Supp.2d 1251, 1259 (D.Colo. 2005). For examples of decisions where courts refused to exercise that authority, *see National Graphics Co. v. Dilley*, 681 P.2d 546 (Colo.App. 1984) (refusing to rewrite a covenant that lacked both geographic and temporal scope); *McGough v. Nalco Co.*, 420 F.Supp.2d 556, 579 (N.D.W.V. 2006). For an interesting discussion of the blue-pencil rule in general, *see Compass Bank v. Hartley*, 430 F.Supp.2d 973, 980-81 (D.Ariz. 2006) (*Compass Bank I*) (discussing Arizona's blue-pencil case law and the practice there of writing "step-down provisions," or fall-back positions, into the scope of a covenant).

23. *Allsopp v. Wheatcroft*, 15 *Law Reports/Master of Rolls and Vice-Chan-cellors* (*L.R. Eq.*) 59, 42 *Law Journal, New Series/Chancery* (*L.J., Ch.*) 12, 27 *Law Times Reports, New Series, All the Courts* (*L.T.*) 372, 21 *Weekly Reporter/ All the Courts* (*W.R.*) 162 (1872).

24. *Id.*

25. *See, e.g.*, the later case, *Gravely v. Barnard*, 18 *L.R., Eq.* 518; 43 *L.J., Ch.* 659; 30 *L.T.* 863 (1874).

26. CRS § 8-2-113(2)(c).

27. Act for Avoiding of Exaction Taken Upon Apprentices, 28 Hen. 8, ch. 5 (1536); Blake, *supra* note 1 at 634.

28. *Reed Mill, supra* note 12 (noting that covenants up to five years and 100 miles "are commonly upheld").

29. *See, e.g.,* Judge Parker's discussion of "total restraints of trade" versus "partial" restraints in *Mallan v. May,* 11 *Meeson & Welsby/Exchequer* 853, 12 *Law Journal, New Series/Exchequer* 376, 7 *Jurist/All the Courts* 536 (1843).

30. *Horner, supra* note 7.

31. *Nordenfelt, supra* note 9.

32. *Energex Enters., supra* note 12 at 1283, noting that:

> Colorado courts applying this fact-driven test have enforced non-competition agreements with durations extending from six months to perpetuity and geographic scopes ranging from county to nation-wide. . . .

Citing Nutting v. RAM Southwest, 106 F.Supp.2d 1121, 1127 (D.Colo. 2000). In *Nutting,* the court discussed the possibility of enforcing a worldwide agreement if, as in *Nordenfeldt, supra* note 9, the evidence established its necessity.

33. *Blake, supra* note 1 at 642.

34. *Hitchcock v. Coker,* 113 *Eng. Rep.* 167 (Ex. 1837).

35. *Id., quoting Gravely, supra* note 25.

36. *Id.*

37. Two recent cases involving Compass Bank bookend the modern analysis of this issue. *Compare Compass Bank I, supra* note 22 at 979 (holding under Arizona law that continued at-will employment is sufficient consideration) *with Olander v. Compass Bank,* 363 F.3d 560, 565 (5th Cir. 2004) (*Compass Bank II*) (holding under Texas law that continued at-will employment is not sufficient consideration).

38. *See, e.g.,* the following three decisions: (1) *Benwell v. Inns,* 24 *Beavan/Rolls* 307, 26 *L.J., Ch.* 663 (1857); (2) *Mumford v. Gething,* 7 *Common Bench Reports, New Series/Common Pleas* 305, 29 *Law Journal, New Series/Common Pleas* 105, 6 *Jurist, New Series/All the Courts* 428 (M.T. 1859); and (3) *Gravely, supra* note 25.

39. *Mumford, supra* note 38.

40. *Jacoby v. Whitmore,* 49 *Law Times Reports, New Series/All the Courts* 335; 32 *Weekly Reporter/All the Courts* 18 (C. A. 1883).

41. At the time, the pound was divided into 20 shillings.

42. *Jacoby, supra* note 40.

43. *Id.*

44. *Id.*

45. *Fitness Experience, Inc. v. TFC Fitness Equipment, Inc.*, 355 F.Supp.2d 877, 888 (N.D.Ohio 2004):

> Thus, the assignment of the Individual Defendants' non-compete agreements is not categorically precluded even though the agreements did not expressly state that they were assignable and even though the Individual Defendants did not expressly consent to the assignment.

Safelite Glass Corp. v. Fuller, 807 P.2d 677 (D.Kan. 1991); *Equifax Serv., Inc. v. Hitz*, 905 F.2d 1355, 1361 (10th Cir. 1990) (holding covenants assignable); *Artromick Int'l, Inc. v. Koch*, 759 N.E.2d 385, 387-88 (OhioApp. 2001); *Reynolds & Reynolds Co. v. Tart*, 955 F.Supp. 547, 556-57 (W.D.N.C. 1997). *C.f., Traffic Control Serv. v. United Rentals Northwest, Inc.*, 87 P.3d 1054, 1058 (Nev. 2004) (discussing cases on both sides, and then holding covenants "are personal in nature and, therefore, unassignable as a matter of law, absent the employee's consent"). Colorado appears to follow the rule permitting assignablity. In an unpublished decision, the Colorado Court of Appeals enforced assigned covenants. *Miller v. Kendall*, 541 P.2d 126 (Colo.App. 1975). *See also Cantwell v. Lemons*, 200 P.2d 911, 912-13 (Colo. 1948) ("Such an agreement not to engage in business is assignable, and upon sale of the business and goodwill will pass to a new purchase and the assignees may enforce it."); *Reed Mill, supra* note 12.

46. *See, e.g., Benwell, supra* note 38; and *Jacoby, supra* note 40.

47. Lothair I, Holy Roman Emperor (b. 795, d. 855).

REASONABLE TEST,
BY CHIEF JUDGE PARKER[1]

[T]he true reasons of the distinction upon which the judgments in these cases of voluntary restraints are founded are, 1st, the mischief which may arise from them, 1st, to the party, by the loss of his livelihood, and the subsistence of his family; 2dly, to the publick, by depriving it of an [*sic*] useful member.

Another reason is, the great abuses these voluntary restraints are liable to; as for instance, from corporations, who are perpetually laboring for exclusive advantages in trade, and to reduce it into as few hands as possible; as likewise from masters who are apt to give their apprentices much vexation on this account, and to use many indirect practices to procure such bonds from them, lest they should prejudice them in their custom, when they come to set up for themselves.

3dly, Because in a great many instances, they can be of no use to the obligee; which holds in all cases of general restraint throughout England; for what does it signify to a tradesman in London, what another does at Newcastle? And surely it would be unreasonable to fix a certain loss on one side, without any benefit to the other.

The fourth reason is in favour of these contracts, and is, that there may happen instances wherein they may be useful and beneficial, as . . . in [the] case of an old man, who finding himself under such circumstances either of body or mind, as that he is likely to be a loser by continuing his trade, in this case it will be better for him to part with it for a consideration, that by selling his custom, he may procure to himself a livelihood, which he might probably have lost, by trading longer.

Notes

1. *Mitchel v. Reynolds*, 1 P. Wms. 181, 24 *Eng. Rep.* 347 (Q.B. 1711).

II

RACE RELATIONS

INTRODUCTION

I t is something of a truism that gold and silver were more significant colors on the Colorado frontier than black or white. African-Americans and Jews, two groups subject to a long history of abuse and persecution in other parts of the world, found Colorado a relatively safe haven during the territory's early days. White Protestant Coloradans were too busy trying to strike it rich — and later, to bring civilized amenities to fledgling cities — to care very much about maintaining rigid religious or class structures.

Colorado's small population of African-Americans included an entrepreneurial class, who found work running their own stores and businesses, particularly in Denver. The black community, while never subject to the extremes of mistreatment common in the South, nevertheless encountered various forms of institutionalized racism, even during the early years. It is undeniable that many whites in the Colorado territory prior to and during the Civil War held Confederate sympathies. Certain patterns of discrimination evidently proved too well entrenched even to break down at high altitude.

One need not look far to find examples of racism in action. Blacks in Central City, for example, were forced to hire a lawyer to compel the town to educate their children in integrated schools, a boon the dozen or so black children in that city did not receive until 1869. The Summit County mining claim stolen from African-American pioneer Barney Ford was known by a racial epithet that added insult to injury until more enlightened sympathies caused the area to be renamed "Barney

Ford Hill" in 1964. And an early proposed constitution for the state of Colorado, drafted during the Reconstruction Era, even denied the vote to African-Americans.

This defect was ultimately remedied after it became clear that the Reconstruction-era Congress would not tolerate such a blatant deprivation of rights to Colorado's African-American citizens. Although various forms of segregation continued, racial relations between whites and blacks continued on a surprisingly even keel until the 1920s, when the Ku Klux Klan gained political dominance in parts of the state and began persecuting African-Americans who were perceived to be seeking greater integration between the state's black and white communities.

Colorado's Native Americans were treated much like those in other parts of the West — subjected to broken treaties, seizure of their land, and ultimately massacre and/or removal. They were, of course, Colorado's earliest inhabitants. But their aboriginal rights counted for little in the face of European ownership structures that favored individual property rights over communal traditions.

The Pueblo People (often referred to as "Anasazi," actually a Navajo word meaning "Ancient Ones" or "Ancient Enemy") built the cliff dwellings found in the southwest corner of the state at Mesa Verde. Archaeologists believe that the Pueblo People abandoned these dwellings in the 13th Century as the result of a combination of factors including population pressures from other tribes and a catastrophic drought lasting 300 years beginning around 1150 A.D. Evidence of prehistoric tribes that preceded the Pueblo People — including the Basket Makers and the Folsom people, known for their distinctive flaked spear-points — has also been found at various locations in Colorado.

Historians mark the end of Colorado's prehistoric period with the year 1540, when Spanish explorer Francisco Vásquez de Coronado led an expedition from Mexico into the region. Ironically, Coronado was said to be looking for gold, a passion that would draw a multitude into the territory three hundred years later. The Spanish developed a number of settlements in southeastern Colorado, thus becoming the first Europeans to settle in the state. Hispanic settlers from Taos, New Mexico, established the first town in Colorado, San Luis, officially incorporated in 1851.

These Spanish settlements were occasionally raided by Native American tribes, who also feuded with each other. The tribes with the longest history in Colorado were the Ute, Apache, and Commanches. The Arapahoe, Cheyenne, and Kiowa tribes also made their home in the state, though at a later date. It is believed that these tribes were driven across the prairie into Colorado by population pressure from the Sioux Indians, who were in turn driven westward by the Chippewas, who had been armed by French colonists. The Pawnee, Shoshoni, and Navajo tribes also found a home in various parts of Colorado.

Non-Hispanic Europeans did not arrive en masse in Colorado until the 1858-59 gold rush. That event, more than any other, sealed the fate of Colorado's Native Americans. Although whites and natives lived together for a while in bemused tolerance, with only occasional outbreaks of violence, soon a drumbeat of eliminationist rhetoric began to be heard in the European-American press. Much to the irritation of reform-minded Europeans, Colorado's Native Americans were simply uninterested in becoming white farmers and ranchers. Esteemed journalists such as Horace Greeley and Henry Villard expressed their chauvinist conviction that the Native Americans were an inferior race that would eventually disappear under a wave of human progress. Cruder men put it more bluntly: "They need killing," one white spokesman chillingly put it.

It did not take long for these sentiments to be translated into practice. In November 1864, Colonel John M. Chivington, a Methodist bishop and Civil War hero, led a rag-tag group of mostly volunteer soldiers in an ambush of a peaceful group of Cheyenne and Arapahoe Indians camped along Sand Creek in Southeastern Colorado. Chivington's men indiscriminately slaughtered at least 160 Native Americans, including women and children. Though he was initially praised by Colorado's European pioneers, after hearings in Washington before a Congressional joint committee Chivington's action was eventually recognized for what it was: a cold-blooded massacre. The town on the eastern plains named for him is now a ghost town, and Chivington is no longer seen as a hero in most quarters.

Another minority group prominent on the frontier was the Chinese. The first Chinese arrived in Denver in 1866, brought in to serve as contract laborers. The "Celestials" as they were called (China being known as the Celestial Kingdom) were willing (or, more correctly, compelled) to work for less than the Irish, Germans, and other Europeans who slaved in the mines and on the railroads. Naturally, the idea that these Celestials were driving down wages drove up resentment among other workingmen.

There were other resentments as well. The Chinese were tarred with various stereotypes. They were heathens. They were effeminate, decadent. They bought their sundries from China rather than patronizing local merchants. They took work from white washerwomen, who were then forced into prostitution or other unsavory livelihoods. They lusted after these same white women, who they ruined by addicting them to opium. This last charge was the most dangerous. Fears of opium abuse among the Chinese led to what may have been America's first full-scale drug panic in the 1880s.

Tensions came to a head in Denver on Halloween night, 1880. After some Chinese men defended themselves from some pool hall hooligans, a full-scale race riot raged through Denver's Chinatown, known then as "Hop Alley." The white mob charged itself with eliminating the "Yellow Plague." They trashed Denver's Chinese-owned laundries and then set fire to them. Chinese who fell into the hands of the mob were beaten, often seriously, and one Chinese man was killed.

Throughout the ordeal, the authorities worked to restore order. Several Denver residents tried to protect the Chinese from the rampaging mob. But when it was all said and done, the 1880 anti-Chinese riot was one of the worst instances of racial intolerance in Denver history.

FOR FURTHER READING

Phil Goodstein, *Denver From the Bottom Up: Volume One: From Sand Creek to Ludlow* (Denver, CO: New Social Pubs. 2003).

Liping Zhu, *A Chinaman's Chance: The Chinese on the Rocky Mountain Mining Frontier* (Boulder, CO: Univ. Press of Colorado 1997).

Robert G. Athearn, *The Coloradans* (Albuquerque, NM: Univ. of New Mexico Press 1976).

Echevaria & Otero, eds., *Hispanic Colorado: Four Centuries: History & Heritage* (Ft. Collins, CO: Centennial Pubs. 1976).

Stephen J. Leonard, *Denver's Foreign Born Immigrants 1859-1900* (Ph.D. dissertation, Claremont Grad. School 1971).

Bill Hosokawa, *Nisei: The Quiet Americans* (New York, NY: William Morrow & Co., Inc. 1969).

LeRoy R. Hafen, *Colorado and Its People,* Vol. II (New York, NY: Lewis Historical Pub. Co., Inc. 1948).

Race, Murder and Criminal Prosecution in Wartime Denver

BY TOM I. ROMERO, II

On May 4, 1942, a startling headline dominated the front page of the *Rocky Mountain News*: "Denver Jap Butchers Wife in Hotel Lobby."[1] In vivid detail, Denverites discovered how George Honda, "a 37 year old Japanese American restaurant operator, slashed his wife to death . . . then attempted to commit hara-kiri with the blood drenched weapon." In reporting the violent act, the Denver paper painted a vivid portrait of murder that rocked a rapidly changing wartime city.

During World War II, Denver and Colorado experienced a major increase of Japanese Americans and Japanese aliens as a result of forced relocation from the West Coast of the United States. Early in the war, the War Relocation Authority adopted regulations to encourage "able-bodied [Japanese Americans] with good records" to move to Denver, Boulder, and other Colorado towns.[2] However, many Coloradans feared such a policy. As one columnist in *The Denver Post* declared:

> The Japs are naturally a treacherous race. Neither [the War Relocation Authority] nor anybody else knows what is going on in their heads. There were a lot of Japs out in California when the war started who were supposed to be loyal citizens of the United States. And they were all set to betray this country, if they got the chance.[3]

The *Rocky Mountain News* headline on Monday, May 4, 1942
Rocky Mountain News/Denver Public Library

Although such images were by no means new, they directly influenced the legal experiences of Japanese Americans moving into Colorado. In one case, some Coloradans even attempted to amend the Colorado Constitution to prevent Japanese aliens from purchasing and owning real estate in the state. Although the measure was barely defeated in 1944, Japanese Americans were in many cases barred from public discussion of the amendment.

It was in this atmosphere that the City and County of Denver prosecuted George Honda. Honda operated the United States Café in the heart of downtown Denver with his Colorado-born wife, Mary Iyama, a Nisei (child of Japanese immigrants). In his murder trial, Honda was tried before a jury composed entirely of white men. From the start of the case, Denver District Court Judge Stanley Johnson attempted to mitigate the racial antagonism generated by the war, as well as the sensationalistic news coverage of the crime:

The defendant, though I am informed he is an American citizen, is of Japanese extraction. Of course we are at war with Japan at this time, and all of us well understand that it is possible for some individuals to have prejudice against anyone of Japanese extraction. . . . I do not need to say . . . that is one of the things that we are in this war for, to protect, and if any individual is drawn into the error of allowing racial prejudice to enter in his service as a juror, he is simply doing that much to destroy the institutions that protect our own liberty as well as that of any person who comes to this country and happens to be charged with a crime.[4]

Despite such pronouncements, the issue of racial difference was imbedded in the case. For example, Honda's own expert witness declared that Honda's "mind is Oriental, he thinks and feels and acts very much like an Oriental . . . [this] has hastened that impulse which resulted in the tragedy."[5] Throughout the trial, both the prosecution and defense made Honda's dissimilarity — from the language he spoke to his citizenship — a central issue. In less than thirty minutes after it received the case, Honda's jury convicted him of murder in the first degree and, as a result, sentenced him to death.

Honda's lawyers appealed, arguing that war against Japan prevented him from receiving balanced treatment by an all-white jury. The Colorado Supreme Court, however, held that Honda received a fair and impartial trial and that accusations of racial improprieties were completely "without merit."[6] In October 1943, the state of Colorado executed George Honda.

The only Japanese American executed during World War II in the United States, George Honda's criminal prosecution revealed the protean impulses working in Denver and Colorado's wartime criminal justice system. Although the trial court made every effort to diffuse racial discrimination, it could not easily separate the case from a social context complicated by war and demographic change.

Original printing: *The Colorado Lawyer*, July 2003. The murder of Mary Honda by her husband George was followed extensively by the *Rocky Mountain News* and *The Denver Post* in 1942 and early 1943. Newspaper clipping files of the murder and the subsequent trial can be found at the Western History Collection at the Denver Public Library. The trial transcript, as well as some physical evidence, is available at the Colorado State Archives. The general experience of Japanese Americans in Colorado during World War II is chronicled in Chang, "Side by Side: Japanese Americans and Colorado, 1941–1945" (1996) (B.A. thesis, University of Denver) and Hosokawa, *Nisei: The Quiet Americans*, rev. ed. (Niwot, CO: University Press of Colorado, 2002).

NOTES

1. *Rocky Mountain News* (May 4, 1942).

2. Atkins, *Human Relations in Colorado: A Historical Record* (Denver, CO: Publishers Press, 1968) at 121.

3. *The Denver Post* (March 17, 1944).

4. Trial transcript appearing in appellate record, *Honda v. People*, 141 P.2d 178 (Colo. 1943) at 5.

5. *Id.* at 186.

6. *Id.* at 182.

Turbulence a Mile High

Equal Employment Opportunity in the Colorado Sky

BY TOM I. ROMERO, II

In 1957, Captain Marlon Green, a distinguished pilot in the U.S. Air Force's Air-Sea Rescue Service, decided he wanted to fly large passenger airplanes. Green subsequently traveled to San Francisco, Chicago, New York, Washington, D.C., and Denver in quest of work as a pilot for the nation's major air carriers. In every instance, Green's superior credentials and experience seemingly held little significance. Despite exemplary service to his country, Green discovered that several air carriers, including Denver-based Continental Air Lines ("Continental"), had rejected his application.

What made Green's experience peculiar, but not all that out of the ordinary, was the fact that he was African American. During the 1950s, no major airlines in the United States employed black aviators. Some airlines argued this was due to the lack of experienced and qualified African American pilots. Others believed that co-workers or paid customers would not accept a black aviator. To challenge such beliefs, Colorado legislators passed increasingly strong fair employment legislation during the 1950s. By 1957, Colorado had one of the most far-reaching civil rights laws in the nation.[1]

Green's experience with Continental seemed an especially clear expression of discrimination. After the company invited Green to Denver

Marlon Green
Courtesy of author Flint Whitlock,
from his book *Turbulence Before Takeoff:
The Life and Times of Aviation Pioneer
Marlon Dewitt Green*

for an interview and flight test, the flight instructor remarked that Green was the "first Negro pilot who ever applied to his company" and, subsequently, he asked Green to complete his application by stating his race on the application form.[2] After the interview, Continental chose not to select Green for its pilot training program, despite the fact that he had substantially more flight time on a multi-engine aircraft than any of the four white candidates selected. Consequently, Green relied on Colorado's nascent civil rights infrastructure for a redress of his grievances.

After extensive hearings, the Colorado Anti-Discrimination Commission ("Commission") found Continental guilty of racial discrimination and ordered the company to give Green the first opportunity to enroll in Continental's pilot training school.[3] Continental, represented by the Denver firm of Holland and Hart, appealed the ruling to Denver's District Court. In his analysis of the case, Judge William Black vocally denounced the form and manner of the Commission's order and eventually held that Colorado's 1957 civil rights statute was an unconstitutional burden on interstate commerce and was preempted by, among other things, several federal acts and Executive Order No. 10557.[4]

A divided Colorado Supreme Court upheld Judge Black's opinion. An effectual fair employment law seemed to be a lost cause. Not long after, however, the U.S. Supreme Court decided to take up the Commission's appeal due to the "the obvious importance" of Colorado's civil rights law. In a case that involved as *amicus curiae* the NAACP, Colorado and national branches of the ACLU, the Anti-Defamation League of B'Nai Brith, American Jewish Congress, Department of Justice, and the attorneys general of several states, Green's complaint had national ramifications.

The U.S. Supreme Court overruled the Colorado high court. It held that Colorado law was not preempted by either the letter or spirit of non-discrimination covered by federal legislation and executive acts.[5] On remand, Continental was compelled to hire Green. After seven years of litigation, Green became the first African American in the United States to be employed as a pilot by a major commercial air carrier.

Green's legal struggles heralded a new era in Colorado employment law. One commentator observed in 1969: "This case, as much as any other ... put employers on notice that in Colorado fair employment is more than just a mere statement of policy."[6] Moreover, Colorado's anti-discrimination statutes and subsequent interpretation by state courts posited human rights found in such legislation as a basic privilege of American life. Colorado Supreme Court Justice Otto Moore, in describing the Court's analysis of Colorado's 1959 fair housing law, stated: " ... there are fundamental and inherent rights with which all humans are endowed even though no specific mention is made of them in either the national or state constitutions."[7] Indeed, Coloradans increasingly asserted these rights with various degrees of success in the second half of the 20th Century.

Original printing: *The Colorado Lawyer*, September 2003. Green's complaint to the Commission provided the Colorado Bar an unprecedented opportunity to "make" national civil rights law in the 1950s and 1960s. Internal and public debates examining the scope and legality of Colorado's Civil Rights Acts can be found in the Commission's files at the Colorado State Archives and Papers of the Mountain States Chapter, Anti-Defamation League of B'Nai Brith, housed in the Beck Memorial Archives at the University of Denver. For a thorough study of this case and the life of Marlon Green, see Whitlock, *Turbulence Before Takeoff: The Life & Times of Aviation Pioneer Marlon Dewitt Green* (Brule, WI: Cable Publishing, 2009).

NOTES

1. CRS 53, §§ 80-24-1 *et seq.*

2. *Colorado Anti-Discrimination Comm'n v. Continental Air Lines, Inc.*, 355 P.2d 83, 87 (Colo. 1960) at 55-60.

3. Civil Rights Comm'n Hearing Case Files Record #83-376, Box 109904.

4. Trial transcript, appellate record, *Colorado Anti-Discrimination Comm'n v. Continental Air Lines*, Civ.Act. No. B-29648 (June 25, 1959).

5. *Colorado Anti-Discrimination Comm'n v. Continental Air Lines*, 372 U.S. 714 (1963).

6. Penwell, "Civil Rights in Colorado," 40 *Denver L.J.* (Spring 1969) at 189.

7. *Colorado Anti-Discrimination Comm'n v. Case*, 380 P.2d 34, 39 (Colo. 1962).

"An Immoral Course of Life"

Vagrancy Conviction for Interracial Marriage

BY FRANK GIBBARD

A generation growing up in a new millennium may find it hard to believe that just over fifty years ago, interracial marriage was illegal in a majority of the states. At its peak, between 1913 and 1948, an anti-miscegenation regime was in force in thirty out of the forty-eight states, covering territory roughly congruent with today's so-called "red states," plus California and Oregon.[1]

Colorado's anti-miscegenation law, in force from its Territorial days, was typical in that it made "all marriages between [N]egroes or mulattoes, of either sex, and white persons . . . absolutely void."[2] The law had a unique local twist, however: it did not prohibit "the people living in that portion of the state acquired from Mexico from marrying according to the custom of that country."[3] "Thus a marriage might be legal in most of Salida, but illegal over in Hollywood Heights. . . . A couple could be legally married in Buena Vista, but guilty of illegal cohabitation if they moved to Leadville."[4]

In 1942, this statute was tested in an unusual way — on appeal from a vagrancy conviction.[5] James W. Jackson was an African-American. His common-law wife, Lydia Jackson, was white. Although they claimed to be married at common law, the Jacksons were convicted of vagrancy for living together, under a statute that prohibited persons from leading an "immoral course of life."[6]

Jackson provides an excellent example of how differences in framing the facts and issues of a case can be used to support radically different outcomes. The *en banc* majority in *Jackson* heaped scorn on the Jacksons' protestation of common-law marriage: The man testified, "I asked her if she would be my wife, she said 'Yes.' She asked me if I would be her husband, I said 'Yes.' Just like that. Nothing more."[7] The majority further de-legitimized Mrs. Jackson's marital claim by repeatedly referring to her as "the woman" and stating, "[i]f there was no marriage the woman's name was Brethaner."[8]

Turning to legal analysis, the majority brushed aside the defendants' argument that their alleged offense did not fit within the common-law definition of vagrancy, finding that under the statute, cohabitation "by such people . . . constitutes gross immorality and a clear violation of the ordinance."[9] The majority found no racial discrimination in the ordinance, because it applied equally to blacks and whites found cohabitating. Since Mr. Jackson admitted that he was African-American and did not claim to be in a part of the state acquired from Mexico, he could not assert that the statute was vague or limited to only a portion of the state.

The dissenting opinion, authored by Justice Otto Bock, seems to have come from an entirely different universe than the majority. It began "Defendants herein, *Mr. and Mrs. James W. Jackson*, were charged separately in a complaint with vagrancy."[10] The dissent castigated the police for "invad[ing] the home of the Jacksons" without a warrant to arrest them at eleven o'clock at night, a "vindictive, rather than a careful, execution of the vagrancy laws."[11] It censured the majority for mentioning a prior vagrancy conviction, finding the reference "purely gratuitous and absolutely immaterial to the issues."[12]

The dissent concluded that the vagrancy conviction, which was based on an allegedly immoral lifestyle, was inappropriate and could not survive the Jacksons' presumptively valid common-law marriage. If interracial marriage was "immoral," then the anti-miscegenation statute, which was valid in only part of the state, had created a "geographical immorality."[13] A course of life that was only immoral in part of the state could not form the basis for a charge of vagrancy.

The dissent in *Jackson* was something of a last hurrah for Justice Bock. He died less than five months after *Jackson* was issued. Colorado's anti-miscegenation statute survived for another fifteen years, before finally being repealed in 1957, in part due to efforts by attorney John E. Gorsuch, chair of the Domestic Relations Committee of the Colorado Bar Association. Ten years later, the U.S. Supreme Court decided *Loving v. Virginia*,[14] holding unconstitutional such laws in the remaining seventeen states that had them.

Original printing: *The Colorado Lawyer*, January 2005. In addition to the resources cited above, the researcher may find the following useful: Cummins and Kane, Jr., "Miscegenation, the Constitution, & Science," 38 *Dicta* 24 (1961); Sickles, *Race, Marriage & the Law* (Albuquerque, NM: Univ. of N.M. Press 1972). The Tenth Circuit upheld Oklahoma's anti-miscegenation statute in *Stevens v. United States*, 146 F.2d 120, 123 (10th Cir. 1944). There also is an interesting chapter on the continued effect of American attitudes toward interracial marriage on legal issues such as adoption in Bell, *Race, Racism & American Law* 253-88, 5th ed. (New York, NY: Aspen Publishers, 2004). The author thanks Dan Cordova for research assistance with this article.

NOTES

1. *See* map in Wellenstein, *Tell the Court I Love My Wife: Race, Marriage, and Law — An American History* 160, fig. 8 (New York, NY: Palgrave, 2002).

2. *See, e.g.,* Colo. Stat. Ann. Ch. 107, § 2, (1935).

3. *Id.*

4. "Colorado Once Had Two States of Marriage," 121 *Colo. Central Magazine* 6 (2004).

5. *See Jackson v. City & County of Denver*, 124 P.2d 240 (Colo. 1942) (*en banc*).

6. Den. Mun. Code §§ 1345, 1346 (1927).

7. *Jackson*, 124 P.2d at 241.

8. *Id.*

9. *Id.*

10. *Id.* at 242 (Bock, J., dissenting) (*emphasis added*).

11. *Id.* at 243.

12. *Id.*

13. *Id.* at 242.

14. *Loving v. Virginia*, 388 U.S. 1 (1967).

III

"THAT OLD
TIME RELIGION"

INTRODUCTION

C hurches sprouted on the Colorado frontier almost as rapidly as saloons. Though the believers were ardent, their early worship structures were often crude and ephemeral. A Mormon log meeting house built in 1846 in Pueblo, for example — reputedly the first non-Indian house of worship in Colorado — operated for only a few years before being swept away by a flood. A more powerful tide, of settlers with their various religious traditions, would soon inundate the territory, bringing with it the seeds of more enduring and beautiful churches and synagogues.

Catholicism sunk early roots in the Southwestern United States, where Catholic missionaries were among the earliest European visitors. Catholicism absorbed native religious sensibilities and flourished among the area's Hispanic population. Under the 1848 Treaty of Guadalupe Hidalgo between the United States and Mexico, Hispanics in what would soon become Colorado territory were guaranteed the right to practice the Catholic religion. This may be one of the few treaty rights accorded former citizens of Mexico that was actually respected in practice.

In 1851, Hispanics from Taos, New Mexico founded the first town in Colorado, San Luis. By 1860, it was clear that an official representative of the faith was needed to minister to believers and convert unbelievers in the frontier settlements. In that year, the Archbishop of Santa Fe appointed a French priest, Joseph Projectus Machebeuf, to a parish consisting of what later became the states of Colorado and Utah.

Bishop Machebeuf proved a tireless and effective toiler in the vineyard of Colorado during his nearly thirty years of service. Among other things, he was responsible for bringing the Sisters of Charity to Denver, where they staffed St. Joseph's Hospital beginning in 1873 and performed many charitable works among Denver's poor.

Later immigrants from Italy brought their own brand of Catholicism to Colorado. Unfortunately, anti-immigrant sentiment eventually led to the rise of both the Ku Klux Klan and the American Protective Association, anti-immigrant and anti-Catholic organizations that gained considerable political power in the state.

By the 1870s, the religiously inclined in the Colorado territory had their choice of a broad spectrum of Protestant worship opportunities. The Methodist, Baptist, Congregational, and Episcopal denominations thrived. There is some truth to the image of the Methodist preacher on horseback, a Bible in one saddlebag and a pistol in the other. St. James Methodist Church in Central City is one of the oldest church buildings in Colorado that still functions as a church. After some initial failures, the Lutheran Church also proved successful at planting congregations with the influx of German immigrants.

Members of the Jewish faith were also well represented on the Colorado frontier, where they frequently (though certainly not exclusively) found work as merchants and grocers. According to tradition, the first Jewish religious service in Denver occurred on *Rosh Hashanah*, September 29, 1859. If the tradition is true, it indicates there were at least ten adult Jewish males in Denver at the time to firm a *minyan* or quorum for the service. While Colorado would have neither a synagogue nor a full-time rabbi until close to statehood, organized Jewish activities continued throughout the territorial period.

The world's third major monotheistic faith, Islam, would not achieve a visible presence in Colorado until later in the 20th Century. Interestingly, however, scholars have identified survivals of Muslim customs and beliefs among African-Americans brought to the antebellum South as slaves.

America was not without its own homegrown religious groups during this period, most of them tied to the Christian tradition. In addition to Mormonism, that quintessentially American faith, Mary Baker Eddy founded Christian Science in 1870s Boston. In the early 1900s, the so-called Azusa Street Revival in Los Angeles sparked the Pentecostal movement that would later spread world-wide. And Denver eventually gained its own charismatic prophetess, a dynamo named Alma White, who founded the famous Pillar of Fire congregation.

In addition to traditional or formal religion, various non-traditional and initiatory groups made an early appearance on the frontier. Many early Colorado pioneers were members of Masonic lodges. A branch of the "New Thought" movement known as Divine Science had early roots in Denver, founded there by the Brooks sisters. Spiritualism was not without influence, and Coloradans embraced various forms of faith healing.

The flip-side of all this religious enthusiasm was a certain skepticism about religion that prevailed among some adventurous denizens of the frontier. The village atheist was not an unknown figure in the frontier days. S.P. Putnam, author of "Four Hundred Years of Freethought," for example, gave lectures attacking traditional religion at the Tabor Opera House. Freethought organizations were reportedly active in various Colorado towns by the 1890s.

The latter half of the 19th Century represented both a high point for traditional religious sentiment in America and an apogee for a positivist scientism that despised traditional religious creeds as the shopworn relics of barbarism. Victorian intellectuals embraced infidelity with an almost smug certitude that may be difficult to comprehend in a postmodern age. Theirs was the age of European skeptics — Marx, Darwin, and (later) Freud. There is evidence that this European attitude fed a homegrown skepticism that flourished in America.

Mark Twain wrote a number of unpublished freethought works mocking the Bible and actually published a book-length attack on Christian Science during his lifetime. In his youth, Abraham Lincoln wrote an attack on religion, which he was wisely persuaded to keep to himself. But the best-known American unbeliever of the times was probably Robert Green Ingersoll (1833-1899), dubbed "The Great Agnostic."

Ingersoll began his career as an outstanding trial lawyer with a remarkable gift for oratory. He later spoke to packed lecture halls across the country on the evils of revealed religion. His books and speeches were full of a rhetorical bombast that sparked a public furor over issues of faith. It was a furor that would remain unequaled until the fall of "godless" Communism and the rise of Islamic terrorism paved the way for the so-called New Atheists (men like Richard Dawkins, Daniel Dennett, and Sam Harris) to proclaim their anti-religious creed to 21st Century Americans.

FOR FURTHER READING

Ferenc Morton Szasz, *Religion in the Modern American West* (Tucson, AZ: Univ. of Az. Press 2000).

Fred Whitehead, *Freethought on the American Frontier* (Albany, NY: Prometheus Books 1992).

Thomas J. Noel, *Colorado Catholicism and the Archdiocese of Denver 1857-1989* (Denver, CO: Univ. Press of Colo. 1989).

Millikin, Mierow, Hopkins & Colwell, *The Bible and the Gold Rush: A Century of Congregationalism in Colorado* (Denver, CO: Big Mountain Press 1962).

Wilson Thomas Hogue, *History of the Free Methodist Church of North America* (Chicago, IL: Free Methodist Publishing House 1915).

Bah Humbug!

Colorado Law and
the Winter Holiday Season

BY TOM I. ROMERO, II

T he winter holiday season in Colorado is often a time of giving. In
    the case of some Colorado citizens, however, it has been a time
fraught with peril. Colorado's legal history provides a glimpse of the
challenges that have confronted the state's jurists and litigants during
the holidays.

On January 1, 1904, members of an African American dance club
found themselves locked out of Arion Hall in the Enterprise Building
located in downtown Denver. Only a week earlier, on Christmas night,
the club held a dance in the very same hall, although building managers
vigorously opposed their use of the facility. Holding a valid contract to
occupy the hall on both nights, members of the club nevertheless were
barred on New Year's night because the Enterprise Building's owners
and management objected to having the hall utilized by African American citizens. The Colorado Supreme Court did not take kindly to such
a view. According to the Court, "[t]he mere fact that [the building's
agent] rented it to those of that race, or that they were objectionable to
the lessor, affords no legal justification or excuse for locking the hall and
excluding [African Americans] who were reputable and orderly and
conducted themselves in a proper manner."[1]

Similar to the holiday behavior demonstrated by the Enterprise Building's management, the actions of some Longmont skaters left much to be desired. A couple of days before Christmas in 1938, Gladys Williams encountered a large crowd "full of fun and revelry, and composed principally of children, adolescents and the younger social set" at Longmont's Sunset Lake. As she skated that night, a sizable group of revelers were playing "crack-the-whip." When the tail of the whip was suddenly "cracked," a detachment of skaters — "having been rent and torn loose from the whip" — slid out of control toward Williams. Within seconds, Williams lay unconscious on the ice. In rejecting Williams's claim against the City of Longmont, the Colorado Supreme Court recognized the near impossibility of a municipality in supervising young holiday revelers. Indeed, the Court suggested that the public policies associated with the holiday season required a relaxation of normal standards of conduct.[2]

Like Gladys Williams, Denver violinist Leonard Austria learned that the holiday season could be physically dangerous. On February 1, 1954, Austria tripped over a wire mesh fence that city workers had erected around elaborate Christmas decorations on the front steps of the municipal building. The post-holiday mishap left Austria with a few broken teeth, several sizable cuts, and a lawsuit against the City and County of Denver. In attempting to avoid liability for Austria's injuries, the City and County of Denver argued that Colorado law (CRS 1953, 36-4) compelled the city to assemble its garish holiday display. The Colorado Supreme Court, however, rejected this line of reasoning, arguing instead "that it is not within the bounds of judicial reasoning to say that placing Christmas decorations on the municipal building or courthouse, and the removal thereof, is a governmental function. The municipal government . . . can operate at full efficiency in every respect without such decorations."[3]

The whole situation may have been avoided if the city had followed the advice of Mayor Quigg Newton not long after he was elected in 1947. At the time, Mayor Newton proposed toning down the gaudy Christmas display at the City and County Building. Rather than getting

Denver Mayor Quigg Newton
Courtesy University of Colorado at
Boulder, University Archives,
University Photolab Collection

support for his proposal, Newton instead incited what one historian called a "public uproar, second in recent times only to the revolt provoked when the legislature tried to remove the mountains from Colorado license plates. Despite groans from a few aesthetes and atheists, Newton bowed to the majority and reinstalled a full array of Christmas figures, ranging from the Baby Jesus to Rudolph the Red-Nosed Reindeer."[4] In a complete rejection of the pronouncements of the Colorado Supreme Court, Denverites made it patently clear that the holiday display at the City and County Building was not only essential to good government, but central to their civic identity.

Ultimately, Coloradans have negotiated a precarious balance in the legal issues that arise during the winter holiday season. Through jurisprudence on such issues, Colorado courts have historically recognized the spirit of community in the holiday season and, correspondingly, have attempted to find good will in the men, women, children, companies, and municipalities that make up the state's many winter holiday celebrations.

Original printing: *The Colorado Lawyer*, December 2002. The early 20th-Century efforts of Colorado's African American community to enjoy equal access to the state's public facilities during the winter holiday season are documented in the pages of the *Colorado Statesman* and the *Denver Star*, located in the Western History Collection of the Denver Public Library. The lavish light display at the City and County Building of Denver is recounted in Stephen Leonard and Thomas Noel, *Denver: Mining Camp to Metropolis* (Niwot, CO: Univ. Press of Colo., 1990). Based partially on Professor Noel's testimony concerning the municipal building's holiday display history, the Colorado Supreme Court ruled in *Conrad v. City and County of Denver*, 724 P.2d 1309 (Colo. 1986), that the city's nativity display did not violate the Preference Clause of the Colorado State Constitution (Const. Art. 2 § 4).

NOTES

1. *Central Business College Co. v. Rutherford*, 107 P. 279, 280 (Colo. 1910).

2. *Williams v. City of Longmont*, 129 P.2d 110 (Colo. 1942).

3. *City and County of Denver v. Austria*, 318 P.2d 1101 (Colo. 1957).

4. Leonard and Noel, *Denver: Mining Camp to Metropolis* (Niwot, CO: Univ. Press of Colo., 1990) at 246.

"Last Night Was the End of the World"
Prohibition in Colorado

BY TOM I. ROMERO, II

Ｎew Year's Eve, 1915, marked the end of an era in Colorado. At midnight 1916, Colorado became one of the first states in the nation to go dry.[1] Mourning not only the ready availability of fine spirits, but the closing of the Western saloon as a central community institution, patrons of Denver's Heidelberg Café sang "Last Night Was the End of the World," as the barkeepers tapped their last glasses on December 31, 1915.

The two-decade-long struggle to prohibit the sale of alcohol ended what many perceived to be the central force driving lawlessness and lewdness in Colorado. As a major component in Colorado's civic life, alcohol and its prohibition encapsulated notions of "American idealism, progressive hopes for a better society, and widespread prejudice against the sorts of people" that did not quite fit a casual definition of a Coloradan or American citizen.[2]

The legal effort to prohibit the sale and consumption of alcohol began almost as soon as Colorado became a state. For example, early farming and ranching towns enacted ordinances mandating that real estate titles and deeds needed to carry a provision that property would revert to its

79

former owner if liquor were sold on the premises. The political movement to ban alcohol statewide received a major boost in 1893 when Colorado became the second state in the United States to grant women suffrage. With their enhanced political clout, members of the Women's Christian Temperance Union ("WCTU") pushed for laws they believed would not only end drunkenness, but also vice, crime, and other social ills.

The cause of the WCTU also was bolstered by a fear of immigration. Articulated most clearly by the Anti-Saloon League, many Prohibitionists associated alcohol and social disorder with anyone who "looked, spoke, or acted foreign," despite the fact that most of Colorado's pre-Prohibition saloonkeepers were long-term English-speaking residents or that many citizens were frequent patrons. One historian stated: "Xenophobic fears that led Coloradoans to join the American Protective Association in the 1890s and the Klu Klux Klan in the 1920s in record numbers also led them to vote Colorado dry in 1914."[3]

The Colorado Bar played an active role in the passage, regulation, and end of Prohibition. Most prominent was Judge Benjamin Lindsey who publicly linked juvenile delinquency with alcohol consumption. Nevertheless, to Lindsey and many others, Prohibition quickly proved to be a failed experiment. Rather than end lawlessness, Prohibition spawned creative circumvention of the law, bootlegging, gang warfare, and class tension. In testimony before Denver's grand jury in the 1920s, Judge Lindsey lamented how the rich openly disregarded the law while poor men and women down on their luck went to jail for minor alcohol violations. Others, like District Attorney Phillip S. Van Cise, recognized early on that the law could not be effectively enforced. As a result of such disillusion, Colorado voters suspended the state's Prohibition laws on July 1, 1933, several months before the U.S. Congress repealed the Eighteenth Amendment in December 1933.

The socio-legal history of the prohibition of alcohol in the early decades of the 20th Century symbolized the deep fissures that shaped law, order, and moral politics in Colorado. While moral crusaders used legal institutions to challenge what they perceived to be vice and immorality, others used legal loopholes and extra-legal authority to protect what they believed to be fundamental rights. Prohibition was the first, but certainly not the last, sustained legal and political conflict over lifestyle in the Mile High State. For Colorado's socially diverse and politically engaged citizenry, Prohibition was not the end of the world, but, instead, resulted in early 20th Century tensions over hotly contested definitions of liberty and freedom.

Original printing: *The Colorado Lawyer*, January 2003. An early Colorado Prohibition case to reach the Colorado Supreme Court involved the Denver Athletic Club, the Denver Club, and the University Club. In *People v. Denver Athletic Club*, 164 P. 1158 (Colo. 1917), the Court declared that separate 1914 charges against each club for selling intoxicating liquors were moot as a result of the passage of Colorado's Prohibition laws. The social, political, cultural, and legal history of prohibition, as well as the centrality of the early western tavern in Denver and Colorado, is recounted in Thomas J. Noel, *The City and the Saloon: Denver, 1858-1916* (Niwot, CO: Univ. Press of Colorado, 1996) and William Elliot West, *Dry Crusade: The Prohibition Movement in Colorado, 1858-1933* (Ph.D. Diss., University of Colorado, 1971). The role of the Colorado Bar in supporting, enforcing, and ultimately challenging Prohibition is told by Phillip S. Van Cise in his autobiographical work, *Fighting the Underworld* (Cambridge: Riverside Press, 1936). In addition, Judge Benjamin Lindsey's evolving understanding of alcohol, delinquency, and crime can be studied in his personal papers housed at the Library of Congress in Washington, D.C. The early story of Colorado women in affecting legal change, including Prohibition, is detailed in Carolyn J. Stefanco, *Pathways to Power: Women and Voluntary Associations in Denver, Colorado, 1876-1893* (Ph.D. Diss., Duke University, 1987). An unfiltered account of the Colorado chapter of the Women's Christian Temperance Union's Prohibition efforts can be found in their newsletter, housed at the Stephen H. Hart Library at the Colorado Historical Society.

NOTES

1. Chap. 98, Sess. Laws of 1915, amended in 1916 under Chap. 82, Sess. Laws of 1917, and by the so-called "Bone Dry Act," Chap. 141, Sess. Laws of 1919, initiated and passed by Colorado citizens in November 1918.

2. Thomas J. Noel, *The City and the Saloon: Denver, 1858-1916* (Niwot, CO: Univ. Press of Colorado, 1996) at 111.

3. Noel, *id.*

The Limits of Tolerance

Alma White and
the Pentecostal Union Crusade

BY FRANK GIBBARD

Both the Colorado and U.S. Constitutions guarantee absolute free-dom of religious belief. The parameters of permitted religious con-duct are less clear. While Americans tend to tolerate a wide variety of religious expression, the principle of "live and let live" has not always won the day.

In 1902–03, Denver residents had their religious tolerance tested by a remarkable woman named Alma White. White was the founder of the Pentecostal Union. Her church stressed personal holiness and vivid expressions of the spirit, vegetarianism, and women's rights, while dis-couraging non-procreative sexual activity. White also was a vehement anti-Catholic and a supporter of the Ku Klux Klan.

White erected a tent at the corner of Eighteenth and Stout Streets with room for 200 souls. To her neighbors, it must have seemed like a great many more souls than that. The noise from the tent soon proved so loud that a group of the Pentecostal Union's neighbors petitioned the mayor of Denver not to renew the tent permit. The protestors included Denver County Coroner W. P. Horan, who claimed that the noise made by the tent worshipers was almost loud enough to wake his customers.

The Alma Temple in Denver was dedicated in 1937 and bears the call letters of what was then the Pillar of Fire radio station (KPOF)
Darlene Johnson

Supporters of the Pentecostal Union filed their own counter-petitions, and Mayor Robert R. Wright renewed the permit.

Encouraged, White took her crusade to the streets. In February 1903, her followers marched down Seventeenth Street from Champa to Larimer Streets, beating a bass drum, waving handkerchiefs, and carrying banners. These activities were not unusual for evangelical groups of the era. What distinguished the Pentecostal Union was their practice of "leaping for joy." "Leaping" produced physical feats rarely seen outside a sports arena. Leapers were known to jump three or four feet into the air, screaming religious sentiments at the top of their lungs. After the leaping frightened the horses, police moved in and arrested fifteen of White's followers for disturbing the peace.

In jail, White's followers continued their singing and leaping. They appeared in court the next day, carrying banners warning of hellfire and judgment, and were released with a warning. The Unionists persisted in their noisy parading, and were arrested at least two more times. After the third arrest, they earned a two-week jail sentence. White, however, prevailed on Mayor Wright to release them. By early 1904, the Pentecostal Union had constructed a large building at 1845 Champa Street, where its members apparently settled down without further incident.

Would the Pentecostal Unionists have been arrested and jailed today for the same conduct? The Colorado Constitution provides that "the liberty of conscience hereby secured [for religious belief] shall not be construed to . . . justify practices inconsistent with the good order, peace or safety of the state."[1] Under U.S. Supreme Court precedent, generally applicable laws will be upheld, even if they have an incidental effect of burdening a religious practice.[2]

These cases must be balanced against a line of authority beginning with *Cantwell v. Connecticut*,[3] in which the U.S. Supreme Court has upheld the right of religious solicitation and proselytizing on free speech grounds. Unfortunately for the Pentecostal Unionists, however, those favorable Supreme Court decisions were still far in the future.

Alma White lived until 1946, active in ministry until the end of her life. In her later years, she served as "Bishop" White in her Pillar of Fire Church, a more sedate institution. Yet for a time, 100 years ago, Denverites must have felt that White's followers had, in the colorful words of the King James Bible, "turned the world upside down."[4]

Original printing: *The Colorado Lawyer*, August 2004. The standard biography of Alma White is Stanley, *Feminist Pillar of Fire: The Life of Alma White* (Cleveland, OH: The Pilgrim Press, 1993). White's extensive writings include her multi-volume autobiography, White, *The Story of My Life & Pillar of Fire*

(Zaraphath, N.J.: Pillar of Fire, 1935–43). An analysis of White's own religious intolerance can be found in Kandt, "Historical Essay: In the Name of God; an American Story of Feminism, Racism, and Religious Intolerance: the Story of Alma Bridwell White," 8 *Am. Univ.J. of Gender, Social Policy & the Law* 753, 790-94 (2000). Visitors to Morrison, Colorado can view the Pillar of Fire Church dedicated to White in 1932, which now serves a non-denominational congregation.

NOTES

1. Colorado Constitution, Art. II, § 4.

2. *See, e.g., Church of the Lukumi Babalu Aye, Inc. v. City of Hialeah*, 508 U.S. 520, 531 (1993); *Heffron v. International Society for Krishna Consciousness, Inc.*, 452 U.S. 640 (1981).

3. *Cantwell v. Connecticut*, 310 U.S. 296 (1940).

4. Acts 17:6.

The Divinely Scientific Edward C. Smith

Prosecution of a Healer for Hire

BY FRANK GIBBARD

The sign in the window above street level at 14th and California Streets[1] read: "Professor Smith, Healer. Office Hours 9 to 12, 2 to 6."[2] The year was 1910. The prospective "patient" who followed the invitation on Professor Smith's door to "walk in" would not have found inside any of the usual accouterments of a medical office. His office consisted of two comfortably furnished and carpeted rooms with chairs, tables, and pictures. Professor Smith had no license to practice medicine.

NATURAL GIFT FROM ON HIGH

What sort of help, then, could the sufferer expect from Edward C. Smith? Professor Smith claimed to have a natural gift from the Almighty.[3] This gift allowed him to cure "any disease a medical man could, and many they could not."[4] He claimed that he could cure people whom doctors had pronounced incurable. What was more, his gift did not depend on medical knowledge or any technique of science. Indeed, he often remedied illnesses without even knowing exactly what he was treating.

Professor Smith denied using drugs or surgery in his treatments. In fact, the only indication of his actual healing technique lies in evidence excluded from his criminal proceeding: the certificate of incorporation of the Divine Scientific Healing Mission — Smith's church.[5] The church, which he alleged had branches "everywhere,"[6] proclaimed one of its tenets to be "healing the suffering humanity by laying on of hands."[7]

Smith's cures, then, were effected through prayer, connected with the "laying on of hands." Ministers in established churches frequently used this method to perform healings.[8] Why, then, did the authorities single out Professor Smith for prosecution?

BUSINESS VERSUS RELIGION

There seem to have been two reasons Smith was the object of such attention. First, the Professor charged for his cures. Granted, he did not charge everyone. In fact, he prided himself in never turning away anyone for lack of payment.[9] Nevertheless, the fact that he did charge some people made it possible for the prosecution to argue that healing was his business, rather than his religion. Second, he gave himself the medical-sounding title of "healer."

Professor Smith was convicted of practicing medicine without a license, and was fined.[10] He appealed to the Colorado Supreme Court. His defenses were that (1) he was not practicing medicine, and (2) he came within a statutory exemption to the medical licensing statutes that protected "the practice of the religious tenets or the general belief of any church whatsoever, not prescribing or administering drugs."[11] The Supreme Court rejected both arguments.

BUSINESS IN DISGUISE

In reaching its decision, the Court emphasized the commercial nature of Professor Smith's healings. In the five crucial paragraphs of its opinion, the Court used variants of the words "business" or "commercial" no fewer than sixteen times, to describe the nature of Professor Smith's healing enterprise, and to enunciate the reasons the state could regulate it.

The Court dismissed Professor Smith's claim to a religious exemption, stating that the exemption "does not . . . authorize one under the cover of religion or a religious exercise to go into healing commercially for hire, using prayer as the curative agency or treatment. Religion cannot be used as a shield to cover a business undertaking."[12] The Court concluded that "[t]he commercial practice of healing by prayer, followed as a moneymaking venture or occupation, is the practice of medicine within the plain meaning of the statute."[13]

ANALYZING THE COURT'S DECISION

Was the Court's reasoning sound, or was some of the evidence concerning Professor Smith's practices deliberately or conveniently ignored? To fall under the statutory exemption, which the Court essentially held was an affirmative defense to prosecution,[14] Professor Smith had to show only that he was practicing the general tenets of his religion or the general belief of his church, and that he was "not prescribing or administering drugs."[15] From the evidence described in the Supreme Court's decision, he seems to have established each of these facts.

The exemption says nothing about whether money is charged for prayer or for the laying on of hands; however, the Supreme Court placed major stress on the commercial nature of Professor Smith's undertaking, even in addressing his claim to exemption. Could it be that paternalism — a desire to protect the people from a suspected charlatan — really was what motivated the decision? If so, it seems to have been a misguided paternalism. In particular, it is unlikely that anyone seeking help from Professor Smith would be fooled into thinking that he was "practicing medicine" or "prescribing or administering drugs." It seems more likely that people came to him for "supernatural" assistance, not medical care. Shouldn't rational adults have been permitted to decide what method of healing they preferred, and even to pay for it if they concluded that "the laborer is worthy of his hire"?[16]

SPECIAL CONCURRENCE

Supreme Court Justice Musser's special concurrence seems to exhibit some discomfort with the focus in the majority's approach on economic factors. The somewhat elliptical wording of the concurrence, however, suggests an attempt to avoid pointed questions. Justice Musser stressed the jury's resolution of the exemption question under the reasonable doubt standard, but did not discuss the specific evidence on which he relied to conclude that standard was met.

FAITH HEALING TODAY

The use of faith healing has become a topic of controversy in Colorado within the past few years. Until July 1, 2001, a parent who chose and legitimately practiced "treatment by spiritual means through prayer" was exempt from prosecution for child abuse solely from the use of that method of treatment rather than traditional medical care.[17] However, that exemption has been repealed. Interestingly, Colorado's dependency and neglect statutes do retain an exemption for children treated "solely by spiritual means through prayer in accordance with a recognized method of religious healing."[18]

Original printing: *The Colorado Lawyer*, September 2006.

NOTES

1. The exact address was 1439 California Street. This building apparently functioned as, among other things, a rooming house. It had connections to at least one well-known Denver name: Mrs. Madge A. Wynkoop, who was listed in the 1903 and 1904 Denver City directories as a resident of the building. Wynkoop worked as a stenographer, and later as a bookkeeper, for Schiele Bros. & Moreland, a Colorado cigar manufacturer.

2. The facts concerning Professor Smith's practice are directly adapted from the Colorado Supreme Court's opinion in *Smith v. People*, 117 P. 612, 614 (1911).

3. *Id.*

4. *Id.*

5. Research turned up no church in Denver known as the "Divine Scientific Healing Mission." The "First Divine Science Church," however, which still exists, was established in 1899 in Denver. *See* http://www.dvscdnvr.org. Interestingly, an early affiliate, the "College of Divine Science" met from 1896 to 1898 at 1410 Curtis Street, three blocks from Professor Smith's office. *See generally* Brooks, *Early History of Divine Science* (Denver, CO: First Divine Science Church, 1963). There is no indication of a connection between Professor Smith and the First Divine Science Church, but the name of the better-known church may have influenced the name he chose for his own.

6. It is difficult to know where, in the spectrum of American religion, Professor Smith's beliefs fell. His use of the term "Divine Scientific" seems to place him within the general orbit of the "New Thought" movement, a sort of quasi-Gnostic approach to religion very popular during the late 1800s and early 1900s, and still influential today. New Thought emphasizes the human ability to transcend bodily limitations such as sickness by realizing the body's essentially divine nature. *See, e.g.,* http://divinescience.com/links/links_newthought.htm. On the other hand, the emphasis on laying on of hands, and Smith's stress that his powers were "the gift of the divine spirit" (*Smith, supra* note 2 at 614), suggests that he may have been influenced by the early Pentecostal-Charismatic movement, which began in Los Angeles during the famous Azusa Street revival in 1906. *See generally* Harvey Cox, *The Legacy of Azusa Street*, http://www.beliefnet.com/story/189/story_18913_1.html.

7. *Smith, supra* note 2 at 614. The tradition of prayer and laying on of hands to cure the sick is a long-standing practice within Christian churches. *See, e.g.,* Mark 16:18 (KJV): "[T]hey shall lay hands on the sick, and they shall recover."

8. "The practice of laying on of hands has deep roots in the apostolic tradition of healing ministry." *See* http://www.redeemerstpaul.org/Healing.htm.

9. *Smith, supra* note 2 at 614.

10. *See* CRS, Ch. 127, § 6069 (1908), which prohibited one who did not have a license to practice medicine from: (1) holding himself out to the public as being engaged in the diagnosis and treatment of diseases; (2) prescribing any treatment for mental or physical ailments with the intention of receiving compensation therefor; (3) maintaining an office for the treatment of diseases or injuries; or (4) attaching any word or abbreviation to his name suggesting that he was engaged in the treatment of diseases or injuries.

11. *See id.*
12. *Smith, supra* note 2 at 615.
13. *Id.*
14. *Id.*
15. *Id.* at 614, *quoting* CRS § 6069.
16. Luke 10:7 (KJV).
17. CRS § 18-6-401(6).
18. CRS § 19-3-103.

Liquor and Dynamite

A One-Man Vice Crusade
Yields Explosive Results

BY FRANK GIBBARD

Two significant events in the history of alcohol prohibition occurred on April 7, 1891. Erstwhile temperance lecturer and circus
impresario P.T. Barnum breathed his last, and the Colorado legislature
passed a new statute, closing all saloons state-wide at midnight every
night and all day on Sunday.[1]

Sunday closing laws had a long pedigree, dating back to New England's 17th Century "blue laws."[2] By 1891, all but four states in the Union
required that saloons be closed on Sunday.[3] Colorado already had a Sunday closing law, as well as many other laws on the books regulating the
liquor business, including prohibitions on selling to Indians and a law
permitting local authorities to forbid the sale of alcohol to "minors, apprentices, insane, idiotic or distracted persons, drunkards, or intoxicated
persons."[4] The Colorado legislature must have concluded, however, that
existing liquor laws had failed to adequately deter saloon-goers from
drinking on the Sabbath.

Public opinion on the new law was sharply divided. For some people,
however, the issues were clear. In particular, the Reverend Florida F.
Passmore of the Breckenridge Methodist Church supported a no-
tolerance approach to enforcement of the statute. He regularly made the

Reverend Passmore's church, now named the Father Dyer Church, restored and still active in Breckenridge

Gary Abrams

rounds of the saloons in Breckenridge to ensure they were not violating the Sabbath with liquor sales. Woe betide the saloon-keeper whom the Reverend Passmore found dispensing spiritous liquors after 12:00 a.m. on a Sunday! The Reverend would not hesitate to report this transgression to the nearest officer of the law. If the officer would not take action, Reverend Passmore would seek forfeiture of the officer's bond for failure to enforce the laws.[5]

The Reverend Passmore's Sunday-closing campaign evidently was a great success, at least from his point of view. An editorial in the *Summit County Journal*, however, took a different view. The Reverend had deprived Breckenridge of the one thing that made life worth living there on Sundays. Editorial writer Jonathan C. Fincher described local miners standing on the sidewalks after the closing law went into effect, on a damp and dreary Sunday, "looking wistfully to the right or left for some retreat from a condition of misery."[6] Fincher raged that the saloon law "was conceived in the brain of a fanatic, enacted by a body of imbeciles, signed by a doughface, and [losing a bit of rhetorical steam] in a camp like Breckenridge, would be enforced only by an impractical enthusiast."[7] Making a connection between organized religion and disorganized vice common in freethought bombast,[8] Fincher noted that the law had been passed in Denver, a place "weighed down with cathedrals, churches, chapels and colleges, and crowded with night prowlers, policemen, preachers, priests, and professors."[9] In Fincher's opinion, the sin of spending Sunday in a saloon could not compare with the decadence of priestcraft-ridden Denver.

We will never know in whose alcohol-deprived brain the desperate plot for revenge on the Reverend Passmore was hatched. Perhaps it was a community effort. The Reverend's striving for higher and better things was epitomized by the elaborate bell and belfry he had installed on the simple structure of his Methodist church. "The bell could be heard through the thin mountain air to call the faithful to services,"[10] and surely was heard with resentment on Sundays by the miners wandering the damp and dreary streets of Breckenridge in a state of enforced sobriety.

On Monday night, August 17, 1891, an unknown person or persons climbed the belfry of the Breckenridge Methodist Church, set a delayed fuse, and dynamited the bell. The resulting explosion sent shards of the demolished bell in all directions and awakened nearly everyone in town.

Undeterred, the Reverend Passmore ordered a new, heavier bell, which arrived a couple of months later. He stepped up his anti-vice crusade, seeking to shut down all gambling in the town, in addition to Sunday drinking. After he was reappointed by the Methodist Church to serve in Breckenridge, the townspeople responded by hanging him in effigy. He was warned to leave town. The Reverend managed to stay another year, however, until his successor was appointed. Ultimately, he was expelled from the ministry after he began giving speeches in which he accused officials of his own denomination of complicity with the liquor trade.

Colorado law currently restricts the sale of liquor on Sundays, as it has since the end of Prohibition.[11] Every so often, the legislature considers repeal of this remaining vestige of the blue laws. The Reverend Passmore surely would not approve. [*Editor's Note:* The law was changed in 2008 to allow Sunday sales of liquor in Colorado.]

Original printing: *The Colorado Lawyer*, May 2006.

NOTES

1. Saloons, House Bill 203, 1891 Sess. L. 315, *codified at* Colo. Stat. Ann., Ch. 36 § 1346d (1904).

2. For a fascinating — if rather jaundiced look — at those laws, *see* Myers, *Ye Olden Blue Laws* (New York, NY: The Century Co., 1921).

3. *The Cyclopedia of Temperance and Prohibition* 622 (New York, NY: Funk & Wagnalls, 1891). The four holdouts were California, Montana, Nevada, and Texas.

4. *Id.* at 280.

5. Fiester, *Blasted Beloved Breckenridge* 186 (Boulder, CO: Pruett Publishing Co., 1973).

6. *Summit County Journal*, Aug. 1, 1891, *reprinted in* Fiester, *supra* note 5 at 186.

7. *Id.* A "doughface" was a Northerner sympathetic to the South during the Civil War. *Webster's New Collegiate Dictionary* 342 (7th ed., 1975).

8. The 1890s were the apogee of free thought in the United States. Robert Green Ingersoll (1833–1899), dubbed "The Great Agnostic," lectured to large crowds on the evils of organized religion.

9. *Supra* note 6.

10. Jessen, *Bizarre Colorado* 147 (Loveland, CO: J.V. Publications, 1994).

11. *See* CRS § 12-47-901(5)(b).

IV

MURDER MOST FOUL

INTRODUCTION

D enver was never quite as "wild" as some other parts of the "Wild West." Though the city experienced a period of lawlessness, it was comparatively brief, lasting mostly for the first two years of its existence during the height of the "gold rush." Nevertheless, the homicide rate during these first two years is alarming by today's standards. There were four reported murders in Denver in 1859, for example, and thirteen in 1860, among a population of just under five thousand people. This is a rate more serious by an order of magnitude than the citizens of Denver experience today.

Prior to the establishment of formal police and judicial structures, vigilante justice held sway in Colorado Territory. Historian Stephen J. Leonard has identified 175 lynchings in Colorado beginning in 1859, for crimes ranging from theft to murder. All but two of these lynchings occurred prior to 1907, making this a true Old West phenomenon. In the 1860s, the high point of the lynching craze, horse thieves, rapists, and outlaws all met their demise at the end of a noose, with or without judicial formalities. The concept that the death penalty should be awarded only for murder, and then only in the worst cases — with appropriate weighing of aggravating and mitigating factors — was unknown on the Colorado frontier.

Some killings carried out by quasi-official groups during this period are hard to classify as lynchings. They fall somewhere between mob action and military force. I have already mentioned the 1864 Sand Creek Massacre of peaceable Cheyenne and Arapaho Indians. What may be less well known is that the Sand Creek Massacre was not the only atrocity committed that year by Colonel John M. Chivington's militia. A few months before he massacred the Native Americans encamped on Sand Creek, Chivington ordered his men to gun down five captured members of a Confederate terrorist group.

These killings allegedly were performed under the guise of foiling an escape attempt. There is evidence, however, that the "escaping" Confederates were still locked in leg irons at the time. Chivington's reputation as a "hero" in the struggle against Confederate sympathies in the territory may only have encouraged him in perpetrating the later and greater atrocity against Native Americans for which he became infamous.

Although the informal and rough justice of the people's courts and miners' courts was superseded by the installation of a territorial government, a glance at Colorado's early session laws shows that justice in cases of murder at least was still swift and unyielding. The 1861 session laws prescribed death by hanging for murder, to be carried out no less than fifteen and no more than twenty-five days after the pronouncement of sentence. The convict's body was not spared the indignity of dissection, which could be ordered on the application to the court by any respectable surgeon. The deceased's friends and relatives were specifically prohibited from claiming the body, even to give it a Christian burial.

These early statutes did recognize various degrees of homicide. In this respect, they occasionally have a Levitical ring to them, as when they define "excusable homicide by misadventure," an event transpiring "when a person doing a lawful act, without any intention of killing, yet unfortunately kills another, as where a man is at work with an axe and the head flies off and kills a bystander, or where a parent is moderately correcting a child, or [a] master his servant or scholar, or an officer punishing a criminal, and happens to occasion death." Colo. Rev. Stat., Ch. XXII, § 33 (1868). (The comment about an axe-head flying off, incidentally, does not appear in the original 1861 session law, but it seems to have been borrowed directly from Deuteronomy 19:5.)

Other interesting features of these early penal statutes include an anti-dueling statute, which provided that participants in a duel resulting in death were subject to conviction of a high misdemeanor, carrying a relatively mild sentence of imprisonment from one to five years but also disqualifying them from public office. The penalty extended not only to direct participants, but to their seconds and other aiders and abettors. The statutes also abolished the separate offense of petit treason, stating that henceforth it would be treated as murder. Finally, a prosecution for murder might await a woman who aborted her viable child.

Other famous murders in early Colorado history include the case of Alfred (or "Alferd") Packer, a gold-seeker who left Provo, Utah for the Colorado goldfields in November 1873. Against the advice of friendly Indians, Packer and his group decided to make the trek from Montrose to Gunnison in mid-February. The group became hopelessly lost and snowbound and eventually ran out of food. Packer, who survived the ordeal, was later accused of killing and roasting some of his companions to stay alive. He escaped from custody but was eventually recaptured, tried, convicted of manslaughter, and given a forty-year sentence, considered very long in those days. He was eventually paroled and purportedly died a vegetarian.

The Ludlow Massacre occurred at the end of the Old West days. It marked the culmination of a period of serious labor unrest that pitted coal miners against mine owners. The quasi-feudal conditions prevailing in company towns, together with extremely hazardous conditions in the mines, led miners to organize with the United Mine Workers of American. In 1913, after the mine owners rejected their demands, the UMW called a strike at several Southern Colorado mines. The miners, who were summarily evicted from their homes in company towns, set up a tent city near Ludlow. The militia reacted by randomly shooting into the tents, killing and maiming some of their inhabitants. For their part, union workers attacked the "scabs," the workers the companies hired to replace the strikers. The Colorado National Guard was eventually called on to restore order.

In retaliation for the murder of a scab, the Guard burned down one of the tent colonies. Eventually, the Guard was withdrawn for financial reasons, but mine company employees were allowed to remain on in

Guard uniforms. On April 20, 1914, a firefight broke out between miners and the militia. In the resulting chaos, a fire broke out in the tent city at Ludlow, resulting in the deaths of thirteen women and children by asphyxiation or burning. Six other people, including miners, militiamen, and one child, also died by shooting in the violence. It was one of the deadliest incidents in a long and violent struggle between miners and those who provided their livelihood.

FOR FURTHER READING

Dick Kreck, *Murder at the Brown Palace: A True Story of Seduction and Betrayal* (Fulcrum Pub. 2003).

Stephen J. Leonard, *Lynching in Colorado 1859 – 1919* (Boulder, CO: Univ. Press of Colorado 2002).

George S. McGovern & Leonard F. Guttridge, *The Great Coalfield War* (Niwot, CO: Univ. Press of Colorado 1996).

Barnaby Conrad, *A Revolting Transaction* (Arbor House 1983).

Paul H. Gantt, *The Case of Alfred Packer, the Man Eater* (Denver, CO: Univ. of Denver Press 1952).

John Husband, "The Colorado Coal Wars of 1913 and 1914: Some Issues Still Debated Today," 26 *The Colorado Lawyer* 147 (June 1997), available at www.cobar.org/tcl.

Law, Order, and Municipal Authority in Colorado's Early Mining Towns

BY TOM I. ROMERO, II

In May 1859, prospector John H. Gregory, vegetable gardener D. K. Wall, and a few select associates returned to the mountain canyons Gregory had explored earlier that winter. Following Clear Creek from its confluence with the South Platte, Gregory brought Wall about thirty-five miles west of Denver to the rich vein of ore that he previously discovered. Without the aid of lawyers, who were admittedly in short supply, Gregory and Wall divided up the most promising claim sites between themselves and returned to Denver to organize and announce to the world the creation of the Gregory Mining District. The action brought a horde of would-be prospectors into the area. Within weeks, miners from Canada, Ireland, Germany, Mexico, and other parts of the United States formed shelters, located claims, and erected the institutions that became the basis of Colorado's earliest municipal mountain settlements in Central City, Mountain City, Nevada City, and Black Hawk.

Literally and figuratively, Central City — established by prospectors and miners in June 1859 — was the vital center of what came to be known as "the richest square mile on earth." Due to the fact that miners dominated the area, municipal organization in Central City and neighboring communities was based solely on mining rules, codes, and regulations. On their face, miners' courts provided a forum to resolve the

"Gregory Gold Diggings, Colorado, May 1859," a wood engraving, appeared in an 1867 book, *Beyond the Mississippi: From the Great River to the Great Ocean*, by Albert D. Richardson
Courtesy David Erickson collection

disputes of an international population. Central City and the mining district it governed granted citizenship rights to all European and American miners who held valid, legally recorded claims. Organized on a popular basis, mining-camp law attempted to provide simple justice, without much legal jargon or technical legislation. Indeed, almost all of the early mining cities barred lawyers from interfering with the collective will and authority of the miners and their courts.

Not surprisingly, miners chafed for years at federal and state attempts to bring them under judicial control and surveillance. For example, in 1861, a Central City miner shot a county deputy appointed by the territorial legislature. After the shooting, the miner turned himself in to the miners' court. After a short deliberation, the miners' court found the miner not guilty because he believed he was defending his property. Later that year, a territorial judge sitting in the Gregory District used a revolver to restrain a mining litigant. When the miner responded by brandishing his own weapon, the spectators — mostly miners — drew their weapons and prepared for a "trial by fire." Although no one was killed, extreme distrust existed between miners and the state government for decades to come.

At the end of years of speculative claims and a decline in the local production of gold in 1864, those entrepreneurial laborers remaining in Central City formed the foundation of civic life. A police court was opened in 1865, and a fire department was organized in 1869. After fire ravaged Central City in 1874, miners, as well as millers, mechanics, and small businesspeople living in the city, vested city officials with the power to create the city's first zoning regulations by limiting new buildings to be constructed exclusively of brick or stone. Finally, in 1875, after miners battled with the city officials regarding mineral and land claims, Central City received its municipal patent. With the patent, the city had the ability to distribute and grant title to municipal properties that did not infringe on mining claims.

Ironically, the municipal patents, charters, and mining claims in Colorado's earliest cities were drawn up and sustained by those lawyers and judges who early citizens had labored so hard to exclude from local law, order, and municipal organization. In the Centennial State, lawyers eventually became as indispensable as mining engineers to the successful maintenance and organization of Colorado's mining communities.

Original printing: *The Colorado Lawyer*, October 2002.

Heat of Passion
A Murder on the Streets of Leadville

BY FRANK GIBBARD

It seems possible that Charles M. Kent knew Thomas G. Bennett professionally before he killed him. The 1882 city directory for the City of Leadville identifies Kent as treasurer of the Globe Theater. Bennett is listed in the same directory as a musician. The third party in the triangle, the woman who called herself "Carrie Bennett," is not listed at all.

Before Charles Kent married her, Carrie had been Thomas Bennett's mistress for about three years. She became Mrs. Charles Kent in April 1882. It was a significant month in Leadville, Colorado. Playwright Oscar Wilde had just arrived on his tour of the West. Leadville's new baseball team, the Blues, played its first exhibition game in April, and was on its way to a spectacular season.

Mrs. Kent was having an exciting time as well. She did not let marriage slow her down. She continued to visit "low dance halls, frequented only by lewd women and men who desired to associate with them."[1] She "hired a room in a house of prostitution for the purpose of meeting men away from her home."[2] In sum, she "continued her dissolute life after marriage as before."[3]

At his murder trial, the testimony indicated that Charles Kent knew of his wife's scandalous activities during their marriage. It is unclear

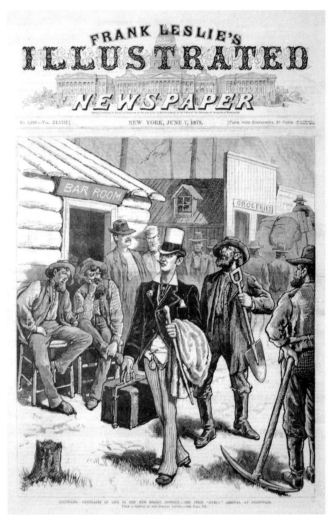

"A Swell Arrives in Leadville," from the June 7, 1879, issue of
Frank Leslie's Illustrated Newspaper
Courtesy David Erickson collection

whether he tried to curtail them. Perhaps he benefited financially from
her exploits, or perhaps he was simply unable to change her behavior.
One thing we do know: Kent and his new bride were known "to speak
of and to each other in the most disrespectful style, using towards each
other in public places the vilest epithets."[4] It seems the Kent marriage
was not one made in heaven.

On July 3, 1882, Kent left home and went into downtown Leadville, intending to travel to Gunnison. We do not know the reason for the trip or why he found himself unable to complete it. When he returned home to Leadville, Kent found Thomas Bennett, Carrie's former lover, in bed with his wife.

Kent did not react violently to this discovery; at least, not right away. Instead, he left and went down the street, where he got drunk and bought a revolver, not necessarily in that order. He later showed off the revolver to witnesses, stating there would be trouble the next time he and Bennett met.

The meeting he had prophesied occurred the next day. On July 4, 1882, witnesses saw Kent and Bennett engaged in a fistfight on Harrison Avenue, the street on which Leadville's City Hall and the famous Delaware Hotel are now located. The two men shoved each other for a few minutes. Then Bennett broke away and ran, attempting to hide behind a bystander. The human shield did not save Bennett. Kent shot Bennett, who staggered across the street, collapsed on the opposite sidewalk, and died a few minutes later.

The issues at Kent's murder trial centered on his state of mind when he killed Bennett. Kent's defense relied on provocation, heat of passion, and self-defense. Witnesses testified that a pair of brass knuckles were found next to Bennett's body, and that Kent had appeared visibly battered when they saw him in jail. In the end, the jury rejected Kent's self-defense theory and convicted him of manslaughter. He was sentenced to ten years in the penitentiary.

On appeal to the Colorado Supreme Court, Kent focused on the complex and confusing jury instructions given at his trial. Kent argued, among other things, that the instructions had improperly shifted the burden to him to prove self-defense. Although the Court found at least one of the instructions misleading, it concluded that in light of all the instructions, Kent had received a fair trial.[5] The Court clearly found the burden of proof issue troubling, however, for its opinion continued on for eleven more pages, during which it conducted a painstaking historical analysis of the common law principles that underlay the burden of proof problem in murder cases.

Tracing the law of presumption in murder cases back to Danish and Norman antecedents and to a case decided by the King's Bench in the days of King James I, the Colorado Supreme Court concluded that once the state had proved an offense beyond a reasonable doubt, it was the defendant's responsibility to produce evidence that would mitigate, justify, or excuse his conduct.[6] Warming to the topic, the Court went on to discuss such extrinsic defenses as alibi and insanity, neither of which had anything to do with Kent's case. The bottom line was that Kent's manslaughter conviction, which the Court concluded was the result of the jury's humane application of the reasonable doubt principle given the evidence against him, was allowed to stand.[7]

Original printing: *The Colorado Lawyer*, May 2005. For more on the Leadville baseball team, the Blues, see Smith, "Baseball Champions of Colorado: The Leadville Blues of 1882," *Journal of Sport History* (Spring 1977) at 51-71. Oscar Wilde's 1882 adventures in Leadville are described in Ellmann, *Oscar Wilde* (New York, NY: Vintage, 1988) at 204-05. There are a number of good, recent books concerning vintage prostitution in Colorado, including Mackell, *Brothels, Bordellos & Bad Girls* (Albuquerque, NM: Univ. of N.M. Press, 2004) and Secrest, *Hell's Belles: Denver's Brides of the Multitudes* (Aurora, CO: Hindsight Hist. Pubs., 1996), rev. ed. (Boulder, CO: Univ. Press of Colo., 2002).

NOTES

1. *Kent v. People*, 9 P. 852, 852 (Colo. 1886).
2. *Id.*
3. *Id.*
4. *Id.*
5. *Id.* at 854-55.
6. *Id.* at 863.
7. *Id.* at 866.

A Case of Gift *Causa Mortis* and the Dead Man's Statute

BY FRANK GIBBARD

> There is only one basic plot for fiction:
> things are not as they seem.
> —Jim Thompson[1]

M ystery writers love the plot device known as "the snap," in which the author reveals some previously unknown fact that twists the reader's entire perspective on the tale. This technique can add spice to a mystery novel, but hidden facts that surface during real-life transactions can be disastrous. Take the case of Charles Conner, who in 1882 attempted to cash in a certificate of deposit for a friend, only to find himself embarked on a six-year voyage through the legal system, including a trip to the Colorado Supreme Court.[2]

PRESENTMENT AND DISHONOR

On January 17, 1882, Conner showed up at the Colorado National Bank of Denver (Bank), bearing a certificate of deposit in the amount of $943.40.[3] The Bank had issued the certificate the month before to Annie Reardon. It was endorsed with Reardon's signature.

The Bank determined, however, that the endorsement on the certificate did not match the signature in its book. Granted, Conner could have had reason to question the Bank's own file signature for Reardon. The Bank's cashier had noted in the signature book that Reardon had "a sore finger" when she signed it.[4] Nevertheless, the Bank refused to pay on the dissimilar endorsement.

CONNER AND ROOT STRIKE A DEAL

Conner returned to the Bank the next day with Amos H. Root, a prominent Denver businessman.[5] The two men had reached an agreement. Root would guarantee the endorsement and obtain the certificate funds from the Bank. Once Conner could demonstrate the genuineness of the endorsement and provide indemnification to Root, Root would pay over the funds to Conner. Root sweetened the pot with a promise of interest at the rate of 10 percent. The Bank, satisfied with Root's guarantee, paid him the money.

THINGS FALL APART

It was precisely at this point, with the deal seemed clinched, that Conner and Root's neat arrangement began to fall apart. On the morning of January 18, 1882, the same day Root and Conner were withdrawing her money from the Bank, Annie Reardon died. Actually, as it turned out, her name was not "Annie Reardon" at all; it was "Joanna Hennessey." Reardon had married a man named Hennessey on January 1, 1882, shortly after she purchased the certificate. To make things worse, the administrator of her estate now announced that the estate was the proper owner of the certificate and its proceeds, not Amos Root or Charles Conner.

A stand-off ensued. Root had the money, Conner had the contract, and Hennessey was beneficiary of the estate. Finally, in October 1882, Conner sued Root on the contract. The estate was permitted to intervene, and a Bench trial proceeded. It was during this trial that the rest of the story surfaced — a tawdry little tale of greed, theft, and brutality fit for a pulp novel.

The A. H. Root Building at 1501 Platte Street in Denver is on the National Register of Historic Properties
Darlene Johnson

THE MYSTERY OF
THE FORGED ENDORSEMENT

At trial, several experts testified that the endorsement of Annie Reardon/Joanna Hennessey was a forgery. The issue of whether Joanna Hennessey had endorsed the certificate to Conner was, however, soon overshadowed by another question: Why would she have done so? Why would a newly married woman hand over a certificate of deposit worth a large sum of money to a friend, instructing him, rather than her husband, to cash it in for her? The answer Conner presented was chilling.

A WOMAN BRUTALIZED

At trial, Dr. Bickensderfer, who attended Joanna Hennessey during her brief, fatal illness, testified that she had fallen ill with pain and fever within a week of her marriage to Hennessey. Conner's attorney asked him what had made her so ill. The court sustained an objection to this question, and Conner made an offer of proof. If permitted, Dr. Bickensderfer would testify that Annie Reardon had been in good health before she married Hennessey, but that Hennessey had treated her so brutally on the first night of their marriage that she had fallen terminally ill. Conner would testify further that Hennessey had used abusive language with his wife and had "nearly turned her out of bed looking for keys."[6] After the events of that night, she regarded Hennessey with such horror that she called on neighbors to keep him away from her until she died, which was only seventeen days later.[7]

There was other testimony about Joanna Hennessey's loathing for her new husband. Maria Clark, an acquaintance of Joanna Hennessey, stated that Joanna told her that her husband had "robbed her [on] the first night of their marriage — robbed her of one hundred and some dollars; had ruined her for life; had murdered her; and said she didn't want him to enter her room at all."[8] Another acquaintance testified that Joanna Hennessey told him, "I made a terrible mistake. I thought I had married a man, but I married a brute."[9]

Other witnesses testified that Joanna Hennessey had signed over the certificate to Conner because she no longer trusted her husband, and that she wanted Conner to pay her debts before she died, as well as her funeral expenses afterward. Any remaining funds were to be given to her friend Maggie Hunt, with whom she previously had operated a restaurant on Larimer Street and who had nursed her in her final illness.[10] Finally, the undertaker testified that Conner had paid Joanna Hennessey's funeral expenses, as instructed.

Given this evidence, one could piece together a tale of a brutalized woman who turned to loyal friends in her dying hour of need. But was this the whole story? More disturbing facts would come out at trial, facts that would cast doubt on Conner and Hunt's tidy explanation of the events. A "snap" was in the offing, and the result would not be pretty for Conner and Hunt.

THE PLOT THICKENS

First, evidence was presented that Joanna Hennessey actually had been too weak to endorse the certificate herself. She did so only with help from Conner, who "took hold of her hand with the pen, and wrote the name on the certificate."[11] By itself, this evidence was ambiguous. It could suggest merely that a dying woman needed help holding her pen. But there was more. Hennessey testified that he was in his wife's room six days before her death, "when she threw a pitcher at Maggie Hunt, and charged that she and Conner were robbing her."[12] According to Hennessey, Maggie Hunt responded that Joanna Hennessey was raving. But Hennessey's story was corroborated by a disinterested witness named Kennedy, who said she heard Joanna Hennessey tell her husband "that the keys were under her pillow, or else in the trunk; to take care of them, that Maggie and Conner would rob her, had done it partly; that she had $150, and it was nearly gone."[13] Finally, there was the interesting fact that Conner and Maggie Hunt were married soon after Joanna Hennessey died.

MANY QUESTIONS

So what really happened? Was Hennessey a monster who stole his wife's money and scared her literally to death, causing her, in desperation, to resort to friends to make sure she at least had a decent burial? Were Conner and Hunt conniving forgers and thieves, stealing a dying woman's property, then perhaps lying about her husband? Was Joanna Hennessey delusional, accusing everyone around her of robbing her, and working herself into a paranoid frenzy just before her death? The answers to these questions may never be known; however, this much is known: the trial court ruled for the estate administrator and, hence, for Hennessey.

THE SUPREME COURT CASE

Conner appealed the court's ruling in favor of the estate administrator, and the case proceeded to the Colorado Supreme Court.[14] The Court began by disposing of a "red herring" — the genuineness of the endorsement. If Joanna Hennessey had gifted the certificate to Conner and Hunt during her final illness, in anticipation of her death (a so-called "gift *causa mortis*"), then she could have done so merely by delivering the certificate to Conner. No written endorsement was necessary.[15] However, Conner still would have to prove, by clear and unequivocal evidence, that a gift *causa mortis* actually had been made.

Contrary to the trial court's verdict, the Supreme Court clearly believed that Conner had gone a long way toward meeting that burden. "Wrecked, as [Joanna Hennessey] was, upon the threshold of her wedded life," the Court opined, "if the cause thereof was according to the evidence offered, it seems but natural and reasonable that she should turn, as it is said she did, from him who was her husband, to her who seemed kind and constant [that is, Maggie Hunt], and, as best she could, divert from him to her, what little of property and money she would have left after her death and burial."[16]

What the Doctor Should Have Said and the Husband Couldn't

The Supreme Court further held that in ruling for the estate administrator, the trial court had made some key evidentiary errors. First, it should have permitted Dr. Bickensderfer and others to testify about her husband's mistreatment of Joanna Hennessey. Testimony "offered to show the nature and cause of [the] illness of the deceased, and the conduct of her husband touching the same" was relevant, because it showed why Joanna Hennessey would have wanted to give the certificate to

Conner and Hunt, rather than to her husband.[17] Second, the court should not have allowed Conner, Hunt, or Hennessey to testify concerning facts that occurred prior to Joanna Hennessey's death, because they were all potential beneficiaries of the certificate.[18] Accordingly, the Supreme Court reversed and remanded for a new trial.[19]

The Dead Man's Statute and Gift Causa Mortis

The bar to testimony that the Supreme Court applied, preventing testimony by interested witnesses concerning the circumstances of a gift from the decedent, is known as the "dead man's statute." The version of this statute in effect at the time of the trial in *Conner v. Root*[20] provided that a party to a civil action or interested person (such as Conner, Hunt, and Hennessey) should not be permitted to present his or her own testimony concerning events involving the deceased, where the administrator of the estate was an adverse party.[21] The statute provided a number of exceptions. For example, it permitted testimony concerning facts that occurred after the death of the deceased.[22]

The former version of this statue, which stood essentially unchanged for 100 years, was criticized for an overbroad approach that led to perceived injustices.[23] The current version takes a different approach. Today, statements made by persons "incapable of testifying" — such as a decedent — are permitted if the statement was made under oath at a time when the person was competent to testify; if the statement "is corroborated by material evidence of an independent and trustworthy nature"; or if the opposing party introduces evidence of a related statement.[24]

The basic law of gift *causa mortis*, however, has not changed since *Conner* was decided. There are essentially three requirements:

1) the gift must be made in contemplation, fear, or peril of death;

2) the donor must die of the illness or peril that he then fears or contemplates; and

3) the delivery must be made with the intent that the title shall vest only in case of death.[25]

The story behind *Conner* shows that the determination of these issues can be very convoluted indeed.

Original printing: *The Colorado Lawyer*, July 2007. The author thanks Daniel B. Cordova, Colorado Supreme Court Librarian, for his extensive and invaluable research assistance on this article.

NOTES

1. *Quoted in* Polito, *Savage Art: A Biography of Jim Thompson* (Alfred A. Knopf, 1995) at 7. Jim Thompson (1906-77) was an American hard-boiled detective novelist. Several films, including "The Grifters," are based on his novels. He is perhaps best known for "The Killer Inside Me," his study of a small-town psychopathic sheriff and his crimes.

2. The facts as described here are taken from *Conner v. Root*, 17 P. 773 (Colo. 1888).

3. This sum of money would be the equivalent in purchasing power of approximately $20,400 in 2009 dollars. *See* "Purchasing Power of Money in the United States from 1774 to 2006," available at www.measuringworth.com.

4. *Conner, supra* note 2 at 774.

5. Root is perhaps best known today for the building in Denver that bears his name, which is located at 1501 Platte Street. The building was constructed in 1890, and is on the National Register of Historic Properties. *See Directory of Colorado State Register Properties* (*Directory*), 16th ed. (Historic Society, 2003) at 100.

According to a biographical account published during his lifetime, Root fought in the Civil War on the Union side and was captured by the Confederates, but managed to escape by swimming the Mississippi River at night; came to Colorado with the Greeley Colony and set himself up there in the hotel business; then relocated to Denver, where he embarked in business as a wholesale dealer in cigars and tobacco. *History of the City of Denver, Arapahoe County, and Colorado* (O.O. Baskin & Co., 1880) at 570. Root also served two terms as a Denver alderman. *See Directory, supra.*

6. *Conner, supra* note 2 at 774.

7. *Id.*

8. *Id.* at 775.

9. *Id.*

10. A "Maggie Hunt" makes several appearances in the Denver newspapers of the time. She may be the same person mentioned in the *Conner v. Root* case. The November 30, 1880, edition of the *Rocky Mountain News* reported that Hunt, identified as a "waiter girl," was arrested on a complaint of assault and battery after she allegedly hit another "waiter girl" named Virginia Delmonico with chunks of coal. Hunt stated she had thrown the coal "in fun," and did not mean to hit Delmonico. *Rocky Mountain News* (Nov. 30, 1880) at 8. A "Mrs. Maggie Hunt" is identified in the 1881 *Denver Directory*, as a chambermaid at the Denver House. There are several other newspaper references to divorce proceedings begun by a "Maggie Hunt" against her husband, "E.R. Hunt," beginning just before the time of Hunt's marriage to Conner. *See Rocky Mountain News* (Jan. 14, 1882) at 3; *Rocky Mountain News* (March 6, 1882) at 7; *Rocky Mountain News* (March 12, 1882) at 6.

11. *Conner, supra* note 2 at 775.

12. *Id.* at 776.

13. *Id.*

14. *Conner, supra* note 2.

15. *Id.* at 776. This ruling must have come as a big disappointment to whoever paid for all the expert handwriting witnesses.

16. *Id.*

17. *Id.* at 776-77.

18. *Id.*

19. It is unclear what happened after the remand. The court file for this case is unfortunately unavailable.

20. *Conner, supra* note 2.

21. Colo. Gen. Stat. 1883, ch. 66, § 3641.

22. *Id.*

23. *See* Nagle, "The Dead Man's Statute (The Dead Man's Curve)," 9 *The Colorado Lawyer* 81 (Jan. 1980). *See also Tompkins v. DeLeon*, 595 P.2d 242, 244-48 (Colo. 1979) (Carrigan, J., dissenting).

24. CRS § 13-90-102.

25. *Brind v. Int'l Trust Co.*, 179 P. 148, 150 (Colo. 1919).

However Improbable His Story
A Controversial Case of Self-Defense

BY FRANK GIBBARD

"At Last He's Vindicated," crowed the July 29, 1897 *Rocky Mountain News*. "After a weary delay Robert J. Boykin, who shot and killed Milton S. Smith, a Negro desperado, while in the discharge of his duties as a policeman, is a free man."[1]

The *News* article made no pretense of objectivity in reporting on the denouement of a very controversial murder case involving racial tensions, law enforcement rivalries, and a shaky claim of self-defense. The article is full of misleading simplifications: that Boykin was "vindicated"; that Smith was a "desperado"; and that the shooting was part of Boykin's "duties as a policeman." The reality concerning the tragic shooting of Sheriff's Deputy Milton S. Smith and Officer Boykin's subsequent conviction of second-degree murder is considerably more complex and ambiguous than the bombastic headlines suggested.

THE SHOOTING

This much is undisputed: Denver police officer Robert J. Boykin shot and killed Arapahoe County Sheriff's Deputy Milton S. Smith at the corner of 20th and Market Streets in Denver at approximately 10:30 p.m. on October 5, 1894.[2] Pretty much everything else about the case is open to interpretation. The most important ambiguities involve Officer Boykin's claim that he acted in self-defense.

Character of the Victim

In a typical self-defense case, the victim's character is examined carefully to determine whether he could have been the aggressor. Opinions differed widely concerning the character of Deputy Smith. The *Rocky Mountain News* described him as a "desperate drunken brute," and stated that he "had the name of being a bad character."[3] It is unclear whether the News relied on testimony to support its statements, and it did not reveal the source of these opinions.

The same *News* article admitted, however, that several officers testified at Boykin's trial that Smith was "a peaceful, law-abiding citizen."[4] The *News* also claimed that Smith had been drinking on the night of his death.[5] Unfortunately, none of this information is discussed in the opinion of the Colorado Supreme Court.

Defendant and Witness Accounts of Events

The Court's opinion does provide an account of Boykin's version of events. Denver's chief of police and five of his officers were standing near the corner of 20th and Market Streets when Smith's girlfriend approached them and asked them to arrest Smith; she said he had been threatening her.[6] Boykin crossed the street, placed his hand on Smith's shoulder, and told him, "I will have to arrest you."[7] Smith replied, "You can't arrest me," and drew his gun.[8] Boykin then began striking Smith with his baton, trying to get him to drop the gun. Another officer crossed the street and joined in the clubbing of Smith. When Smith pointed his gun at Boykin, Boykin drew his own gun. Boykin, in fear for his life, shot Smith, killing him.

Other testimony at Boykin's trial, however, appears to have painted a very different picture of the events in question. Witnesses for the prosecution said there was no need for Boykin to shoot Smith. These witnesses suggested that Boykin deliberately picked a fight with Smith to seriously injure or kill him.

JUDGMENT AND SENTENCE

After hearing all of the evidence, a jury returned a verdict of second-degree murder against Boykin. Public opinion, as reflected in contemporary newspapers, seems to have regarded the jury's verdict as a miscarriage of justice.[9]

Attempts to free Boykin began almost immediately. He filed a motion for a new trial, which was argued to Judge Butler, the trial judge, in a marathon court session lasting nearly ten hours. In the end, Judge Butler denied the motion and sentenced Boykin to ten years' imprisonment. An attempt by Boykin's wife to obtain a pardon for her husband from the governor was not successful.[10]

APPEAL TO THE COLORADO SUPREME COURT

Boykin appealed his conviction to the Colorado Supreme Court, raising several challenges to the district court's rulings at trial and to the sufficiency of the evidence. The Supreme Court summarily rejected most of his contentions. The Court held, however, that some of Boykin's objections to the jury instructions had merit and required reversal.

The most significant problem with the instructions involved what is called the "duty to retreat." The jury was instructed that Boykin could succeed on this claim that the shooting was in self-defense only if Boykin was in danger of great bodily harm or death, and if "he could not otherwise escape the injury threatened, or defend himself without shooting the deceased."[11] Another instruction required the jury to find that Boykin "was not able to escape from such injury or death, or to prevent the same by retreating, or in other manner than by shooting the deceased."[12]

The problem with these instructions, the Court said, was that if Boykin legitimately was acting as a police officer, he did not have a duty to retreat and could in fact use deadly force without retreating. A police officer who does not provoke an assault "is not obliged to retreat or flee to save his life, but may stand his ground, and even, in some circumstances, pursue his assailant until the latter has been disarmed or disabled from carrying into effect his unlawful purpose."[13] If the jury believed Boykin's version of events, it could find that he had acted legitimately and had no duty to retreat.

Based on this and other errors in the instructions, the Court as "a matter of regret" remanded for a new trial.[14] The reluctant tone of the Court's opinion suggests that it had some residual doubt about the legitimacy of Boykin's self-defense theory.

It may have appeared improbable that Boykin was so compelled to take Smith's life to save his own life — considering there were four other policemen just across the street from Boykin when he was engaged in clubbing Smith. Nonetheless, the Court concluded that Boykin had a right to the judgment of a jury, aided by instructions of the court regarding the laws of self-defense.[15]

BOYKIN'S RELEASE

Boykin was never "vindicated" — in the sense of being found not guilty of the murder. He was, however, released from prison in 1897, a year after the Supreme Court issued its decision. His release was required because two terms of court had elapsed without the state taking any action toward retrying him.

HISTORICAL AND POLITICAL CONTEXTS OF THE CASE

The historical context of this case may shed some light on the attitude of the press and the public toward the verdict. First, there is the racial overlay. Deputy Smith was African American, and Officer Boykin was white. In the year 1894, when Smith was killed, at least 134 African

Americans were lynched, the second-highest annual number ever.[16] For many white Americans in 1894, ensuring careful treatment of African Americans suspected of a crime was not a priority.

Second, at the time Boykin shot Smith, there were interdepartmental rivalries between the law enforcement agencies to which the men belonged. The Colorado Supreme Court observed that "bad blood" existed between the Denver Police Department and the Arapahoe County Sheriff's Department.[17] It is not clear what caused this animosity, but it may have played a role in the course of events.

Finally, there is a political angle to consider. The strong editorial slant the *Rocky Mountain News* took toward the case may have been due as much to politics as to race. The *News* article suggests that Boykin's prosecution and conviction were the result of a political vendetta maintained by conspirators who opposed his involvement in the Colorado Populist Party. Thomas Patterson, the owner of the *Rocky Mountain News* at the time, was a moderate Populist himself,[18] so it may not be surprising that he was all too ready to believe that Boykin's conviction was the result of persecution for his Populist affiliation, rather than an appropriate punishment for a murder. It surely did not reduce the level of political paranoia that the Arapahoe County Sheriff appears to have selected the veniremen who became jurors at Boykin's trial,[19] although the Colorado Supreme Court later held that any issue on this point had been waived.[20]

What seems most remarkable about the case, given that it took place in 1894, is that a jury convicted a white police officer of murder and sentenced him to prison for killing an African American man. Whether this result occurred because the jurors were actually color-blind, or because there was a political "fix," remains — like so much else about this case — a matter of speculation.

Original printing: *The Colorado Lawyer*, May 2008. The author is grateful for the research assistance of Dan Cordova and Lynn Christian of the Colorado Supreme Court Law Library.

NOTES

1. "At Last He's Vindicated," *Rocky Mountain News* 3 (July 29, 1897).

2. "In Self Defense," *Boulder Daily Camera* 1 (Oct. 6, 1894).

3. "At Last He's Vindicated," *supra* note 1 at 3.

4. *Id.*

5. *Id.*

6. *Boykin v. People*, 45 P. 419, 421 (Colo. 1896). The *Rocky Mountain News* article adds that Smith had been beating her, but this allegation is not reflected in the Court's opinion. *See id.*

7. *Boykin, supra* note 6 at 421.

8. *Id.*

9. *See* "The Fee Fiends Foiled," *Boulder Daily Camera* 1 (April 20, 1895). In reporting on the Colorado Supreme Court's denial of a *supersedeas* bond to Boykin, this story noted that "Boykin is serving a long time sentence for an act public opinion does not hold him criminally liable."

10. "At Last He's Vindicated," *supra* note 1 at 3.

11. *Boykin, supra* note 6 at 422.

12. *Id.*

13. *Id.*

14. *Id.* at 423.

15. *Id.*

16. *See* "Lynching: By Year and Race," statistics provided by the archives at Tuskegee Institute, available at www.law.umkc.edu/faculty/projects/ftrials/shipp/lynchingyear.html.

17. *Boykin, supra* note 6 at 421.

18. *See* Jameson, *All That Glitters: Class, Conflict and Community in Cripple Creek* 166 (Univ. of Illinois Press, 1998).

19. "At Last He's Vindicated," *supra* note 1 at 3. The story states that "The defendant had to face a prejudiced jury, selected by a prejudiced sheriff."

20. *Boykin, supra* note 6 at 419-20.

Corpus Delicti
Three Unusual Colorado Cases

BY FRANK GIBBARD

A common misconception concerning the principle of *corpus delicti* is that the prosecution is required to produce the body of the deceased to obtain a conviction for murder; however, this is incorrect.[1] The word "*corpus*" does not refer to the victim's dead body; it refers to the "body" of the crime — that is, the evidence that a crime took place.[2] In the case of a homicide, it usually requires "evidence of a death and of a criminal agency as its cause."[3]

In each of the following three Colorado cases, the existence of a body was not the problem for the state's case; there was in fact a body in each case, and there was no question about the decedent's identity or the fact that he or she had died. However, *corpus delicti* was still at issue, because the cause of death was in question.

Before the age of modern crime scene analysis and forensic science, law enforcement officials had fewer tools to determine the precise cause of death. These decisions demonstrate that the Colorado courts still applied the principle of *corpus delicti* to hold the prosecution to an exacting standard of proof on the question of whether the decedent's death actually resulted from a homicide.

THE McBRIDE CASE

The first case, *McBride v. People*,[4] dates from 1891, when modern medical science was still in its infancy.[5] Mr. and Mrs. Edward McBride ran a grocery store in Arapahoe County where they sold beer and hard liquor. They had a lamentable tendency to consume the inventory. In the words of the Colorado Court of Appeals, they were "confirmed inebriates" who for a number of years had a habit of getting "stupidly drunk, sometimes jointly or in company with each other, and at other times individually and separately."[6]

When they were drunk "jointly or in company with each other," they turned to quarreling and violence. Any nearby object could serve as a missile. They threw cups, bottles, sticks — even brickbats — at each other. There was no evidence that any of Edward McBride's missiles ever hit his target;[7] still, testimony concerning his projectile behavior and aptitude was elicited from several witnesses at his subsequent trial for murdering Mrs. McBride.

Mrs. McBride's "individual and separate" drinking bouts were as dangerous to herself as those she engaged in with her husband — perhaps even more so. Toward the end of her life, she was almost always drunk, sometimes helplessly so. She had a series of nasty falls, including one time when she tumbled down some cellar stairs. On another occasion, she was found passed out "some distance from the house, in a ravine, without cover or consciousness, in cold, inclement weather."[8] Her final act of excess, culminating in confinement to her deathbed, consisted of drinking two gallons of hard liquor during a two-week period without any other form of nourishment.

The Medical Evidence

Dr. Bilby, who was summoned to Mrs. McBride's bedside, testified that when he observed her, she was vomiting blood and her throat looked like she had been drinking carbolic acid. She was pale, emaciated, and suffering from abdominal pain. He saw her five times between December 28 and New Year's Eve 1891, the day she died.

Attorney George F. Dunklee,
one of the attorneys for Edward
McBride on appeal to the Colorado
Supreme Court, and later president
of the Denver Bar Association
(1902–03)
Denver Bar Association

In addition to her inflamed throat, the doctor noted the presence of several bruises on her body. Her 12-year-old son later testified that Edward McBride had assaulted his mother a few weeks before her death, hitting her with a boot and shoving her out the door. When asked about the cause of death, Dr. Bilby testified that it resulted from "[l]ack of nutrition and loss of blood, caused by some internal injury."[9] He further stated that the internal injury had been caused by blows delivered to her exterior.

Other medical testimony, delivered by a physician who autopsied Mrs. McBride, was more favorable to her husband. Dr. R. B. Knight found no rupture of her internal organs. However, he did find plenty of other medical problems: she had an old inflammation of the mitral valve of her heart; she was in the last stages of Bright's disease;[10] and she was hemorrhaging blood from her nostrils, which settled in her stomach and was then "thrown off by vomiting."[11] None of the bruises on her body would have resulted in internal injuries, Dr. Knight testified. Even assuming she was violently assaulted before her death, he opined, the death itself resulted not from a beating but from exhaustion, chronic alcoholism, and Bright's disease.

Dying Declarations

The prosecution presented evidence of statements made by Mrs. McBride before her death. When Dr. Bilby asked her "what brought you on," she told him that her husband had struck her with his fists, knocked her down, jumped on her, and kicked her.[12] These statements were hearsay, of course, but they were admitted at trial as her dying declaration.[13] Other witnesses testified that she knew she was dying, and that she blamed her husband for killing her.

Challenging Corpus Delicti on Appeal

The jury convicted Edward McBride of second-degree murder, and he received a life sentence. On appeal, he argued that it had been improper to introduce evidence of his previous, nonfatal fights with his wife before establishing the *corpus delicti*. The court of appeals agreed. Admitting such evidence to bolster a doubtful *corpus delicti* by pointing out the husband's violent intentions toward his wife amounted to putting the cart before the horse. The existence of a homicide had to be proved first.

The other evidence allegedly pointing to a murder did not prove *corpus delicti*, because it did not "absolutely establish the death resulting from violence, and clearly negat[e] the possibility, or, at least probability, of death from natural causes."[14] Indeed, "[t]he cause or causes of death were not obscure, but patent, — [sic] alcoholism, exposure, and exhaustion."[15] Moreover, Mrs. McBride's "dying declarations" were dubious because she (1) made statements to Dr. Bilby when she still had hope of living; (2) made statements to other witnesses that were merely opinions; and (3) only nodded her head in response to questions from other witnesses about the cause of death. None of her statements met the evidentiary requirements for a dying declaration. The court of appeals therefore reversed Edward McBride's conviction.

THE COBIANCHI CASE

Before the Supreme Court legalized abortion in 1973, Colorado recognized a rather unusual crime known as "murder by abortion." The crime was unusual because the victim typically consented to the medical procedure that resulted in her death, but not to its fatal consequences.[16] To prove murder by abortion, it was, of course, necessary to prove that an abortion had taken place. Sometimes, that could be more difficult than it might seem.

A "Rabbit Test," Followed by Death

In *Cobianchi v. People*,[17] the victim is referred to only by her first name, Geraldine. On October 1, 1941, Geraldine consulted with a doctor by the name of Holt for a pregnancy examination. He gave her a bottle and told her to return the next day with a urine sample. (Why he didn't have her provide the sample in his office is not explained.) She returned as instructed and "presented what Dr. Holt assumed was a sample of her urine, though he had no knowledge of that fact."[18] He then performed the famous "rabbit test" on the sample, and achieved a "positive" result, indicating that Geraldine was pregnant.

Within two months, Geraldine was dead from generalized peritonitis, secondary to an acute infection of the uterus and ovaries. It was the state's theory that the infection resulted from an illegal abortion performed on her by the defendant, Dr. Cobianchi. The state managed to convince a jury of this theory, and the doctor was convicted of second-degree murder.

There was one major weak spot in the evidence, however. An autopsy revealed no evidence that Geraldine had had an abortion or that she had ever been pregnant. There was only a pelvic abscess that could have been caused by a number of other conditions, and which could have existed even in a male patient.

The state thus was placed in the position of proving a pregnancy and an abortion without any direct physical evidence from the body of the victim. To make its case, it presented what would seem to be some rather damning circumstantial evidence. Even so, the Colorado Supreme Court was unconvinced.

The State's Medical Evidence

The state introduced the positive pregnancy test, administered by Dr. Holt, to prove that Geraldine had been pregnant before her death. The Supreme Court did not find this evidence very persuasive. The Court went to great lengths to describe how the rabbit test (known more formally as the "Zondek-Aschelm test") works and how its result in the Cobianchi case could have been fallible. As the Court explained it:

> This is done properly by injecting a quantity of the urine of the woman suspected of pregnancy into the blood stream of a virgin female rabbit that has been kept away from proximity to a male rabbit, and which is from four months to seventeen weeks old and weighs about four pounds. Forty-eight hours after such injection the rabbit is killed and its ovaries examined. If the woman is pregnant, certain changes in the appearance of the rabbit's ovaries ordinarily occur, discernible to one skilled in making such tests. If the woman is not pregnant, ordinarily no change is produced in the appearance of the ovaries.[19]

The Supreme Court pointed out a number of potential flaws and omissions in the evidence that could have produced a false positive result in the rabbit test performed in Geraldine's case: (1) the test was only 90 percent accurate; (2) the urine sample might not have been Geraldine's; (3) the rabbit might not have been a virgin; (4) the rabbit might not have been isolated from male rabbits; (5) the rabbit might not have been the right age or weight; (6) Geraldine might have had a tumor that would have invalidated the test; and (7) Geraldine might have had some other condition that would have invalidated the test.

Other Evidence — A Doctor, a Nurse, and Geraldine's Fiancé

The prosecution also presented evidence of Geraldine's statement to another doctor, Dr. Dwyer, who examined her at St. Luke's Hospital on October 21, 1941. Geraldine told Dr. Dwyer that "she had attempted an abortion on Saturday, October eleventh, and that a doctor, whose name she did not state, had curetted her on the following Sunday, October twelfth."[20] The medical evidence disclosed that curettage is the procedure used after an abortion.

Geraldine's fiancé, Jack Fixler, provided evidence against Dr. Cobianchi. He stated that he spoke with the doctor at Geraldine's apartment. Without describing her condition, Dr. Cobianchi told Fixler not to worry, that Geraldine would be well taken care of. Fixler later took Geraldine to see Dr. Dwyer, at which point Geraldine described to him the attempted abortion.

After Geraldine returned to her apartment from St. Luke's Hospital, Dr. Cobianchi visited her there once or twice more. He asked Fixler to call him "James" whenever they spoke on the telephone, because he feared his phone was tapped.

After Geraldine died, Fixler took a long car ride with Dr. Cobianchi, who told Fixler he "felt badly over her death and told him what a fine girl she was and also 'that was the first case he lost in his practice.'"[21] He told Fixler to "stick to my story [that] Geraldine [had] done the job herself."[22] Dr. Cobianchi then allegedly began handing out money to various people, including Fixler and Geraldine's mother, perhaps to encourage their corroboration. Fixler testified that Dr. Cobianchi had told him "it was the first [abortion] case he had lost in twenty-five years."[23]

Finally, a nurse who attended Geraldine after her return from St. Luke's Hospital testified against Dr. Cobianchi. Her statements, however, did not add much to the case against him. She merely testified that Dr. Cobianchi had visited Geraldine and called every day inquiring about her condition.

No Proof of Abortion

On appeal, the Colorado Supreme Court found insufficient evidence to establish the *corpus delicti* required for a death by abortion. As in McBride, the Court followed a two-part test, which required the state to prove "(1) [d]eath as the result of an act performed, or a wound inflicted; [and] (2) that such act was unlawfully performed, or such wound was unlawfully inflicted by another."[24] Here, the medical evidence did not establish that an abortion had even occurred; none of the expected placental tissue was found during the autopsy, and the evidence of pregnancy was established only by the "rabbit test," which the Court found unreliable. Moreover, even if Geraldine had been pregnant, her own hearsay statement to her doctor was that she had attempted to bring about an abortion on herself and had a curettage the next day by an unnamed doctor.

Dr. Cobianchi's own somewhat suspicious statements might be explained by the fact that he had performed only a curettage and not an abortion. His conduct in handing out money could be explained by a sense of guilt about her death as the result of this procedure. This fell short of proof of the required element — that Dr. Cobianchi had caused her death by use of instrumentation during an abortion.[25] His conviction was reversed.

THE TATE CASE

Occasionally, the facts of a case seem so odd that they almost belong in the realm of the surreal. This is certainly true of the case of *Tate v. People*,[26] where Ella Hewitt Tate was convicted in the early 1950s of second-degree murder for killing her ex-husband, Dot T. Hewitt.

To Be or Not to Be Married

Dot T. Hewitt married Ella in Oklahoma in 1936, during the middle of the Great Depression.[27] She was approximately 23 years old at the time. He was much older when they married — in his mid-50s. Two children were born of the marriage.

Dot Hewitt's health — both physical and mental — began to deteriorate during his marriage to Ella. He had had some operations, possibly for cancer. He frequently spoke of suicide, and had made a few unsuccessful attempts at killing himself. He also had grown alarmingly eccentric.

In 1945, out of the blue "he displayed what he claimed was a Reno divorce decree to [Ella], saying that he had paid a Denver lawyer $200 to get it for him."[28] Taken aback, Ella decided to consult a lawyer to see whether the decree was valid. Hewitt responded by actually traveling to Reno and making sure he obtained a valid divorce from her. He returned to Colorado, where he resumed living with his now ex-wife.

A strange, quasi-marital existence grew between the former Mr. and Mrs. Hewitt. He still lived in the family home. Ever restless, he took little trips around the country, but would come home to stay with the children on occasion while Ella was at work.

An Unconventional Living Arrangement

Dot and Ella Hewitt knew a serviceman named Mr. Tate. Hewitt suggested that his ex-wife should marry Tate so that he could support her and help take care of the children. Ella took Hewitt's advice and married Tate — in the words of the Colorado Supreme Court, "apparently without too much romance."[29]

The three of them — Mr. and Mrs. Tate and Hewitt — lived together after that. Their living arrangement was more or less harmonious at first. However, Tate turned out to be an alcoholic who spent all of his earnings on drink. By 1947, Ella had divorced him.

After that, Hewitt remained with Ella in the home, "sick and complaining most of the time and talk[ing] about suicide at least two or three times a week."[30] Ella took care of him, nursing him through his various illnesses. Hewitt signed over his property to Ella, but apparently did not have any life insurance. Ella refused to allow visitors to speak of him as her "ex-husband"; she wanted the children to think they still were married.

There was evidence that during "the last several years of his life [Hewitt] did strange and unexplainable things."[31] Unfortunately, the Supreme Court's opinion does not reveal what those things were. We do know that the old man was fascinated by unusual inventions. One such bizarre "invention" would later play a role in his death.

The Death of Hewitt

Ella Tate provided the following account to the police concerning her husband's death. She spent the morning of February 10, 1950 as she often did, caring for others. At around 7:30 a.m., she drove her son, who was nearly blind, to a school for blind children in Denver. Before she left, she and Hewitt discussed that he should put the cats out of the house. Nothing seemed unusual in their interaction that morning. She then traveled to Bannock Street in Denver, to call on an elderly lady who was ill. After that, she returned to the family home in Adams County, arriving at the back door around 11:15 a.m.

When she entered the house, she noticed an odor. She moved through the kitchen toward her husband's bedroom. She found him in the bedroom, seated but slumped over in a chair. She stood there, frozen in place, while her eyes took in the scene. Hewitt was tied to the back of the chair with strands of binder twine attached to the handles of a nearby chest of drawers. The twine was connected to a contraption made of four or five coat hangers. Inside this contraption was an automatic pistol that had been in the house for a number of years. Then, she saw the blood—on the back of Hewitt's head, on his hip, and on the floor. It appeared he had been shot several times.

Ella Tate Tidies Up

Ella quickly realized that her ex-husband had finally moved from talking about suicide to actually doing it, and in his own peculiar way. She decided to remove his body from the room and to bury it in the back yard before the children came home. She made a valiant effort to conceal the corpse. She cut the twine; wrapped the body in a quilt, papers, and a gunny sack; and dragged Hewitt's remains down the stairs and approximately seventy-five feet. There, near a little house in the backyard, she dug a shallow grave and rolled Hewitt into it. She poured fuel oil over the body and the dirt (but apparently did not ignite it); covered the grave with a sheet of corrugated iron; and piled pieces of lumber and fence posts on top of it. As a crowning touch, she dragged a chicken coop on top of the improvised grave.

Back in the bedroom, she had her work cut out for her. First, she disassembled her ex-husband's strange apparatus. Then, she collected the pistol shells off the floor, and took them, the twine, the coat hangers, and an old pillow to the incinerator and burned them. Finally, she cleaned the bloody floor thoroughly with Clorox*, removing every trace of the ghastly scene.

She finished tidying up in time to pick up the children from school. Their first words to her were, "How is Daddy?"[32] She told them he had left and was going to see relatives. Given his frequent absences, it may not have been difficult to persuade them of this story.

A Trip to the Sheriff

Soon after, Ella Tate became ill with the flu. Apparently, her conscience gnawed at her and she became very troubled and distressed. On February 28, a few weeks after the impromptu burial of her ex-husband, she drove herself and the children to the sheriff's office in Brighton. She told the sheriff she had something to say and that she wanted to say it in front of the children. She then related to him the story of her ex-husband's death and the burial.

The Physical Evidence

The sheriff went to the family home, removed what was left of the incinerator contents, including the hangers and the shells, and recovered Hewitt's body. The body was turned over to a pathologist at Denver General Hospital, who later testified that Hewitt had been underground for "some time." He had been shot five times. Four bullet wounds were superficial; however, one bullet had entered the jaw and exited under the ear on the opposite side of his head. It would have been fatal, possibly killing Hewitt within thirty seconds.

Not all of the physical evidence supported Ella's story about how Hewitt died. None of the five bullets was ever found, nor were any bullet marks found in the room, the house, or anywhere on the premises.

No blood was detected, either. The pathologist testified that Ella Tate's thorough cleansing of the room could have removed all traces of blood. He opined that a death by suicide, involving all five shots, was at least "remotely possible."[33]

Acting on information from Ella Tate, officers recovered the automatic pistol. A ballistics expert testified at trial that it had a heavy trigger pull, about ten or twelve pounds. No fingerprints were taken and there was no evidence concerning powder marks or burns. No one attempted to reconstruct the twine, coat hanger, and pistol apparatus Ella had described.

The jury convicted her of second-degree murder. She was sentenced to fifteen to twenty years in the state penitentiary.

Ella Tate Appeals

Ella's motion for a new trial raised fifty-two grounds of error. It was overruled. She then raised ten grounds for reversal to the Colorado Supreme Court. Although the Court concluded that reversal would have been appropriate simply on the ground that the evidence did not support the verdict, it reversed on a number of other grounds, including "that the corpus delicti, namely, the body of the offense and the essence of the crime was not established."[34]

Simply put, the evidence pointed to suicide, not murder. In the 565-page record, the Supreme Court noted: "[T]here is not the slightest whisper or indication of any kind of motive for a killing on the part of defendant, nor any outsider."[35] The Court noted the harmonious family relationships in the Tate/Hewitt household; the deceased's lack of property or life insurance; the lack of evidence that Ella Tate was romantically involved with anyone; and the fact of her free and voluntary confession to the sheriff and the coroner. The Court concluded:

[I]n face of the testimony of the autopsy physician that the gunshot wounds causing death could have been self-inflicted, and that it was possible the case was one of suicide, we must say that all other circumstances are not sufficiently cogent or sufficient to exclude every reasonable hypothesis except guilt; and that the circumstances are not convincing to a moral certainty; therefore, from the record, we must, and do determine that the corpus delicti was not established.[36]

The panel assigned to hear the case reversed the judgment of conviction and remanded with directions to dismiss the complaint.[37] Then, an odd thing happened. The case was reheard *en banc* and the disposition was altered by the entire Court. The opinion remained the same, except that instead of dismissing the complaint, the Court awarded Ella Tate a new trial.[38] This may indicate a compromise vote by the entire Colorado Supreme Court, perhaps based on a failure to agree on the sufficiency of the evidence as a ground for reversal. Had the evidence been insufficient, double jeopardy principles would have required dismissal of the complaint.[39]

CONCLUSION

Corpus delicti prevents the state from relying on conjecture and speculation to convict the defendant of a crime. It represents a powerful protection for the defendant in cases where the evidence of the cause of death is ambiguous. It remains an important principle of the criminal law.[40]

Original printing: *The Colorado Lawyer*, March 2009. The author is grateful for the research assistance of Dan Cordova and Lynn Christian of the Colorado Supreme Court Law Library.

NOTES

1. *See* Hahn, *Colorado Criminal Law* 37 (Courtright Pub. Co., 1963) ("Corpus delicti does not mean 'dead body.'").

2. Garner, *A Dictionary of Modern Legal Usage* 226 (2d ed., Oxford Univ. Press, 1995).

3. *Id.*

4. *McBride v. People*, 37 P. 953 (Colo.App. 1894).

5. As late as the 1870s, American medical schools often accepted anyone who could pay the required tuition:

> No medical school in America allowed medical students to routinely either perform autopsies or see patients, and medical education often consisted of nothing more than two four-month terms of lectures.

Barry, *The Great Influenza* 32 (Penguin Viking, 2004).

6. *McBride, supra* note 4.

7. *Id.* None of the witnesses could say that any of the items thrown by Edward McBride actually struck Mrs. McBride. Perhaps some lingering affection for his wife threw off his aim, or maybe he was just too drunk to throw straight.

8. *Id.*

9. *Id.* at 954.

10. Bright's disease refers to several different types of kidney ailments, primarily an inflammation of the kidney, commonly called nephritis. *See* Stedman, *Stedman's Medical Dictionary* 458 (Golden Jubilee ed., Lippincott Williams & Wilkins, 1961).

11. *McBride, supra* note 4 at 954.

12. *Id.*

13. *See* CRS § 13-25-119 (making dying declarations of a deceased person admissible as evidence in civil and criminal trials).

14. *McBride, supra* note 4 at 957.

15. *Id.*

16. A typical formulation can be found in CRS § 40-2-23 (1953), which provides in part that

> if the woman should die as the result of an attempt to procure the miscarriage of any woman then being with child, the person administering or causing to be administered [an abortifacient] poison, substance or liquid, or using or causing to be used any instrument [to produce an abortion], shall be deemed guilty of murder, and if convicted, to be punished accordingly, unless it appear that such miscarriage was procured or attempted by or under advice of a physician or surgeon with intent to save the life of such woman or to prevent serious and permanent bodily injury to her.

17. *Cobianchi v. People*, 141 P.2d 688 (Colo. 1943).

18. *Id.* at 689.

19. *Id.*

20. *Id.* at 690.

21. *Id.* at 691.

22. *Id.*

23. *Id.*

24. *Id.*

25. Justice Burke dissented. He felt that the majority opinion had usurped the province of the jury, which should have been permitted to draw its own inferences from the evidence concerning Dr. Cobianchi's guilt. *Id.* at 693 (Burke, J., dissenting).

26. *Tate v. People*, 247 P.2d 665 (Colo. 1952) (*en banc*).

27. Ella Tate may not have been Hewitt's first wife. The 1930 U.S. Census shows a "Dot T. Hewitt," born around 1882, living in Colorado with his wife Catherine.

28. *Tate, supra* note 26 at 667.

29. *Id.*

30. *Id.*

31. *Id.*

32. *Id.* at 668.

33. *Id.* at 669.

34. *Id.* at 670.

35. *Id.* at 669.

36. *Id.* at 670.

37. Judge Alter dissented from the disposition; he felt that reversal was appropriate, but not because the evidence was insufficient.

38. It is not clear whether such a trial was actually held.

39. *See, e.g., People v. Williams*, 183 P.3d 577, 580 (Colo.App. 2007).

40. *See, e.g., People v. Robson*, 80 P.3d 912 (Colo.App. 2003).

"A Fine Old Whiskey"
The Murder-by-Mail Slaying of Josephine A. Barnaby

BY FRANK GIBBARD

The 1891 murder trial of Dr. Thomas Thatcher Graves brought national attention to the state of Colorado. The case of *People v. Graves*[1] had it all: wealth, sex, scandal, and mystery. The accused was an accomplished gentleman whose lofty credentials inspired immediate respect in Victorian society.[2] The victim was a wealthy widow of questionable morals. The killing was a first: it was accomplished through the U.S. Mail from a distance of 2,000 miles.

THE ACCUSED: DR. GRAVES

Dr. Graves was a Mason, a devoted Congregationalist, a scientific researcher, and a public lecturer who had achieved success both as a military man and as a physician. After compiling a stellar academic record as a young man, he enlisted in the Union Army, where he quickly attained the rank of Major.

Graves was chosen to escort President Abraham Lincoln on his tour of the fallen Confederate capital in Richmond, Virginia in 1865. He later wrote a published account of his experiences during the Southern occupation.[3]

In 1871, six years after the Civil War ended, he graduated first in his class at Harvard Medical School. He married a beautiful young woman and settled into practice in Providence, Rhode Island.[4] In 1891, when the murder of Mrs. Josephine A. Barnaby occurred, he was 50 years old and appeared "tall, well dressed and startlingly handsome," with full sideburns and a moustache, and penetrating eyes.[5]

THE VICTIM: MRS. JOSEPHINE BARNABY

Josephine Barnaby's great-grandson has left us a vivid portrait of the victim. According to his account, she was not endowed with much of Dr. Graves's ambition, wit, or intelligence.[6] What she did have, though, was money — lots of it. Her home — the Barnaby mansion known by locals as "the Castle" — stood just across the street in Providence from the more modest house where Dr. Graves and his wife Kitty lived.

Josephine became acquainted with Dr. Graves after one of her family servants began working for the Graves family. Though still an attractive woman at age 55, she was no longer the beauty she had once been. Years of fondness for fine food and drink had left her a little pudgy, with a drinker's veins showing in her cheeks.[7] But she quickly found herself captivated by the dashing, handsome physician.

JOSEPHINE BARNABY'S
FORTUNE AND TRAVELS

At the time of her death, Josephine enjoyed a generous sum of money from the estate of her late husband, Jerothmul Bowers Barnaby. J.B., as he was known, had been a rather overbearing and self-centered man who owed his fortune to a chain of men's clothing stores known as the J.B. Barnaby Company.[8] He was rumored to have had numerous extramarital affairs. One morning in 1889, while sitting in his horse-drawn carriage, he suddenly slumped over and died at the age of 59.

Josephine fancied herself a *bon vivant*. Life with her boorish and inattentive husband, whom she had married when she was just 21 years old, must have been a sort of a cross to bear on her delicate shoulders. After

2226 Williams Street in Denver, site of a murder by mail
Darlene Johnson

J.B. died, she began to live it up. She spent his money on travel. She took friends with her on her journeys, including her special friend, Dr. Graves.

Dr. Graves had a legitimate medical reason for attending to Josephine. He specialized in diseases of the nerves, and she had suffered partial paralysis of one of her arms since giving birth to one of her children.[9] What Kitty Graves thought of her husband's travels with a wealthy woman five years older than he was not recorded. The exact nature of Dr. Graves's relationship with Josephine also is uncertain,[10] but before long, as some sources describe it, she had become little more than his slave, whose life was in his hands.[11]

A FINE OLD WHISKEY

In the spring of 1891, Josephine and her friend from Pennsylvania, Mrs. Edward Worrell, traveled to Denver. They stayed with Mrs. Worrell's son, Edward, Jr., and her daughter-in-law at the Worrell home located at 2226 Williams Street. Dr. Graves remained behind in Providence.

On April 13, 1891, the day of her murder, Josephine and Mrs. Worrell spent the day on a ranch in the country near Denver. On the ride home in their open carriage, Josephine became chilled. Mrs. Worrell suggested they each enjoy a hot toddy. Josephine quickly agreed, and proposed that they try the present from her "unknown admirer."

The present she referred to was an odd bottle that Josephine had received several days earlier in the mail. The package she received had been dispatched to her from Boston — bearing no return address — in care of the office of Edward Worrell, Jr. Inside a wooden box marked "Liebig's Extract of Meat," Josephine found a glass bottle full of a reddish fluid. The bottle was not commercially labeled. It had a handwritten label on it that read: "Wish you a happy New Year. Please accept this fine old whiskey from your friends in the woods."[12]

Josephine's comment when she opened the package was, "It must be from [Edward] Bennett." The person she was referring to was a gentleman friend who lived in the Adirondacks.[13]

The Unfriendly Woods

The phrase "friends in the woods" must have had a bittersweet resonance for Josephine. "The Woods" was the name of her favorite resort in the Adirondack Mountains, run by her friend Edward Bennett. She liked the place so much, in fact, that she had proposed to buy a house or property nearby. This proposal had produced an alarmed response from Dr. Graves.[14] He wrote her a letter informing her that the executors of her late husband's estate were very displeased with her investment plans and that if she persisted in them, they would doubtless take steps to have a guardian appointed for her.[15] Dr. Graves later admitted that he had lied to her in the letter.[16]

The prosecution would make much of this letter, contending it was written with ulterior motives. Dr. Graves, the state theorized, had squandered some of Josephine's estate and was afraid she would find out the money was missing and demand an accounting. To prevent this from happening, he eventually murdered Josephine.[17]

Poisoned Whiskey

On that April evening in 1891, both Josephine and Mrs. Worrell drank some of the liquid in the gift bottle. Mrs. Worrell drank a whole glass of it quickly, and then complained of the taste. Josephine sipped it slowly.[18] Within minutes, both women were in horrible agony. Mrs. Worrell eventually recovered, but Josephine suffered a slow, painful death. Analysis of the bottle later showed it contained 132 grains of arsenic — enough to kill nearly seventy people.

ENTER JOHN HOWARD CONRAD

Suspicion did not focus immediately on Dr. Graves; in fact, there was plenty of finger-pointing to go around. The Worrells came under suspicion, if for no other reason than their proximity to the bottle and their opportunity to have supplied its deadly contents. Josephine's friends at The Woods also were scrutinized.

Even Josephine's daughters had reason to resent her and were not above suspicion. When J.B. Barnaby died, he had left Josephine only $2,500 per year in his will, claiming she was too flighty to handle a larger sum of money.[19] At Dr. Graves's urging, Josephine had sued her daughters for a larger share of the estate — and won. The victorious attorney, Daniel R. (Colonel) Ballou, paid Dr. Graves a finder's fee of $500, something the prosecution later found quite suspicious. As a result of the litigation, mother and daughters had become completely estranged by the time of her death.

One of Josephine's daughters, Mabel, was married to a strong-willed man named John Howard Conrad. He was a wealthy Montana rancher, miner, and businessman. When Conrad heard of his mother-in-law's death, he vowed to find the murderer, whatever it took.

Early on, Conrad settled on Dr. Graves as the murderer, and attempted to build a case against him. To this end, he hired a bevy of shady characters: Orinton C. Hanscom, a Pinkerton agent; James McParlan, a notorious informer; Edwin McHenry, a private detective; and a newspaperman for the *Boston Herald* with the improbable name of Henry G. Trickey.[20] Their campaign relied heavily on trickery and deceit. After "interviewing" Dr. Graves, for example, Trickey published an article in the *Boston Herald*, alleging that Dr. Graves had called Josephine "a vile woman with vile lovers"; that he had described seeing her lying drunk on the floor of an icehouse in the Adirondacks with Bennett, "with every indication of a previous revolting transaction having taken place"; and that he had called her a "damned whore," which was very strong language for those days.[21] Accurate or not, the article proved damaging for Dr. Graves; it planted seeds of suspicion in the public's mind by suggesting that he was less loyal and dedicated to his patient than he should have been, and that he disliked her so much in fact that he might even have murdered her.[22]

A BLOCK OF ORANGE STAMPS

For all his deceitfulness and dubious investigative tactics, Conrad actually uncovered one legitimate piece of evidence that pointed toward Dr. Graves as the murderer. The package with the deadly bottle inside had been mailed from Boston. When Josephine opened the package at Edward Worrell's office, Worrell's partner saved the wrapper with the stamps for his son, who collected them. The partner later supplied Conrad with the postmark and the stamps.

Conrad then traveled to the Boston post office to see if anyone remembered the sender of the package. There, a clerk told him something significant. The stamps could not have been purchased in Boston.

They were orange Daniel Webster stamps, which had not been available in Boston for some time, because they had been replaced by a commemorative issue of blue Henry Clay stamps. Conrad had Pinkerton agent Hanscom's men check all 9,122 post offices in New England to see which ones had carried the orange Daniel Webster stamps at the time the package was mailed. As it turned out, there was only one — in Providence, Rhode Island, hometown of Dr. Graves.

THE TRIAL

Conrad played a huge role in the prosecution of Dr. Graves, so much so that the trial took on the aura of a personal vendetta. First, he performed much of the investigation of the case. Then, he tricked Dr. Graves into traveling to Colorado by using a bogus telegram. Finally, he paid a small fortune to transport all the witnesses in the case to Colorado, where he put them up in hotels at his own expense during the four-week trial.

Opening Statements

The prosecutor began his opening statement with a rhetorical flourish, tracing the history of poisoning to the decadence of the declining Roman Empire and the ancient Egyptians. He then cast aspersions on Dr. Graves's skill as a medical man, claiming that his practice was "not very extensive nor very lucrative," and that he was not even a member of the Rhode Island State Medical Society.[23] Instead, the prosecutor argued, Dr. Graves made his money by siphoning it from the Barnaby estate.

The prosecutor noted Dr. Graves's professional sideline of compounding patent medicines and selling them by mail. He contended that Dr. Graves "succeeded in working himself into [Josephine's] goodwill and good graces, through his attentions as a physician, and through his profession of disinterested friendship for the woman herself."[24] He described the circumstances of the murder, and the state's theory that Josephine had intended to withdraw her accounts from

Dr. Graves's management, thus exposing his fraud and depriving him of future opportunities to embezzle from her. The prosecutor devoted most of the remainder of his opening statement to describing Dr. Graves's self-serving conduct after the murder. Most telling, he promised to show that Dr. Graves had actually confessed on more than one occasion to Conrad's detectives that he sent the whiskey, with the pusillanimous disclaimer that "it was good whiskey when I sent it."[25]

Defense counsel, Henry Marshall Furman,[26] began his opening by confessing to his "many, many imperfections" and his "liability to make a mistake, perhaps to say something I should not say, perhaps for want of ability not properly understanding the case."[27] He pled with the jury not to act like Pontius Pilate, giving in to the shouts of the crowd to crucify Dr. Graves, unless or until the prosecution proved its case. Noting Dr. Graves's competence as a scientist and doctor, he argued that had the doctor wanted to kill Josephine, he could easily have done so by using a poison that left no trace, rather than employing the amateurish tactic of sending a bottle of arsenic-laced whiskey. Defense counsel disputed many of the prosecution's facts, including its claims that Josephine had been dissatisfied with Dr. Graves's management of her money before her death and that she had commented that perhaps he had sent the whiskey.

State's Witnesses

The state began with testimony that established the basic facts of the case. It presented testimony from postal employees about the orange stamps on the package sent to Josephine; from a chemistry professor concerning his analysis of the arsenic-laced liquid, along with the fact that an unskilled person could not have prepared it; from an analytical chemist who examined Josephine's tissues and detected large quantities of arsenic in them; and from Josephine's attending physicians, who testified to the cause of her death. The state then called several witnesses who testified about the receipt of the package and the circumstances of Josephine's illness and death.

These witnesses presented testimony about what Josephine said to them before she lapsed into a coma and died. Mrs. Worrell's daughter-in-law testified that she asked Josephine whether she thought the Bennetts — her friends in the woods — had sent the bottle, and Josephine said no. When she asked whether she thought Dr. Graves had sent it, Josephine did not answer.

Mrs. Worrell's grandmother, Nancy B. Allen, testified that she had asked Josephine whether anyone would benefit from her death. "She replied that she left Dr. Graves $50,000 in a will," and that the doctor knew he was a beneficiary.[28] She also complained that Dr. Graves had not supplied her with adequate money from her funds when she needed it.

Hattie Carrier, Edward, Jr.'s mother-in-law, testified that she had spoken with Josephine before her death. Josephine stated that she and the Bennetts were the best of friends and they could not have sent her the bottle. Josephine then asked, "I wonder if it can be possible that Dr. Graves could do such a thing?"[29]

Edward Worrell, Sr. testified that Josephine had told him, during a visit to his home in Pennsylvania in January 1891, that she thought she had left Dr. Graves too much money in her will. The elder Worrell dispatched a letter to Dr. Graves, asking for return of the will. Dr. Graves stalled on returning it. Josephine then drafted a new will, leaving Dr. Graves $25,000 instead of the $50,000 in her previous will. Mrs. Worrell, who also had been poisoned by the "whiskey" but had recovered, testified to Josephine's dissatisfaction with Sallie Hanley, the maid provided by Dr. Graves, whom Josephine believed was spying on her. Mrs. Worrell also testified to Josephine's desire to reduce the amount bequeathed to Dr. Graves in her will.[30] She said Josephine had told her that "Dr. Graves would ruin her yet."[31]

Edward Bennett testified that Josephine had stated she had become "dissatisfied with Dr. Graves and his management," and that she was going to make a new will.[32] Mary Hickey, Josephine's former servant, stated that Josephine wrote her a letter shortly before her death, stating "You watch Dr. Graves. I have reason to mistrust him."[33] Hickey also said Dr. Graves told her not to be surprised if Josephine "got a shock" and ended up declared insane, with himself appointed as her guardian.[34]

Trickey, the *Boston Herald* newspaperman, also took the stand. According to his testimony, once Josephine died, Dr. Graves said many harsh things about her, including that she had to pay blackmail money and the blackmailer had probably killed her, and that he "was sorry he ever met her and that she was not a woman he would admit into his family circle."[35] Charles E. Lincoln, a *Boston Herald* correspondent who had helped Trickey interview Dr. Graves, repeated Dr. Graves's statement that Josephine had been a "damned whore in her instincts," and that he had seen her lying drunk on the floor with Mr. Bennett "with all the indications of a previous revolting transaction."[36]

Hanscom, the Pinkerton detective, testified that he had pretended to be Conrad's brother to get Dr. Graves to talk. Dr. Graves had repeated his theory that the bottle had been sent as part of a blackmail plot. Most damning, according to Hanscom, Dr. Graves admitted to having sent Josephine a bottle of pure whiskey.[37]

Conrad testified to his conversations with Dr. Graves. He said Dr. Graves had apologized profusely for the things he said about Josephine. Dr. Graves also tried to finger the Bennetts for the poisoning, and "mentioned a red-headed Irishman who had blackmailed [Josephine] out of money."[38] He also testified that Dr. Graves admitted to sending Josephine a bottle of whiskey, but would never admit it publicly, because he had denied it to his friends and family and felt he would be ruined if he changed his story. Conrad characterized Josephine as a woman of excellent character and then stated (perhaps laying it on a bit thick), "[t]here was never an unkind feeling between [Josephine] and her daughters."[39]

The prosecution called several handwriting experts, who testified that the handwritten label on the bottle matched Dr. Graves's handwriting in his letters to Josephine. With that, the state rested.

Defense Witnesses

The first important witness for the defense was Colonel Ballou, who also was one of Dr. Graves's attorneys in the trial. He stated that Josephine had been a very bright woman who was clear and cogent in her expression, that she had asked him to draft her will, and that she had asked him to deliver the will to Dr. Graves. He had seen one of Dr. Graves's letters about a guardianship, but believed he wrote it out of genuine concern for Josephine and the possible consequences of her profligate spending.

The defense then presented its own handwriting experts, whose testimony, as it turned out, was far from helpful to Dr. Graves. Charles Clinton was a cashier at the German National Bank. On direct examination, he testified that Dr. Graves's letters and the label on the bottle were not in the same handwriting, and that the label-writer was probably a woman. On cross-examination, however, he admitted that he now had discovered similarities between Dr. Graves's handwritten letters and the bottle label that made him uncertain whether it was the same. Worse, he stated that the handwriting on the bottle label was also similar to that of Sallie Hanley, the maid whom Dr. Graves had assigned to accompany Josephine on her travels. The second handwriting expert, testifying favorably to Dr. Graves on the one hand, admitted that he was not an expert at handwriting comparison.

The defense presented testimony from a veterinary surgeon, who testified that arsenic with potash was a common remedy used in livery stables and that arsenite of potassium, the compound used to kill Josephine, was not particularly difficult to make. On cross-examination, the prosecution pounded him, forcing him to admit that he did not graduate from any college and to deny that he was a "homeopathic horse doctor."[40] Another witness, a druggist and chemist from Copenhagen, also testified that arsenite of potassium is simple to make, but admitted on cross that he had never sold any of it since coming to the United States years earlier.

Next came Sallie Hanley, who tried to place a positive spin on her ill-fated employment with Josephine. She testified that Josephine had told her that the Bennetts had put her up to buying a house near The Woods, even though it was expensive and she had no use for it. On cross-examination, the prosecution produced a devastating letter from

Sallie Hanley to Josephine, complaining about being discharged, requesting $75 for her trouble, and threatening, if that sum were not paid, to go to the executors for Josephine's estate and reveal how she had spent her money, which "would make a great deal of trouble for you."[41] In the letter, Hanley raised the specter of a guardianship and told Josephine that if she were called on to testify before the executors, Josephine would do better to have her as a friend than as an enemy.

Finally, it was time for Dr. Graves to testify on his own behalf. He presented an entirely innocent version of events. It was Josephine, he said, who pressed him to manage her money, in spite of his initial refusals, and Colonel Ballou insisted he accept the $500 finder's fee. Although he had received Josephine's will, he kept it sealed, and had placed it in a safety deposit box. He had not sent the will when requested earlier in the year because it was inconvenient to go and get it from the deposit box. He had proposed Hanley as a traveling companion to Josephine, but only at Josephine's request.

Dr. Graves said he viewed Josephine's plan to buy a house as foolish extravagance, and that is why he threatened her with a guardianship. For managing her funds, Josephine paid him $2,500 per year.

He had nothing to do with the poisoning, of course, and was "very, very much shocked when I learned Mrs. Barnaby had been poisoned."[42] After her death, he showed a list of his investments for her, and Conrad seemed satisfied with them. He later showed Conrad the stocks, bonds, and other investments he had made, and Conrad told him, "You are entitled to credit instead of censure for the manner in which you have administered upon Mrs. Barnaby's estate."[43]

Dr. Graves denied ever telling Conrad that he had sent a bottle of whiskey to Josephine. He stated that Conrad exercised continuous pressure on him to admit to sending the bottle, telling him that the unresolved affair was hurting Conrad's political chances in Montana. Conrad finally exploded and made the startling statement that "the East is your country, the West is mine; if you are taken to Denver, I will pack a jury on you; you will never have a fair trial, for with my money I will buy up a jury and you will be convicted anyway."[44]

On cross-examination, Dr. Graves denied saying it was the Bennetts who sent the bottle; in fact, he never believed they sent it. He flatly denied making most of the damaging statements attributed to him, or at least denied memory of them. Furman, Dr. Graves's attorney, pronounced himself satisfied with the cross-examination, and asked Dr. Graves no questions on redirect.

Finally, the defense called several witnesses who testified that a stable hand named Dan Smith may have taken a drink out of the Barnaby bottle when it was sitting in the buggy at Worrell's office. Smith himself was called to the stand, though, and denied drinking from the bottle. If he had, with no ill effects, this would have fit the defense's contention that the poison was introduced only later into the bottle.

On rebuttal, the state offered a letter Conrad had received, threatening him with exposure of skeletons in his family closet. An expert witness testified that the handwriting on the letter was that of Dr. Graves. With that, the evidence was closed.

CLOSING ARGUMENTS

In its closing argument, the prosecution spun a conspiracy theory. It denounced the "tramp of a doctor and adventurer of a lawyer who conspired to deprive this feeble, paralytic old lady of her estate and administer deadly poison to their victim."[45] The prosecutor's theory was that Colonel Ballou had launched the contest of J.B. Barnaby's will to get more funds in the hands of Josephine, from which he and Dr. Graves could then steal. The Barnaby family, he said, had been a perfectly happy one until Dr. Graves and Colonel Ballou became involved, poisoning Josephine's mind before Dr. Graves poisoned her body.

By the time Dr. Graves sent the deadly bottle, the prosecutor explained, he had secured control of all of Josephine's funds, much of which he invested with his brother-in-law. He was named in her will to serve as her executor, without bond; however, she had drafted a new will, and her dissatisfaction with him indicated that she intended to withdraw the power of attorney. To prevent this from happening, Dr. Graves concocted the deadly compound, and sent it to her at Worrell's business address, all the better to cast suspicion on the Worrells. Finally, the prosecution laid great emphasis on Josephine's statements during her dying hours that exonerated the Bennetts and on her refusal to exonerate Dr. Graves.

Colonel Ballou led off the defense closing, in which he made the following points: (1) the second will did not actually reduce the amount that Dr. Graves would receive on Josephine's death, which had always been $25,000; (2) in her financial dealings with Dr. Graves, Josephine had acted shrewdly and in her own interests; (3) Dr. Graves's conduct after the murder did not show guilty knowledge; (4) Dr. Graves would not have resorted to such a clumsy and dangerous scheme to eliminate Josephine; (5) the newspapermen had slandered Dr. Graves and their testimony should be disregarded; and (6) the chain of custody of the bottle was irrevocably tainted.

Thomas Macon, who was quite ill by this point and allowed to remain seated during his closing, went next for the defense. In an argument laced with scriptural references, he first defended Colonel Ballou, who was now on trial almost as much as the defendant, as an "honorable, high-minded, intelligent, and conscientious gentleman and lawyer."[46] With dripping sarcasm, he noted that the true conspiracy was that of the Conrad family, who stood to control a great sum of money from Josephine's estate if Dr. Graves were executed. The "happy and affectionate" nature of the Barnaby family, he continued, was illustrated by the paltry $2,500 per year J.B. Barnaby left his wife, and by the fact that she had chosen to travel far away after her husband's death rather than staying with her "affectionate and dutiful son-in-law."[47]

Macon then launched an attack on the prosecutor, accusing him of using perjury to falsely convict Dr. Graves, making him little better than a murderer himself. The government's case was weak, he insisted. Dr. Graves was right to caution Josephine against extravagant spending. As for the prosecution's claims that Sallie Hanley was a spy sent by Dr. Graves to control Josephine, Macon claimed she was just a poor working girl who had tried to protect herself from Josephine. Rather than embezzling Josephine's money, Dr. Graves had wisely invested it.

The evidence pointed to the Worrells having adulterated the whiskey, rather than Dr. Graves. It was the Worrells who tried to get Josephine to believe that Dr. Graves had poisoned her, not the other way around. Finally, Josephine had been satisfied, rather than dissatisfied, with Dr. Graves's management of her money.

On rebuttal, the prosecutor reminded the jury that they could convict on circumstantial evidence. He then went back through the evidence, again emphasizing each point that cast suspicion on Dr. Graves, whom he called a "quack."[48] He then tarred and feathered Colonel Ballou, stating that "any lawyer who allowed that woman to will to a vendor of patent medicines and medicinal tramp, without consideration, the sum of $25,000, and made him executor, ought to be [disbarred] for professional misconduct."[49]

Finally, he asked the jury to remember that Dr. Graves had boasted that the state of Colorado was too poor to prosecute him, and implored it to enter a guilty verdict to maintain the dignity of the state.

The jury retired to consider its verdict on January 2, 1892, at 6:30 p.m. A little more than an hour later, at 7:35 p.m., the jury returned a guilty verdict. Two-thirds of its time in deliberation had been spent reading the instructions of the court and comparing the inscription on the bottle to the writing in Graves's letters. The first and second ballots were 11 to 1 for conviction, and by the third ballot, the jury was unanimous.

THE APPEAL

On appeal, the Colorado Supreme Court focused on the statements Josephine had allegedly made on her deathbed about the Bennetts and Dr. Graves. These statements, the Court noted, were hearsay.[50] The government argued that the statements were admissible as "dying declarations," but the Court disagreed, noting that it took several days for Josephine to die, and at the time the statements were made, she expected to recover.[51] Also, the statements were not part of the *res gestae* of the crime, because they were made long after Josephine consumed the fatal drink.

In reversing Dr. Graves's conviction, the Court noted that:

In all criminal prosecutions[,] the law of the land guarantees to every accused person a fair trial, and a right to meet the witnesses against him face to face. [Dr. Graves] has not had such a trial. Suspicions and statements of the deceased not even having the sanction of her oath were put in evidence against him, in violation of fundamental principles.[52]

DEATH OF DR. GRAVES

Before his conviction was reversed, a rather odd story describing the manner in which Dr. Graves would be executed appeared in *The New York Times*.[53] The article explained that Colorado authorities had adopted a Rube Goldberg contraption[54] that would spare the executioner from actually killing Dr. Graves. Instead, Dr. Graves's own weight on a platform would set in motion machinery that would cause a heavy weight to drop and for him to be hanged.

Ironically, in light of subsequent events, the article began by explaining that although Dr. Graves would thus "hang himself," he had promised "on entering the prison, with right hand outstretched to heaven . . . that he would not attempt to take his own life."[55] The warden's concern may have come from reports that Dr. Graves had stated, "I will never live to have a new trial."[56]

Once the Court entered its decision ordering a retrial, things initially looked good for Dr. Graves. The cost of assembling the witnesses against him once again might prove prohibitive even for Conrad. Then, something very unfortunate occurred — at least from the doctor's perspective. A new witness from Massachusetts came forward who said that he had been approached in November 1890 in Boston by a man who paid him a quarter to write a note word-for-word identical to that on the whiskey bottle sent to Josephine. Armed with this new evidence, the prosecutor went to the County Commissioners, who appropriated $3,000 to pay the cost of witnesses for a new trial in Denver.

A report concerning this new evidence appeared in the Denver newspapers on September 1, 1893. Two days later, Dr. Graves was found dead in his cell. He had, ironically, killed himself with poison, by ingesting flypaper. In a letter to the Denver Coroner that was discovered in his cell, he attributed his death to "persecution," stating he was "worn out" and "exhausted."[57]

CONCLUSION

The Graves trial is a reminder that no matter how sensational and reprehensible the defendant's alleged crime, he is entitled to a fair trial. We will never know how a second trial — with proper observation of the rules of evidence — would have ended in the case of Dr. Thomas Thatcher Graves.

Original printing: *The Colorado Lawyer*, July 2010. The author is grateful for the research assistance of Dan Cordova and Lynn Christian of the Colorado Supreme Court Law Library.

NOTES

1. *People v. Graves* (Arapahoe County Dist. Ct. 1891).

2. Detailed descriptions of Dr. Graves and Josephine Barnaby, along with many other interesting details about the case, are provided in a fascinating true-crime book about the Barnaby murder, written by her great-grandson Barnaby Conrad. *See* Conrad, *A Revolting Transaction* (Arbor House, 1983). Conrad's was not the only book written about the case. Two other contemporaneous accounts are: Barnaby, *Dr. Graves: His Trial and His Suicide: or, the Famous Barnaby Mystery Being a Complete Account of the Arrest, Trial and Conviction of Dr. T. Thatcher Graves for the Murder of Mrs. Josephine A. Barnaby of Providence, R.I., and the Suicide in Prison of the Accused* (1893); and Day, *Death in the Mail: a Narrative of the Murder of a Wealthy Widow, and the Trial and Conviction of the Assassin, her Physician, Dr. Thomas Thatcher Graves* (1892).

3. Johnson and Buel, eds., "The Occupation — by Thomas Thatcher Graves, Aide-de-Camp on the Staff of Gen. Weitzel," *Battles and Leaders of the Civil War* 726-28 (1888).

4. Kitty formerly was one of Dr. Graves's patients. Her parents brought her to him for mental health treatment after "she had been found totally nude in

a meadow at midnight, babbling lines of Ophelia from *Hamlet*." Conrad, *supra* note 2 at 57.

5. *Id.* at 37.

6. *Id.* at 28.

7. *Id.* Josephine Barnaby would be referred to as an "old woman" during Dr. Graves's trial, which is perhaps attributable to the shorter life expectancies than today that prevailed in the 19th Century. It was also a tactic used by the prosecution to create sympathy for the victim.

8. Bayles, ed., "Jerothmul Bowers BARNABY," *History of Providence County, Rhode Island* 684-85 (W.W. Preston & Co. 1891).

9. The Colorado Supreme Court's opinion in the case indicates that she suffered from "partial paralysis of one side of her body." *Graves v. People*, 32 P. 63, 63 (Colo. 1893).

10. In what may have been delicate language, the Colorado Supreme Court called Dr. Graves Josephine's "confidential friend." *Id.*

11. *See, e.g.,* Lawson, ed., *American State Trials* 258 (Thomas Law Book Co., 1921).

12. *Graves, supra* note 9 at 64.

13. Lawson, *supra* note 11 at 257.

14. *Graves, supra* note 9 at 63.

15. One of the letters, later read to the jury, was extremely harsh. Dr. Graves explained the prospective guardianship as follows:

> You could not sign a paper legally. You could not borrow money, you could have nothing charged more than a six-year-old child. You never could step foot again in the Adirondacks, for you could not even leave town, as you could not raise funds.

Lawson, *supra* note 11 at 341.

16. *Graves, supra* note 9 at 64.

17. *See id.*

18. As Dr. Graves later explained, a large overdose of arsenic can lead to vomiting and expulsion of the poison; a smaller dose may be absorbed, proving fatal. Conrad, *supra* note 2 at 43.

19. To add insult to injury, he allegedly left a mistress $100,000.

20. Trickey and McHenry would later achieve infamy for their role in the "Trickey–McHenry affair," which involved a fabricated newspaper story about

the Lizzie Borden axe-slaying case. *See, e.g.,* www.lizzieandrewborden.com/
CrimeLibrary/CastofCharacters.htm.

21. Conrad, *supra* note 2 at 55.

22. The author of the account in *American State Trials* found this newspaper report quite damning, but did not question its dubious source with the discredited reporter. Lawson, *supra* note 11 at 259.

23. *Id.* at 265.

24. *Id.*

25. *Id.* at 283-84.

26. Henry Marshall Furman was one of Dr. Graves's three defense attorneys. He was a well-known criminal lawyer from Oklahoma who served on the Oklahoma Court of Criminal Appeals. *See* en.wikipedia.org/wiki/Henry _Marshall_Furman.

27. Lawson, *supra* note 11 at 290.

28. *Id.* at 332.

29. *Id.* at 333.

30. Josephine found Ms. Hanley vulgar, because she rode a horse "man-fashion" rather than in the more lady-like "side saddle" style. *Id.* at 342.

31. Lawson, *supra* note 11 at 339.

32. *Id.* at 342.

33. *Id.* at 346.

34. *Id.*

35. *Id.* at 348.

36. *Id.* at 349.

37. This admission (if Dr. Graves actually said it) made little sense, in light of the other evidence at trial. Other scientific witnesses had testified that, by chemical analysis, the bottle contained no whiskey. Also, Dr. Graves would have had no reason to disguise a bottle of real whiskey with a label indicating it was from "friends in the woods."

38. Lawson, *supra* note 11 at 353.

39. *Id.* at 358.

40. *Id.* at 364.

41. *Id.* at 366. In a remark laden with sexual innuendo, the prosecutor later called Hanley "that pliant, jaunty, slippery, serpentine piece of Rhode Island bric-a-brac." *Id.* at 408.

42. Lawson, *supra* note 11 at 369.

43. *Id.* at 371.

44. *Id.* at 373-74.

45. *Id.* at 385.

46. *Id.* at 398-99.

47. *Id.* at 399.

48. *Id.* at 408.

49. *Id.* at 409.

50. *Graves, supra* note 9 at 65.

51. *Id.*

52. *Id.*

53. "Graves to Hang Himself: How the Murderer of Mrs. Barnaby Will Die," *The New York Times* 16 (Jan. 24, 1892).

54. *See* "Rube Goldberg — biography, general information, art work, art ideas," available at www.rube-goldberg.com.

55. "Graves to Hang Himself: How the Murderer of Mrs. Barnaby Will Die," *supra* note 53.

56. Lawson, *supra* note 11 at 448. Sixty years later, a letter appeared in the *Rocky Mountain News*, in which the writer insisted that Dr. Graves committed suicide after it was discovered that he "stepped into a small railway station in some far Eastern state and had asked the depot agent to address the package for him, saying that his hand had been injured." *See* "More on Graves Case," *Rocky Mountain News* 45 (Jan. 25, 1953). This is further proof that the *Graves* case has never ceased to fascinate newspaper readers.

57. Lawson, *supra* note 11 at 449. *See also* "Dr. Graves' Death," *Rocky Mountain News* 1 (Sept. 4, 1893).

V

OUR FELLOW
CREATURES

INTRODUCTION

A mong famous figures of the Old West, few possess a more ambivalent reputation than William Frederick "Buffalo Bill" Cody (1846–1917). On the credit side of the ledger, Bill showed both courage and compassion. As a young boy he helped rescue his father, who had been stabbed, from a pro-slavery mob. A few years later, after his father eventually died from his wounds, a young and fatherless Bill took on hazardous jobs like scout and pony express rider. His service as a cavalry scout later won him the Medal of Honor. His Wild West show employed many Native Americans who might otherwise have sunk into destitution. And Bill appears to have genuinely supported expanded rights for women and Native Americans.

On the debit side, Bill's participation in the destruction of Native American culture and life (as a so-called "Indian fighter") cannot be ignored. The Wild West shows exploited Native Americans, and may have perpetuated stereotypes concerning them. The most significant tarnish on Buffalo Bill's reputation, however, lies in his association — whether or not justified — with the eradication of American buffalo from the western plains.

From time immemorial, humans have exploited animal resources in one of two basic ways: hunting and domestication. In the beginning, our ancestors hunted animals. Their tribal lives and religious sentiments often were built around the hunt. Later, they learned to domesticate animals, so that carnivorous activity became more sedentary and regularized.

165

Early hunters sometimes drove a species to extinction, as evidenced by the disappearance of some prehistoric animals. But such overkill appears to have been largely accidental, a by-product of increasing hunting skill. By contrast, the great buffalo hunt on the western plains was something new: a deliberate attempt to destroy an entire native species of animal as an act of war. It is estimated that by 1887, only twenty wild buffalo remained in the State of Colorado.

It could be argued that we are still paying a price for this indiscriminate slaughter. There are certainly trade-offs in choosing factory farming of imported animals over the cultivation of native species. In any event, cattle and fenced ranges took the place of buffalo and the open prairie. The change was so successful that it has now been estimated that the average American eats three hamburgers a week.

Such fast food has deep roots. Human beings have domesticated farm animals for at least the past 9,000 years. The domestication of cattle has been greatly significant in the rise of civilizations all over the world. Today, domesticated cattle are ubiquitous, from the herds of Masai tribesmen in East Africa to the longhorn steers of Texas, from the pampas of Argentina to the pampered cows of Kobe, Japan.

There are reasons for this success. Skeletons of early agriculturalists tell us that they on the whole were less healthy than their hunter-gatherer counterparts. For many of our ancestors, the additional calories provided by the milk and flesh of domestic animals must have made the difference between survival and starvation.

Given this crucial dependence, it is not surprising that the friendly beasts have had a role to play in human religious understanding. Christians adore their manger scenes, and the paschal lamb has been significant in Judaism, where it is connected with the celebration of Passover. Both Islam and Judaism proscribe the consumption of certain types of animals. But it is paganism that may provide us with the most exotic examples of animal symbolism.

To give one example, altars to the ancient Persian god Mithras have been found throughout Europe. Christian churches were built over many of them. Mithras appears in a characteristic scene known as the *tauroctony*, where he is shown sacrificing a sacred bull. The precise meaning of the *tauroctony* is still debated in academia. Mithraism, the faith of the Roman legions, was an early rival of Christianity. There is evidence that some of its initiates were actually baptized in the hot blood of a freshly-slain bull. Some have even argued that Spanish bull-fighting is a curious remnant of this ancient cult.

Rodeo, another sport involving men and animals, has a more prosaic history. It began right here in Colorado on July 4, 1869. On that day, a group of cowboys assembled near Deer Trail to show off their skills as ranch hands and to compete to determine whose skills were best. Today, though the number of people actually working as cowboys has gradually decreased, rodeo has grown in popularity and hundreds of rodeos throughout the United States offer millions of dollars of prizes for exhibition of superior cowboy talent.

As farm animals became domesticated, people also turned to animal companions like dogs and cats. These animals, unfortunately, were sometimes subject to abuse, even as organized entertainment. Robert Darnton describes appalling acts of cruelty perpetrated on cats as a form of amusement in France's *ancien regime*. The British were also known to enjoy their cock-fighting and bear baiting. Here in the United States, live pigeons and doves were shot, dozens at a time, for the purpose of target practice. One entire native species of pigeon, known as the Passenger Pigeon, was entirely exterminated though it numbered in the billions when settlers arrived.

The first humane societies dedicated to the prevention of cruelty both to animals and human children were organized in Great Britain in the early 1800s. The concept soon spread to the United States. By the 1880s, Colorado had its own Humane Society. Wolfe Londoner, Denver's famous grocer and politician (who is featured in "Official Misconduct: Wolfe Londoner and the Denver Mayoral Election of 1889," in this book), served as an early president. Though today the Society is known mostly for running animal shelters, in the early days it had police powers and its agents wore badges and could arrest those suspected of abusing children and animals.

FOR FURTHER READING

Kathryn Shevelow, *For the Love of Animals: The Rise of the Animal Protection Movement* (New York, NY: Henry Holt & Co. 2008).

Joel H. Bernstein, *Wild Ride: The History and Lore of Rodeo* (Layton, UT: Gibbs Smith 2007).

Whisker, *The Right to Hunt* (2d ed., Merril Press, 1999).

Tester, *Animals & Society: The Humanity of Animal Rights* (New York, NY: Routledge 1991).

Ritvo, *The Animal Estate: The English and Other Creatures in the Victorian Age* (Harvard Univ. Press 1987).

The Docked Horse's Tail
Cruelty and the Commerce Clause

BY FRANK GIBBARD

I do not deny that beasts feel: what I deny is, that we may
not consult our own advantage and use them as we please,
treating them in the way which best suits us.
—Benedict de Spinoza, *Ethics,* Pt. IV, Prop. XXXVII, n.1.

I care not much for a man's religion whose
dog and cat are not the better for it.
—Abraham Lincoln[1]

I am betting that the reader will find Lincoln's sentiment more con-
genial than Spinoza's. The Romantic Era, which succeeded the Age
of Reason, has made Spinoza's 17th-Century logic seem cold and un-
feeling to modern ears.

As attitudes about cruelty toward animals have evolved, thorny ethical and legal issues have co-evolved, to bedevil commentators and legislators alike. In the words of the old saw about the Puritans: Do we
outlaw bear baiting because it causes the bear pain or because it gives
the spectators pleasure?

The Colorado Supreme Court addressed this issue a century ago, in
two cases involving the curious practice of horse docking. "Docking"

is a cosmetic procedure performed to shorten a horse's tail. It is not as harmless as it sounds. Docking does not simply involve clipping the hair that forms the tail; it is a surgical operation that removes a majority of the vertebrae in the horse's tailbone.[2] Docked horses were considered quite stylish around the turn of the last century. Unamused, the Colorado legislature passed a statute prohibiting the docking of horses and the importation of docked horses into the state. Owners of such horses were given ninety days to register their horses. Use of an unregistered docked horse was made illegal.[3]

In the 1904 case of *Bland v. People*,[4] the owner of an unregistered docked horse was charged under the anti-docking statute. The legislation was unconstitutional, he claimed, because it deprived him of the use of his property, the horse, without compensation. He also argued that the prohibition on the use of an unregistered horse was not a valid exercise of the state's police power, because it did not protect the health, comfort, or good morals of the community.

The Colorado Supreme Court disagreed. In a remarkable decision, it found that horse docking ran afoul of *both* prongs of the old Puritan dilemma.[5] First, docking was cruel to the horse, "not only because of the torture inflicted by the operation," but because it deprived the horse of its tail, "a weapon supplied him by nature for his protection from the myriads of winged pests that infest the land."[6] Second, docking also was an offense against morals, because "seeing frequently the mutilated and disfigured animals sears the conscience and hardens the minds of the people."[7] These two rationales were sufficient to justify the statute under the state's police power.

The horse-docking statute fared less well against a Commerce Clause challenge three years later in *Stubbs v. People*.[8] The defendants were charged under the portion of the statute that prohibited bringing docked horses into the state. The legislature passed an exception to the anti-docking statute that permitted docked horses to be brought into the state for breeding and exhibition purposes. The Supreme Court recognized that this knocked the blocks out from under its anti-cruelty rationale in *Bland*.[9] This time, the Court agreed with the defendants that the challenged portion of the statute that prohibited bringing docked horses into the state for domestic use was unconstitutional because it offended the dormant Commerce Clause — by prohibiting the importation of docked horses, the Colorado legislature had attempted to legislate concerning interstate commerce, a field reserved to Congress.

Justice Robert W. Steele was not impressed by the Commerce Clause rationale. In a heartfelt concurrence, he deplored "the importation and use of mutilated animals — mutilated not because of a tender solicitude for the welfare of the animals, nor for the benefit of society, but cruelly mutilated, from sordid motives, to supply the demands of the devotees of an ephemeral and senseless fashion."[10] Nevertheless, given the legislative retreat on the importation of such horses for exhibition and breeding, Steele concluded that the Court's previous decision in *Bland* could no longer stand, and the defendants must be discharged. Later prosecutions under the Colorado anti-docking statute were rare. The statute was repealed in 1971.

Original printing: *The Colorado Lawyer*, November 2005. For a discussion of the legal and ethical aspects of various cosmetic procedures that continue to be performed on horses, including docking, see Tozzini, "Hair Today, Gone Tomorrow: Equine Cosmetic Crimes and Other Tails of Woe," 9 *Animal Law* 159 (2003). For an interesting sociological study of the evolution of attitudes toward animal protection, see Tester, *Animals & Society: The Humanity of Animal Rights* (New York, NY: Routledge, 1991).

NOTES

1. See the July/August 2001 issue of *Quest* magazine, available at www.theosophical.org.
2. *See* West's Ann. Cal. Penal Code § 597n (1999) (defining "docking").
3. Colo.Sess.L. 1899, p.175, c.93.
4. *Bland v. People*, 76 P. 359 (Colo. 1904).
5. *Id.* at 363.
6. *Id.* at 360.

7. *Id.* at 361.

8. *Stubbs v. People*, 90 P. 1114 (Colo. 1907).

9. *Id.* at 1114-15.

10. *Id.* at 1120 (Steele, C.J., specially concurring).

When Doves Died
A Case of Animal Cruelty in El Paso County

BY FRANK GIBBARD

"The quintessential feature of modern man, at least since the
Neolithic age, is that he need not hunt for survival. . . . We hunt
now to amuse ourselves, not to survive."[1]
"[L]ate Victorian critics of hunting . . . characterized
enjoyment of the sufferings of the hapless victims of butchery as
a remnant of the barbarism in our natures, one that would
slowly but surely die under the influence of a higher and a
gentler civilization."[2]

Can hunting be morally justified if it is undertaken primarily for
amusement rather than survival? Are there any limits on the ways
we may use animals to satisfy our desire for such amusement? More
than a century ago, the Colorado Supreme Court took up these questions in *Waters v. People*,[3] and reached a surprising result.

THE DOVE SHOOT

Frank A. Waters was a member of a country club in El Paso County,
Colorado. Concerned that Colorado's animal cruelty statute might be
construed to prohibit shooting live, captive birds for sport, he agreed
to be a test case for the statute.

173

Waters and other country club members purchased about forty live doves. On January 12, 1895, they assembled for a test of skill. One by one, the caged doves were released. Waters and other country club members fired on them. Some of the doves were killed outright. A few of the birds escaped unhurt. Others were wounded. The wounded birds were killed by attendants hired for that purpose.

Waters and the others took the dead birds home and ate them. Afterward, the Colorado Humane Society (Society) brought Waters in front of an El Paso County Justice of the Peace and charged him with cruelty to animals.

A History of Live Bird Shoots

Waters' dove shoot was not that unusual for its time. By the late 1800s, the related sport of live pigeon shooting had been going on for at least a century. An English sporting magazine published in 1793 appears to provide the first mention of live bird shoots in print.[4]

Live pigeon shooting was big sport in America during the 19th Century and often went hand-in-hand with other exhibitions of skill with firearms, including contests involving shooting at glass balls.[5] Trophies and prize money were awarded to the shooters with the highest accuracy, some of whom lived like celebrities, "[t]raveling in lavish railroad cars, dining on the best food, shooting the finest shotguns and living in the best hotels."[6]

In Paris in 1900, for the first and only time in Olympic history, live pigeon shooting was featured at the Olympics.[7] The shoot at the Olympics marked an apogee of sorts in the sport of live pigeon shooting. During the next decade, society quietly moved away from the shooting of captive birds for sport. The clay target (or "clay pigeon")—a hard clay disk that was ejected into the air and fired on—began to be substituted for live birds.[8] More important, live bird shoots increasingly were viewed as a form of cruelty to animals. Most states eventually outlawed them.[9]

Colorado Humane Society

Today, the Society, which brought the charges against Waters in 1895, generally is thought of as a private organization charged with running animal shelters.[10] At the time Waters was charged, however, the Society had significant "police powers" under state statute.[11] Its agents were entitled to wear badges and had the power to arrest and bring charges against those suspected of animal cruelty or cruelty to children.[12]

The Society tried its first case of animal cruelty in August 1881, successfully prosecuting a Denver man who beat his horse.[13] In its early years, the Society cast its net wide, looking into many activities involving animals, including the new sport of rodeo and abuse of a donkey, "which the people of Cottage Lane, in the bottoms, [were] charged with inducing to drink beer, thus getting the animal drunk."[14]

The Supreme Court Case: Waters v. People

After the Justice of the Peace found Waters guilty and sentenced him to pay a fine, he appealed to county court. The county court affirmed the conviction and fine. Waters then appealed to the Colorado Supreme Court.

The parties agreed on the facts. At issue was the interpretation of Colorado's animal cruelty statute. The statute provided that "[e]very person who . . . tortures, torments, . . . or needlessly mutilates or kills . . . any animal, or causes or procures it to be done, . . . shall, upon conviction, be punished."[15] "Torture," "torment," and "cruelty" were defined to include "every act, omission or neglect whereby unnecessary or unjustifiable pain or suffering is caused, permitted, or allowed to continue when there is a reasonable remedy or relief."[16] The Colorado Supreme Court appeared uncomfortable attaching too much stigma to Waters' actions, which it found morally ambiguous. The Court stated:

> As an abstract question, men of equal refinement and intelligence . . .
> might well differ as to the moral obliquity of the act of shooting live
> doves as they were released from a trap. The scholarly ascetic, whose
> chief pleasures are found in the library, or the man whose life is de-
> voted to the welfare of the lower animals, might suffer excruciating
> pain if such an act was committed in his presence; while the sports-
> man, whose recreations are gunning and fishing, might look with plea-
> sure upon what, to him, was "an ancient and honorable pastime."[17]

The Supreme Court noted "the progress of civilization" and the
"tender solicitude for the brute creation which keeps pace with man's
increased knowledge of their life and habits." It stated that the Court's
duty was "to give proper effect to [the animal cruelty] legislation"
spawned by these concerns.[18] Citing a number of cases from other jurisdictions that had reached conflicting results, the Court determined
that the holdings of the courts that had prohibited live bird shoots were
predicated on language very similar to the Colorado statute and were
"in harmony with the advance in enlightened public opinion at this day
as to the protection of dumb animals" and therefore were more in tune
with the intent of the Colorado legislature.[19]

> [T]he killing of captive doves as they are released from a trap, merely
> to improve one's skill of marksmanship, or for sport and amusement
> . . . is, within the meaning of this act, unnecessary and unjustifiable.[20]

The shooting skill the sportsmen desired could be achieved by other
means that did not involve cruelty to animals, and the pain and suffering
caused by shooting the birds was disproportionate to the end sought. The
Supreme Court therefore upheld Waters' conviction.

AFTERMATH

As noted, by the end of the first decade of the 20th Century, live pigeon
shoots had been outlawed in most American states. There may be good
reasons this particular form of "hunting" eventually was banned. Hunt-

ing wild animals pits human cunning against the animal species in their own habitat. The development of alternatives to shooting at live birds for target practice, such as clay pigeons, offered a more "civilized" way to demonstrate and improve one's shooting skill.

Original printing: *The Colorado Lawyer*, March 2008. The author is grateful for the research assistance of Dan Cordova and Lynn Christian of the Colorado Supreme Court Law Library.

NOTES

1. Whisker, *The Right to Hunt* 3 (2d ed., Merril Press, 1999).

2. Ritvo, *The Animal Estate: The English and Other Creatures in the Victorian Age* 132 (Harvard Univ. Press, 1987) (quotations omitted).

3. *Waters v. People*, 46 P. 112 (1896).

4. *See* Hamilton, "Bogardus, Elliott and Gilbert Make Big Money in the Pigeon Rings," available at www.traphof.org/Equipment-Artifacts/early-pigeon -rings.html.

5. *See id.*

6. *See id.*

7. Myths abound concerning this event. It has been suggested that the sport was so new to the Olympics that the gold medal winner, an Australian named Donald MacKintosh, apparently did not even know he was in the Olympics. He believed he was shooting as part of the "Paris Exhibition," to which the Olympics that year were attached. *See, e.g.,* "Olympics Sydney 2000: Shooting," available at www.abc.net.au/news/olympics/sports/shooting.htm. However, other reputable sources state that pigeon shooting was not an official Olympic event, and list the official winner of the non-Olympic event of live pigeon shooting at the 1900 Olympics as Leon de Lunden of Belgium, with Donald MacKintosh coming in third place. *See* en.wikipedia.org/wiki/ Shooting_at_the_1900_Summer_Olympics.

8. *See* Hamilton, *supra* note 4.

9. *Id.*

10. *See* Colorado Humane Society website, www.coloradohumane.org.

11. *See* Mills' Ann. Stat., Ch. 4, §§ 108-110, -115, and -116 (1891).

12. *See id.*

13. "A Beater Beaten," *Rocky Mountain News* (Aug. 14, 1881). J.F. ("Honest John") Shafroth, future governor of Colorado and U.S. Senator, presented the case for the prosecution. For a profile of John Franklin Shafroth, *see* Shafroth, "Six of the Greatest: John Franklin Shafroth," 33 *The Colorado Lawyer* 15 (July 2004). Wolfe Londoner, future mayor of Denver, was president of the Colorado Humane Society at the time, and attended the proceedings. For more on Wolfe Londoner, *see* Gibbard, "Official Misconduct: Wolfe Londoner and the Mayoral Election of 1889," in this book.

14. "Amusements," 8 (col. 7) *Rocky Mountain News* (Feb. 14, 1882).

15. Mills' Ann. Stat., Ch. 4, § 104 (1891).

16. *Id.* at Ch. 4, § 117.

17. *Waters, supra* note 3 at 113.

18. *Id.*

19. *Id.* at 114-15.

20. *Id.*

VI

POLITICS AS USUAL

INTRODUCTION

Colorado territorial politics developed in the shadow of the Civil War. In the beginning, this meant the territory was governed by Republicans, the party that had elected Lincoln to the White House in 1860. The first territorial legislature, chosen in an election held August 19, 1861, was solidly Republican. William Gilpin, the first territorial governor, switched from the Democratic to the Republican Party before Lincoln appointed him. The Territory's first congressional delegate in Washington, Hiram Pitt Bennet, was known to be a pro-Lincoln man.

Though Colorado was officially pro-Union during the Civil War, there was substantial Southern sentiment in the territory. This led to some harrowing conflicts as hostilities intensified between the North and South. Although no major battles were fought in Colorado, and many Southerners merely voted with their feet — departing the territory and returning to the South to enlist in the Confederate forces — the War Between the States was not without impact in the nascent Colorado territory. Pro-Confederate militia roamed the new territory committing acts of terrorism in the name of their cause. There were acts of violence in Denver between northern and southern sympathizers. Worst of all, Confederate forces routed Union enclaves in New Mexico and by early 1862 were poised to turn northward and invade Colorado.

Territorial Governor William Gilpin dealt with this threat by organizing a regiment of volunteer Colorado infantry. The only problem with this otherwise laudable step was that Congress had not appropriated any funds for defense of the territory. Gilpin solved the problem by issuing warrants, signed by himself, totaling $375,000 and payable on the United States Treasury. The merchants who later presented these "Gilpin Drafts" for payment were dismayed to find the United States Treasurer disavowing any knowledge of them. The resulting controversy led President Lincoln to dismiss Gilpin and to appoint John Evans as a substitute governor. This story has a happy ending, however, as the Treasury eventually honored most of the "Gilpin Drafts," and in time the regiment he had organized successfully drove the rebels from New Mexico.

When Colorado's first push for statehood came, in 1864, it was motivated in part by national political considerations. By admitting Colorado to the Union as a pro-Republican state, Lincoln stood to gain additional support in the Electoral College for his re-election as President. Though Lincoln gave the nod to pro-statehood forces, voters within the territory decisively rejected statehood. Voters in Denver may have seen distinct advantages in becoming a state, but they were unable to convince their brethren in other parts of the territory. Lincoln easily won re-election without Colorado, which would not become a state until three more tries and twelve years later.

Unfortunately, the end of the Civil War did not bring an era of peaceful cooperation to Colorado governance. The years following the conflict were marked by power struggles and insider politics. There was no agreement on even such a basic issue as where the territorial capitol should be located. Denver, Golden, and Colorado City all housed the legislature at various points, and Central City and Pueblo had their supporters as well. In addition to the intrigue concerning the capitol, political insiders were suspected of favoring their cronies under a Republican administration that was viewed as increasingly corrupt.

The endemic corruption even infected the third branch of government. There were scandalous rumors concerning the clerk's office at the fledgling Colorado Territorial Supreme Court. The clerk allegedly was soliciting bribes and kickbacks in connection with the award of lucrative publishing and printing contracts. These problems at the Supreme Court had a silver lining, however: they were partly responsible for the appointment of Moses Hallett, a courageous and uncompromising justice, to the high court.

By 1875, movers and shakers in the territory were ready to make what would be a fourth attempt to bring statehood to Colorado. This time, the national political stakes could not have been higher. The 1876 presidential election was one of the closest in history, in which every vote in the Electoral College would be needed. In light of this, both Republicans and Democrats stumped for statehood.

On the Democratic side stood Thomas M. Patterson, a politically astute Denver lawyer and journalist who had helped break the Republican monopoly on politics in Colorado territory by getting himself elected as the territory's congressional delegate in 1874. He worked to convince national party leaders that Colorado would swing Democratic in the next election. Patterson reached an odd alliance with Republican Jerome Chaffee, who had been a powerhouse in Colorado politics until he had a falling-out with President Ulysses S. Grant, allegedly over a card game.

Chaffee arranged a back-room deal with Henry Teller of Central City. Teller agreed to work for statehood if he was chosen as one of Colorado's first senators. He was, and Chaffee was chosen as the other. (This all took place, of course, before the Seventeenth Amendment established direct election of senators by the voting public, in 1913.) This time around, the voters approved statehood, and in 1876, Colorado became the Centennial State. What is more, Colorado's three electoral votes provided Republican Rutherford B. Hayes with the margin he needed to gain the presidency.

Though Patterson had miscalculated the extent of Democratic sentiment in Colorado, his tireless stumping had won bipartisan support for Colorado statehood. As expected, Hayes's election had been far from a sure thing. The deal by which he clinched the office featured backroom manipulations to resolve disputes in the Electoral College. As part of the deal, Reconstruction was formally ended. This proved a bad thing for African-Americans in the South, because it withdrew federal protections from them, caused them to be excluded from political participation, and inaugurated an era of violence including lynching. Coloradans, however, had little reason to mourn the end of Reconstruction. In Colorado territory, Republican rule had been associated with rampant corruption.

Though Republicans remained dominant in the state for another decade, a prairie wildfire movement composed of farmers and laborers called Populism would sweep the state in the 1890s, breaking the Republican monopoly and forging new alliances.

One other significant political development from Colorado's early days deserves mention. In December 1869, Wyoming territory passed an amendment giving women the right to vote. On February 14, 1870, Esther Hobart Morris became the first female justice of the peace in the territory, an event now celebrated in statues in front of the Wyoming capitol building and in Washington, D.C. Giving women the right to vote was a strategic move in the sparsely populated Wyoming territory; it increased the number of eligible voters for statehood. But it also inspired their sisters in Colorado to insist on the same right.

By 1876, a Colorado Women Suffrage Association had been founded. Soon, the state was teeming with advocates of woman suffrage, including national figures like Lucy Stone, Henry B. Blackwell, Margaret Campbell, and Susan B. Anthony, all of whom came to the state to promote the cause. On the other side, religious authorities, including the famous Bishop Machebeuf, proved some of the most vociferous opponents of giving women the right to vote. Despite tireless efforts by its advocates, a referendum on woman suffrage (in which only men could vote) went down to defeat in 1877. It would take another 16 years and the rise of the Populist reform movement before women gained the right to vote, in 1893.

FOR FURTHER READING

Rebecca J. Mead, *How the Vote Was Won: Woman Suffrage in the Western United States, 1868-1914* (New York, NY: New York University Press 2004).

Phil Goodstein, *Denver From the Bottom Up, Volume One: From Sand Creek to Ludlow* (Denver, CO: New Social Publications 2003).

Sybil Downing & Robert E. Smith, *Tom Patterson: Colorado Crusader for Change* (Niwot, CO: University Press of Colorado 1995).

Robert C. McMath, Jr., *American Populism: A Social History, 1877-1898* (New York, NY: Hill & Wang 1992).

Law and Equity in Colorado's 19th Century Suffrage Movement

BY TOM I. ROMERO, II

Ellis Meredith was an optimistic and forward-looking woman. Described by one historian as "educated, egalitarian, and entrepreneurial," Meredith represented the type of activist who could appeal to a broad cross-section of the electorate.[1] In August 1893, however, Meredith was beginning to have her doubts about the possibility of women gaining the vote in Colorado.

In a letter to nationally known suffragist Susan B. Anthony, Meredith articulated her concerns about anti-suffrage materials characterizing women voters as uneducated and ill informed. In response to such caricatures, Meredith responded: "We . . . are pushing our claims for suffrage simply and solely on the grounds of right and justice. Whether we use the ballot for 'a bonnet or a bustle' . . . it is no one's business" (emphasis added).[2] Indeed, for suffragists like Meredith, the meaning of the phrase "right and justice" was at the heart of legal and political equality they sought in the women's suffrage movement.

First advocated by Territorial Governor Edward McCook and his wife in 1870, the right to vote finally was extended to women in Colorado on November 7, 1893. Colorado thus became the second state in the Union, after Wyoming, to extend the franchise to women. To be

Photo from October 1907 article in *Circle Magazine* entitled "The Truth About Women's Suffrage in Colorado"
Courtesy Colorado Historical Society - #10025803

sure, until 1911 when California extended its suffrage laws, Colorado boasted the largest city (Denver) in the nation allowing women to vote.

In the late 19th-Century struggle to secure voting rights, Colorado and national suffragists articulated an ambivalent conception of law and equity. Suffragists first targeted Colorado after the U.S. Supreme Court declared in 1874 that the U.S. Constitution neither extended nor prohibited suffrage to women. Accordingly, the Court left it up to individual states to determine the parameters of who would and would not be extended full political citizenship.[3]

The movement to end Colorado's territorial status in 1875 and 1876 provided the first significant opportunity to inscribe gender equality into a state constitution. Indeed, the National American Woman Suffrage Association saw a certain symmetry and, in turn, symbolism in Colorado's admittance to the Union as a full and equal partner when "they advanced a 'free-women-on-the anniversary-of-men's freedom' plea."[4]

However, these early efforts to extend women the franchise pitted the rights of women against those of other minorities in the state. In 1866, William Byers, publisher and editor of the *Rocky Mountain News*, argued in an editorial that white women deserved the vote more than the nation's recently emancipated African Americans.[5] Then, during the 1876 Constitutional Convention, national suffragists blamed "the Mexican vote" for the failure of men to grant the franchise to women in an 1877 general election, even though Agapita Vigil, a Spanish-speaking legislator representing Huerfano and Las Animas, was a vocal and active supporter of women's suffrage.[6]

By the 1890s, Colorado suffragists realized the importance of building coalitions. They galvanized the support of the Women's Christian Temperance Union, Young Women's Christian Association, the Grange Movement, and the Populists, as well as the support of more than thirty-three newspapers across the state. Like the 1877 election, the issue of U.S. nativity played a role as Colorado citizens feared the influx of foreign immigrants to Colorado and their potential political influence in the state's urban enclaves. According to one historian, "by enfranchising women, natives gained more ballots than did the foreign-born."[7]

It has been 110 years since Colorado men extended the franchise to women. Nevertheless, full inclusion of women into Colorado's public life continues to evolve. It was not until 1944 that Colorado voters amended the Constitution, officially allowing women to sit on a jury. As late as the 1990s, gender bias remained prominent in the state's judicial administration.[8] Today, the wages of women still lag behind those of men for similar work. Although suffragists secured one aspect of the battle for "right and justice" in 1893, the march toward equity continues.

Original printing: *The Colorado Lawyer*, May 2003. The movement to extend women the right to vote in Colorado has long fascinated historians. Barnes Jensen in "Let the Women Vote," *Colorado Magazine* 42 (Winter 1964) and "Colorado Women's Suffrage Campaigns of the 1870s," *Journal of the West* (April 1973) remain the best academic resources on Colorado's suffrage campaigns. The role of the Colorado Bar in the 1893 suffrage campaign is suggested in Bohning, "Six of the Greatest: Jared Warner Mills" 29 *The Colorado Lawyer* 5 (July 2000) at 8. For primary research into the sources of Colorado's suffrage movement, see Goldstein and Hunt, "From Suffrage to Centennial: A Research Guide to Colorado and National Women's Suffrage Sources," *Colorado Heritage* (Spring 1993). Among the collections that Goldstein and Hunt document is the voluminous Ellis Meredith Collection located at the Colorado Historical Society in Denver.

NOTES

1. Marilley, *Women Suffrage and the Origins of Liberal Feminism in the United States*, 1820-1920 (Cambridge, MA: Harvard Univ. Press, 1996) at 132.

2. Ellis Meredith Collection, MSS #427, Box 1, FF 5, Stephen H. Hart Library, Colorado Historical Society, Denver, CO.

3. *Minor v. Happersett*, 88 U.S. 162 (1874).

4. Faherty, "Regional Minorities and the Women Suffrage Struggle," 33 *Colorado Magazine* 214 (July 1956).

5. *Rocky Mountain News* (Jan. 31, 1866).

6. See Elizabeth Cady Stanton, Susan B. Anthony et al., *IV The History of Women's Suffrage* (Rochester, NY: Charles Mann, 1887) at 317.

7. Leonard, "Bristling for their Rights: Colorado's Women and the Mandate of 1893," *Colorado Heritage* 12 (Spring 1993).

8. *See* Tamblyn and Wood, "Final Report, Colorado Supreme Court Task Force on Gender Bias in the Courts" (Denver, CO: Office of the State Court Administrator, 1990).

Of Roosters and Eagles
Colorado's Voting Emblem Cases

BY FRANK GIBBARD

Butterfly ballots, overvotes, hanging chads — the technical difficulties associated with the 2000 presidential election seemed, for a brief moment, to call the electoral process itself into question. Yet in one sense, this was nothing new. Courts have been called on throughout American history to resolve disputes about electoral ballots.

Ballot disputes kept the Colorado Supreme Court particularly busy over a century ago, during the 1890s. Ironically, this may have been the result of attempts to reform the electoral process. In 1891, in an effort to curb some of the abuses associated with previous voting methods, the Colorado legislature passed what was known as the "Australian Ballot Law."[1]

The key feature of the new voting system was that the state prepared a single ballot on which all the eligible candidates were listed, permitting voters to choose among them. Americans take this form of balloting for granted now, but it is actually only about 150 years old. Prior to the adoption of Australian balloting, political parties pre-printed their own ballots, sometimes containing only the names of their candidates, and handed them out to voters at the polls. The voters then placed these ballots in the voting boxes. The ballots often were printed with distinct colors and unique designs or emblems, and could easily be recognized

To Vote a Straight Party Ticket place a Cross (X) with Ink in the Square Opposite Your Party Emblem.

Republican Ticket.

Democratic Ticket.

People's Party Ticket. X

Prohibition Ticket.

If you have not Voted a Straight Ticket above Place a Cross Mark (X) with Ink Opposite Each Name You wish to Vote for in the Blank Space left for that pu

ongress, First Congres- (Vote for One.)	Mark in this column	For Auditor of State.	(Vote for One.)	Mark in this column	For State Senators, First Distr
Republican.		H. C. Bolsinger.	Prohibition.		David Boyd.
People's Party.		Frank C. Carney.	People's Party.		J. Gratz Brown.
Prohibition.		William R. Kennedy.	Democrat.		Wilbur F. Cannon.
		Harry Tarbell.	Republican.		Archie Pirk.
					A. T. Gunnell.

Sample ballot from 1894
Daniel B. Cordova
Ballot courtesy Denver Public Library, Western History Collection

from a distance. This led, as one might imagine, to cases of bribery and voter intimidation.

Although Australian balloting solved some of the problems associated with earlier, more visible forms of voting, it was not a panacea. The state's involvement in printing the ballots and in certifying the candidates who would appear on them inevitably spawned litigation by disappointed office-seekers or entire parties who failed to appear on the ballot. Predictably, voters also found the new ballots more difficult to use.

In a nod to the former system (and also, perhaps, a sad concession to illiteracy among Colorado voters), parties were permitted under the new law to have their emblems appear on the ballot as a guide to voters. Voters could select the entire slate of candidates for a given party by simply placing an "x" or cross next to the emblem, or they could vote *a la carte* by placing their mark next to a candidate's name. Sometimes, they did both, giving the election officials real headaches.

The "emblematic" ballots contained some colorful and creative representations for the parties. The Democratic Party was represented on the ballot by an emblem of a rooster. Republicans used an eagle. The "Miner Party" used a figure of a miner. The People's Party used a cottage home. This use of emblems also spawned an impressive amount of litigation. A summary of a few of these cases will show the kinds of issues the Supreme Court had to deal with once party emblems became significant.

In *Smith v. Harris*,[2] a disappointed candidate for county judge contended that the county clerk had incorrectly printed his name beneath the rooster emblem instead of the miner emblem, after two factions of the Democratic Party had held separate conventions. The Supreme Court held that he failed to state a claim for relief.

Two factions of the People's Party fought over the cottage home emblem in *People ex rel. McGaffey v. District Court of Arapahoe County*.[3] The Supreme Court refused to grant a writ of prohibition to restrain the district court's order granting the Pueblo faction, rather than the Denver faction, the right to the emblem.

In *Dickinson v. Freed*,[4] the losing Republican candidate for county treasurer protested that the successful Democratic candidate had received votes for the party slate placed next to the rooster emblem, even though the county Democratic convention had not been permitted to use that emblem for its candidates. The Supreme Court ruled that the challenge was untimely; the candidate should have protested the proposed ballot before the election.

In *Kratzer v. Allen*,[5] the National Silver Party was permitted to use the face of its candidate for Denver mayor as its emblem on the ballot, even though the Supreme Court opined that later developments might make this choice seem ridiculous. Finally, in *Schaefer v. Whipple*,[6] the Socialist Labor party was permitted to adopt an emblem, even though its nominees had been made by a petition of electors rather than at a party convention.

Perhaps it was all this litigation that persuaded the legislature to do away with ballot emblems in 1899.[7] The memory of emblem balloting has proved to be a long-lasting one. More than 100 years later, the current Colorado statutes still contain the following prohibition: "[N]o emblem, device, or political party designation shall be used on the official ballot at any election by which an eligible elector may vote for more than one office by placing a single cross mark on the ballot or by writing in the name of any political party or political organization."[8]

Original printing: *The Colorado Lawyer*, January 2006. An excellent history of Australian balloting can be found in Fredman, *The Australian Ballot: The Story of an American Reform* (East Lansing, MI: Michigan State University Press, 1968). The Supreme Court also provided an interesting discussion of Australian balloting in *Timmons v. Twin Cities Area New Party*, 520 U.S. 351, 356-57 (1997).

NOTES

1. 1891 Colo. Sess. Laws at 143; *as amended*, 3 Mills' Ann. Stat. § 1625r (1894 Colo. Sess. Laws at 62).

2. *Smith v. Harris*, 32 P. 616 (Colo. 1893).

3. *People ex rel. McGaffey v. District Court of Arapahoe County*, 46 P. 681 (Colo. 1896).

4. *Dickinson v. Freed*, 55 P. 812 (Colo. 1898).

5. *Kratzer v. Allen*, 50 P. 209 (Colo. 1897).

6. *Schaefer v. Whipple*, 55 P. 180 (Colo. 1898).

7. 1899 Colo. Sess. Laws, Ch. 94 at 177.

8. CRS § 1-5-409.

Official Misconduct

Wolfe Londoner and the Denver Mayoral Election of 1889

BY FRANK GIBBARD

The front-page headline in the *Rocky Mountain News* was a shocker. It read: "Sold Like Cattle: Voters in Spring Election Handled Like Herds of Hogs."[1] The invective continued in smaller type: "A Day of Reckoning Has Come, and the Political Harlots Tremble in Fear." Headlines went on to decry the "Nefarious Plot to Cheat Honest Citizens."[2]

The article described the previous day's testimony in a suit against Republican Mayor Wolfe Londoner. Key witnesses were Charles Connor and Jefferson Randolph Smith, who was better known by his infamous sobriquet "Soapy."[3] The two had given devastating testimony in Denver District Court about rampant ballot box stuffing in the 1889 Denver mayoral election. Their testimony would help sway the jury against Londoner and cause his ouster from office.

WOLFE LONDONER: A BRIEF HISTORY

Who was Wolfe Londoner? How did he become Denver's twentieth mayor,[4] and the only one to resign his office because of voter fraud? What caused his downfall? To answer these questions, we have to go back another thirty years, to a time when the city of Denver was little more than a mining camp.

Arrival in Denver

The year was 1860, and Wolfe Londoner, then 21, had just walked 700 miles from Atchison, Kansas, to the Rocky Mountain foothills. The dirty, broke, and exhausted young man who shuffled his way through Denver's dusty streets was born in 1839 to a Jewish family of wealthy New York merchants. He had set off for Denver after some family friends at the merchandising firm of Hanauer, Dold & Co. engaged him to work in their Denver office. Like many who made the trek west, he came with a wagon train.

On the first day of his journey from Atchison, Londoner found himself a comfortable seat in a merchandise wagon. About five miles outside Atchison, the burly Mexican wagon master discovered him. Refusing to believe the young man's story about his employment with the Hanauer firm, the wagon master ordered him off the wagon. He was forced to walk the rest of the way. Londoner arrived in Denver dead on his feet, with only $1.50 left in his pocket.[5]

"I Married a Widow"

It was an uncharacteristic humiliation for Londoner, who usually came out on top of any transaction. Just prior to his long foot journey to Denver, for example, he had "pulled a fast one" on a steamboat captain in Dubuque, Iowa. Londoner's father, living in St. Louis after a business reversal, sent $20 to Dubuque, instructing his son to use the money for expenses until he could send more money to transport the family to St. Louis. Londoner, however, made up his mind to bring the family to St. Louis immediately. The only problem was the steamboat fare: $15 per passenger was far more money than Londoner could afford.

Undeterred, Londoner persuaded the steamboat captain to transport him "and his family" for a mere $25—$20 of which was to be paid up

Wolfe Londoner
Courtesy Denver Public Library,
Western History Collection

front. Imagine the captain's consternation when he found that instead of being occupied with a young man, his wife, and a child or two, the ship's berths were filled with seven members of the Londoner family and all of their household goods. When the captain angrily protested that Londoner had deceived him, the young man had a quick answer: "I married a widow. What's a man to do when he's in love?"[6]

It is a mark of Londoner's charm that, even after the captain discovered that Londoner was in fact a bachelor, the two men became friends. Londoner was allowed to complete the journey to St. Louis and, eventually, made his way to Denver.

Fortune and Fame

Fortune smiled on Wolfe Londoner throughout his life, but never so much as during his first years in Colorado. After a few months in West Denver, Hanauer, Dold & Co. sent him to Cañon City to start another store in their chain. Londoner arrived to a community in turmoil, full of miners eager to strike their claim during the first year of the great California Gulch gold rush. The Gulch, located near Leadville, was then home to 10,000 men, and its placer mining claims were yielding $1 million a season.[7]

Londoner's store did a booming business, but he soon resigned to pursue greener pastures — this time in government service. He served as county clerk and recorder of Lake County, Colorado from 1861 to 1865. In those days, the office holder's pay was based on fees for services provided. During two of the wildly busy years of his tenure, Londoner made $10,000 a year,[8] a sum equivalent to more than $200,000 today.[9] He took this money to Denver, where in 1865 he opened a wholesale and retail grocery business that soon began operating in four states and grossed $1 million per year.[10] In 1887, he moved the grocery business to the "Londoner Block," located at 1624–1630 Arapahoe Street.[11]

Denver in the 1890s has been described as an unusually friendly city to people of Jewish descent — at least to Jews of the professional and managerial class to which Londoner belonged; however, anti-Semitic incidents and attitudes were not unheard of in the city's early days.[12] If Londoner ever felt intimidated by ethnic prejudice, he did not let it keep him from becoming one of Denver's most prominent citizens. He was especially well known for his hospitality to visitors to the city and to Denver journalists. He liked to regale members of Denver's newspaper community with delicacies — cheeses, sausages, caviar, and tropical preserves — served in a special basement room called the "Cyclone cellar," located in the Londoner Building on Arapahoe Street.[13] How ironic, then, that providing hospitality of another sort would soon land him in very hot water, castigated in newspapers by reporters of the very sort he considered his friends.

THE ELECTION

The Denver mayoral election of 1889 was one of the most colorful and corrupt in the city's history. An unusually large slush fund allowed the Londoner campaign to buy votes outright, purportedly for $2 and two beers a head.[14] A more cynical and disturbing tactic — amply detailed in testimony during the subsequent *quo warranto* proceeding that was instituted in Denver District Court — involved ballot box stuffing at saloons in the Eighteenth, Nineteenth, and Thirtieth Precincts. Voter names were inscribed on hundreds of blank ballots pre-marked with a straight Republican ticket.[15] "Voters" then submitted these ballots to corrupt election officials, often voting several times. If the voter whose name was inscribed on the ballot showed up at the polling place, he was informed that he already had voted, or that he was ineligible to vote.

In the end, Londoner won the election by seventy-seven votes. During a high-level meeting after the election, Colorado Senator Henry M. Teller asked Londoner if he knew that he actually lost by 2,000 votes and won only through vote fraud. Londoner did not respond to the Senator directly; he turned to his chief of police and said, "You know I told you that I did not want to take this office under the circumstances I was elected."[16] But he did take office.

PEOPLE EX REL. BARTON *v.* LONDONER (ROUND ONE)

Londoner's opponent in the election, a man named Elias R. Barton, did not take his loss lying down. Given the rampant fraud, he considered himself the rightfully elected mayor of Denver. He went so far as to take the oath and demand admission to the office; however, he was refused. He then instituted a *quo warranto* proceeding in Denver District Court.

Initially, things went badly for Barton in court. Londoner demurred to his suit, citing a provision of the Denver City Charter that stated that in the case of a contested mayoral election, the Denver Board of Supervisors would hear the contest.[17] He also cited provisions of the Colorado Constitution concerning the conduct of election contests. The district court agreed with his position and dismissed the *quo warranto* suit for lack of jurisdiction. Barton appealed to the Colorado Supreme Court.

The Supreme Court considered whether the provision in the Denver City Charter, or the provisions in the Colorado Constitution dealing with contested elections, deprived the courts of *quo warranto* jurisdiction. In an opinion that placed high value on the historic writ, the Court held that they did not. Because there was no language vesting sole or exclusive jurisdiction in the Board of Supervisors, the courts retained concurrent jurisdiction to proceed by information in the nature of *quo warranto*.[18] Similarly, constitutional provisions for election contests did not displace *quo warranto* proceedings, which were brought by the People of the State of Colorado.[19] As a "freeholder, resident, and elector" of the city of Denver, Barton was empowered to proceed in the name of the People.[20] Accordingly, the Supreme Court reversed the dismissal of his complaint.

LONDONER *v.* PEOPLE EX REL. BARTON (ROUND TWO)

The *quo warranto* action proceeded to trial in district court in March 1890. By this time, Londoner was about half way through his term as mayor. Unfortunately for him, after devastating testimony including that of his erstwhile associates Connor and Smith, the jury found in favor of Barton.

The district court's findings, based on the jury's responses to interrogatories, left no doubt where its verdict lay. It concluded that "certain persons combined and confederated together to procure the casting of illegal ballots" for Londoner; that "such persons did procure . . . fraudulent and illegal ballots," and that election judges participated in the fraud.[21] It entered a "judgment of ouster" against Londoner.

Londoner appealed. The Supreme Court entered a brief order dismissing the appeal, ruling that under a Colorado Code provision relating to appeals dealing with a franchise or freehold, no appeal was available from a judgment of ouster.[22]

LONDONER *v.* PEOPLE EX REL. BARTON (ROUND THREE)

In light of the judgment dismissing the appeal, it is surprising to find it resurrected for a third decision a few months later. In its third decision in the case, the Colorado Supreme Court was careful to emphasize that Londoner had not been personally implicated in the fraud.[23] Toward the fraud itself, however, the Court was unsparing. Noting that "we have found no instance where the extent of the official misconduct surpasses that disclosed in the case at bar,"[24] it rejected each of Londoner's arguments in favor of retaining his office.

It was Londoner's burden, the Court said, to prove that he would have been elected even without the fraud. He had not met that burden.[25] The People did not have to show who had falsely cast ballots for Londoner — "most of the men who perpetrate frauds of this kind belong to the criminal class, or are transients" — and it would be impossible to track them down.[26] Londoner was not even entitled to continue in office until his successor was qualified. In sum, "[t]he case seems to have been tried with unusual care, and we find nothing in the record that justifies a reversal."[27]

AFTERMATH

Ironically, for all his efforts, it does not appear that Barton ever took office as Denver mayor. By the time Wolfe Londoner resigned his office, soon after the Supreme Court rendered its decision, there was only a month left to his te]'rm. Durand Packard, President of Denver's Board of Supervisors, served out the remaining month.[28]

Wolfe Londoner lived until 1912, beloved by many in Denver, but never again to dabble in politics. Always a character, in later years he worked as a journalist and won additional fame by claiming to have discovered a stone-aged city in Colorado. Although he neglected to disclose the location of this prehistoric city, the story was picked up by papers in the East and the National Geographic Society prepared to launch an expedition. Londoner had made up the whole thing and left town to avoid embarrassment. However, he later was vindicated when Mesa Verde was discovered. "That's the City I found!" he claimed; no one was willing to argue with him.[29]

CONCLUSION

Wolfe Londoner was a friendly and generous man, with a tendency to be a bit too clever in his business dealings and perhaps indiscriminate in his choice of friends. Although he succeeded at nearly everything else he tried, his venture into mayoral politics ended under a cloud.

Original printing: *The Colorado Lawyer*, November 2007. The author appreciates the research assistance of Daniel B. Cordova of the Colorado Supreme Court Law Library.

NOTES

1. *Rocky Mountain News* 1 (March 20, 1890).
2. *Id.*
3. Jefferson Randolph (Soapy) Smith (1860–98) was a legendary frontier con man. He got his start at the age of 18, selling cheap trinkets and counterfeit jewelry at county fairs. From there, he graduated to short con games, such as shell games and three-card Monte. He organized a large gang of wrongdoers and eventually dealt in larger schemes, along the lines of fake lotteries, gambling halls, and even a phony stock market investment firm. He earned the name "Soapy" through a con game in which he auctioned off packages of soap, some of which he claimed contained money. Shills in the audience retrieved any currency there was to be had; all his victims got was overpriced soap. Smith died on July 8, 1898, shot by an angry mob of vigilantes in Juneau, Alaska. *See* www.soapysmith.net.
4. Londoner is sometimes accounted Denver's nineteenth mayor. *See, e.g.,* a list of Denver mayors on Wikipedia.
5. Everett, "Story of Buried City in Colorado Startled Nation," *Denver Catholic Register* 4 (March 13, 1941).
6. *Id.*
7. *Id.*
8. *Id.*
9. *See* "Purchasing Power of Money in the United States from 1774 to 2009," available at www.measuringworth.com.

10. Everett, *supra* note 5.

11. *See* www.blongerbros.com/graftersClub/bios/Londoner.asp.

12. An interesting discussion of this period, with references to Londoner and Denver's Jewish community, can be found in Pozzetta, *Immigrant Institutions: The Organization of Immigrant Life* 213-14 (Routledge, 1991).

13. Everett, *supra* note 5.

14. *See* "Denver Decides—2003," available at www.umaitech.com/portfolio/Suffrage_in_Colorado.pdf.

15. The names were recorded in books, one of which somehow ended up in the hands of Western legend Bat Masterson. *See Rocky Mountain News, supra* note 1 at 2.

16. *Rocky Mountain News, supra* note 1 at 2.

17. Denver City Charter, art. 4, § 9, *quoted in People v. Londoner,* 22 P. 764, 765 (Colo. 1889).

18. *Londoner, supra* note 17.

19. *Id.* at 767.

20. *Id.* at 768.

21. *Londoner v. People ex rel. Barton,* 26 P. 135, 136 (Colo. 1891).

22. *Londoner v. People ex rel. Barton,* 25 P. 183 (Colo. 1890).

23. *Londoner, supra* note 21 at 138.

24. *Id.*

25. *Id.*

26. *Id.*

27. *Id.* at 140.

28. Fleming, "Denver's Most Controversial Mayor," *Post Empire Magazine* 18 (May 8, 1960).

29. Everett, *supra* note 5.

Divorce by Jury
Governor Gilpin's Matrimonial Ordeal

BY FRANK GIBBARD

In his 1889 biography of William Gilpin, Hubert Howe Bancroft imagined Denver as a "new Athens," and the erstwhile Colorado governor as "her Plato, the first of philosophers and the first of men."[1] Bancroft's hyperbole was not entirely disinterested: Gilpin paid him $10,000 to pen the biography.[2]

Even so, in many respects, Gilpin did fit the mold of a platonic philosopher-king. By all accounts, he was an educated and well-read man, highly successful in his military and political endeavors. His matrimonial experiences also may have made him philosophical, at least if he followed Socrates' famous advice to a friend: "[G]et married. If you find a good wife you'll be happy; if not you'll become a philosopher."[3]

ORIGINS OF A MARRIAGE

If there ever was a man who needed a philosophic frame of mind to cope with a difficult marriage, it was William Gilpin. By the time he married Julia Pratte Dickerson in 1874, Gilpin was accustomed to hardship. But none of his prior experiences could have prepared him for his marriage to Julia.

Before serving as Territorial Governor of Colorado in 1861–62, Gilpin attended the U.S. Military Academy at West Point (1834–35); served as a Lieutenant in the Second Seminole War in Florida, also known as the Florida War (1837–38);[4] traveled as a pioneer in Oregon and throughout the Western wilderness (1843–45); volunteered to fight as a U.S. soldier in the Mexican-American War (1846–47);[5] and was hired on as an Indian fighter (1847–50).[6]

Julia Pratte was the daughter of Bernard Pratte, Jr., an army general and the former mayor of St. Louis, Missouri. Gilpin proposed to Julia for the first time in 1856, but she refused him, choosing instead to marry an army captain named John H. Dickerson. She had four children with Dickerson before he died in a mental hospital. Julia's enemies later would speculate that she drove Captain Dickerson insane.[7]

After Captain Dickerson died, Gilpin resumed his courtship of Julia in St. Louis, attending many parties with her during the winter of 1873–74. Both Julia and her father consented to Gilpin's renewed proposal of marriage in early 1874.

At the time of their nuptials in 1874, Gilpin was 59 and Julia was 37. Problems surfaced in the marriage as early as their honeymoon trip to California, when Julia accused him of leaving her alone with a sick child.[8] The couple smoothed things over and within three years, Julia gave birth to three more children — a set of twins and a son.

Julia proved to be a charming hostess at their comfortable Denver home, which was located at 443 Champa Street. Her delight in lavish entertainment, however, soon sparked one of the enduring tensions in their marriage.

TENSIONS IN THE GILPIN HOUSEHOLD

"Julia took her role of society's leader very seriously, [but] William could not get accustomed to spending a fortune after too often knowing what he liked to call 'secret hunger.'"[9] Like many other Western entrepreneurs, Gilpin had experienced financial hardship and failure,

Governor William Gilpin
Courtesy Colorado Historical Society - #10025405

including foreclosure proceedings as the result of his land speculation in Missouri. Now, at a relatively advanced age, Gilpin sought a measure of financial stability, something that was less important to his wife, who had never known poverty and hardship.

Other problems further stressed the marriage, such as their conflicting religious beliefs. Julia was very religious, and Gilpin was not. There also were troubles with the in-laws. Julia's siblings, for example, had a reputation for emotional instability. Her brother allegedly tried to kill Gilpin after an argument in 1884, and was prevented from doing so only when Julia thrust herself between them.[10] Later, it was Julia's turn to attempt violence on Gilpin — with a paper cutter — before the children's teacher intervened.[11] Gilpin eventually hired bodyguards to protect him from his wife and her children.[12]

The tensions roiling the marriage were not all one-sided, of course. A Gilpin biographer noted that his "intense, powerful personality" and "occasionally very odd behavior" also contributed to the growing rift between the Gilpins.[13] Julia later would charge him with his own forms of violence and cruelty, complaining of his strict discipline of the children, his intolerance, and his violent temper. His obsession with money also had practical consequences for Mrs. Gilpin; she alleged that, on occasion, he left her to run the household without a cent.[14]

GILPIN FILES FOR DIVORCE

By March 1887, Gilpin had had enough of his marriage to Julia, and he filed for divorce. His complaint made no attempt to sugarcoat his grievances after thirteen years of marriage. He charged that Julia had been guilty of extreme cruelty toward him from the beginning of their married life; that she was subject to frequent outbursts of passion and "ungovernable" frenzy; that she made the home a scene of continual strife; that she taught his children to hate, despise, and avoid him; that she entered into conspiracies with her relatives and friends to bereave him of his children and to deprive him of his fortune, seeking to accomplish these ends by threats and intimidation, and by declaring it to be their intention to take his life; that she had, on two or three occasions, violently assaulted and struck him with her hand or small "weapons" that happened to be nearby; that on one occasion she had caused him to be assaulted, struck, and knocked down by her 22-year-old son Sidney; and that this assault and beating was based on an alleged arrangement among Julia, her son, and others to draw him into a quarrel and take his life under color of self-defense.[15]

Julia responded in kind, denying Gilpin's allegations and crossclaiming for custody of their children. She "charged [Gilpin] with extreme cruelty towards herself and her children, specifying details of a most violent character; that plaintiff, by reason of his disordered fancy and ungovernable temper, his disposition to cruel and severe punishment, and his austere and intolerable demeanor, was unfit to have the care, custody and tuition of the infant children of plaintiff and defendant."[16]

THE JURY DECIDES

Had this proceeding been filed in 2007, a divorce would have been granted; the only remaining issues would have concerned custody and visitation, the division of property, and maintenance and support for the children (and, perhaps, a restraining order against one or both of the parties). However, this was 1887, and no-fault divorce was decades away in the Western world.[17]

The situation was complicated by the fact that, despite her own complaints about her husband's behavior, Julia did not want a divorce.[18] She had moral scruples against divorce due to her strong Catholic beliefs.[19] Gilpin's attorney later would mock her for considering the divorce filing a "martyrdom" that left her "immolated upon the shrine of her church."[20] Nevertheless, she was perfectly within her rights to oppose a divorce under the law then in effect. Colorado law dictated what to do when one party to a marriage wanted a divorce and the other did not: let a jury decide.[21]

"Extreme cruelty" was a recognized ground for divorce in 1887.[22] The Denver superior court empaneled a jury to determine whether Julia was guilty of such "extreme cruelty." After testimony from the parties and other witnesses, and five hours of deliberations, the jury returned with its verdict, in favor of Governor Gilpin. To make matters worse (from Julia's perspective), the court not only granted the divorce, it awarded custody to Gilpin and denied Julia's request for alimony and the costs of the suit. Gilpin, accompanied by an officer of the court and three detectives, later seized his children by force from the family home.[23]

APPEAL TO THE COLORADO SUPREME COURT

Julia appealed to the Colorado Supreme Court. She raised a number of objections to the trial proceedings. The Court found that her objections had merit. It reversed the superior court's decision, and remanded.

The Court reversed the jury's verdict on two evidentiary grounds. Gilpin had testified that after receiving a signal from Julia, her son Sidney had struck him a blow that knocked him to his knees. Julia then called out, "Run, Sidney, he is armed, and will kill you."[24] During her testimony, Julia was asked whether she had in fact made that statement. Gilpin's counsel objected, and the objection was sustained. The Supreme Court found this inexplicable: denying her the right to give her testimony about her alleged statement "was certainly contrary to the rules of evidence, and may have greatly prejudiced her cause in the minds of the jury."[25]

The Supreme Court also found error in permitting a witness to testify that the Gilpins' son, Willie, had told her his "papa was a thief, and everybody belonging to him[] and his mamma could put them in the penitentiary; that his mamma said so."[26] The Court found this to be hearsay, not within any exception, and its admission was manifest error.

Finally, the Court found fault with numerous instructions given to the jury.[27] Although the instructions specifically had not been challenged, the Court felt constrained to point out the errors, in the event that the case proceeded to retrial on remand.

Throughout its opinion, the Court used language that suggests it sympathized with Julia's desire to keep the marriage together, notwithstanding the enmity between the parties. The Court opined:

> In the opinion of many good people, the family household may be . . . too easily broken up and destroyed. The institution of marriage lies at the foundation of our civilization. It is the safeguard of education and true religion, the promoter of public and private morals, and the conservator of social order. Public policy favors the continuance of the marriage relation, and the courts should not lend their influence to dissolve the same, except in obedience to strict law.[28]

PROCEEDINGS ON REMAND

A second trial ensued on remand, which resulted in a hung jury. What happened next may be hard to believe. In spite of the mutual accusations of cruel behavior and even conspiracy to commit murder, the Gilpins reconciled their differences and lived together (happily ever after, if later accounts are to be believed) until his death in 1894.

THE GILPIN CASE –
RETROSPECTIVE CONSIDERATION

In 1971, Colorado adopted no-fault divorce under the Uniform Disso-lution of Marriage Act.[29] Opponents of no-fault divorce argue that it makes divorce too easy to obtain. Supporters of no-fault divorce point to the harm caused when spouses accuse each other of detestable acts to obtain a divorce. The Gilpin case, decided under a prior, fault-based system, suggests that there may be some truth to each position. The Gilpins spattered each other with vitriol in a public trial because Gov-ernor Gilpin wanted a divorce and Mrs. Gilpin did not. However, in the end, when neither side could persuade a jury of the rightness of its cause, something between necessity, exhaustion, and the latent embers of rekindled love brought the couple back together until natural death did them part.

Original printing: *The Colorado Lawyer*, January 2008. The author is grateful for the research assistance of Dan Cordova and Lynn Christian of the Col-orado Supreme Court Law Library.

NOTES

1. Bancroft, *History of the Life of William Gilpin: A Character Study* 1 (The History Company, 1889). Bancroft's encomium continues in turgid prose, de-scribing Gilpin as

> [he] whose thoughts fly in air, preferring symbol to syllogism; who if he needs a religion makes one, or if a government, formulates one; who if he lacks incident, falls back on inspiration, having always at hand that philosophy of philosophies which makes men and nature its own.

Id. at 1-2. The entire text of Bancroft's airy tome, part of a series called "Chronicles of the Kings," is available at books.google.com.

2. Karnes, *William Gilpin, Western Nationalist* 337 (University of Texas Press, 1970).

3. The Socrates quote is ubiquitous, available at many locations, including www.wisdomquotes.com/quote/socrates.html.

4. For information about the Second Seminole War, *see* en.wikipedia.org/wiki/Second_Seminole_War.

5. For information about the Mexican-American War, *see* en.wikipedia.org/wiki/Mexican-American_War.

6. *See generally* Karnes, *supra* note 2 at 19-211.

7. *See id.* at 335.

8. "The Gilpin Divorce Suit," *Denver Republican* 8 (June 18, 1887).

9. Karnes, *supra* note 2 at 334.

10. *Id.* at 335.

11. *Id.*

12. "The Gilpin Divorce Suit," *supra* note 8.

13. Karnes, *supra* note 2 at 334.

14. "The Gilpin Divorce Suit," *supra* note 8.

15. *Gilpin v. Gilpin*, 21 P. 612, 613 (Colo. 1889).

16. *Id.*

17. The Bolshevik rulers of what later would become the Soviet Union were among the first authorities in the modern Western world to institute a system of "no-fault" divorce, following the Russian Revolution in 1917. *See, e.g.*, Antokolskaia, "The Process of Modernisation of Family Law in Eastern and Western Europe," *Electronic Journal of Comparative Law* (vol. 4.2, Sept. 2000), available at www.ejcl.org/42/art42-1.html. Dictator Joseph Stalin later countermanded many of the early Bolsheviks' liberalized measures involving divorce.

18. *Gilpin, supra* note 15 at 613.

19. *Id.* at 615.

20. "Verdict for Mr. Gilpin," *Denver Republican* 8 (July 2, 1887).

21. Colo. Gen. Stat., Ch. XXXII, § 1097 (1883).

22. *Id.* at § 1093.

23. "Scenes at the Gilpin Home," *Denver Republican* 6 (Dec. 9, 1887).

24. *Gilpin, supra* note 15 at 614.

25. *Id.*

26. *Id.*

27. *Id.* at 615:

> One instruction leaves out of view the provocation which may have been given for the supposed misconduct; another leaves out of consideration the probability of condonation; and still another calls specific attention

to the conduct and demeanor of defendant, as asserted by plaintiff and
his witnesses.

28. *Id.* at 614.
29. *See* Laws 1971, H.B. 1229, § 1.

The House Un-American Activities Committee Visits Denver

A Crossfire of Accusations

BY JEFFREY P. KELSON

In early 1956, two newly minted Colorado lawyers had lunch with William Doyle,[1] who was a prominent member of the Denver legal community. The two new lawyers were considering the prospect of representing individuals who had been subpoenaed to appear before the House Un-American Activities Committee ("HUAC"), the Congressional committee that was conducting a wide-ranging investigation of Communism in the United States. The HUAC had subpoenaed more than thirty Coloradans to testify at hearings that were held in Denver in May 1956.[2]

Doyle advised the two young lawyers not to represent these clients. His advice was based on practicality, not politics or philosophy. Doyle feared that, by representing suspected Communists, the two young lawyers might draw retribution that would cause serious damage to their careers.[3] One thing was certain: The Denver HUAC hearings would bring a furious crossfire of accusations.

THE CROSSFIRE

The HUAC is a symbol of the legendary anti-Communist fervor in the United States in the 1950s. Legions of Americans supported the anti-Communist ardor. Throughout the HUAC's Denver hearings, the committee and its supporters consistently expressed a belief that an insidious and threatening Communist conspiracy had infiltrated the federal government, the professions, and labor organizations, and had colonized industry.[4] From the HUAC perspective, American Communists were deceitful traitors who were conspiring to undermine the Constitution and overthrow the government.[5]

The *American Heritage® Dictionary* defines "McCarthyism" as "the practice of publicizing accusations of political disloyalty or subversion with insufficient regard to evidence" and "the use of unfair investigatory or accusatory methods in order to suppress opposition."[6] That definition synthesizes the view of the proceedings held by the suspected Communists who were subpoenaed to testify before the HUAC in Denver. From the perspective of the suspected Communists, the HUAC used lies, fear, and the persecution of political beliefs to betray the Constitution.[7]

The stakes at the Denver HUAC hearings were particularly high, because the hearings were preceded by well-publicized criminal trials in which several Coloradans, based on their alleged activities as Communists, had suffered federal criminal convictions for violating the Smith Act.[8] According to testimony at the Smith Act trials, some of the Coloradans subpoenaed to testify at the Denver HUAC hearings had been labeled "Communists." The primary topic at the Denver HUAC hearings was alleged Communist activity (1) in the Denver office of the War Labor Board during World War II; (2) at the University of Colorado; and (3) in the International Union of Mine, Mill, and Smelter Workers, which was headquartered in Denver.

THE STAR WITNESS

The committee's star witness was Bellarmino Joe Duran.[9] When questioned by Richard Arens, the committee's counsel, Duran testified that he joined the Communist Party of Colorado in the fall of 1948, and was expelled from the party on April 3, 1955.[10] Duran said he was a member of the party solely at the behest of the Federal Bureau of Investigation ("FBI"), and that he reported to the FBI periodically while he was a member of the party.

Duran testified that he contacted the FBI in 1948 after he saw and heard "Communists in the Progressive Party in the Denver area who were using a sound truck to carry out their propaganda in Spanish and English."[11] He described attending what he called "a youth Marxist-Leninist study group" that was "conducted in the Sam Kaplan grocery store at Decatur and West Colfax."[12] He said this was a "school to try to indoctrinate people before they came into the party."[13] Duran also described many meetings, conventions, and schools conducted by the party in the Denver area that he had attended. For each event, Duran listed the names of several individuals who were organizers, participants, or attendees. He specified the address of each meeting conducted in Denver, and he described meetings at the Ute Ranch outside Idaho Springs and at the YMCA in Estes Park.[14] During his testimony, Duran named several individuals and testified that he was certain that each was a member of the Communist Party.[15]

During Duran's testimony, committee counsel Arens asked Duran to assess "the menace of the Communist Party in this area. Is it just a few crackpots or is it a serious menace to the integrity of this State and Nation?"[16] Duran responded:

> [T]he American people and the American government are in worse trouble today than at any one time. . . . The local Communists are no longer working only on issues; they are fighting hand in glove from Moscow down to here. I can see it very plainly.[17]

It should be noted that Duran described only one situation that might be seen as involving a directive from the Soviet Union, and that description was vague. He was asked by committee counsel Arens if there was any democratic procedure in the "Communist operation." Duran responded that "in 1951 we had a report that the Communist Party had entered a revolutionary stage and it would operate with less democracy.

It was read from the Communist Party of the Soviet Union."[18] Duran was not asked to elaborate further.

At the conclusion of Duran's testimony, HUAC Chairman Francis E. Walter told Duran: "You have made a fine contribution. I am sure that those who have heard you are thoroughly convinced of the integrity and the honesty and sincerity of the position you have taken and of your testimony."[19]

THE COUNTERPOINT

Of course, not everyone who heard Duran's testimony was convinced. The suspected Communists who testified before the committee saw Duran and the other cooperating witnesses as despicable, dishonest "stool pigeons." Witness David Eakins stated the countervailing view quite bluntly. When committee counsel Richard Arens asked David Eakins to identify himself to the committee, Eakins said: "My name is David Eakins.[20] I would like to make this very clear because a stoolpigeon [sic] called me 'Eekins' and my name is properly pronounced Eakins [A-kins]. My friends know that."[21]

MR. ARENS: Mr. Eakins, a stoolpigeon [sic] is one who testifies falsely or gives false information. Isn't that right?

MR. EAKINS: A stoolpigeon [sic] is any man who is paid for testimony and spies on his neighbors and his friends and relatives.

MR. ARENS: Are you asserting that any witness appearing before this committee in the last several days has been paid by this committee for giving false information?

MR. EAKINS: This witness [indicating Duran] was paid for his testimony.

MR. ARENS: Did he give false information to your knowledge?

MR. EAKINS: Stoolpigeons [sic] always give false information. Traditionally they give false information.

MR. ARENS: Then I take it you must assert that the witness who identified you as a member of the Communist Party gave false information to this committee, is that correct?

MR. EAKINS: I am not answering that question because it is none of your business.[22]

Eakins's counsel, Harry Nier, says Eakins risked being cited for contempt of Congress with his confrontational "it is none of your business" response, which Eakins repeated frequently.[23] Eakins elaborated at one point, citing the Fifth Amendment and other constitutional provisions as bases for his refusal to answer, but "it is none of your business" was Eakins's shorthand for the assertion of his constitutional rights.[24]

With the echoes of the Denver Smith Act prosecutions still ringing loudly, many witnesses invoked the Fifth Amendment in response to the committee's questions. The questioning of witness Eunice Dolan typifies the exchanges between the committee and hostile witnesses over the Fifth Amendment. Dolan had been implicated as a Communist in one of the Denver Smith Act Trials, and her husband was employed by the International Union of Mine, Mill, and Smelter Workers, a union the committee suspected to be a Communist front.[25] Dolan told the committee that she belonged to the PTA, the AAA, and the Bluebird Mothers Club, but she repeatedly invoked her Fifth Amendment rights in response to other questions.

MR. ARENS: Were you a member of the Communist Party at the time you were identified with the Women's International League of Peace and Freedom?

MRS. DOLAN: I refuse to answer that question on the grounds previously stated [Fifth Amendment].

MR. ARENS: Do you honestly apprehend if you gave a truthful answer to that question you would be supplying information which might be used against you in a criminal proceeding?

MRS. DOLAN: I refuse to answer that question on the same grounds.

MR. ARENS: I respectfully suggest, Mr. Chairman, that the witness be directed to answer that question.

THE CHAIRMAN: You are directed to answer the question.

MRS. DOLAN: Mr. Chairman, I refuse to answer on the same grounds.

MR. ARENS: Are you now a member of the Communist Party?

MRS. DOLAN: I refuse to answer that question.[26]

Over the course of four days of hearings, this exercise was repeated with most of the witnesses who testified before the committee. At some points, suspected Communists who refused to answer questions were accused of hiding behind the Fifth Amendment to conceal the vast Communist conspiracy. [27]

Some witnesses expressed the view that the committee's primary purpose was the persecution of left-wing political beliefs, and not just the protection of the country against violent revolution. Asked if he was a member of the Communist Party, witness Eugene Deikman challenged the constitutionality of the law that empowered the committee's investigation. That law authorized the committee to investigate "the extent, character, and objects of un-American propaganda activities in the United States."[28] Deikman, a Denver lawyer, argued that an investigation of propaganda is much broader than an investigation of those seeking to "overthrow the Government by force and violence," and that an investigation of such breadth is unconstitutional.[29]

Representative Harold H. Velde of Illinois, former HUAC Chairman and member of the present committee, objected to the continuation of Deikman's testimony "if it is to be a lecture. We know all about the type of man that he is. We don't have to be informed about the ... [r]esponsibility of this committee by you."[30] Noting that he was required to state the basis for his refusal to answer, Deikman continued his testy exchange with the committee, citing several constitutional provisions as bases for his refusal to answer.[31]

The members of the committee apparently felt that anyone who believed in Communism was, by definition, a participant in a conspiracy to overthrow the U.S. government by force. Some of the witnesses expressed the view that one could hold a political view in support of Communism without also being a conspirator working for the violent overthrow of the government. The stark contrast between these two viewpoints is reflected in the testimony of Edward Scheunemann, also a Denver lawyer.

Scheunemann had been accused of being a Communist, but he openly denied the accusation.[32] However, Scheunemann testified that he had worked with New York attorney Nathan Witt when the two of them represented the International Union of Mine, Mill, and Smelter Workers on a number of matters in the 1940s.[33] To some, Nathan Witt was a renowned labor lawyer. To the committee, Witt was an infamous hard-core Communist labor lawyer, and any association with him was suspicious.[34] Scheunemann said he never had discussed Communism with Witt, and that his only discussions with Witt were in connection with "practical, immediate problems."[35] Scheunemann also described having lunch with Witt several weeks before the Denver HUAC hearings. Committee counsel Arens clearly was appalled that Scheunemann would associate with Witt.

MR. ARENS: Did you have a sense of indignation toward Nathan Witt, who would have the gall to call you and invite you to lunch when he has been repeatedly identified as a hard core member of the Communist conspiracy in this Nation?

MR. SCHEUNEMANN: None whatever.

MR. ARENS: Did you have any qualms of conscience in undertaking to solve practical immediate problems with a person who has been repeatedly identified as a hard-core agent of the international Communist conspiracy?

MR. SCHEUNEMANN: I have no problems whatsoever. I respect the right of a man to be a Communist if he chooses to be one. I do not share his beliefs.

MR. ARENS: Do you respect the right of a man to be a traitor if he chooses to be one?

MR. SCHEUNEMANN: No, I do not.

MR. ARENS: Do you make a distinction between a traitor and a member of the Communist conspiracy?

MR. SCHEUNEMANN: I certainly do.[36]

THE AFTERMATH

There is no indication that anyone engaged in the crossfire at the Denver HUAC hearings changed their view of the other side. Closing

James W. Wilson, one of the few
attorneys willing to defend witnesses subpoenaed by the HUAC
Jeffrey P. Kelson collection

the hearings, committee Chairman Walter indicated that he still saw a
vast Communist conspiracy. He said he did not want to leave the impression "that we have looked at all of the ramifications of the Communist conspiracy in this particular area."[37] Representative Velde called
for a "constant watch" for Communism.[38] "[T]here is no question there
are still hard core party members operating here."[39] On the other hand,
Harry Nier, counsel for David Eakins, recalls feeling that the committee
had been set back a bit in Denver.[40] Nier remembers thinking that the
committee had come to Denver seeking information in support of its
illicit quest, but that it left Denver with no new information.

Many people will testify to the sometimes devastating retribution that
was imposed on those suspected of being a Communist or those associated with an accused Communist during the Joseph McCarthy era.
William Doyle had feared that the two young lawyers who sought his advice before the Denver HUAC hearings might suffer such retribution in
the inevitable crossfire. Despite the fear of retribution, the two young
lawyers who sought Doyle's advice, Chuck Montfort and Jim Wilson,
each represented two witnesses who were hostile to the committee.[41]
Many years later, Montfort said the fear of retribution was very real, but
he and Wilson were motivated by the fact that the witnesses who had

Attorney Chuck Montfort (right) representing a client during
the HUAC hearings
Jeffrey P. Kelson collection

been subpoenaed by the HUAC needed legal representation, and willing
lawyers were few and far between.[42] Both Montfort and Wilson represented suspected Communists in the fury of crossfire at the Denver
HUAC hearings, but neither felt that he ever suffered any retribution because he had represented a client who held a HUAC subpoena.[43]

Original printing: *The Colorado Lawyer*, November 2006. James W. Wilson,
who represented two witnesses in the Denver House Un-American Activities
Committee hearings, was Kelson's father.

NOTES

1. William E. Doyle later served as a Justice of the Colorado Supreme
Court, as well as a Judge of the U.S. District Court for the District of Colorado
and the U.S. Court of Appeals for the Tenth Circuit.

2. The hearings were conducted from Tuesday, May 15 to Friday, May 18, 1956, in the courtroom of the U.S. Court of Appeals for the Tenth Circuit. That second floor courtroom now is part of the Byron White U.S. Courthouse in Denver. The members of the House Un-American Activities Committee ("HUAC") who were present were: Representative Francis E. Walter of Pennsylvania, HUAC Chairman; Representative James B. Frazier, Jr. of Tennessee; and Representative Harold H. Velde of Illinois, former HUAC Chairman.

3. Interview with Charles D. Montfort, attorney at law (Feb. 2001).

4. Investigation of Communist Activities in the Rocky Mountain Area: Hearings Before the Committee on Un-American Activities, House of Representatives, 84th Cong., 2nd Session, Parts I and II (May 15–18, 1956) at 4074 (*hereafter* "Hearings").

5. *See, e.g.*, Hearings at 4137, 4142–43, 4246–48.

6. *The American Heritage® Dictionary of the English Language*, Fourth Ed. (Boston, MA: Houghton Mifflin Company, 2000).

7. *See, e.g.*, Hearings at 4113–14, 4121–24, 4288–95.

8. The Smith Act makes it a crime for anyone knowingly or willfully to advocate, abet, advise, or teach the duty, necessity, desirability, or propriety of overthrowing the Government of the United States or of any State by force or violence, or for anyone to organize any association that teaches, advocates, or encourages such an overthrow. 18 U.S.C. § 2385. After the Denver HUAC hearings, some convictions under the Smith Act were reversed as unconstitutional. *See, e.g., Yates v. U.S.*, 354 U.S. 298 (1957), *overruled on other grounds, Burks v. U.S.*, 437 U.S. 1 (1978).

9. Hearings at 4125–50.

10. Hearings at 4126.

11. *Id.*

12. Hearings at 4127.

13. *Id.*

14. Hearings at 4133, 4135.

15. *See, e.g.*, Hearings at 4129, 4132.

16. Hearings at 4137.

17. *Id.*

18. Hearings at 4149.

19. Hearings at 4150.

20. Telephone interview with Harry Nier, attorney at law, counsel for David & Ann Eakins (Aug. 26, 2006).

21. Hearings at 4293.

22. Hearings at 4293–94.

23. Nier, *supra* note 20.

24. Hearings at 4293–95.

25. Hearings at 4169, 4201.

26. Hearings at 4202.

27. *See, e.g.*, Hearings at 4109, 4122.

28. Public Law 601, 79th Congress (1946), Chapter 753, 2nd Session.

29. Hearings at 4289–90.

30. Hearings at 4289.

31. Hearings at 4289–90.

32. Hearings at 4121–22.

33. Hearings at 4119, 4123.

34. Nathan Witt represented several witnesses at the Denver HUAC hearings.

35. Hearings at 4124.

36. Hearings at 4122, 4124.

37. Hearings at 4301.

38. *Rocky Mountain News*, May 19, 1956, at 12.

39. *Id.*

40. Nier, *supra* note 20.

41. Hearings at 4200, 4248, 4267, 4286.

42. Montfort, *supra* note 3.

43. *Id.*; numerous conversations with James W. Wilson, attorney at law, counsel for Eunice Dolan & Alfonso Sena (1976–99).

VII

PLIGHT OF
THE WORKING MAN

INTRODUCTION

The popular image of the early Colorado miner is that of a solitary and rugged individual, with his pan, his pick, and his mule, working his claim and living in a log cabin he built with his own hands. While there is certainly some truth to the stereotype, particularly when we consider the early days of the Colorado gold rush, most of Colorado's real mining wealth came from industrial-scale exploitation. Placer mining could recover only relatively small quantities of gold and silver. The major finds were extracted using shafts cut into hard rock.

Significant capital was required to purchase the machines that ran the hard rock mines. Investors, many of whom came from the Eastern United States and Europe, could afford the gigantic equipment that dug the shafts, pumped out the water, and ran the ore up into hoppers. These wealthy investors built the mountain smelters that purified the ores, and brought the mountain railroads that transported the raw materials. As Thomas G. Andrews points out in his book, *Killing for Coal*, all this machinery required a power source, and the best local candidate was Colorado coal, abundant in the southern part of the state.

Soon Colorado was filled with workingmen, many of them recent immigrants to the United States, who were nothing like the stereotypical independent fifty-niner placer miners living out under the stars and breathing pure Rocky Mountain air. Industrialists needed colliers who were willing to spend most of their days underground digging coal. They required smeltermen who could feed the coal into hellish smelters. These workers had to be willing to work long hours, often six or seven days a week, ten or twelve hours a day, doing back-breaking work under inhuman conditions. Many workingmen, in fact, died from their labors or from accidents in the mines.

Technological advances, though they improved productivity, did not always lead to better conditions for workingmen. The pneumatic hammer drill, for example, enabled a miner to do his work many times faster than with previous drills but stirred up fine particles of silica dust. Over time, miners who worked with such pneumatic drills developed silicosis, a scarring of the lung tissue that caused them premature death by asphyxiation.

Ironically, early advertisements for the state emphasized its salubrious air, making claims that now seem quaintly optimistic about the health benefits of the clear Colorado skies. Before long, though, residents in parts of the larger mining and industrial regions of the state found themselves blanketed in fog of black coal smoke every bit as bad as the "brown cloud" that would descend on Denver in the automotive age. Not that there were many who complained about this, in those days. Industrial expansion was seen as the key to Colorado's future.

Gold and silver miners generally fared better than colliers. They resisted attempts by mine owners to reduce their traditional prerogatives, summarized as "eight hours and three dollars a day." The pressure to cut wages became especially acute after the crash in silver prices in 1893 destroyed the wealth of many of the silver barons.

Miners of all varieties were ready to resort to strikes when they felt ill-used. Miners went out on strike early on, for example, in Black Hawk (1865) and Erie (1871). By 1874, Colorado had its first permanent miners' union.

Unionism reflected a struggle between miners and mine owners that would last through the 1920s. Strikes during this period would be marked by convulsive acts of violence and heavy-handed behavior by management. A 1903 strike of gold miners in Cripple Creek, for example, led by the World Federation of Miners, prompted Colorado Governor James H. Peabody to declare martial law and call out the militia, a decision upheld by the Colorado Supreme Court. The worst incident of labor violence, however, was the 1914 Ludlow Massacre, during which militiamen burned a miners' tent city, resulting in the suffocation deaths of thirteen women and children, and killed numerous other people in a gun battle with striking miners.

In 1892, the winds of change swept through Colorado. The state elected a Populist governor, Davis H. Waite. Long-overdue workers' rights legislation seemed to be in the offing. But although the Colorado legislature passed a law setting an eight-hour work day for miners and smeltermen, the Colorado Supreme Court declared the act unconstitutional as an infringement on the workers' right to contract.

The Court's decision was a typical one during what is now known as the *Lochner* era. This period of laissez-faire economic jurisprudence, named for a representative Supreme Court case, *Lochner v. New York*, 198 U.S. 45 (1905), ran from the late 1890s until the New Deal era in the late 1930s. During the *Lochner* era, courts applied the Fourteenth Amendment to strike down legislation regulating the conditions under which workers could sell their labor to employers. The Supreme Court took a dim view of many kinds of economically based legislation during this period, in fact. It was only after President Franklin D. Roosevelt's struggle with the Court during the Great Depression that the prevailing doctrine gave way to a more permissive attitude toward legislative regulation of business.

FOR FURTHER READING

Duane A. Smith, *The Trail of Gold & Silver: Mining in Colorado, 1859-2009* (Boulder, CO: Univ. Press of Colorado 2009).

Thomas G. Andrews, *Killing for Coal: America's Deadliest Labor War* (Cambridge, MA: Harvard University Press 2008).

Lukas, *Big Trouble: A Murder in a Small Western Town Set Off a Struggle for the Soul of America* (New York, NY: Simon & Schuster 1998).

Seligson & Bardwell, *Labor-Management Relations in Colorado* (Denver, CO: Sage Books 1961).

George Orwell, *The Road to Wigan Pier* (New York, NY: Harcourt, Brace 1958).

Langdon, *The Cripple Creek Strike* (Denver, CO: Great Western Pub. 1904).

Charles H. Moyer
Martial Law and the Great Writ

BY FRANK GIBBARD

Habeas corpus be damned, we'll give 'em post mortems!
Sherman M. Bell, 1903

Sherman Bell, Commander of the Colorado National Guard, could be an embarrassment at times, even to his superiors. During a 1900 presidential campaign stop in Colorado, Theodore Roosevelt found it necessary to restrain Bell's homicidal rage after a mob surrounded them.[1] With his expensive gold-braided uniform, left hand tucked into his shirt, Bell must have reminded some people of a tin-pot Napoleon.[2] Colorado Governor James H. Peabody once responded to one of Bell's strident proclamations by stating that he hoped and believed no one would take Bell seriously.[3]

Bell's deficiencies did not keep Governor Peabody from ordering him to Cripple Creek in September 1903 to quell a gold-mine strike. Peabody cited a "reign of terror" in the district.[4] Whether there really was a reign of terror is disputed, but Bell certainly became responsible for one after he arrived. He and his troops essentially created a military despotism in Cripple Creek and Telluride.[5]

On March 26, 1904, Bell's militia arrested and jailed Charles H. Moyer, President of the World Federation of Miners, in Telluride for

Charles Moyer
Courtesy Denver Public Library,
Western History Collection

"flag desecration." Moyer had printed a poster bearing the headline: "Is Colorado in America?" Below the headline appeared an American flag, each of whose stripes contained a provocative inscription denouncing military rule.[6] After Bell defied a state district court decree ordering Moyer's release from military custody, Moyer took his case to the Colorado Supreme Court.

Moyer argued that Governor Peabody had no power to suspend the writ of *habeas corpus* or to declare martial law.[7] Even if the governor had such power, Moyer contended, he had not expressly invoked it in this case, and Moyer's detention was therefore illegal.[8] The Supreme Court did not resolve these issues. It simply noted that under the Colorado Constitution, "The governor is ... empowered to call out the militia to suppress insurrection."[9] Since the Constitution granted this power exclusively to the Governor, the Court could not review it.[10]

Moreover, the power carried with it an implicit grant of authority to use "all necessary means" to suppress insurrection.[11] The Court placed no explicit time limit on Moyer's detention, which could continue until the Governor determined the "insurrection" was at an end.

Justice Robert W. Steele filed a forty-six-page dissent. He concluded that the power asserted by Governor Peabody was unconstitutional. If the Governor had unchecked power to declare a state of rebellion, he reasoned, then any citizen could be subjected to arbitrary arrest and detention at the whim of the executive department of government.[12]

Moyer was eventually released. He was later re-arrested and charged with the murder of Idaho Governor Frank Steunenberg, but these charges against him were dropped as well, after jurors acquitted other labor defendants in the case.

The post-script to this case came more than twenty years later, during another round of labor disturbances in 1927–28. Once again, the Colorado Governor called out the militia, relying on his power to suppress insurrection rather than an explicit declaration of martial law. This time, it did not work. Judge John Foster Symes of the federal district court concluded that unless martial law had been declared, "no rogatory body can lawfully go around in this state depriving individuals of the rights that the Constitution . . . guarantees."[13] The decision of Judge Symes in the *Palmer* case speaks to us with renewed significance today, as courts seek to parse the limits of legitimate executive action in the face of international terrorism.

Original printing: *The Colorado Lawyer*, March 2004. The author expresses sincere appreciation to Dan Cordova and Catherine Eason for their research work. A biography of Judge Symes can be found in Logan, ed., *The Federal Courts of the Tenth Circuit: A History* (Denver, CO: U.S. GPO 1992) at 54-60 and Treece et al., "Six of the Greatest," 19 *The Colorado Lawyer* 1284 (July 1990). Papers of Governors James H. Peabody and William H. Adams are available through the Colorado State Archives. A useful general history of labor relations in Colorado is Seligson and Bardwell, *Labor-Management Relations in Colorado* (Denver, CO: Sage Books, 1961). For a related civil rights case brought by Moyer against Governor Peabody, see *Moyer v. Peabody*, 148 F. 870 (D.Colo. 1906), *aff'd*, 212 U.S. 78 (1909). An enlightening historical perspective on the use of *habeas corpus* can be found in Rehnquist, *All the Laws But One: Civil Liberties in Wartime* (New York, NY: Vintage Books, 1998).

NOTES

1. *See* Lukas, *Big Trouble: A Murder in a Small Western Town Sets Off a Struggle for the Soul of America* (NY: Simon & Schuster, 1998) at 225.

2. *Id.*

3. *See Labor Disturbances in the State of Colorado*, S. Doc. 122, 58th Cong., 3d Sess., Vol. 3 (1905) at 213.

4. *Id.* at 175.

5. *See generally* Lukas, *supra* note 1 at 230-31.

6. For an account of the facts surrounding the Moyer *habeas* case, *see Labor Disturbances, supra* note 3 at 229-46; *see also* Langdon, *The Cripple Creek Strike* (Denver, CO: Great Western Pub., 1904) at 296-307. In Lukas, *supra* note 1, a photograph of the flag poster appears following page 224.

7. *In re Moyer*, 85 P. 190, 192 (Colo. 1904).

8. *Id.*

9. *Id.*; *see* Colo. Const. Art. 4 § 5.

10. *Id.*

11. *Id.* at 193.

12. *Id.* at 194 (Steele, J., dissenting).

13. *U.S. ex rel. Palmer v. Adams*, 26 F.2d 141, 144 (D.Colo. 1927).

Smeltermen Dealt a Blow

A *Lochner*-Era Case Tosses the Eight-Hour Workday

BY FRANK GIBBARD

Mining takes place out of sight, literally beneath the surface of things. The public often is left blissfully unaware of the sweat and toil that go into extracting the essential minerals on which our economy depends. Perhaps no one has described the heroic endurance demanded from miners better than George Orwell, who spent some time in English coal mines during the Great Depression. Orwell filed a harrowing dispatch describing the coal mines

> like hell, or at any rate like my own mental picture of hell. Most of the things one imagines in hell are there — heat, noise, confusion, darkness, foul air, and, above all, unbearably cramped space.[1]

Orwell depicted men walking for miles underground, hunched over, just to get to their jobsite; their backs bearing a line of scabs along the vertebral column from frequent collisions with overhead timbers.[2]

WORKING CONDITIONS

Imagine, then, having to perform this sort of back-breaking labor for ten or even twelve hours at a time; or putting in a twelve-hour shift at a smelter, whose fires are used to melt solid metal. This was the fate of mining company employees in turn-of-the-century Colorado.[3] Not surprisingly, Colorado's minefields became a hotbed of labor agitation.[4]

PROTECTIONS FOR MINERS

Populist pressures eventually drove Western state legislatures to enact protections for mine workers. When these new laws reached the courts, however, a surprising thing happened. Some courts did not hesitate to throw out progressive legislation that they determined interfered with the right of working men and employers to enter into labor contracts, no matter how "hellish" the working conditions provided for under those contracts might seem.

LOCHNER v. NEW YORK

The most famous such case, undoubtedly, was *Lochner v. New York*,[5] which gave its name to an entire era of Supreme Court jurisprudence. *Lochner* involved a New York statute that prohibited employees from being required or permitted to work in bakeries for more than sixty hours a week or ten hours a day. A bakery operator in the city of Utica was convicted of a misdemeanor after he required or permitted one of his employees to work more than the statutorily prescribed sixty hours. The Supreme Court overturned the conviction, reasoning that the individual's Fourteenth Amendment right to sell his labor trumped the state's use of its police power to "seriously limit[] the right to labor or the right of contract in regard to their means of livelihood between persons who are *sui juris*."[6] In dissent, Justice Oliver Wendell Holmes took issue with the conservative political stance that he found reflected in the majority's opinion, famously opining that "[t]he 14th Amendment does not enact Mr. Herbert Spencer's Social Statics."[7]

HOLDEN v. HARDY

Interestingly, *Lochner* distinguished one of the Court's prior decisions, *Holden v. Hardy*,[8] which had upheld a Utah law limiting workmen in

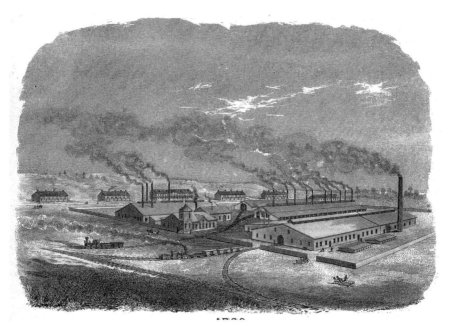

An 1881 etching of the Argo Smelting Works northwest of Denver
Courtesy David Erickson collection

underground mines and smelters to an eight-hour day. The *Lochner* Court noted that the Utah law had included a clause permitting workers to exceed the hours specified in cases of emergency, a feature not present in the New York bakery law.[9] The Court also appears to have determined that working in a bakery was not as "unhealthy" as mining and smelting.[10]

IN RE MORGAN

Between *Holden* and *Lochner*, the Colorado Supreme Court decided its own working-hours case: *In re Morgan*.[11] The Colorado law at issue — setting an eight-hour workday for miners and smelter employees — was virtually identical to the law upheld in *Holden*.[12] Anticipating *Lochner*, however, the *Morgan* Court threw out the Colorado law, reasoning that it was necessary to jettison the law to uphold the liberty of workers to form their own contracts.

The Colorado court's rhetoric in *Morgan* often seems to exceed the bounds of rationality. The Court stated:

> If, to protect the health of workmen engaged in these two occupations, the legislature may limit them to 8 hours' labor per day it may hereafter ... enact that workmen must labor at these occupations 14 or 16 hours per day.[13]

Such a law would be open to an obvious attack on Thirteenth Amendment grounds, a fact that should not have escaped the notice of the Colorado Supreme Court. The Court continued in the same vein, however, comparing the law to

> that period in English history when parliament busied itself in passing numerous acts interfering with the freedom of conscience in religious matters, and in prescribing minute regulations of the personal conduct of the individual, against which our ancestors rebelled.[14]

CONCLUSION

The *Morgan* Court took no notice of an obvious rejoinder to its own labor contract theory — that an individual miner had no bargaining power to haggle for any sort of flexible arrangement of hours or working conditions. Indeed, it would be the rise of collective bargaining, together with a more liberal attitude by the courts, that ultimately would tip the scales in favor of more favorable hours and pay for those who do the arduous and dangerous work that keeps industrial civilization alive.

Original printing: *The Colorado Lawyer*, July 2006. The author thanks Daniel B. Cordova for research assistance with this article.

NOTES

1. Orwell, *The Road to Wigan Pier* (New York, NY: Harcourt, Brace, 1958) at 21.

2. *See id.* at 25, 28.

3. Advances in mining technology did not always improve things. Prior to the adoption of water-flushed drilling in the 1890s, miners who breathed the dust kicked up by new-fangled pneumatic drills were left with lungs "appearing to be almost petrified . . . . Under the microscope the [silica] dust was shown to possess murderously sharp edges — the miners had been breathing in millions of Lillputian razor blades. This dust scarified and altered the lung tissues until the miner literally smothered to death." Young, *Western Mining* 207-08 (Norman, OK: Univ. of Okla. Press, 1970) at 207-08.

4. The resulting chaos, which at times resembled civil war, is described thoroughly in a well-known report by the Commissioner of Labor to the U.S. Senate. *See* "A Report on Labor Disturbances in the State of Colorado from 1880 to 1904, Inclusive," S. doc. 122, 58th Cong., 3d Sess. (1905).

5. *Lochner v. New York*, 198 U.S. 45 (1905).

6. *Id.* at 53-54.

7. *Id.* at 75 (Holmes, J., dissenting). Herbert Spencer (1820–1903) was a strong believer in social Darwinism, the idea that society evolves by favoring the "fittest," and that government should take a *laissez-faire* attitude toward business relations. The entire text of Spencer's book, *Social Statics*, is available online at http://oll.libertyfund.org/Texts/LFBooks/Spencer0236/SocialStatics/0331_Bk.html.

8. *Holden v. Hardy*, 169 U.S. 366 (1898).

9. *Lochner, supra* note 5 at 55.

10. *See id.* at 59. The majority was called to task on this point by three of the dissenting justices, who emphasized the horrible working conditions under which bakers labored and their traditionally low life expectancy. *See id.* at 70-71 (Harlan, J., dissenting).

11. *In re Morgan*, 58 P. 1071 (Colo. 1899).

12. A fact acknowledged by the *Morgan* Court. *See Morgan*, 58 P. at 1077.

13. *Id.* at 1076 (*emphasis added*).

14. *Id.* at 1077.

"In Hell or Aspen by Christmas"
A Railway Accident and Its Aftermath

BY FRANK GIBBARD

In the fall of 1887, the Colorado Midland Railway Company (Colorado Midland) built its Leadville to Aspen line.[1] The job required laying track at a high elevation, in adverse weather, under extreme deadline pressure. The company cut corners to beat the clock. The accident that resulted injured or killed dozens of railroad workers. This is the story of that accident, and of a mutilated victim whose case for compensation eventually reached the Colorado Supreme Court.

NO DUDES ON THIS JOB

It had been storming the morning of September 13, 1887. The workmen on the Leadville–Aspen line were hunkered down in their boarding camp near Lake Ivanhoe. The work of handling and bedding railroad ties was arduous under the best of conditions. Faced with a roadbed that was "water-soaked, soft, and muddy," it would be downright dangerous.[2]

To get to the jobsite, known as the "front," the workmen had to leave camp and travel four or five miles on a construction train. The train wound through the mountains to a railhead near Hell Gate tunnel.

That morning, Michael O'Brien and several other workmen approached Henry Banker, the head track-layer for Colorado Midland.

They told Banker they wanted to stay in camp and not go to the front. Banker had no sympathy for men who didn't want to work. He told the men they could go to the front or pick up their pay and be fired.

"I don't want any dudes on this job," he announced. "I'm going to be in hell or Aspen by Christmas!"[3]

A PRIOR UNFORTUNATE INCIDENT

As it happened, the hand of fate had fired a warning shot across Henry Banker's bow less than two weeks before, during construction of the Colorado Springs to Leadville stretch. Banker's boss, a man named Nelson, had ordered that all the rails be carefully spiked — double-spiked on curves of three degrees or more.[4] Nelson left the jobsite, leaving Banker in charge.

Under pressure to reach Leadville as quickly as possible, Banker instructed a subordinate to single-spike the rails on the curves and to omit every fourth tie. The defective spiking caused a construction train to derail. In the derailment, a workman lost a foot below the ankle. Incredibly, after this incident, which resulted in a tort judgment against the railroad, Banker remained employed as the head track-layer for the Colorado Midland.

MICHAEL O'BRIEN BOARDS
THE CONSTRUCTION TRAIN

Banker's calumny aside, workman Michael O'Brien was no "dude." He was thirty-nine years old, in good health and physically strong, six feet, one-and-a-half inches tall. Working on the railroad was a temporary job for him. His usual occupation was in merchandising and iron mining, at which he earned $100 a month.[5]

However, a paycheck was a paycheck. O'Brien and the other men overcame their hesitation and boarded the construction train. This alarmingly minimalist conveyance "consisted of an engine and tender, a flat-car carrying two large water-tanks holding several hogsheads each, and a flat-car loaded with broad-gauge curved steel rails and other material."[6]

Railroad workers on the Atchison Topeka & Santa Fe
Courtesy Colorado Historical Society - #10038367

A total of 287 men rode the train that day.[7] Forty or fifty workmen
were permitted to occupy the train's engine, tender, and tank-car. The
remaining men, including O'Brien, were packed standing up, as close
together as they would fit, on the second flatcar. They shared this car
with eighty steel rails, which weighed from 600 to 650 pounds each.
The human and metallic load on the flatcar was later estimated at
75,000 pounds, more than thirty-seven tons. The car's carrying capacity was 50,000 pounds.

THE ACCIDENT

The train pulled away from camp and began its trek through the
mountains. It had not gone very far before it reached a "soft, marshy
place in the road-bed."[8] Here, the track passed over an embankment
built on the swampy ground. O'Brien knew the place. He had worked
earlier with Banker's assistant foreman repairing the track at precisely
this spot. Unfortunately, the roadbed had not been given time to settle.[9]

The train was running downgrade about eight miles an hour over the embankment when disaster struck. The train hit a curve. Its front cars lurched to one side on the mushy rails. The track began to slip as the densely packed flatcar rolled over it. The flatcar leaned to the right. Twenty-four tons of steel rails shifted and slid toward the ditch. The car's front wheels jumped the track, followed by the tender car and the engine. The tender tipped over. The flatcar turned sideways, its front wheels sliding down the embankment.

The men on the edges of the flatcar could jump and try to save themselves. Men in the middle, like O'Brien, had no chance. Steel rails and workmen alike cascaded off the flatcar into the ditch, the rails smashing and mangling bodies as they fell, burying some of the men. When it was all over, sixty men were injured, forty of them so badly they required treatment at hospitals in Leadville and Colorado Springs. Three men were dead, including Banker, who had been riding on the engine.[10]

Michael O'Brien's legs were crushed under a load of steel rails. A witness later described the horrifying scene:

> I saw O'Brien after the accident — after the steel had come off. . . . His limbs at the time he was taken out resembled a dish-rag. I could see blood all over his pants, and masses of raw flesh under his overalls, and blood where his overalls were torn by this iron, and I could see, where his garments were gone, his legs were all crushed up. After he got out it looked to me as if they were literally ground to pieces — bone, flesh and muscle all mingled together.[11]

THE AFTERMATH

The doctors did what they could for Michael O'Brien. They amputated both of his legs, one four inches above the knee and the other five inches below. They fitted him for artificial limbs. However, after a long and painful period of recovery, he was still unable to straighten his legs at the knee joints. With the crude prostheses available in 1887, it appeared he would never walk again. "[H]is only mode of personal locomotion [was] by dragging himself upon his knees."[12]

To make things worse, O'Brien had no means of support besides his own labor. At a time before workers' compensation laws, he had only one option: to sue his employer for his personal injuries from the accident. He was successful. The jury awarded him $13,000 against the railroad, a sum equivalent in today's dollars to about $316,000.[13]

THE *COLORADO MIDLAND* CASE

The railroad appealed, raising several issues to the Colorado Supreme Court. Some of the railroad's arguments may seem callous, but they were common defenses in those days. Essentially, they consisted of pointing the finger at others to blame them for the accident, absolving the railroad itself of fault.

Colorado Midland contended that the accident was Banker's fault. It contended that he caused the train to be overloaded and to travel over the weak and dangerous roadbed. Because Banker was O'Brien's co-worker or "fellow servant," the railroad argued that O'Brien could not sue Colorado Midland for his injuries.[14] The Supreme Court disagreed, holding that Banker had "full power and control" over the employees and was the railroad's representative; hence, his negligence was attributable to Colorado Midland itself.[15]

Doctrine of Contributory Negligence

The railroad also argued that O'Brien's injuries were his own fault, through the doctrine of contributory negligence. It pointed to O'Brien's knowledge of the hazardous conditions on the track to the front. In fact, the railroad contended, O'Brien had earlier worked on the very spot where the accident occurred.

The Supreme Court reasoned that O'Brien was merely following his employer's instructions. That would defeat the contributory negligence bar, unless the employer's instructions were so unreasonable that it was imprudent for him to follow them. However, even if the instructions were unreasonable, the Supreme Court stated, O'Brien still should win, because there was a conflict in the evidence about whether he had acted prudently.

O'Brien denied knowing of the unsafe condition and that he previously had worked at the location of the accident. Any such dispute, the Supreme Court insisted, was a factual question for the jury to resolve. The jury had spoken in favor of O'Brien.[16]

Finally, the Court addressed the issue of damages. Was the verdict excessive? Given the severity of O'Brien's injuries, the Court held that it was not:

> The record before us does not disclose nor lead to the conclusion that the jury were influenced either by passion, prejudice, or other unworthy motive in arriving at their verdict. Under the circumstances, we do not feel warranted in declaring the damages excessive.[17]

The Supreme Court thus upheld the jury's verdict for O'Brien.

CONCLUSION

Industrial accidents were a common feature of early railroad construction in Colorado. Until 1919, when the legislature adopted workers' compensation laws, injured workers often were forced to fall back on tort remedies. These remedies required the worker to run a gauntlet of common law defenses that could defeat recovery. Michael O'Brien was fortunate to receive compensation for his injuries.

Original printing: *The Colorado Lawyer*, September 2007. The author appreciates the research assistance of Daniel B. Cordova and Kristin M. Karr of the Colorado Supreme Court Law Library.

NOTES

1. In 1887, the Colorado Midland Railway Company and the Denver and Rio Grande Railroad competed to become the first to complete rail lines to the town of Aspen. The Denver and Rio Grande Railroad won. Its line reached

Aspen by October; the Colorado Midland Railway line did not arrive at the town's Maroon Creek Crossing until December. *See Directory of Colorado State Register Properties*, 16th ed. (Historic Society, 2003) at 245 (discussing Maroon Creek bridge). *See* http://coloradohistory-oahp.org/programareas/register/1503/cty/pt.htm.

2. The facts are taken from *Colorado Midland Ry. Co. v. O'Brien*, 27 P. 701, 701 (Colo. 1891), and from Abbott, *Colorado Midland Railway: Daylight Through the Divide* (Sundance Pubs. 1989) at 67-68.

3. *O'Brien, supra* note 2 at 701.

4. The facts concerning this previous accident are taken from *Colorado Midland Ry. Co. v. Naylon*, 30 P. 249 (Colo. 1892). "Spiking" refers to securing the rails with metal spikes to the railroad ties beneath them.

5. *O'Brien, supra* note 2 at 704.

6. *Id.* at 702.

7. Abbott, *supra* note 2 at 67, *quoting* an unnamed newspaper account of the accident.

8. *Id.*

9. Abbott, *supra* note 2 at 68, *quoting* an unnamed newspaper account of the accident.

10. *O'Brien, supra* note 2 at 703. The newspaper account quoted in Abbott, *supra* note 2 at 58, states that four men died, and gives their names. Despite his boast, Banker never made it to Aspen by Christmas. Whether he made it to hell is beyond mortal ken.

11. *O'Brien, supra* note 2 at 702.

12. *Id.* at 705.

13. *See* "Purchasing Power of Money in the United States from 1774 to 2009," available at www.measuringworth.com.

14. Prior to 1901, the "fellow-servant rule" exempted an employer for liability for negligence of a fellow servant or employee. *See, e.g., Denver and Rio Grande R.R. Co. v. Sipes*, 47 P. 287, 288 (Colo. 1896).

15. *O'Brien, supra* note 2 at 703. The disposition of this argument thus turned on who was a "fellow servant," a perennial issue in Colorado until the legislature abolished the "fellow-servant" rule in 1901. Colo. Stat. 1905, Ch. 37, § 1511f.

16. It should be noted that the doctrine of contributory negligence has since been abolished for actions pursued under the Workers' Compensation Act. *See, e.g., Employers Mut. Ins. Co. v. Indus. Comm'n of Colo.*, 230 P. 394, 395 (1924).

17. *O'Brien, supra* note 2 at 705.

"I'd Rob Him and Skip"
Digging for Gold in an Old Miner's Heart

BY FRANK GIBBARD

Like most of us, Andrew S. Meldrum had some good luck in his life, and some bad. On the good luck side of the ledger, in August 1882, he became one of the discoverers of the Yankee Girl Mine, "one of the richest and most famous silver mines in the history of mining in the United States."[1] Even better, Andy gained interests in three other profitable silver mining claims: Guston, Robinson, and Elnora.

On the bad luck side, he married Mary Bond, a rancher's daughter with a heart of pitchblende. During the couple's brief marriage, Mary took Andy for everything she could grab — so much so, in fact, that a district court decree and a Colorado Supreme Court decision were required to restore some of Andy's property to him. Unfortunately, no court decree could ever restore his dreams of a happy marriage with Mary, for she had never loved him.

A BLACKSMITH WHO MADE GOOD

Beginning in the 1870s, the Red Mountain Mining District (District) in southwestern Colorado produced millions of dollars worth of gold, silver, lead, zinc, and copper.[2] Although the mines operated for only a few decades, they were extraordinarily productive. The mining industry helped to build the nearby towns of Silverton and Ouray and, sixty miles away, the town of Delta.

Not everyone who staked a claim in the District became rich, of course. The great fortunes were confined to a lucky few. Andy Meldrum was one of them. He started out as a blacksmith at the Sheridan Mine. Through careful management of his money, he grubstaked other miners (including John Robinson, who found the Yankee Girl mine), using his stake money to enter into lucrative partnerships with them.[3]

In the early 1880s, Andy and his partners sold "Yankee Girl" for $125,000, a tidy sum in those days. Andy bought a ranch with his money. He and his partners went to work on their other mining claims. Things were looking up for Andy. Then, he fell in love.

A "GOLD-DIGGER" GOES TO WORK

Mary Bond, also known as "Polly," had a problem: she hated living on her parents' ranch in Delta County. The solution she devised was both clever and cruel: she would marry Andy Meldrum, a local silver magnate, and squeeze out of him every penny she could. It is unclear when she developed the cruelest part of her plan: to divorce him after she fleeced him, and then run away and start a new life. It's possible she planned that from the beginning.

Some "gold-digging" spouses possess a hint of genuine affection for their chosen victims; not so with Mary. Mary never loved Andy at all. In fact, over time, she grew to despise him. Her own words reveal that the marriage was all about Andy's money—first, only, and always.

Mary made no secret of her intentions, except of course to Andy. William Robinson, a witness in the lawsuit Andy later filed against Mary, testified that Mary told him before the marriage that "she was going to marry Meldrum, and get some money out of him."[4] After the marriage began, Robinson heard Mary talking to her mother about extracting money from Andy. Her mother cautioned her to "be careful about Andy, how you talk to him, and behave nicely to him, and get

The Meldrum House, which Andy built in Delta, Colorado, after his divorce
Chris Weldon

that $10,000 out of him."[5] Mary replied: "[Y]ou leave it to me. I know how to work him. I'll get all I can out of him, you bet."[6]

CASHING IN

So she did. Andy and Mary were married on December 3, 1884. At the time, his estimated resources totaled approximately $50,000. Hers totaled zero.[7] Over the course of their fifteen-month marriage, she persuaded Andy to give her his ranch in Delta County, valued at $7,500; a Denver property that had cost him $12,500; and several cash gifts, including one for $2,000.[8] In just over a year, she had acquired nearly half of Andy's net worth.

Perhaps Mary thought she'd earned it. She later told a friend, "I just hate him. I just shiver when he touches me. If he would bring his money home [in cash], honest to God I'd rob him and skip."[9] Mary told her friend that she wished Andy would die: "[A]fter he gets the money [from his mining claims,] I wish to God he would fall down and break his neck."[10]

Mary knew that Andy planned to sell his interest in the Guston mine in February 1886. Once that happened, she planned to cajole him out of the proceeds, take the money, and run for it — but could she wait that long? In November 1885, after less than a year of marriage, she told her mother, "Mamma, I can't stand it to live with him. . . . I can't wait until February."[11] Her mother, coldly practical as usual, told her to "[t]ry to love him, and wait until the first of February, and then he will get his money. Then you can go to Europe or New York, and you can stay [away] a year, and send him a divorce, and have a good cry, and that will be the last of it."[12]

ANDY BUYS A HOUSE

As expected, in February 1886, Andy sold his interest in the Guston mine. Flush with cash, he decided to buy a house in Denver where he and Mary could live. Mary approved of the plan — but with one stipulation. She insisted that the Denver property be personally conveyed to her.

Andy, showing some uncharacteristic backbone, pointed out that he had already given her their ranch home in Delta. "[Y]ou better let me have this one," he said.[13] She then offered to give him back the place in Delta, if he would let her have the home in Denver. Andy, demonstrating a lack of comprehension of what was at stake, treated the whole thing as a joke. Evidently, he teased her that maybe he would not give her the Denver home after all.

It was then that Mary unleashed her ultimate weapon — she burst into tears. Her mother, who was present, asked what she was crying about. Mary responded that "Andy don't want to deed me that house."[14] Her weeping intensified. Her mother reassured her, in words clearly designed for Andy's benefit, that "he don't say he won't deed it to you."[15] Faced with a weeping wife and a guilt-inducing mother-in-law, Andy gave in. He had the deed to the Denver home recorded in Mary's name.

THE SEPARATION

Soon thereafter, Andy and Mary moved into their — well, Mary's —
new Denver home, which Andy paid to furnish. It was at this point that
Mary showed her hand. According to Court records:

> About the time they became settled in the house, and the day after the
> carpets were laid, and the last of the furniture put in place, [Mary],
> making a pretext of some slight disagreement with [Andy] about the
> use of a horse and buggy which he had purchased for her recreation
> and amusement, drove [Andy] out of the house, and notified him of
> her intention to apply for a divorce.[16]

Andy must have been stunned.

THE "DEAR ANDY" LETTERS

Andy could not fathom that she really intended to divorce him. The
letters she sent him shortly thereafter likely brought some bracing clarity to the situation. They certainly cast a chilling light on the workings
of his wife's mind.

The first letter, written to him on March 1, 1886, was full of odd
threats and promises. Mary informed Andy that she did not love him
and never would. "Now, don't you think it is best to give me a divorce,
as long as I want one?" she asked.[17] If he gave her a divorce, she promised, she would not sell anything he had given her, including the house
in Denver; however, if he did not divorce her, she would sell the house
and move away. Mary, who cared for the house far more than for Andy,
must have viewed this as a persuasive argument. Andy probably found
it less compelling. He also was unlikely to put much stock in her other
dubious promise: if he granted her a divorce and three months later they
decided they really did love each other, she would remarry him.[18] After
all, she had just finished telling him that she would never love him.

The second letter, written just three hours later, was replete with a new
round of threats and promises, perhaps inspired by Mary's consultation

in the interim with her lawyer. Mary advised Andy that "the easiest way to [get a divorce would be] for you to come here and say, in the presence of [a witness,] that you are going to leave the state for good, and bid me good-by[e]."[19] Apparently, she thought a tidy and convenient end to the marriage would appeal to Andy as much as it would to her; however, if he would not take the easy way out, she threatened that her lawyer "will do [it] another way, which will cost you all the money you have, and all the money I have, and besides that, it will give us both a bad name."[20] Mary promised Andy that if they did things the easy way, neither of them would have to go to court. He would not actually have to leave the state; he only had to say that he would. It is unclear whether Mary understood that the consequent divorce would be granted on the basis of abandonment, or whether she simply was hiding this unpleasant truth from Andy. In any event, he refused to go along with her charade, and she was compelled to file for divorce.

PROCEEDINGS IN DISTRICT COURT

Mary proceeded with her divorce action. In an ugly twist, she falsely swore in the petition that Andy had left Colorado with no intention of returning. She then served him by publication. Andy, finally disabused of any idea that the marriage could be saved, answered and filed a cross-complaint for a decree of divorce. The district court granted his complaint, and a final decree of divorce was entered.

It was at this point that Mary's scheme began to unravel. Andy sued her to get his property back.[21] He filed a complaint charging Mary with "undue influence, misrepresentation, deceit, and fraud . . . in procuring [his] property to be conveyed to her."[22]

The abstract of the subsequent trial to the district court ran to 346 pages.[23] Mary presented her side of the story, which had Andy giving her the house in Denver without any compulsion on her part, and even as a surprise to her.

The district court did not prove to be as gullible as Andy had been. In the end, the court divided the "gifts" to Mary into two categories.

First, there were those gifts that Andy made during the first year of their marriage, before Mary had been shown to have formed an intention to abandon him; these, she would be allowed to keep. Next, there were those gifts made shortly prior to their separation, after she had determined to leave the marriage; these, she was ordered to return to Andy.

The latter category of gifts, of course, included the Denver home, the jewel in the crown of Mary's fraudulent acquisitions. Its loss may explain why she appealed to the Colorado Supreme Court.

SUPREME COURT DECISION

On appeal, the Colorado Supreme Court had no trouble upholding the district court's finding that Mary had defrauded Andy by pretending to love him and by obtaining property when she intended to leave him. The more difficult question was whether a court of equity could offer Andy any relief. Given the clear evidence of fraud, the Court decided that it could.

Most cases of fraudulent seizure of property through marital pretense, the Court noted, had involved husbands who perpetrated a fraud on their wives to obtain property the wives brought into the marriage. Given the recent legislative moves toward equalizing a wife's property rights with those of her husband, however, the Court saw no reason not to apply the same rule where it was the wife who exercised fraud and undue influence over her husband. A party, male or female, who abuses the marriage contract to defraud a spouse "has no right either in morals or law to property thus acquired."[24]

"That [Andy] acted foolishly will not be denied," the Court continued.[25] "He, with his strong passion and ardent love, was not able to cope with [Mary]. She, with her deceit and false professions of affection, held complete mastery over him, which she did not fail to exercise to her great benefit, and to his great disadvantage."[26] Accordingly, the district court acted properly in imposing a constructive trust on the property in favor of Andy.

ANDY'S LATER LIFE

After he regained his property, Andy's good fortune continued, at least for a while. In 1891, he built the Meldrum House, a brick structure that still stands at 461 Palmer Street in Delta and currently houses a radio station.[27] By 1898, work had begun on the so-called Meldrum Tunnel, a railroad tunnel project that would permit a narrow-gauge freight train to run from the District to connect to an existing Rio Grande Southern Railroad line, thus hopefully reviving mining in the District.[28]

Andy sunk all of his remaining energy and money into this last project, which he hoped would solve the many problems that had plagued mining efforts in the District for years.[29] He managed to raise capital from overseas investors, but when this dried up, he had to quit, leaving the project unfinished. His efforts left him a pauper and, when he died, Andy was buried in an unmarked grave in the Cedar Hill Cemetery in Ouray.[30] His luck had finally run out.

Original printing: *The Colorado Lawyer*, September 2010. The author is grateful for the research assistance of Dan Cordova and Lynn Christian of the Colorado Supreme Court Law Library.

NOTES

1. Smith, *Mountains of Silver: The Story of Colorado's Red Mountain Mining District* 36 (Pruett Pub. Co., 1994). Smith reports that on August 14, 1882, while deer hunting, John Robinson accidentally discovered the claim that became the Yankee Girl. Robinson and his partners, including Meldrum, later dug a shaft and found the "mother lode" at the site. Reports that Meldrum himself found the Yankee Girl (*see, e.g.,* Crane, *Gold and Silver: Comprising an Economic History of Mining in the United States* 67 (John Wiley, 1908)) appear to be spurious.

2. *See* Smith, *supra* note 1 at 4-5.

3. *Id.* at 189.

4. *Meldrum v. Meldrum*, 24 P. 1083, 1085 (Colo. 1890).

5. *Id.*

6. *Id.*

7. *Id.* at 1083.

8. *Id.*

9. *Id.* at 1085.

10. *Id.*

11. *Id.*

12. *Id.*

13. *Id.*

14. *Id.* at 1085-86.

15. *Id.* at 1086.

16. *Id.*

17. *Id.* at 1083.

18. *Id.*

19. *Id.*

20. *Id.*

21. The Supreme Court's opinion makes it clear that Andy brought his action against Mary after the final decree of divorce had been entered. *See id.* The Court concluded that for jurisdictional reasons, Andy could not have asserted his fraud claims in the county court divorce proceeding. *See id.* at 1088.

22. *Id.* at 1083.

23. *Id.* at 1086.

24. *Id.* at 1087 (quotation omitted).

25. *Id.*

26. *Id.*

27. *See* "Delta Building Tour," available at www.deltacolorado.org/histtour2.html.

28. Smith, *supra* note 1 at 189. Andy may have carried a torch for Mary even into his later years, or perhaps he just had a wicked sense of irony. Twelve years after she first demanded a divorce, he named a placer mine the "Polly." *See Kirk v. Meldrum*, 65 P. 633, 634 (Colo. 1901).

29. These problems included poor drainage and high costs of transportation from the isolated mines in the District. *See* Smith, *supra* note 1 at 189.

30. *Id.*

VIII

WATER FOR
AN ARID LAND

INTRODUCTION

The Homestead Act, passed in 1863, may have been the biggest land giveaway in history. Congress promised to deed 160 acres of government land to whoever would farm them. The Homestead Act filled America's backyard with immigrant farmers, many of them from Germany where the failed Revolution of 1848 arguably proved as potent a stimulus to emigration as the potato famine in Ireland.

Once immigrants reached the 100th Meridian, however, they discovered something disheartening. In this region, 160 acres was not quite enough to support a family. For west of the 100th lay the arid west: a region with scant rainfall and poor soils. The axiom that "rain follows the plow," which held that if farmers just tilled the soil their sod-busting activities would release moisture into the atmosphere and change the climate, was quickly revealed as a myth. No amount of tillage would bring water to the West.

What would bring water was irrigation. The Great American Desert was full of rivers that flowed south and east from the Rocky Mountains into the great Mississippi. It was only a question of harnessing these mighty waters, and of managing their extreme seasonal fluctuations to serve the purposes of agriculture, that would make the desert bloom.

Irrigation was nothing new. It was first practiced in the Middle East in ancient times and contributed to the rise and maintenance of civilizations throughout the world. On the American continent, Hispanic farmers with their *acequia* system and Mormons in Utah developed

261

extensive irrigation systems that served as a model for later projects elsewhere in new states and territories.

It soon became clear that large-scale action was needed to tame the Western rivers and set them to beneficial use. In 1877, Congress passed the Desert Land Act, increasing the allotment of land for the home-steader to 640 acres. A new agency known as the United States Recla-mation Service (later renamed the Bureau of Reclamation) was created to build dams throughout the West. (Its counterpart, the Army Corps of Engineers, built dams in the Eastern United States, where water was more plentiful.) The Bu Rec, as it was popularly known, constructed some of the best-known dams in the West, storing water to be used for irrigated farming and recreational activities and also in the generation of hydroelectric power.

There was just one problem. Water law as it had developed in the Eastern United States did not take into account the scarcity of water that existed in the West. To prevent disputes and create an orderly exploita-tion of water resources, a different approach to water law was needed. Colorado, like several other Western states, adopted the doctrine of prior appropriation — recognizing it in the 1882 Colorado case of *Cof-fin v. Left Hand Ditch Co.*, 6 Colo. 443 (1882). Prior appropriation gives priority to earlier diversions from the same stream for beneficial use over those made later in time. It relies on a system of head-gates, which shut off water to users with lower priority during times of scarcity.

Although large-scale irrigation with prior appropriation has worked well in practice, there are still disputes that must be resolved by the courts. When a river flows through several states, for example, the rights of appropriators in each state vis-à-vis those in other states must be de-termined. This is usually done through an interstate compact. When the states cannot resolve issues arising under such a compact, however, they often call on the U.S. Supreme Court to exercise one of its few instances of original jurisdiction by issuing decrees apportioning river water.

Another issue that has caused disputes involves in-stream flows. If river water is backed up behind a dam, it deprives the river bed beyond the dam of its seasonal flow. This can have severe adverse effects on wildlife and plants that rely on the flow of water. A release of water solely for environmental purposes could be viewed as waste of valuable water under traditional prior appropriation principles. Over time, however, the value of in-stream flows has gradually been recognized.

In recent years, concerns have also arisen concerning overuse of fragile and limited water resources. Aquifers in many states are being depleted for industrial and urban uses at a rate much faster than they can be replenished by natural processes. Dams also tend to silt up with time, rendering them useless. As Marc Reisner reminds us in his book *Cadillac Desert*, many ancient civilizations that relied on irrigation disappeared from history because their water use proved unsustainable over the long run.

FOR FURTHER READING

Steven Solomon, *Water: The Epic Struggle for Wealth, Power, and Civilization* (New York, NY: HarperCollins 2010).

Marc Reisner, Cadillac Desert: The American West *and Its Disappearing Water* (New York, NY: Penguin Books 1993).

Raging Waters at Cub Creek
A Homesteader
Confronts Prior Appropriation

BY TOM I. ROMERO, II

Lawyers, judges, and historians have widely praised the historical development of Colorado's water law for bringing certainty and reliability to one of the most precious resources in the American West. One court case in 1914 became a piece of Colorado water history.

Josie Bassett Morris settled near Dinosaur National Monument and attempted to use nearby Cub Creek to water her livestock. Not long after she settled at this site, a neighbor challenged her use of the water in Cub Creek by taking her to court. In applying the prior appropriation doctrine to the facts of the case, the court determined that Josie's neighbor had the senior property right. The court ruled that Josie could not continue to draw water from Cub Creek and that, if any water from the spring on her property drained into the creek, the spring could be considered a tributary of Cub Creek and the neighbor also would be entitled to that water.

To comply with the court's decision, and still preserve her option to use the spring, Josie built several small ponds to catch spring water. She even flooded some of her own pastures to prevent any spring water from washing into the creek. Thus, only by "impounding" her own water and, thereby, wasting much of it was she able to preserve her sole right to use

Josie Morris's cabin near Cub Creek
National Park Service

it. Josie's experience symbolized one of the many ways Coloradans have attempted to exercise their water rights. Flexibility, imagination, and a whole lot of courage were traits necessary to forge a home in this arid state.

Original printing: *The Colorado Lawyer*, July 2002. Many articles on Josie Bassett Morris can be accessed on the Internet. *See, e.g.*, www.hodgman.org/travel/dino-2000/dnm-cabin.html and www.nps.gov/dino/historyculture/josiebassettmorris.htm.

Wyoming v. Colorado
A "Watershed" Decision

BY FRANK GIBBARD

A side from sports rivalries, Coloradans tend to get along pretty well with their neighbors to the north. There is one area, however, that has divided them over the years: water rights. Both Colorado and Wyoming are west of the 100th meridian, making them part of the "arid west." Both states have always relied heavily on river water to supply their cities, industries, and agriculture. Early on, both states adopted the doctrine of prior appropriation, which gives priority to earlier diversions from the same stream for beneficial use over those made later in time.[1]

Of course, rivers do not respect state boundaries. An interesting issue arose once water users became big and powerful enough to conduct major diversions from interstate rivers. If prior appropriation governs reciprocal rights of users within a state, what happens when a river or stream begins in one state and then flows, downstream, into another? Can the users in an upstream state, like Colorado, take all the water, leaving none for the downstream state? No, said the U.S. Supreme Court in *Kansas v. Colorado*.[2] The decision in that case laid the groundwork for the decision in *Wyoming v. Colorado*,[3] another major western water law case.

Although the principal parties in *Wyoming v. Colorado* were the two named states, the actions that precipitated the lawsuit were those of the

Larimer County Ditch Company of Colorado. Larimer Ditch set its eyes on the Laramie River, which begins high in the Rocky Mountains in Colorado, then flows down into Wyoming before joining the Platte. (The Laramie River actually flows north, heading downstream and downhill into Wyoming from its headwaters in the mountains in Roosevelt National Forest in Colorado, before turning to the west in the state of Wyoming. Then it continues downstream where it joins the Platte River.) Larimer Ditch had plans to drill a tunnel under the Never-Summer Range, and to divert water from the Laramie River into another watershed.

Wyoming, a heavy downstream user of the Laramie River, balked at this proposal. It filed suit on the U.S. Supreme Court's original docket in 1911, but the case was not decided until eleven years later, in 1922. Justice Willis Van Devanter, the only justice from Wyoming ever to sit on the U.S. Supreme Court, wrote the opinion for the Court.

Wyoming's argument was this: The prior appropriation doctrine contemplated that when a farmer took water from a river to irrigate his or her fields, the runoff would find its way back downstream, benefiting users farther down the river. The plan Larimer Ditch proposed, however, would take the water it diverted out of the watershed altogether. The state of Wyoming argued that this sort of diversion violated the prior appropriation doctrine. The U.S. Supreme Court disagreed, noting that "[d]iversions from one watershed to another are commonly made in both states and the practice is recognized by the decisions of their courts."[4] The Court then engaged in a complex equitable apportionment of Laramie River water between users in Colorado and Wyoming.

The practical effect of this decision was huge, because it helped force downstream states as far away as California to hammer out the Colorado River Basin Compact, which in turn resulted in the construction of Lake Mead and the Hoover Dam. As for Colorado and Wyoming, the decision in *Wyoming v. Colorado* unfortunately did not result in permanent peace and harmony. They were back in court on Laramie River issues in 1932, 1936, and 1940, before a modified decree was entered in 1957, leading to a few decades of peace.

Construction of Lake Mead and the Hoover Dam resulted from various water compacts among Western states
Nancy Garman

It was not yet time, however, to close the water law division in the Colorado and Wyoming state Attorneys General offices. In fact, *Wyoming v. Colorado* was not the only case involving the allocation of the Platte River that would make its way to the U.S. Supreme Court. In the

1980s, Nebraska sued both Colorado and Wyoming over alleged violations of another apportionment decree, dating back to 1945, involving the North Platte River. That litigation continued until 2001, when the states and other parties involved finally settled it.[5]

For this case, the Court had wisely appointed a special master to do the heavy lifting, an assignment for which he received the Court's thanks and the sum of more than $2 million for fees and costs, paid by the parties. *Nebraska v. Wyoming* appears to have settled matters on the North Platte for the time being. Nevertheless, an honest observer of Western water law issues might have grounds to believe that this will not be the last interstate case fought on the issues of equitable apportionment.

Original printing: *The Colorado Lawyer*, March 2005. Congress included a provision recognizing the beneficial use/prior appropriation principle in the 1877 Desert Land Act (19 Stat. 377, codified as amended at 43 U.S.C. §§ 321-23), perhaps recognizing that 640 acres does not do anyone much good in this part of the country unless there are water rights to go with it. Originally published in 1948, David Lavender's book, *The Big Divide: The Lively Story of the People of the Southern Rocky Mountains from Yellowstone to Santa Fe* 260-65 (Edison, NJ: Castle Books, 2001), contains a colorful discussion of the circumstances surrounding the dispute in *Wyoming v. Colorado*. Also of general interest on the history of Western water issues is Reisner, *Cadillac Desert: The American West and Its Disappearing Water*, rev. ed. (New York, NY: Penguin Books, 1993).

NOTES

1. *See, e.g., Coffin v. Left Hand Ditch Co.*, 6 Colo. 443, 446 (1882); *Wiley v. Decker*, 73 P. 210, 215 (Wyo. 1903).

2. *Kansas v. Colorado*, 206 U.S. 46, 100-18 (1907).

3. *Wyoming v. Colorado*, 259 U.S. 419 (1922).

4. *Id.* at 466.

5. *See Nebraska v. Wyoming & Colorado*, 534 U.S. 40 (2001) (decree approving final settlement stipulation).

IX

INFRASTRUCTURE

INTRODUCTION

Colorado came of age during a time of rapid industrialization. The state's municipal infrastructure developed chaotically at first, but eventually yielded to efficiencies created by the succession of technologies, the concentration and rationalization of public utilities, and a reliance on economies of scale. The progress was remarkable. Over an eighty-year period beginning with the gold rush and ending with the Second World War, gas lighting replaced kerosene and candlepower, and was itself replaced by electric lighting; railroads replaced the stagecoach; streetcars replaced horses; indoor plumbing replaced outhouses; paved streets replaced dirt streets and trails; and gas ovens replaced coal stoves.

Often there was a transitional period, during which a prior technology competed with its successor or operated synergistically with it. Thus, for a time, commercial businesses and streets were equipped with the new electric lighting while their owners still depended on gaslight at home. One example of a less successful synergy was an early Fort Collins ordinance that required outhouses to "connect" to a public sewer — a case of bureaucratic bungling at its most egregious.

One of the earliest and most important forms of infrastructure was public transportation. Effective transportation was essential because it brought goods and people into and out of the new territory. Early on, as historian Thomas J. Noel tells us, Denver won a valuable stagecoach connection in exchange for 53 lots and nine shares in the Denver town company that the town founders deeded to the Leavenworth and Pikes

Peak Express Company. The first stage under this concession arrived in the city in May 1859. But really effective transportation for people and goods did not arrive until 1870, when Denver finally obtained a connection to the nation's railway system.

Between 1860 and 1870, Denver seemed moribund. The territory's first big mining boom was over, and while the city was well placed to benefit from mining and agricultural traffic, it was unclear whether Denver would continue to grow in the coming decades. The 1860 census showed 4,749 residents in Denver. By 1870, the city had managed to increase its population by only ten souls, to 4,759. After 1870, however, Denver's population increased significantly. One reason for this was the city's new railroad connections.

Denver fought hard to have the transcontinental railroad built by Union Pacific run through the city. Union Pacific was not impressed by the city's boosterism, however. The problem was one of economics: a railroad running through Cheyenne, Wyoming would be easier and less expensive to build than one running through Denver. So, the U.P. laid its tracks through Cheyenne and left Denver to wilt on the vine.

Fortunately for Denver, U.P. had also shunned another city further east to the benefit of its northern neighbor. St. Louis had been left out in the cold in the railroad's plans, in favor of Chicago. St. Louis responded by planning a railroad line that would travel from that city through Kansas to the West Coast. The Kansas Pacific (as the line was eventually called) would run through Denver — if the price was right. When Denver balked at the cost, the Kansas Pacific threatened to run its trains through Pueblo instead. Denver caved in, and obtained a spot on the Kansas Pacific line.

The connection to Denver was actually a great benefit for the Kansas Pacific. Developments were afoot that would enable Kansas Pacific to reach the West Coast through Denver on the Union Pacific line. Denver was negotiating with Union Pacific for a railway link between Denver and Cheyenne. By the late 1860s, Denver obtained the link, for an exorbitant cost. The Kansas Pacific reached Denver within two months of the completion of the Denver-Cheyenne stretch of the Union Pacific, in 1870. Denver's decade-long struggle had finally brought the railroad to town.

Another early improvement sought by boosters of several Colorado cities and towns was municipal lighting. Baltimore was the first city in the United States to employ a system of gas streetlights, in 1816. During the frontier period, effective lighting of city streets became a matter of municipal pride, as important a symbol of status as an opera house or a first-class hotel. This may explain why cities hardly worthy of the name made bold plans for street lighting long before they could carry them into effect. Between 1859 and 1868, for example, Denver awarded franchises for its own gas streetlight system to a number of investors. All of them failed to deliver. It was not until 1871 that the city finally had a working gas streetlight system in place. Ironically, given the delay Denver experienced in developing that system, gas streetlights would last for only about fifteen years before they were in turn succeeded by electric lighting.

On April 21, 1880, residents of Denver were treated to an exhibition of electric arc lighting from a plant built within the city. Within a year, investors had formed the Colorado Electric Company (CEC). To gain further publicity for the new utility and to wean the city from its gaslight system, between 1881 and 1885 CEC built a system of eight iron towers 150 to 210 feet high near the city, each of them sporting 3000 candlepower arc lights that earned them the title "Lighthouses on the Plains." These towers were dismantled in 1891, but by then they had served their purpose, of "turning people on" to electricity.

For a while, gas lighting competed with electricity, but the new technology eventually proved irresistible. The Daniels and Fisher store in Denver was the first to employ electric lighting, in 1881. Four years later, in 1885, Denver scrapped its gaslight system for electric street lighting. Leadville was another early adopter; it had electric street lighting installed by 1883. Electricity also came to the state's mining regions; by 1890, for example, a water wheel was running an electrical generating plant at the Gold King Mill in Telluride.

Gas and electric lighting is merely one example of successive technologies that competed for consumer loyalty, often without the monopoly power we now associate with public utilities. While the lack of barriers to entry arguably led to rapid technological advance and an expansion of consumer choice, it also could produce inefficient and even bizarre results. Nowhere is this more clear than the example of the Denver streetcar business. At times in the early days, there were so many different types of streetcar lines running down the city's streets — serving electric trolleys, cable-car railways, and horse-drawn streetcars simultaneously — that there was hardly room for any other traffic, even on the city's broad streets. Eventually the electric railway system won out, until shut down in the 1950s, abandoned in favor of automobiles.

Telephone service in Colorado was also subject to some early competitive jousting. After Alexander Graham Bell invented the telephone, the American Bell Telephone Company aggressively asserted its patent and licensing rights. For a while, however, Western Union resisted Bell's monopoly, and provided telephone service for Colorado's mountain towns. Eventually, though, Bell won its patent infringement suit, and those who wanted phones had to deal with the Bell system. By 1879, investors in Denver had done just that. The Denver telephone exchange opened in February of that year. Over a century later, the service it spawned would ultimately become part of the gigantic Qwest Corporation.

FOR FURTHER READING

Jack McCroskey, *Light Rail and Heavy Politics: How Denver Set About Reviving Public Transportation* (Denver, CO: Tenlie Pub. 2003).

David Haward Bain, *Empire Express: Building the First Transcontinental Railroad* (New York, NY: Penguin Books 2000).

Dan Robertson, Morris Cafky & E. J. Haley, *Denver's Street Railways* (Denver, CO: Sundance Pubs. 1999).

Mark H. Rose, *Cities of Light and Heat: Domesticating Gas and Electricity in Urban America* (University Park, PA: Penn. State Univ. Press 1995).

Stephen J. Leonard & Thomas J. Noel, *Denver: Mining Camp to Metropolis* (Boulder, CO: University Press of Colo. 1990).

Thomas J. Noel, *Larimer Street: Main Street, Skid Row & Urban Renaissance* (Denver, CO: Historic Denver, Inc. 1981).

Forming the Environmental Citizen
Colorado's Early Legal Efforts at Protecting Outdoor Recreation

BY TOM I. ROMERO, II

Not long after the rush to the Rockies in 1859, Colorado acquired a reputation as the "climate capital" of the United States. With lush forests, towering peaks, abundant wildlife, and fresh mountain air, the state became a mecca for those desiring a healthier life. One visitor even argued that it was nearly impossible to get sick while in Colorado. As evidence, the visitor explained that he "once knew a man who tried to make himself ill in order to get off serving on a jury. He ate nothing but pork fat and drank nothing but lemonade for a week, but he couldn't do it. . . . The air that you breathe in Colorado enables you to avoid anything."

Although many of the first settlers in Colorado ventured to the territory with their minds focused on extracting the riches beneath the ground, the state's beautiful scenery and abundant resources inspired early efforts at conservation and environmental protection. These early Coloradans took full advantage of the area's outdoor activities and, from the outset, served as an example to all future generations of the need for the state's natural resources to maintain its civic identity.

Although Colorado's early legislators and governors were concerned about the state's environmental and natural resource challenges, most influential in the early development of Colorado's environmental laws were Colorado sportsmen and citizen groups. Founded as early as 1886, sportsmen pioneered the strategy of mobilizing concerned citizens to *legally* protect the state's vast natural resources. Troubled by commercial hunters and buyers — called by one Colorado jurist as "the most persistent and heartless enemies of the game, and at the same time the most difficult to detect and punish"[1] — sportsmen groups assisted in enacting the state's first and most comprehensive fish and game laws (*see below*).

Not surprisingly, the Colorado Bar recognized Coloradans' long-standing relationship with the state's wildlife and landscape. In his dissent in *Hartman v. Tresise*,[2] Justice Bailey of the Colorado Supreme Court noted that Colorado's settlers were the latest in a long line of "energetic, freedom-loving people, excessively fond of outdoor sports, hunting, and fishing." As a result of arguments made by those like Justice Bailey and the persistence as well as success of sportsmen in trying to preserve many of the state's natural resources, Colorado became known as "America's playground." Soon, other influential citizen groups were born. Colorado chapters of the Sierra Club and the Audubon Society saw their beginnings in the years after the adjudication of these early Colorado legal battles at the beginning of the 20th Century. In this regard, Colorado's purple mountains, fresh rivers, majestic wildlife, clean air, and outdoor enthusiasts provided the foundation for the collective environmental movement that emerged in the 1950s.

Original printing: *The Colorado Lawyer*, November 2002. In 1899, the Colorado legislature passed the state's most comprehensive 19th Century law concerning the licensing and protection of game and fish in the state. "An act to protect game and fish" (Sess. Laws 1899, § 98, 184) provided for state ownership of all game and fish not already under private ownership, a limitation on the time and manner in which one could hunt or fish, and a restriction on what one could legally hunt. Colorado courts reaffirmed the validity of the Act in *Hornbeke v. White*, 76 P. 926 (Colo.App. 1904), and *Hartman v. Tresise*, 84 P. 685 (Colo. 1905). In other cases, early Colorado courts came down hard on mining companies that dumped tailings and other pollutants into Colorado's public waters. *See Suffolk Gold Min. & Mill. Co. v. San Miguel Consol. Min. & Mill. Co.*, 48 P. 828 (Colo. 1897). For insights into the environmental conscience of Colorado's sportsmen clubs, see the Western History Collection at the Denver Public Library and the Stephen H. Hart Library at the Colorado Historical Society, which contain records of such groups as the Vallejo Gun Club and Mile High Duck Club. Some of the legal arguments made by these groups are recounted in Frederick S. Titsworth's report on the annual proceedings of the Colorado Scientific Society in 1910: "Notes on the Legal Aspects of the Conservation Problem" housed at the Hart Library. Finally, the environmental development of Colorado's legislators and chief executives can be found in the public and personal papers of Colorado's governors located at the Colorado State Archives in downtown Denver: http://www.archives.state.co.us.

NOTES

1. *Hornbeke v. White*, 76 P. 926, 930 (Colo.App. 1904).
2. *Hartman v. Tresise*, 84 P. 685, 689 (Colo. 1905).

Rocky Mountain Riches

Law and the Extraction of Colorado's Mineral Wealth

BY TOM I. ROMERO, II

John Gregory was a professional miner. Having mined in Georgia for much of his life, Gregory traveled to Colorado in 1858 to find his fortune. He began prospecting the mountain streams to the south of Fort Laramie. Along Clear Creek in 1859, Gregory found a vast amount of gold lying in the stream-bed. A dazed Gregory allegedly muttered, "My wife will be a lady and my children will be educated."[1] Gregory's strike eventually produced $85 million worth of gold, "but, like many a prospector, the original discoverer died a poor man," because he had neither the means nor, most important, the legal know-how to fully develop the natural resource.[2]

Prospectors soon found that reaping the rewards from Colorado's diverse natural resources would prove a difficult task. Much would be needed to extract such minerals as lead carbonates, oil shale, and molybdenum. The process would require new technologies, underground mines, smelters, massive amounts of capital, a wage-labor workforce, and, most important, lawyers. Not surprisingly, Colorado became the battleground for testing the feasibility of the nation's mineral laws on its rough and hazardous mountain terrain.

U.S. District Court Judge Moses Hallett, who decided
many important early mining claim cases
Courtesy Denver Bar Association

During his tenure, Judge Moses Hallett, of the U.S. District Court for
the District of Colorado, "handed down forty-two decisions on mining
claims."[3] Most important were the cases interpreting the 1872 General
Mining Act ("1872 Act").[4] Because the law used obscure terminology
and made little distinction between minerals and their extraction processes, lawyers early on became indispensable to developing Colorado's
natural resources above and below the ground. Indeed, the issues surrounding the 1872 Act became so complex and at times convoluted that
"miners took to calling mines 'lawyer pits' and quipped that 'the surest
way of discovering a bonanza was to check the court records.'"[5]

One Colorado case that eventually reached the U.S. Supreme Court
exemplifies many of the challenges posed in the application of the Act.
In *Del Monte Min. & Mill. Co. v. Last Chance Min. & Mill. Co.*,[6] the own-

ers of three mining claims patented in 1893 and 1894 asserted their rights to the mineral veins running through each mountain parcel. Although the evidence conclusively demonstrated senior and junior patent rights, as well as the locations of the three claims, the Court confronted several complex questions regarding the 1872 Act. These included the "extralateral" rights of the junior lode location, the worth of each claim, the legal "end lines" of each parcel, the owner of a vein if its apex was found on the "end line" and "side lines" of two claims, and the ability of an owner to follow a vein downward beyond its "side line" and under the surface of another owner's land.[7]

Justice Brewer of the U.S. Supreme Court, in the *Last Chance Min. & Mill. Co.* case, summed up many of the problems associated with law and resource development in 19th Century Colorado:

> If the surface of the ground was everywhere level, and veins constantly pursued a straight line, there would be little difficulty in legislation to provide for all contingencies; but mineral is apt to be found in mountainous regions where great irregularity of surface exists, and the course or strike of the veins is as irregular as the surface, so that many cases may arise in which statutory provisions will fail to secure to a discoverer of a vein such an amount thereof as equitably it would seem. . . .[8]

Despite the complexities that mineral law posed, the insatiable mineral demands of Colorado, as well as the American West and the nation in general, fueled continued exploration and excavation. In mining such resources as lead, zinc, oil shale, vanadium, and uranium, Colorado's abundant mineral wealth drove further excavation and resource development into the twentieth and twenty-first centuries. The 1872 Act, largely unchanged since its inception, continued to be the primary legal instrument regulating the extraction of resources from the state.[9] As the state's history with mining law has continually demonstrated, those who have the gumption, resources, *and* lawyers are most likely to extract, develop, and gain from Colorado's diverse Rocky Mountain mineral riches.

Original printing: *The Colorado Lawyer*, November 2003. The legal history of Colorado mining law is literally rich with resources. Wilbur Fiske Stone's four-volume treatise, *A History of Colorado* (Chicago, IL: S. J. Clarke, 1918–19), provides detailed information about mining and law in the early history of Colorado. The University of Colorado at Boulder Norlin Library Archives and the Stephen H. Hart Library at the Colorado History Museum in Denver contain the public and legal records of many of the state's early mining ventures. In addition, the Archives for the State of Colorado contain the records of the Colorado Department of Natural Resources, the agency that regulates oil, gas, and mining operations in the state.

NOTES

1. Hollister, *The Mines of Colorado* (Springfield, MA: S. Bowles, 1867) at 59.

2. Athearn, *The Coloradans* (Albuquerque, NM: Univ. of New Mexico Press, 1976) at 13.

3. Kane and Elfenbein, *From Guns to Gavels: A History of the Federal Territorial and District Courts of Colorado* (unpublished manuscript, 1991) at 28.

4. 30 U.S.C. § 22.

5. Kane and Elfenbein, *supra* note 3 at 28.

6. *Del Monte Min. & Mill. Co. v. Last Chance Min. & Mill. Co.*, 18 S.Ct. 895 (1898).

7. *Id.*

8. *Id.*

9. *See, e.g.*, Werth, "Where Regulation and Property Rights Collide: Reforming the Hardrock Act of 1872," 65 *U.Colo. L.Rev.* 427 (1994).

Vision Quest
Coal and Culture in Colorado's Native Lands

BY TOM I. ROMERO, II

In 1862, the U.S. government asked a delegation of American Indian leaders to come to Washington D.C., the home of the "Great White Father." The government feared that Indian nations might take up arms as a result of repeated incursions by miners and land-seekers onto Native lands. Only one leader, Chief Ouray of the Confederated Band of Utes, made the trip to Washington. Although Chief Ouray was not happy with the federal government, he recognized that conflict over the land was inevitable.[1] At issue was the vast mineral wealth in the lands held by Colorado's Southern Utes. Through treaties, Chief Ouray attempted to legally preserve his people's way of life in the face of land-hungry immigrants seeking homesteads on Colorado land.

However, in 1879, continued hostilities between Utes, federal agents, and miners finally led Congress to pass a bill that attempted to destroy the Utes' way of life.[2] In subsequent years, during what came to be known as the "allotment period," the United States opened much of Ute land to homesteading and mineral (in particular, coal) exploration and excavation. In 1934, the economic and cultural devastation that allotment created for American Indians led Congress to pass the Indian Reorganization Act.[3] The Act "returned to tribal ownership the remaining . . . lands of any Indian reservation that had been open to

Chief Ouray of the Confederated Band of Utes superimposed over a coal mine like the ones that would later be the subject of legal battles between the Ute tribe and oil companies
Graphic by Katherine Haas

homesteading." In 1938, Congress strengthened the goals of the Act by conveying "the coal previously reserved to the United States . . . to the Southern Ute Tribe."[4] Despite having title to approximately 200,000 acres of coal, at that time, the Southern Ute Tribe lacked the skill and resources to develop their natural resources.

One of these resources was coal-bed methane gas ("CBM"), which "had little value as an energy resource," and its existence posed a "nuisance and a safety hazard" not only to energy developers, but also to residents of surrounding communities.[5] In the 1970s and 1980s, the U.S. Department of Energy was able to develop technologies for transforming CBM into a fuel source. As a result of federal tax credits, cheaper technology, and exemptions from environmental regulation, Southern Utes entered the CBM business. By the 1990s, the Southern Utes started their own production and pipeline operations to develop CBM on the reservation. The Tribe hoped that CBM would help them achieve self-determination over natural resources located on their land.

In 1991, the Southern Ute Tribe sued oil companies over ownership of the CBM contained in the coal estate that the Tribe acquired through the Indian Reorganization Act.[6] The case eventually reached the U.S. Supreme Court, which held that CMB was not part of the original coal estate held by the Tribe.[7] Amoco subsequently entered into an agreement with the Southern Utes to develop the mineral estate jointly.

Today, many members of the Tribe view CBM pumps and compressors as "a cancer. . . . There will be portions of our land that will be so contaminated that they'll be unusable for future generations."[8] Nevertheless, the agreement with Amoco has given the community a stake in the development of their own resources. CBM drilling "presents a conundrum for Southern Utes who, as shareholders of tribal land and mineral rights, profit so much that they're known as one of the nation's wealthiest tribes."[9]

According to Dick Baughman, a member of the Southern Ute Tribe: "I have a sense of place in this land. My ancestors once roamed it. It didn't belong to them. They left it as they found it. . . . Now, it's in extreme danger of overproduction. I'm sure the Creator would want us to exercise some discretion and restraint."[10] Despite such views, unemployment and underdevelopment have forced "a growing number of Indian tribes to exchange the spiritual view of their once pristine environment for a commercial one."[11]

In negotiating claims to such contrasting interests, Colorado courts have had to balance a variety of different visions — from Chief Ouray to Amoco. As 21st Century energy demands drive high levels of mineral development in the American West, understanding the legal history provided by these early visions affords insight into the choices and consequences Coloradans have had to make about their lands.

Original printing: *The Colorado Lawyer*, January 2004. Primary materials regarding the Southern Utes, Indian policy, and mineral development in Indian Country can be found at the Rocky Mountain Branch of the National Archives and Records Administration, located at the Federal Center in Lakewood, Colorado. An analysis of the legal dispute between the Southern Utes and Amoco can be found in Callard, "A Conflict Over What Killed the Canary," 33 *Tulsa L.J.* 909 (1998).

NOTES

1. Atkins, *Human Relations in Colorado: A Historical Record* (Denver, CO: Publishers Press, 1968) at 43-44.

2. 10 Cong. Rec. 2059, 2066 (1880).

3. 25 U.S.C. § 463.

4. Francis, "Mining Law — Ownership of Coalbed Methane: A Judicial Step Toward Efficient CBM and Coal Development," 33 *Land & Water L. Rev.* 469, 471 (1998).

5. *The Sunday Denver Post and Rocky Mountain News* (Sept. 9, 2001) at 1A.

6. *Southern Ute Indian Tribe v. Amoco Prod. Co.*, 874 F.Supp. 1142 (D.Colo. 1995).

7. *Amoco Prod. Co. v. Southern Ute Indian Tribe*, 526 U.S. 865 (1999).

8. *The Sunday Denver Post and Rocky Mountain News* (Sept. 9, 2001) at 9A.

9. *Id.*

10. *Id.*

11. Martella, Jr., Note, "'Not in My State's Indian Reservation' — A Legislative Fix to Close an Environmental Loophole," 47 *Vand. L.Rev.* 1863 (1994).

The Original "Sod Squad"

Dry Lawns, Dirty Cars, and the Legality of Water Restrictions in the 1950s

BY TOM I. ROMERO, II

In 1954, Coloradans faced what, until that time, had been the most severe drought in the history of the state. Hit especially hard was the Denver metropolitan area, which, due to its climate, life-style, economy, and affordability, had become one of the fastest growing metropolitan areas in the nation. From 1945 to 1954, Denver's population increased 43 percent. Such growth put an incredible strain on a water system that already had included several transmountain diversions to dozens of reservoirs. Alarmingly, more people had been added to the Denver water system between 1946 and 1954 than in the entire twenty-eight-year period since the City and County of Denver acquired the system in 1918. Accordingly, water consumption grew as much from 1940 to 1954 as during the entire proceeding period from its inception way back in 1872.

In 1954, to further exacerbate matters, a lack of snow and rain in Colorado, in conjunction with above-average temperatures, decreased water levels to all-time lows. In response, the Denver Water Board ("DWB") promulgated regulations that restricted residents and users of Denver water to use the resource only for irrigation purposes during certain hours and certain days of the week. For the first time in its

Glenn Saunders, legendary counsel for the Denver Water Board, defended use of the "Sod Squad"
Courtesy Denver Water, 2010

history, the DWB instituted its first "Sod Squad" to "discover a use of water contrary to the rules and regulations of the Board." If found in violation, the DWB's Sod Squad issued a warning for the first violation, imposed a "special charge" of $5 for the second violation, $25 for the third, and $100 for each subsequent violation.

The ability of the DWB to impose a "special charge" on its customers raised a host of novel questions in Denver's legal community. Did the charge constitute a "penalty" or was it a permissible action extended to the DWB by Article XX of the Colorado Constitution and Article XIX of the City Charter? Indeed, what constituted "practicable" and "low" water rates that still delivered "good service" to the DWB's burgeoning customer base? In defending the new practice, the legendary Glenn Saunders, long-time counsel for the DWB, equated the powers of the DWB with those of the City Council, a status seemingly implied in the 1951 case, *City of Englewood v. City and County of Denver*, stating that the Colorado Public Utilities Commission had no jurisdiction over the DWB.

In operating the precious water system, Saunders argued that Denver voters vested the DWB with the necessary powers to distribute, regulate, restrict, and, in certain cases, impose a fine in the flow of the municipal resource. Although the "special charge" and the deployment of the Sod Squad raised legitimate questions about the extent of municipal government power, its success in dealing with Denver's water crisis and subsequent decisions respecting the DWB's autonomy introduced a new understanding of citizenship in the city. Denver residents' lawns were a little browner and cars were less clean. However, with the help of the DWB, Denver's citizens — new and old alike — worked to avoid the practical and legal consequences of drought in the "Queen City" of the Rocky Mountain West.

Original printing: *The Colorado Lawyer*, September 2002. The creation of Denver's first "Sod Squad" and the "special charge" imposed by the DWB was chronicled extensively in the summer of 1954 by *The Denver Post* and *Rocky Mountain News*. The legality of the regulations was analyzed by George Gibson and Lee Hamby in 31 *Dicta* 349 (Sept. 1954). Denver's first water crisis was analyzed extensively in the "Report on Future Water Supply Denver Municipal Water Works" (March 1955), submitted to the DWB and available in the government document section of Norlin Library at the University of Colorado-Boulder. Although the Colorado Supreme Court has never had occasion to consider the constitutionality of such regulations, the autonomy of the DWB was first assessed in *City of Englewood v. City and County of Denver*, 229 P.2d 667 (Colo. 1954), and later reaffirmed in *Board of County Comm'rs of Arapahoe County v. Denver Bd. of Water Comm'rs*, 718 P.2d 235 (Colo. 1986).

The Skyline Project
Urban Renewal and the Demolition of Old Denver

BY FRANK GIBBARD

Travel to most of the larger mountain towns in Colorado and you will find large portions of their historic business and residential districts preserved intact. Blocks of aging hotels, shops, and mansions, often dating from the 19th Century, have been renovated and serve as quaint reminders of bygone days. Denver is different. Here, historic buildings often seem like islands of faded glory in a sea of more utilitarian structures. When one reflects on the huge scale of what was once historic Denver, the magnitude of the loss is stunning. What is more amazing is that most of it disappeared almost overnight.

In the decades following the end of World War II, nearly everyone agreed that something had to be done about the increasingly dilapidated condition of downtown Denver. The suburbs were booming, but downtown seemed to be rotting away at its core. Civic boosters complained that Denver's skid row, that demimonde of transient hotels, bars, cheap eateries, pawn shops, missions, and secondhand stores, was spreading to blocks of vacant storefronts as more respectable downtown businesses folded.

March 1958 saw the creation of a public agency known as the Denver Urban Renewal Authority ("DURA"). In 1966, voters approved a

Denver's treasured Mayan Theater, saved from the wrecking ball by historic preservationist groups

Darlene Johnson

referred ordinance adopting a massive urban renewal scheme, known as the Skyline Project ("Skyline"). In 1969, DURA presided over the first stages of Skyline, which ultimately demolished nearly thirty blocks of Denver's urban core. Skyline was accomplished with surprising speed, and with comparatively little concern for the historic structures that it leveled.

A sense of the loss can be gleaned from the auction DURA conducted of pieces of doomed buildings, "sometimes wondrous items like columns and cornices, marble panels and ornamental iron work to smaller memorabilia like terra cotta trim, brass mailboxes and doorknobs."[1] By the time the last Skyline building, the Tabor Center, was opened in 1984, the Project had refashioned skid row and other depressed neighborhoods into the modern city in which Denverites live today.

Urban renewal sparked resistance from historic preservationists. In 1967, the city of Denver created the Denver Landmark Preservation Commission, giving it power to recommend landmark designation for historic structures and to delay their demolition. A private organization known as Historic Denver, Inc. also managed to salvage many individual buildings and historic neighborhoods from the wrecking ball. We can thank these organizations for, among other things, helping to preserve such landmarks as the Molly Brown House, Brown Palace Hotel, Boettcher Conservatory, and Mayan Theater.

The Colorado courts played a significant role in the struggles over urban renewal. Early on, the Colorado Supreme Court upheld the constitutionality of the Urban Renewal Act of 1958, paving the way legally for the Skyline Project.[2] A number of interesting cases involved attempts to resist the destruction of historic religious structures.

Twice, the Colorado Supreme Court considered First Amendment challenges by the Pillar of Fire Church to the condemnation of its historic Memorial Hall at 18th and Champa Streets, constructed in 1903–04.[3] The Court ultimately upheld DURA's right to condemn the church property.[4] DURA also tangled with the Order of the Friars Minor of the Province of the Most Holy Name, when it sought to condemn a church parking lot as part of the Auraria Higher Education Complex.[5] Sometimes, issues of religion and valuation overlapped, as when owners of an old stone chapel at 10th and Lawrence Streets sought unsuccessfully to obtain replacement cost for the building, even though it had not been used for religious purposes in years.[6]

The second Pillar of Fire decision marked the end of an era. By the time it was decided, in late 1976, the demolition phase of Skyline was essentially complete. The old Denver was gone, and a new one was poised to rise from its ruins.

Original printing: *The Colorado Lawyer*, August 2005. Many good resources on urban renewal in Denver are available at the Western History and Genealogy Collection at the Denver Public Library. In addition to the cases cited and resources noted above, I recommend Thomas J. Noel's *Larimer Street: Main Street, Skid Row & Urban Renaissance* (Denver, CO: Historic Denver, Inc., 1981). An excellent discussion of urban renewal by Tom Noel can be found online at www.denvergov.org/AboutDenver/history_narrative_8.asp. The human costs of urban renewal are discussed in Jane Jacob's classic *The Death and Life of Great American Cities* (New York, NY: Vantage, reissue ed., 1992).

NOTES

1. *Denver Renewed: A History of the Denver Urban Renewal Authority 1958-1986* (Denver, CO: The Denver Foundation, 1992) at 265.

2. *See Rabinoff v. District Court*, 360 P.2d 114 (Colo. 1961).

3. For more on the Pillar of Fire Church and its origins, see "The Limits of Tolerance: Alma White and the Pentecostal Union Crusade" in this book.

4. *DURA v. Pillar of Fire*, 552 P.2d 23 (Colo. 1976); *Pillar of Fire v. DURA*, 509 P.2d 1250 (Colo. 1973).

5. *Order of Friars Minor v. DURA*, 527 P.2d 804 (Colo. 1974).

6. *DURA v. Pogzeba*, 558 P.2d 442 (Colo.App. 1976).

Fear and Desire for Streetcars
Denver's Early Electric Railway Wars

BY FRANK GIBBARD

There are many hazards involved in the job of constructing a municipal electric railway. Being arrested for doing your work usually is not one of them. How, then, do we explain the unfortunate fate of five employees of the Denver Tramway Company ("Denver Tramway"), arrested by Denver's chief of police on December 9, 1889, and charged with trespassing?[1]

The workers had been digging holes at the intersection of West Eighth Avenue and Santa Fe Drive for the erection of electric poles. The arrest could not have come as a complete surprise, because four other Denver Tramway employees had been arrested for the same offense at the same intersection two days before. In each case, the police asserted that the workmen had no permission or authority to erect electric lines at that intersection.[2] These arrests were the culmination of a seething controversy that embroiled the newspapers, the public, and the courts of Denver, and very nearly stalled the construction of the city's overhead electric street railway grid.[3]

Just a few years earlier, Denver had been the home of one of the first electric street railways in the world. In 1885, Sidney H. Short, a professor at the University of Denver, constructed an electric streetcar line that ran through downtown along Fifteenth Street, between Court

Restored streetcar that runs near I-25 in Denver
Katherine Haas

Place and Larimer Street. The line was cheap and efficient, estimated to cost only one-fourth of a streetcar line pulled by horses.[4] Unfortunately for this early enterprise, the power cables were not well insulated and unwary pedestrians were likely to have a "shocking" experience when they touched both the rails and the power conduit. Horses also received shocks, and there were rumors that dogs had been electrocuted. Concerns about safety caused this pioneering electric railway to be eclipsed for a few years by its principal competitors — cable railway and horse cars — until new technology employing high-voltage overhead wires made electric-powered trolleys more efficient and safe.

This new electric technology, however, brought with it new forms of controversy. Property owners along the trolley lines did not like the unsightly poles that held the wires. They also were afraid of electric shock from downed wires. Things went from bad to worse when two

Denver newspapers, the *Denver Republican* and the *Denver Times* ("*Times*"), took opposite sides in a controversy over stringing power lines along South Broadway.[5] The *Times* soon became a staunch opponent of electric trolleys and, in a fateful front-page article on November 7, 1889, it opined that the Denver Tramway franchise gave the tramway company no authority to operate an electric-powered tramway.[6]

Denver's new mayor, Wolfe Londoner, was paying attention. He had been elected that spring in one of the most corrupt elections in Denver history.[7] The shenanigans were so bad that he would later become the only mayor of Denver ever forced to resign his office because of election fraud.[8]

One month after the story in the *Times*, Mayor Londoner instructed Denver's chief of police to arrest the Denver Tramway employees. It was a strange step, given that the city council of Denver had passed an ordinance only a few months before authorizing the city engineer to grant permits for the construction of an electric railway system. Acting on this authority, the engineer had issued excavation permits to Denver Tramway.[9] The right hand of Denver government, it seemed, did not know what the left hand was doing.

Denver Tramway, which had invested at that point more than $100,000 in erecting fifteen miles of electric street railway[10] — a small fortune in those days — did not take the arrests lying down. It rushed to state district court to obtain an injunction against further arrests. The district court initially granted an injunction, but later reversed and dismissed the case. Denver Tramway appealed to the Colorado Supreme Court, which issued a *per curiam* decision five years later reversing the dismissal.[11]

The issue before the Colorado Supreme Court was whether the city of Denver ("City") had authorized the construction of an electric trolley system. If it had, obviously, it could not arrest employees who merely were fulfilling their duties in constructing the system. The problem was that Denver's 1883 City Charter, while permitting the City to authorize the construction of a city railway, did not specifically mention electric railways.[12] An 1885 city ordinance had granted Denver Tramway's predecessor the right to construct an electric railway line, but the parties now conceded that this ordinance exceeded the powers provided under the City Charter. An 1889 amendment to the City Charter later rectified this omission, specifically authorizing the construction of an electric railway line.[13] Could it do so retroactively? The Supreme Court held that it could; the 1889 Charter amendment cured the *ultra vires* effect of the earlier ordinance and ratified the City's contract with Denver Tramway.[14]

The electric trolley system soon displaced the horse cars and cable railways, and lasted until the early 1950s, when it was put out of business by the automotive industry. The electric trolleys have now returned with a vengeance, however, in the form of Denver's burgeoning light-rail system.

Original printing: *The Colorado Lawyer*, March 2006. The author thanks Daniel B. Cordova of the Tenth Circuit Library for research assistance with this article.

NOTES

1. Details concerning this incident can be found in Don Robertson, Morris Cafky & E.J. Haley, *Denver's Street Railways*, at 179 (Denver, CO: Sundance Publications, Ltd., 1999).

2. *Id.*; *see also Denver Tramway Co. v. Londoner*, 37 P. 723 (1894).

3. Robertson, Cafky & Haley, *supra* note 1 at 175-76.

4. *See id.* at 83. Further information about Professor Short's electric streetcar line can be found in Jack McCroskey, *Light Rail and Heavy Politics: How Denver Set About Reviving Public Transportation* (Denver, CO: Tenlie Publishing, 2003).

5. *See* Robertson, Cafky & Haley, *supra* note 1 at 175-76.

6. *Id.* at 175.

7. *See* "Official Misconduct: Wolfe Londoner and the Denver Mayoral Election of 1889" in this book.

8. *Id.*

9. *Denver Tramway Co., supra* note 2 at 725.

10. *Id.*

11. *See generally id.* at 723.

12. *Id.* at 724-25.

13. *Id.* at 725.

14. *Id.* at 725, n.11.

Cooking with Gas
John Koll Takes a Stand

BY FRANK GIBBARD

Our 21st Century world does not yet feature flying cars or weekend trips to Mars, but we do have some gadgets that would have made our forebears jealous. Consider the top-of-the-line propane gas grill. These stainless steel behemoths make available to backyard chefs the cooking power of an industrial-sized kitchen, coupled with a push-button convenience usually associated with the Jetson family.[1]

Even in this day of such mechanical marvels, there are still backyard barbecuers who eschew cooking with gas. They insist on employing a more primitive but time-honored method involving matches, charcoal briquettes, lighter fluid, and an almost shamanic sense of patience and ritual. These barbecuing purists might find much to admire in the stance taken by (aptly-named) John Koll, chef at the Windsor Hotel in 1889.

THE WINDSOR AND ITS CHEF

Denver's magnificent Windsor Hotel opened its doors on June 23, 1880.[2] The 140-person staff at the hotel incorporated some highly specialized talent. In addition to the usual desk clerks and cleaning staff, the roster included a pastry cook, a baker, an engineer, a superintendent of woodwork, a package and key clerk, an assistant elevator man, and a billiard room keeper.[3] John Koll originally was hired as its "second head cook."[4]

Things went well for Koll during his first eight years at the Windsor. By August 1888, he had been promoted to head chef, with an annual contract. Had it not been for the management's decision to upgrade the kitchen, he might have continued working there for years to come.

ENTER THE GAS

The Windsor Hotel abounded with Victorian niceties.[5] Everything seemed designed to demonstrate that Denver, the Queen City of the Plains, was much more than a rough-and-tumble mining town. The hotel's kitchen was no exception. Measuring thirty-seven by seventy feet, it included multiple exits to the hotel's three dining rooms, each with double-doors to prevent any kitchen smells from disturbing diners.[6] Inside, the kitchen contained "a baker's oven, several ranges, [and] six vegetable steamers" along with nickel-plated coffee, tea, and egg boilers.[7] The "modern" ovens, however, were still coal-fired.

Trouble came to the Windsor kitchen sometime between August 1888 and February 1889. During this time period, the hotel replaced its coal-fired ranges with gas ranges. The owners, William H. Bush and W. S. Morse, had seen gas used for cooking in hotels back East, and they were enthused with the new technology.

In fact, cooking with gas was almost a century old by that time. In 1802, a Moravian chemical manufacturer named Zachäus Andreas Winzler had served food to his guests at dinner parties that was prepared on a primitive gas cooker.[8] By 1834, the Northampton Gas Company in England was selling commercial gas cookers.[9] Gas cooking became popular in the 1880s with the introduction of schemes for renting the cooking equipment.[10]

The Windsor Hotel's owners probably believed they were just following the wave of the future; Chef Koll, however, did not take kindly to the change.

The stately Windsor Hotel in downtown Denver
Courtesy Denver Public Library, Western History Collection - #H-557

KOLL'S RESISTANCE

Once the gas stoves were in place, the Windsor's head chef began a campaign of passive and not-so-passive resistance to the new technology. His employers wanted him to cook with gas instead of coal, did they? Fine. He would cook with gas — with lots of gas. Before long, he was using three times the amount of gas that the manufacturer of the ranges recommended for cooking meals. The costs became extravagant. When the owners complained, he told them he was doing the best he could.[11]

The hotel's owners found other reasons for dissatisfaction with Koll's performance. They discovered the stove burners were stopped up with grease, causing food to be either underdone or overdone. As one owner put it, "There was continual trouble in the kitchen."[12]

Things came to a head on the evening of February 9, 1899. The hotel's owners testified that around dinnertime, Koll simply refused to go on working for them. Worse, he "aided, abetted, and counseled the other employees . . . then engaged in the kitchen and dining room of the hotel to refuse to work for [its owners]."[13] Koll's walkout left them, the owners claimed, with many hungry guests to feed, but without a chef to feed them.

THE LAWSUIT

It was Koll who sued, contending that the Windsor's owners had wrongfully discharged him.[14] He introduced into evidence his terse contract with them, which read in pertinent part as follows:

> The said parties of the first part [the Windsor partners] have this day employed John Koll as chef at the Windsor Hotel, for the term of one year, at a monthly salary of one hundred and thirty dollars ($130). The said party of the second part [Koll] agrees to give his entire attention to the business for which he is employed, and to render good and satisfactory service.[15]

Koll complained that his service had been good and satisfactory, and that since leaving the Windsor, he had been unable to find work. He demanded judgment in the sum of $827.66 plus costs, presumably representing the unpaid balance due him on the contract.

One suspects that by the time it reached the jury, the suit was about much more than money. Koll wanted vindication for his behavior. This led to both parties putting on considerable testimony "with reference to the capacity and utility of ranges to roast meats, cook potatoes, hard and soft boiled eggs, and, in fact, all of the usual articles that are enumerated upon the hotel menu or bill of fare."[16] What the jurors thought of all this cumulative culinary testimony the court of appeals opinion does not say; however, the jury awarded Koll a judgment of $413.83.

COURT OF APPEALS' OPINION — ROUND ONE

The hotel owners appealed. The Colorado Court of Appeals found all the testimony about gas stoves and coal stoves irrelevant. The real issue was which party, if any, had breached the contract. To the two jurists in the majority — Judge Richmond and Judge Reed — the answer to that question seemed obvious:

> Here is a plain, simple, unambiguous contract, susceptible of easy construction, so simple that he who can read and write ought to be able to understand. The contract is absolute and specific. By its terms plaintiff covenanted that his work should be satisfactory, not to himself, but to his employers. That it was not satisfactory is shown by the evidence of defendants, and is corroborated by that of plaintiff. Had plaintiff's services been eminently satisfactory to his employers, but his position unsatisfactory to himself, he could have quit, and they would have been remediless. To retain him in a state of revolt, and while influencing and demoralizing his subordinates, was impossible.[17]

In other words, the majority read the hotel owners' promise to employ Koll and to pay him for the term of the contract to be conditioned on his service as an employee being satisfactory to them. The owners, the majority reasoned, were the only persons who could say whether Koll's service was satisfactory. Any other reading, the majority opined, would allow Koll to say:

> I am the servant, but I am employed for a year, and for that one year I propose to exact my salary, and compel you, regardless of your wishes, to submit to my management and my dictation, to my manners and my methods, in running this hotel. I care nothing for your guests or your hotel enterprise; as chef for one year I propose to remain.[18]

This reading of the contract violated its plain language, which permitted the employer, rather than the employee, to determine whether his service had been satisfactory.

By a sort of judicial sleight-of-hand, the court of appeals' majority turned a contractually based employment into an employment essentially at will. In an at-will employment situation, the employer can discharge an employee for any reason, whether that reason seems justifiable or not.[19] Here, under the majority's theory, the hotel could fire Koll at any time, simply by declaring that his services were "unsatisfactory," so long as the hotel acted in good faith. Given this power, the majority reasoned, and the employer's statement that Koll's services were in fact unsatisfactory, the jury could not have ruled in Koll's favor. The fact that the jurors did so "demonstrates . . . that their conclusion was the result of prejudice."[20]

THE DISSENT

Judge Bissell, in dissent, saw things differently. First of all, he noted that the hotel owners had not defended the suit at trial on the basis that they had the right to fire Koll at will. Instead, they claimed that they had not discharged him, but that he had quit; therefore, it was improper for the majority to grant judgment in their favor on a theory of at-will employment.

Second, the majority should have followed the rule that, as long as there is evidence to support the jury's verdict, the court of appeals should not second-guess the jury's resolution of the facts. Here, the unpaid portion of the employment contract occurred after Koll either was fired or had quit. Because there could be no showing of dissatisfaction with services that had not yet been rendered, the hotel owners should have been prepared to show that Koll's previous services had been unsatisfactory. However, if they had been dissatisfied, why had the hotel kept him on for so long?[21]

In support of his argument, Judge Bissell carefully parsed the owner's testimony. Owner Bush had remarked on the fact that after he installed the gas range, "there seemed to be a disposition on the part of *every one in the kitchen* to fight it."[22] The testimony of owner Morse was nearly identical. Given these facts, the jury

> might easily have found that Koll's services as cook had been entirely sat-
> isfactory, and that the only trouble in the world was with the employe[e]s
> generally, because of the change in the implements furnished.[23]

Having set out these threshold quibbles with the majority's approach, Judge Bissell now turned to his main point: the majority's
approach was improper under the rules of contract interpretation. In
particular, he stated, the majority had disregarded the rule that words
in a contract should be taken according to their ordinary and usual
sense, unless there are indications that the parties intended otherwise.
Also, the majority should have followed the maxim "*ut res magis valeat
quam pereat,*" meaning that the contract should be read as a whole in
such a way as to permit each part to be given its proper meaning.[24]

Applying these two principles, Judge Bissell concluded that the
promises of the parties (the owners' promise to pay, and Koll's promise
to perform satisfactory work) were not conditioned on each other;
they simply reflected the undertakings made by each of the parties to
the contract. Koll's agreement to perform "satisfactory" work simply
meant that he agreed to live up to his obligation to do good work as
the Windsor's chef. It was not intended to set up a standard by which
the hotel could decide whether he would continue to be employed and
paid for his work. Therefore, Judge Bissell would have affirmed the
jury's verdict.

COURT OF APPEALS' OPINION – ROUND TWO

By stating that no jury could have ruled in favor of Koll, the majority's
opinion essentially had dictated the result on remand. After the case
came back to the district court, the defendants moved for a judgment
in their favor. Finding that "the defendants' testimony is conclusive on
the question of whether the plaintiffs' services were satisfactory to
them or not," the district court granted the motion.[25] Koll made an

offer of testimony from a witness who would have corroborated his story that the hotel had been satisfied with his services; however, the district court stated: "It would not make any difference if there were fifty witnesses to the same effect."[26]

Koll appealed. The court of appeals basically repeated its reasoning from its prior opinion. Although it found the first opinion conclusive as to the issues raised, this time around, in view of the previous dissent, Chief Judge Reed devoted some additional attention to describing the evidence and issues.[27] In his view, the evidence showed that Koll "was responsible for the entire management [of] subordinates, and, following his lead, the whole troop made war upon the gas range."[28] Although Koll had testified that Bush told him to take his money and get out, Bush recounted a very different story:

> I found the dinner all ready, and, the hour for serving the dinner having arrived, and everything off the gas range and on the steam tables for serving, I found the gas, as usual, turned on at full head. I walked around, and turned it off, and said in a very quiet way: "John, I don't want you to use this gas except when you have use for it. Don't have it turned on in this way. I have been to Chicago and other places, and seen them work these, and I know all about it. I know I ought to be able to tell you." He said, "If you know so damned much about it, you don't need my services." I said, "No, sir; I don't," and walked out of the kitchen. That was everything that passed between Koll and myself.[29]

The court of appeals noted the lack of other witnesses to support Koll's version of events. It then turned to the contractual language that had troubled Judge Bissell in the previous decision. Again, it seemed obvious to the court that the phrase requiring that Koll perform his duties in a "satisfactory" manner meant that they must satisfy his employers. Any other interpretation, the court suggested, was not only implausible but perhaps even advanced in bad faith. The court dismissed Koll's attorneys' arguments on this point as "specious, ingenious, and sophistical . . . a mere waste of time and words."[30] The court also found it significant that the salary was to be paid in monthly installments, from which it concluded that the hotel had not agreed to employ Koll for the entire year. It therefore affirmed the judgment for the hotel's owners.

CONCLUSION

Since the *Koll* decisions, Colorado courts have developed a body of law elaborating the effect of employment contracts, express or implied, on the general presumption of at-will employment. As the law now stands, a claim of at-will employment can be defeated not only by an express contract (such as Koll claimed to have), but also by the employee's claim that his or her termination violated public policy or an implied contract or promissory estoppel.[31] Nevertheless, this expanded body of law would not have solved the problem with the Koll contract, which suffered from a lack of clarity concerning the parties' expectations.

Original printing: *The Colorado Lawyer*, November 2009. The author is grateful for the research assistance of Dan Cordova and Lynn Christian of the Colorado Supreme Court Law Library.

NOTES

1. *The Jetsons* was a television series that originally aired during the early 1960s. It featured an animated space-age family.
2. For more history on the Windsor, *see* Gibbard, "Healer or Slayer? A Case of Cyanide Poisoning," in this book.
3. "The Windsor," *Rocky Mountain News* (June 23, 1880).
4. *Id.*
5. For a poetic description of the Windsor Hotel's vanished glories, *see* Buchanan, *A Story of the Fabulous Windsor Hotel* 9-16 (2d ed., A.B. Hirschfeld Press, 1956).
6. *See* "The Windsor," *supra* note 3.
7. *Id.*
8. *See* www.gasmuseum.co.uk/cooking.htm.
9. *Id.*

10. *Id.*

11. *Bush v. Koll*, 29 P. 919, 920 (Colo.App. 1892).

12. *Id.*

13. *Id.*

14. The Windsor's owners counter-sued, but the jury did not rule in their favor, and the court of appeals upheld this decision.

15. *Bush, supra* note 11 at 919.

16. *Id.* at 920.

17. *Id.*

18. *Id.* It should be noted, however, that the court of appeals pointed to no evidence that Koll sought to "run the hotel" or that he "care[d] nothing for the Windsor's guests or [the] hotel enterprise." He simply didn't like cooking with gas.

19. *See, e.g., Wiseheart v. Meganck*, 66 P.3d 124, 127 (Colo.App. 2002).

20. *Bush, supra* note 11 at 921.

21. This argument might be construed as sophistry. Surely the hotel had to pick a specific date to fire an unsatisfactory employee. That they had retained him until that date did not necessarily mean they were satisfied with his service until that time.

22. *Bush, supra* note 11 at 922 (Bissell, J., dissenting) (emphasis added).

23. *Id.*

24. *Id.* at 923.

25. *Koll v. Bush*, 40 P. 579 (Colo.App. 1895).

26. *Id.*

27. Although Judge Bissell was still on the court, for some reason he did not recapitulate his dissent the second time around. *See* www.state.co.us/courts/sctlib/ctapp.95.htm (listing Judge Bissell's terms in office).

28. *Koll, supra* note 25 at 580.

29. *Id.* at 580-81.

30. *Id.* at 581.

31. *Jaynes v. Centura Health Corp.*, 148 P.3d 241, 243 (Colo.App. 2006).

Driven to Distraction

Some Tragic Accidents from a Pre-Automotive Age

BY FRANK GIBBARD

E ffective December 1, 2009, drivers 18 years of age or older are forbidden from text messaging (texting) while operating a motor
vehicle in Colorado.[1] Drivers under 18 are forbidden any use of a cell
phone while driving.[2] It's not surprising that the legislature has imposed these restrictions. Eighty-nine percent of American adults surveyed in a 2007 Harris Interactive poll believed texting while driving
was dangerous and should be banned.[3] Studies have shown that persons talking on cell phones while driving are four times as likely to
have an accident than those not distracted by a cell phone; for those
texting while driving, the likelihood of an accident is six times greater.[4]

Driving is an activity that can be carried on subconsciously while
the conscious mind is otherwise engaged.[5] This may cause us to over-
estimate our ability to multitask while driving, leading to accidents.
Similar lapses in concentration have allegedly contributed to recent incidents involving railroad conductors[6] and airline pilots.[7]

As evidenced in a number of pre-1900 Colorado cases, however, such
accidents cannot be attributed solely to the ubiquity of wireless communi-
cations and other modern digital distractions. They also are due to limits

in the attention system of the human brain, which scientists believe has not changed much in at least 20,000 years.[8] As these old cases demonstrate, one need not be driving an automobile to be "driven to distraction."

WARNINGS IGNORED –
CITY OF DENVER *v.* PETERSON (1894)

On April 7, 1892, the City of Denver (City) sent a steamroller northbound up Market Street toward City Park "to be there used by its board of public works in rolling the park."[9] An engineer and a fireman were on board.[10] Mounted policemen were supposed to precede the steamroller, alerting other traffic of the oncoming machine. In this instance, however, a witness later testified that he did not notice any mounted escort.

The plaintiff, Karen Peterson, was driving a horse-and-buggy southbound on Market Street. The City presented testimony that before she reached the corner of Market and 25th Streets, a policeman warned her that the steamroller was ahead. He told her she should turn onto 25th Street to avoid it. However, "she was absorbed in conversation with a woman who was her companion in the buggy, and gave no heed to the warning."[11] She was warned a second time; the engineer riding the steamroller called out to her to turn around and go back. Peterson later testified that "she did not see the policeman or the engineer, and heard no warning from any source."[12] Peterson's companion in the buggy corroborated this testimony.

When Peterson failed to turn around, the engineer shut off the steam and stopped his machine. Moments later, as Peterson's buggy approached the steamroller, the safety valve on the machine opened and let off a "snort of steam." The noise or the sight of this so frightened Peterson's horse that it "turned suddenly around, overturned the buggy, throwing [Peterson] violently to the ground, and causing her to sustain serious injury."[13] A jury awarded her damages against the City.

The essential questions on appeal were: Who was responsible for this accident? Was the City liable for failing to adequately warn the plaintiff, or did her own negligence cause her to ignore the warnings she received? The Colorado Court of Appeals made three key rulings that supported the jury's verdict on behalf of the plaintiff and against the City.

The court held first that the City was liable for negligence involving the transportation of the steamroller. The machine was under the control of the City's Board of Public Works; therefore, negligence involving its transportation was attributable to the City.

Second, the court held that the jury could have found that the City's negligence was the proximate cause of the accident. The court of appeals reasoned that because the steamroller "by reason of its construction and appearance and the manner of its operation [was] calculated to frighten horses," the City should have chosen a time of day when the streets were less occupied to roll the steamroller through the city streets.[14] Also, if the City had in fact dispatched a mounted policeman to warn people, it would have discharged its duty of care, regardless of the time of day the steamroller was moved. However, because the evidence was in conflict concerning whether there was such a police escort — at least three witnesses for the plaintiff said there was not — the jury was entitled to decide this issue against the City.

Finally, and perhaps most interesting, the court ruled that the plaintiff's own negligence did not contribute to the accident so as to bar recovery. The court stated:

There is no doubt that travelers upon the highway are bound to look out, and must use the faculties with which they are endowed by nature; but the degree of such watchfulness and use of his faculties, in a given case, to which an individual will be held to escape the charge of contributory negligence, depends largely upon the circumstances of that particular case. It is not necessary that one, while driving upon an unobstructed street of a city, should proceed with the same circumspection and caution as if he were crossing railroad tracks upon which locomotives and trains are frequently passing and repassing.[15]

The court of appeals therefore affirmed the jury's verdict.

WALKING THE TRACK –
KENNEDY v. DENVER,
SOUTH PARK & PACIFIC RAILWAY CO. (1887)

The accident in *Kennedy v. Denver, South Park & Pacific Railway Co.*[16] also involved failure to heed a warning, although it concerned more than simple inattention. It was likely attributable both to the plaintiff's physical disability and failure to exercise common sense, as well as to some surprisingly callous behavior by the railroad.

On January 27, 1883, the plaintiff, George O. Kennedy, began walking down the defendant railroad company's track between Dawson's switch station and Dome Rock.[17] He was partly deaf, but was physically and mentally in very good health. He had walked this stretch of track many times before. When he entered on the track at Dawson's switch station, Kennedy looked for trains and saw none; so, he began walking the track.

At the location where the train struck him, there was an unobstructed view for 900 feet behind Kennedy. The train was equipped with air brakes, and could have stopped at a distance of 125 to 150 feet; but the train did not stop. Instead, the engineer blew its whistle six times in short blasts, and gave one long, final seventh blast. Kennedy failed to heed the warning and was struck down by the train and seriously injured (but not killed). The district court granted a non-suit in favor of the railroad, on the basis of Kennedy's contributory negligence in trespassing and walking the track.

On appeal, Kennedy challenged the exclusion of certain evidence that cast a very different light on the occurrence. He contended the evidence, had it been considered, would have shown gross negligence or wanton conduct on the part of the railroad, sufficient to defeat its contributory negligence defense. According to Kennedy's son, on the day of the injury, he approached the conductor of the train and told him that his father had started walking the track to Dome Rock about five or ten minutes earlier and was partially deaf. He asked the conductor to watch out for his father and not to run him over. The conductor callously replied, "[I]f [his father] was deaf, he had no business on the

The conductor had retired to the caboose when the train struck
George Kennedy
Darlene Johnson

track, and would get killed or run over."[18] The conductor then retired
to the train's caboose, apparently without warning the engineer that
there was a partially deaf man walking the track.

Later, after the train struck Kennedy and he was taken to the station
in serious condition, the conductor showed almost psychopathic lack
of feeling, telling a witness at the station that he had "caught that
man."[19] The Colorado Supreme Court did not find this evidence sufficient to demonstrate gross negligence or wanton conduct; in fact, it
opined that "the train was operated with the care required, under all

the circumstances."[20] The Court therefore affirmed the dismissal of the plaintiff's complaint.

Justice Beck dissented. He did not find Kennedy's contributory negligence nearly as serious as the majority did, nor was he quite so willing to excuse the railroad's misconduct. Justice Beck noted that the reason Kennedy did not make inquiry concerning timetables for the railroad's trains was because he found no one at Dawson's switch to ask. While walking the track, Kennedy stepped off the track whenever he could, and he always looked for trains when he stepped back onto it. He had walked this section of the track before, and heard the train whistle on those occasions; he did not realize how badly his hearing had deteriorated. These factors might not have mattered in isolation; however, when coupled with the fact that the railroad's employees knew Kennedy was hard of hearing and was walking the track, Justice Beck felt that something more was required of them than just blowing the whistle before running him over.

STOP, LOOK, AND LISTEN — BEHRENS v. KANSAS PACIFIC RAILWAY CO. (1880)

Justice Beck had reached a different conclusion seven years earlier, in a case that also involved a train striking an unwary pedestrian.[21] Behrens worked for the Kansas Pacific Railway as a repair hand in its track yard. At about 10:00 in the morning on the day of the accident, his foreman ordered him to carry some blocks of wood from the south side of the track to its north side. That morning, an engine had been passing up and down the section of track Behrens would be crossing, switching cars in the yard.

Behrens picked up a block of wood that was approximately six or seven feet long, twelve inches wide, and six inches thick, and slung it over his left shoulder. Held in this manner, the wooden block obstructed his view of the track leading to the train depot. To make matters worse, Behrens did not look to see whether the engine was coming before he crossed the track.

As he was crossing the track, the engine came chugging along at ten miles per hour from the direction of the depot, with several cars attached. This violated protocol in at least two ways. First, when running a train inside the rail yard, the rate of speed allowed was only six miles per hour. Second, when passing men working on the track, the engineer was supposed to ring the bell to alert them; this time, he didn't.

According to the plaintiff's testimony, he "neither saw nor heard the train until he was struck, although his eyesight and hearing were both good."[22] Had Behrens looked down the track, he would have seen the train. The track was level and straight for about 1,000 feet between where he was working and the depot. Because he did not look, the train hit him.

Behrens sued the railroad for damages from his accident. The district court granted the railroad's motion for a non-suit. On appeal, Behrens argued that the railroad's negligence was a factual question that should have been submitted to the jury. The court of appeals rejected this argument. The focus, it said, should not be on the railroad's negligence, but on the plaintiff's own opportunity to have avoided the accident. The court stated: "[I]f a plaintiff so circumstanced might have avoided the injury by the exercise of ordinary care, he cannot recover, though the defendant was negligent."[23] Here, the accident was the result of Behren's "mere inattention and carelessness."[24] His conduct, not the railroad's, was the proximate cause of his accident. The Colorado Supreme Court affirmed the non-suit in favor of the railroad.

DISTURBING WORDS – BURLINGTON & MISSOURI RIVER RAILROAD *v. BUDIN* (1895)

The last case does not involve carelessness by the plaintiff, but by his distracted co-employee. James Budin was a workman on the Burlington and Missouri River Railroad. He and three other laborers were lifting a heavy steel rail to carry it across the main rail to a switch they were installing. Two men carried each end of the rail. When they reached their destination, the men at the opposite end of the rail from

Budin suddenly dropped their end. This caused Budin and his partner to drop their end. The rail struck Budin's "great toe . . . crushing it, and also inflicting some lesser injuries upon some of its fellows."[25]

Why did the men drop their end of the heavy steel rail? The explanation that Budin presented at trial was rather unusual. He elicited testimony from one of the men who dropped the rail, who blamed their unsafe conduct on mental upset and distraction. However, this distraction was not caused by something that happened when they were carrying the rail; it was caused by events that had transpired nearly a half-hour earlier.

The disturbing events involved their road master, a man named McDonald. Like many railroad bosses in those days, McDonald had a tendency to be "rather boisterous" and "rushed or hurried the work."[26] This led to an argument with a workman named Shinwall. Apparently, McDonald and Shinwall used some strong language with each other — very strong language. Although "the language was not shown in evidence," feelings ran so high that Shinwall either quit or was discharged on the spot.[27]

The strong language so traumatized the onlooking workmen that its "paralyzing effect lasted for nearly half an hour after the altercation ended."[28] Its "mental effect remained, incapacitating even the hearers." It was Budin's theory that this mental anguish and distraction caused them to drop the rail.[29]

One cannot help suspect this interpretation of the facts was designed to circumvent the "fellow servant rule."[30] It shifted the blame for the accident from Budin's clumsy co-workers to his supervisor McDonald and his intemperate language — and hence, by the legal theory of *respondeat superior*, to the railroad. Had Budin's co-workers been solely responsible for dropping the rail, Budin would not have been entitled to any compensation from his employer.

A jury awarded Budin $200 for his injuries; however, the court of appeals found his theory that foul language was the proximate cause of the accident less than convincing. The supervisor's conduct, it said, was simply too remote from the injury to establish causation. The court therefore reversed the jury's verdict in favor of Budin.

CONCLUSION

Legal cases before 1900 show that long before the digital age, distractions contributed to unfortunate accidents. Whether the distraction was considered the proximate cause of the accident depended heavily on the facts of each case.

Original printing: *The Colorado Lawyer*, March 2010. The author is grateful for the research assistance of Dan Cordova and Lynn Christian of the Colorado Supreme Court Law Library.

NOTES

1. CRS § 42-4-239(1)(d)(3).

2. CRS § 42-4-239(1)(d)(2). An exception is made for emergencies or for drivers who are contacting public safety entities.

3. *See* Mello, Jr., "Road Texting: An Accident Waiting to Happen," Tech-NewsWorld (Aug. 8, 2007), available at www.technewsworld.com/story/58714.html. The results of the 2007 Harris Interactive poll also revealed that 57 percent of those surveyed admitted to texting while driving, and 66 percent of drivers surveyed had read text messages while behind the wheel. Further information about this survey is available from the author.

4. *Id.*

5. This phenomenon is sometimes referred to as "highway hypnosis" or "white-line fever." *See* en.wikipedia.org/wiki/Highway_hypnosis.

6. "L.A. Train Engineer Was Texting Before Fatal Crash," Associated Press (Sept. 18, 2008), available at www.foxnews.com/story/0,2933,424344,00.html.

7. Hosenball, "Flight 188: Pilots 'Distracted by Their Laptops,'" *Newsweek* (Oct. 26, 2009), available at blog.newsweek.com, type in "Flight 188."

8. *See* Klingberg, *The Overflowing Brain: Information Overload and the Limits of Working Memory* (Oxford Univ. Press, 2008).

9. *City of Denver v. Peterson*, 36 P. 1111, 1112 (Colo.App. 1894).

10. According to Drake and Rhode's history of American steamrollers, the appearance of a steamroller on city streets was at one time cause for excitement and celebration. This was the era when construction of paved roads was a feature of civic pride. In their book, the authors include a photograph of a

1918 parade in Denver featuring four steamrollers moving north on Broadway past the State Capitol Building. Drake and Rhode, *Classic American Steam Rollers, 1871–1935* at 5 (Iconografix, 2001).

11. *Peterson, supra* note 9 at 1112.

12. *Id.*

13. *Id.*

14. *Id.* at 1113.

15. *Id.* at 1114.

16. *Kennedy v. Denver S. Park & Pac. R.R. Co.*, 16 P. 210 (Colo. 1887).

17. The Dome Rock station, in unincorporated Jefferson County near Buffalo Creek, served as a combination depot and living quarters, www.co.jefferson.co.us, type in "Dome Rock Station." It operated until no later than 1938, when the South Park railroad line was discontinued. *See also* www.fs.fed.us/r2/psicc/recreation/trails/spl_colorado_trail_seg2.shtml, type in "South Park Railroad."

18. *Kennedy, supra* note 16 at 211.

19. *Id.*

20. *Id.* at 212.

21. *Behrens v. Kansas Pac. Ry. Co.*, 5 Colo. 400 (1880).

22. *Id.* at 402.

23. *Id.* at 403.

24. *Id.*

25. *Burlington & Mo. River Ry. v. Budin*, 40 P. 503, 504 (Colo.App. 1895).

26. *Id.*

27. *Id.*

28. *Id.*

29. *Id.*

30. The "fellow servant rule" provided that an employer was not liable for injury to an employee caused by the negligence of his fellow employees. *See, e.g., Denver & R.G.R. Co. v. Sipes*, 47 P. 287, 288 (Colo. 1896). It eventually was abolished in connection with the adoption of the workers' compensation laws. *See Jacobson v. Doan*, 319 P.2d 975, 981 (Colo. 1957) (quotation omitted).

From the Outhouse to the Courthouse
Keeping a Privy Private

BY FRANK GIBBARD

The settling of the American West coincided with a revolution in household plumbing technology. During the 1840s, the decade when the trickle of westbound settlers became a flood, and the railroad boom helped open the West to development, indoor plumbing with "running water and water fixtures entered homes of people in a broad spectrum of incomes."[1] These new plumbing fixtures in homes and in businesses required an extensive infrastructure to provide water for domestic uses and to carry away household waste. Americans rose to the challenge, and by the turn of the century and the closing of the frontier, "most urban dwellers, regardless of the size of their city, were enjoying the benefits of underground sewerage."[2]

In rural regions of the American West, however, outhouses remained ubiquitous well into the 20th Century. These outhouses were only gradually replaced by indoor plumbing, and some of them are still in use today. Outhouses, which are stand-alone wooden structures without running water, pipes, or fixtures, are inconsistent with municipal sewerage systems, which rely on water flow to operate. For this reason, the Colorado Legislature eventually gave cities the power to promote uniformity and to improve sanitation by prohibiting outhouses within sewer district boundaries. This statutory scheme, based on the incompatibility of outhouses and modern municipal plumbing, was challenged when the City of Fort Collins enacted an ordinance that led to one of the more unique prosecutions in Colorado history.

AN UNUSUAL ORDINANCE

In 1907, the Colorado Legislature passed a statute permitting smaller cities in Colorado to create municipal sewer systems. Cities were permitted to regulate and control the disposal of sewage in four ways:

1) by dividing the city into sewer districts;

2) by compelling the owners of buildings within the district or abutting established sewers to connect with the sewers;

3) by prohibiting the maintenance of outhouses within the sewer district or within 400 feet of an established sewer; and

4) by regulating "the construction, maintenance, and use of all vaults, closets, privies, and cesspools within the city limits not within the prohibited districts or proximity of any established sewer."[3]

Purportedly relying on these powers, the City of Fort Collins (City) passed an ordinance that managed to merge its ability to require sewer hookup with its ability to prohibit outhouses within a sewer district. The ordinance required that:

> Every vault or privy in, upon, or belonging to any residence, factory, mill, warehouse, outhouse, store, office or other building . . . be connected by the owner or owners of such property . . . with [the] public or district sanitary sewer.[4]

It is not clear exactly how this law was supposed to operate. Outhouses function by force of gravity, composting, and the use of landfill rather than by water-flushing. They do not ordinarily contain running water or pipes that would permit them to connect with a municipal

Outhouse still in existence in Weld County
Ellen Buckley

sewer;[5] however, that is what the ordinance required. Things soon came to a head (so to speak) when the City cited John H. Gault for maintaining an unconnected outhouse, in violation of the ordinance.

Who Was John Gault?

John H. Gault owned a vacant lot inside the Fort Collins city limits. His lot adjoined streets and alleys through which the municipal sewer system ran. At the back end of his lot, near the alley, stood the outhouse.

Although he later contended that the City gave him no notice that he would be required to connect with the sewer, Gault must have known the City was unhappy with his structure. Even before legal action began, he "offered to remove the privy if given a reasonable time, and a few days afterwards cleaned it out, filled up the vault with dirt, and nailed a board over the seat."[6] This did not keep the City from issuing him a summons to police magistrate's court, where he was convicted of violating the ordinance.

Gault appealed to county court. Here, he would be permitted to explain his circumstances to a jury — or so he thought.

THE JURY TRIAL

Gault's appeal was heard in Larimer County Court before Hon. Fred W. Stover and involved a *de novo* trial to a jury.[7] However, whether Gault received a fair trial is questionable. Judge Stover excluded any evidence of the fact that the privy stood on a vacant lot, its distance from the nearest habitation, and the frequency of its use. He also directed a verdict for the prosecution. After the prosecution rested, the judge gave the jury this single instruction:

> Gentlemen of the jury, you are instructed by the court to find the defendant in this action guilty as charged, and you are to fix his fine at such an amount, not exceeding the sum of one hundred ($100) dollars as in your judgment would seem fit and proper for the violation of this ordinance, under the circumstances set forth in the evidence.[8]

The jury was understandably perplexed. It retired to deliberate, but later returned to the courtroom, where the foreman told Judge Stover:

> I am up against a proposition. Now we don't understand whether we are bound by the instructions of the court to find the defendant guilty.[9]

The court responded:

> Those are the instructions you are to follow. The amount of fine is for
> the jury to fix, but as to the question of guilt you must follow the in-
> structions of the court.[10]

The jury again retired, and returned a verdict of guilty, fixing Gault's
fine at a nominal one dollar.

SUPREME COURT APPEAL

Gault appealed to the Colorado Supreme Court. The Court found the
Fort Collins ordinance inconsistent with the powers granted in the
statute:

> The power . . . conferred by statute is to compel owners of buildings to
> connect them with the sewer. No power is given to compel parties to
> connect outside vaults or privies with the sewer.[11]

The Court explained that the statute did not give the City "power
to compel one to connect an outside or open privy or vault with the
sewer, who does not desire to make the connection."[12] If the privy was
a public nuisance, the City could abate it — that is, require the owner
to remove or abolish it — but that was the extent of its powers. Finally,
the Court held that the district court "was mistaken in holding as a
matter of law that, merely because the privy was not connected with
the sewer, the evidence sustained the demand and defendant was
guilty of violating the ordinance."[13] Given this mistake, Gault's conviction was reversed.

PETITION FOR REHEARING

The Supreme Court's opinion left one nagging question unanswered:
If the state statute on which the City had relied was passed in 1907, and
the City's ordinance was enacted in 1905, how could the City have relied on a statute that did not yet exist? Though the Court's opinion

noted the years in which the statute and the ordinance were passed, it did not mention the temporal inconsistency.

The City, however, hired a new attorney and filed a petition for rehearing, raising exactly this point. The City's new counsel contended that the City could not have relied on the 1907 statute. He argued that it had instead relied on several 19th Century Colorado statutes governing public health, the abatement of nuisances, and the maintenance of public sewer systems.

The Court was unimpressed by this argument. It noted that under the first statute newly cited:

> No power is given the city here by ordinance to compel a privy like this to be connected with the sewer. More than this, [Gault] is not charged with violating rules and regulations of the board of health of the city of Ft. Collins in this regard. He is charged with failing to connect a building in a sewer district with the sewer.[14]

Moreover, none of the other statutes could justify an ordinance requiring the owner of an outdoor privy on a vacant lot to connect to the municipal sewer system. Accordingly, the Court upheld its earlier decision reversing Gault's conviction.

CONCLUSION

The move to indoor plumbing represented an important development in improving sanitation and comfort for most Americans. As with any technological improvement, however, it took time to move completely from the old system to the new. The City of Fort Collins attempted to bridge the gap by enacting a statute, but the legislation made little sense in light of the new paradigm. It took an unjust prosecution to expose this unworkable approach.

Original printing: *The Colorado Lawyer*, May 2010. The author is grateful for the research assistance of Dan Cordova and Lynn Christian of the Colorado Supreme Court Law Library.

NOTES

1. Ogle, *All the Modern Conveniences: American Household Plumbing, 1840–1890* (Johns Hopkins Univ. Press, 1999) at 8.

2. *Id.* at 96.

3. *Gault v. City of Fort Collins*, 142 P. 171, 172 (Colo. 1914) (summarizing CRS § 6564 (1908)).

4. Fort Collins Ordinance No. 13, § 20 (1905) (quoted in *Gault, supra* note 3 at 172).

5. *See* en.wikipedia.org/wiki/Outhouse ("An important feature which distinguishes an outhouse from other forms of toilets is the lack of connection to plumbing, sewer, or septic system").

6. *Gault, supra* note 3 at 173.

7. Judge Stover was a Fort Collins native, born on September 25, 1878. He graduated from the University of Denver Law School in 1904 and served as a judge in Larimer County Court from 1907 to 1917. Lewis and Stackelbeck, *Bench and Bar of Colorado* 176 (Bench and Bar Publishing Co., 1917).

8. *Gault, supra* note 3 at 172.

9. *Id.*

10. *Id.*

11. *Id.*

12. *Id.* at 173.

13. *Id.*

14. *Id.* at 174.

X

NIGHTMARES AND TRAGEDIES

INTRODUCTION

Colorado's early pioneers faced a level of hardship and suffering unknown in today's more technologically advanced society. Life expectancy was then around forty-eight years, less than two-thirds of what it is now. The cost of basic goods such as foodstuffs was outrageously high, reaching fifteen dollars a bushel for potatoes and forty dollars for a hundred pounds of flour in the mining camps at a time when miners were paid three dollars a day. Medical care, when available, was lamentably primitive. Working conditions were also often appalling, with mining, smelting, and railroad accidents an all-too-common phenomenon. There was no system of worker's compensation.

Arid conditions west of the 100th Meridian posed challenges unknown to farmers in more humid climes. Without irrigation, farmers struggled to bring in a profitable crop. To make things worse, a severe drought in the late 1880s and 1890s drove all but the most determined prairie farmers out of business. As if these early sod-busters did not face enough of a challenge from an arid climate and primitive living conditions, they also had to contend with a plague of Biblical proportions: a swarm of grasshoppers known as Rocky Mountain locusts that devastated farming regions west of the Mississippi during the years 1874 to 1877. The swarm, estimated at 12.5 trillion insects weighing 27.5 million tons, blackened the skies over several western states and destroyed nearly 50 percent of the harvest during the worst years of the infestation.

Settlers also found themselves at war with the region's original inhabitants, Native Americans chiefly of the Cheyenne and Arapaho tribes. As in other parts of the West, the history of interactions between settlers and the tribes is a story of misunderstandings, broken treaties, massacres, and ultimately, displacement. Things came to a head during the so-called "Colorado War" of 1863 to 1865, fought between settler militias and the United States Army on one side, and members of the Kiowa, Comanche, Arapaho, and Cheyenne tribes on the other. This period included the notorious Sand Creek Massacre in 1864. It culminated in the removal of the remaining Native Americans other than the Utes from Colorado to Indian Territory (the area that later became the state of Oklahoma).

Early in its history, Denver suffered from both fire and flood. The fire came on April 19, 1863, when a party-goer at the Cherokee House at 15th and Blake Streets kicked over a fire box in the wee hours of the morning. The resulting blaze soon swallowed the Cherokee House building. The flames were quickly carried by high winds to the other wooden structures nearby. In all, by the time it died down, the fire had destroyed seventy buildings comprising half a dozen blocks of downtown Denver. This cloud had a silver lining, however, as it resulted in Denver and other nearby municipalities enacting codes requiring brick buildings, many of which buildings still exist today.

The flood came a year later, when Cherry Creek overflowed its banks during a particularly damp spring. Native Americans and mountain men supposedly had warned the residents of Denver not to build so close to the creek. These warnings went unheeded. Then, in May 1864, after a torrential downpour, the Creek overflowed its banks and a flood covered much of the City of Denver in five feet of water. Among other things, the printing press for the *Rocky Mountain News* was swept away by the current and only found years later, buried under a dozen feet of mud.

As noted, medical care on the frontier was nothing to write home about. Unsanitary conditions led to outbreaks of diseases such as typhus and cholera. Gradually, medical talent made its way to the state and Colorado established a State Board of Medical Examiners in 1881. But a third of the places on the Board were reserved for homeopathic and eclectic practitioners, practitioners who would not even be considered doctors by most licensed physicians today.

Not that the allopathic doctors were much better in those days. During the first half of the 19th Century, doctors were still blistering, bleeding, and purging their patients. It is no wonder that settlers not only relied on alternative medicine but also made heavy use of home remedies, and even borrowed some medicinal knowledge from Native American sources.

For those who succumbed to illness, accident, or natural disaster, there were plenty of pioneer cemeteries in the state to accommodate them. Settlers who died here could and did also have their remains shipped back East for burial in the family plot. The methods used to preserve the body for shipment by rail were often crude. Embalming was virtually unknown until after the Civil War. Early embalming relied on toxic substances like arsenic and mercury to keep the cadaver from decomposing until it arrived at its destination. Because of this, leaching of hazardous materials from early cemeteries is even today considered a threat to local watersheds. The possibility of unwanted supernatural activity may be the least worrisome effect of failing to remove bodies from abandoned burial grounds.

FOR FURTHER READING

Steele, *Bleed, Blister & Purge: A History of Medicine on the American Frontier* (Missoula, MT: Mountain Press Pub. Co. 2005).

Jeffrey A. Lockwood, *Locust: The Devastating Rise and Mysterious Disappearance of the Insect That Shaped the American Frontier* (New York, NY: Basic Books 2005).

Iserson, *Death to Dust* (Tucson, AZ: Galen Press 1994).

Shikes, *Rocky Mountain Medicine: Doctors, Drugs, and Disease in Early Colorado* (Boulder, CO: Johnson Books 1986).

Consequential Damages That Decomposed on Appeal
A Mortifying Experience

BY FRANK GIBBARD

Before the Civil War, Americans rarely embalmed their dead. Americans of the 19th Century viewed embalming of corpses as something exotic, a custom of the ancient Egyptians rather than of the modern world.[1] If preservation was needed prior to burial, ice sometimes was used to slow decomposition.[2]

The Civil War changed all that. Families who wanted to have their sons returned from distant battlefields for burial began to hire embalming surgeons to preserve them.[3] By the early 1880s, building on experience gained in the war, embalmers developed safe and relatively simple methods of embalming. The improved methods came into general use for cadavers transported, often by railway, for burial. By the 1920s, almost all dead bodies were embalmed.[4]

BOARD OF EMBALMING EXAMINERS

In 1913, prompted by concerns about the spread of infectious diseases from improperly embalmed or preserved bodies, the Colorado State Board of Embalming Examiners was founded.[5] The Board was empowered to examine and license embalmers[6] and to revoke licenses for "gross incompetency, dishonesty, habitual intemperance, or any act derogatory to the morals or standing of the practice of embalming."[7] As it happened, 1913 also was the year in which the Colorado Court of Appeals decided *Hall v. Jackson*,[8] a case that underlined the concern about the need for uniformity and competency in embalming practices.[9]

THE *HALL v.* JACKSON CASE

It would be difficult to improve on the summary of the trial facts contained in the Colorado Court of Appeals' opinion in *Hall*.[10] The court stated:

> [The evidence showed that defendant, an experienced undertaker,] agreed and undertook to properly prepare for shipment to Pennsylvania the body of . . . Charles D. Jackson, and notwithstanding the body was shipped by the most direct route from Denver to its destination in Pennsylvania, it arrived there in an advanced state of decomposition; that the odor arising from the body contained in the casket was so offensive and disagreeable that it became necessary to leave the casket in the open air near the house while the funeral ceremonies were being conducted therein; that the ceremonies were attended by 75 or 100 friends, but the remains could not be viewed, owing to the bad condition of the body; that mortification was due to the negligent and unskillful manner in which the body was prepared for shipment by the defendant, by reason of which plaintiff suffered great and trying mental anguish, humiliation, and distress of mind.[11]

The regrettably putrid Mr. Jackson, who had the misfortune of perishing in a streetcar accident, then of being subjected to an autopsy,[12] was not even permitted to "attend" his own funeral.

It was Mrs. Jackson, however, who truly was mortified. For her mental anguish, occasioned by the defendant's negligence in failing to carry out the terms of their contract, the jury awarded Mrs. Jackson $1,000. The defendant undertaker appealed.

Contractual Damages for Mental Anguish

In addressing the award, the court of appeals was faced with a dilemma, which arose from the way Mrs. Jackson had pled her case. Given her contractual relationship with the undertaker, Jackson had proceeded in contract, rather than tort. The only damages she sought were for mental anguish, distress, and humiliation due to the breach. Were such damages available in an action *ex contractu*?[13] The court of appeals concluded they were not.

Analyzing prior cases involving tort and contract claims based on mental anguish, the court discerned a system of triage. In a pure tort case, with no contractual relationship between the parties, damages were available for mental anguish, even absent a physical injury or a pecuniary loss.[14] In cases where a breach of contract was alleged, the plaintiff still could recover for mental suffering, provided that the acts relating to the breach involved "willful, insulting, or wanton conduct."[15]

In cases where a mere passive breach of contract was alleged, however, and where the defendant was not engaged in a business of a "quasi public nature" and the breach was not accompanied by any wanton, willful, or insulting act by the breaching party, compensatory damages would be unavailable for mental anguish and suffering.[16] The court of appeals found that Mrs. Jackson's allegations fell into the third category, requiring it to vacate the award of substantial compensatory damages, and remand for an award of nominal damages for breach of contract.[17]

Fate of the Hall Case

Hall was overruled in part in 1978, by the *en banc* Colorado Supreme Court. The Court concluded that there was no requirement in a negligent infliction of emotional distress claim that the plaintiff show that he had been physically injured or impacted at the scene of the accident.[18] However, the Court later reaffirmed *Hall*'s adoption of a "willful and wanton" rule for non-economic damages in contract cases.[19]

CURRENT REGULATORY ENVIRONMENT

Embalming practices are only a small part of the practices regulated today by Colorado's Mortuary Science Code, which governs many aspects of the treatment of dead bodies.[20] Among other things, the Code requires that all dead human bodies kept more than twenty-four hours after death be properly embalmed or refrigerated.[21] Bodies of suspected crime victims, however, may not be embalmed without the permission of a coroner, deputy coroner, or district attorney.[22]

CONCLUSION

Care of the dead is a significant acknowledgment of the value of human life, more so because the one whose remains are cared for can do nothing to thank the person providing the care or reciprocate the gesture. The true beneficiaries of funeral rites are the deceased's living loved ones. Failure to honor the dignity of the departed may represent a betrayal of the deceased's reasonable expectations, which may not adequately be compensated through the legal system.

Original printing: January 2007. The author thanks Daniel B. Cordova for research assistance with this article.

NOTES

1. Iserson, *Death to Dust* (Tucson, AZ: Galen Press, 1994) at 186.

2. *See id.* This led to the expression "to put someone on ice," referring to a murder.

3. *See, e.g.,* the excellent discussion of this topic at www.historynet.com/magazines/american_civil_war/3034086.html (last visited Oct. 31, 2006).

4. Iserson, *supra* note 1 at 187.

5. *See* Colorado Dep't of Regulatory Agencies, Office of Policy Research, "Funeral Service Practitioners 2002 Sunrise Review" (Oct. 15, 2002) at 12, available at http://www.dora.state.co.us/OPR/archive/2002FuneralService PractitionersSunrise.

6. Colo. Laws 1913 at 270, § 3, *reprinted* in Cortright's Colo. Stats. § 5029-C (1914 ed., 1913 supp.).

7. Colo. Laws 1913 at 271, § 6, *reprinted* in Cortright's Colo. Stats. § 5029-F (1914 ed., 1913 supp.).

8. *Hall v. Jackson*, 24 Colo.App. 225, 134 P. 151 (Ct.App. 1913).

9. For an annotation containing several cases on this rather morbid topic, *see* Brazener, *Civil Liability of Undertaker in Connection with Embalming or Preparation of Body for Burial*, Annot., 48 A.L.R. 3d 261 (1973).

10. *Hall, supra* note 8.

11. *Id.* at 226–27, 134 P. at 151–52.

12. *Id.* at 226, 134 P. at 151.

13. The court of appeals phrased the issue this way:

> Will an action lie for breach of contract against a defendant not engaged in business of a quasi public nature to recover substantial damages, founded only upon mental anguish, humiliation, and distress of mind, where the breach is unattended by physical injury to the party bringing the action, and where there is an absence of wanton or willful conduct on the part of the one violating the contract?

Id. at 227, 134 P. at 152.

14. *Id.* at 228, 134 P. at 152.

15. *Id.*

16. *Id.*

17. *Id.* at 237-38, 134 P. at 155-56.

18. *Towns v. Anderson*, 195 Colo. 517, 579 P.2d 1163 (Colo. 1978) (*en banc*).

19. *Giampapa v. Am. Family Mut. Ins. Co.*, 64 P.3d 230, 238–41 (Colo. 2003) (*en banc*).

20. CRS §§ 12-54-101 to -109.

21. CRS § 12-54-105.

22. CRS § 12-54-104(a).

Healer or Slayer?
A Case of Cyanide Poisoning

BY FRANK GIBBARD

In 1880, at the height of Colorado's "silver boom," a consortium of British investors known as the Denver Mansion Company, Ltd., constructed the Windsor Hotel at the corner of 18th and Larimer Streets. The Windsor soon earned a reputation as one of Denver's grandest hotels. Guests admired its spacious lobby filled with sumptuous statuary and artwork, gilded pillars, and diamond dust mirrors. When in session, the Colorado Legislature assembled informally at the Windsor's extravagantly furnished bar to conduct business.[1]

Over the next eighty years, the Windsor experienced cycles of decline and renewed popularity. Silver "King" Horace Tabor died in relative poverty in his room there in 1899.[2] The hotel spent most of the 1920s and 1930s as a flophouse[3] before being renovated and restored to some of its former grandeur in 1938. By the time it was torn down in 1959, the Windsor had hosted the famous and the infamous, including Horace Tabor's wife "Baby Doe"; former U.S. President Ulysses S. Grant; con artist Jefferson Randolph "Soapy" Smith[4]; and lawman and gunman Tom Horn.[5] Writers Oscar Wilde and Jack Kerouac also spent time there.

Like many old hotels, the Windsor had its share of ghosts and dark tales.[6] One such tale unfolded on March 14, 1892, on the hotel's fifth floor. What transpired in Room 519 was not only shocking and tragic

— it sparked a twelve-year course of litigation that included two jury trials and two appellate decisions.

ROOM 519

At about 3:00 on the afternoon of March 14, 1892, Denver businessman Adolph Schayer arrived on the fifth and highest floor of the Windsor Hotel. He did not know it yet, but he was already too late. He knocked on the door to Room 519. No one answered. The room was locked from the inside.

Schayer was deeply worried. An hour earlier, his close friend Jacob Boehm, a partner in the respected Denver firm of Boehm & Co., had come to the hotel alone to rent a room. When he left Schayer earlier, Boehm had been visibly distressed by a business reversal. He was not a habitué of the Windsor Hotel; this was his first stay there, in fact. When checking in, he told the hotel clerk that he needed a room where he could lie down.

When there was no response to his knocks, Schayer solicited the assistance of a boy who happened to be passing by, and boosted him through the transom. The boy unlocked the room from the inside.

A Ghastly Scene

Inside the room, Schayer was stunned by what he saw. Boehm's corpse lay on the bed, flat on his back. His head was thrown back at a 45-degree angle. His mouth was open, his eyes were partially open, and his body was still warm. His fingernails were blue. He had removed his shoes and his coat, unbuttoned his vest and shirt collar, and untied his necktie.

In Boehm's vest pocket, Schayer found a one-ounce vial labeled "Sol. Cyanide of Potassium." The label bore the name of a druggist, Neil Dahl. Later, testimony would show that Boehm had obtained the bottle of cyanide from his family physician, Dr. Muir.

Schayer also found a tumbler with a brownish liquid in it, the same color as the liquid in the vial. In an act of courage, or perhaps foolhar-

A fatal dose of cyanide led to a twelve-year court battle
Katherine Haas

diness, Schayer smelled and tasted the liquid in the glass, which he found was like bitter almonds. Other witnesses also described the bitter almond smell. The undertaker later stated that he also detected the smell on Boehm's lips.

Testimony would show that the smell of bitter almonds is consistent with cyanide. Testimony also would show that Boehm knew that potassium cyanide is a deadly poison.

THE INSURANCE POLICY

On October 23, 1891, about six months before his death, Boehm had purchased a life insurance policy in the amount of $30,000 with the Germania Life Insurance Company of New York (Germania). He assigned the policy to his creditor, the First National Bank of Denver (Bank), naming George E. Ross-Lewin as trustee. After Boehm's death, Ross-Lewin and the Bank demanded payment on the policy. Germania refused to pay, citing a provision of the policy that absolved it of liability if, within three years of issuance, the insured died by suicide.

ROSS-LEWIN SUES GERMANIA

Ross-Lewin and the Bank sued Germania to recover on the policy. Germania answered that recovery was barred, because Boehm had killed himself. The only real question was whether Germania had presented sufficient evidence of suicide to go to a jury. After Germania presented its case, the district court decided it had not, and entered a directed verdict for the plaintiffs. Germania appealed.

FIRST APPEAL – TO THE COLORADO SUPREME COURT

The two appellate decisions in the Ross-Lewin case make for interesting reading. The Colorado Supreme Court's decision in 1897[7] does not mention many of the facts that the Colorado Court of Appeals found crucial to its decision in 1904. It is not clear whether the Supreme Court ignored facts that would have undermined its decision, or whether these facts did not surface until after the second trial. It seems unlikely, however, that many of the facts in favor of Ross-Lewin that the Colorado Court of Appeals described in its decision were unavailable to the Colorado Supreme Court, given the district court's directed verdict in favor of Ross-Lewin.

The issue in both appeals, stripped to its essentials, was the same: could the evidence support a verdict that Boehm committed suicide? The two courts reached opposite results.

Strange Behavior at the Arcade Restaurant

The evidence discussed by the Supreme Court showed that Schayer's concern for his friend began several hours before he discovered the body in Room 519. Around noon on March 14, Schayer, Boehm, and a man identified only as Mr. Farmer dined at the Arcade Restaurant on Larimer Street. After the three men sat down at the table, Boehm ate some soup and then suddenly excused himself, saying he needed to telephone his partner, Mr. Steinbok, to let him know where he was. When he returned from the telephone call, Boehm appeared pale and agitated. He told his friends he no longer wanted to eat and that he wanted to leave instead. The other men said they would leave with him.

When they left the restaurant, the three men stopped at a cigar stand, where Boehm purchased cigars for himself and his two friends. Boehm told Schayer he wanted to speak to him alone about some business. The two men separated from Farmer, and walked along Larimer Street, toward Boehm's store.

Boehm's Last Encounters

As they walked, Boehm became very agitated. "Adolph," he told his friend, "they have got me; the sheriff is in possession of the place now."[8] "My God," he continued, "I didn't think George would do it!"[9]

Schayer asked what he was talking about. Boehm explained that the First National Bank of Denver had seized the assets of Boehm & Co. under a writ of attachment. Boehm then stopped on the sidewalk and said, "Adolph, I want you to promise me one thing. I want you to be as good a friend to my wife as you have been to me."[10]

Boehm's words alarmed Schayer. He became so concerned that he decided to search his friend right there on the sidewalk. It is not clear what he was looking for. Perhaps he thought Boehm had a gun. He ran his hands over Boehm's hip pockets and searched his clothes, but found nothing.

Schayer resolved to stay with his friend until the crisis passed. However, when they reached the Boehm & Co. store, Boehm entered without him. While Boehm was inside the store, Schayer made a brief but fateful trip to the office of a nearby doctor. When he returned to Boehm & Co., Boehm was gone.

Testimony later showed that while Schayer was visiting the doctor, Boehm met with his attorney, Earl B. Coe. It is not known what they discussed. Coe left Boehm, going first to his own office, then to Boehm's residence. The two men separated around 2:00 p.m. It was the last time Coe saw Boehm alive.

Somehow, Schayer figured out that Boehm had gone to the Windsor Hotel. He traveled to the hotel to find his friend. The hotel's register indicated that Boehm had checked into Room 519.

Supreme Court's Decision

The Colorado Supreme Court faced two significant issues in the insurance company's appeal. First, Germania contended that the trial court had erred in excluding the coroner's verdict ruling Boehm's death a suicide.[11] The Supreme Court upheld the trial court's decision excluding the coroner's verdict. The Court held that a coroner's verdict should not be admitted for the purpose of proving suicide, because "the purpose of inquisitions of this character is merely to furnish the foundation for a criminal prosecution in case the death is shown to be felonious."[12] The Court further noted that:

> [l]aw writers of late have frequently animadverted upon the carelessness with which such inquests are frequently conducted, and to allow inquisitions to be used in a suit between private parties growing out of the death of the deceased, as in this case, would be to introduce an element of uncertainty into the practice, which, we think, would be contrary to public policy, and pernicious in the extreme[.][13]

The second assignment of error was more problematic. Germania had sought to introduce the testimony of a highly qualified expert witness, Dr. John T. Eskridge,[14] for the purpose of proving that Boehm's death was consistent with cyanide poisoning. The district court excluded the testimony, because Dr. Eskridge "had no actual experience with poisoning from cyanide of potassium."[15] The Supreme Court held that the district court committed clear error by excluding this testimony. The district court's rule was impractical and unduly restrictive. The Court noted that:

> [n]ew poisons are constantly being discovered by scientists, and under the rule announced by the district court all inquiry as to the result of such new poisons upon the human system from experts would be excluded.[16]

If experts were permitted to testify only concerning the effect of known poisons with which they had actual experience, this "would offer a premium to the ingenuity of criminals and others in the selection of rare and unusual poisons to destroy human life."[17]

Given this error, the question arises as to whether the evidence in favor of the insurer was sufficient to require reversal of the directed verdict for the plaintiffs. The Supreme Court held that it was. Initially, this result may seem strange. The insurance company had a strong circumstantial case, even without Dr. Eskridge's testimony, that it was cyanide that killed Boehm. The real problem was whether Boehm took the cyanide intending to kill himself, or whether he died by accident or for some other reason.

The sufficiency of evidence on that issue was hardly discussed at all in the Supreme Court's analysis. The Court simply concluded:

> We are of the opinion that the evidence properly admitted, and that which was offered and erroneously refused, was sufficient to entitle the defendant to have the defense of suicide submitted to the jury; and although such plea, to prevail, must be established by clear and satisfactory evidence, it may, nevertheless, be so established by circumstantial evidence.[18]

Perhaps the insurer focused its appellate issues primarily on the question of exclusion of evidence rather than its sufficiency. In any event, it was an omission that would come back to haunt the case seven years later, requiring a second appellate decision.

SECOND APPEAL – TO THE
COLORADO COURT OF APPEALS

On remand, the district court held a jury trial. The jury reached a verdict for the insurer — that Boehm had committed suicide. This time, it was Ross-Lewin's turn to appeal.[19]

The court of appeals began its decision by summarizing the evidence presented at the second trial. Much of the evidence was identical to that described in the Supreme Court's previous decision. However, there were additional facts this time around that cast a whole new light on the case. These facts also help explain why the district court initially had directed a verdict in favor of Ross-Lewin.

Additional Evidence: The Prescription

The Supreme Court had noted that the cyanide vial in Boehm's pocket contained the name of a druggist. The court of appeals filled in additional details about how Boehm obtained the cyanide. It had been prescribed for Boehm by Dr. Meuer[20] and compounded by the druggist from the prescription, just four days before Boehm's death.

Additional Evidence:
Medical Uses of Cyanide

The Supreme Court had described cyanide as a deadly poison. The court of appeals noted that although potassium cyanide is a virulent poison, it is "sometimes prescribed by physicians as a medicine."[21] Dr. Meuer testified that "he had used cyanide of potassium as a medicine a good deal; that he had used it mainly for lung troubles; that it was also used for neuralgic troubles, and for diseases of the respiratory organs." He also testified that it could not cure disease and that he used it to provide temporary relief only.[22] A. J. Ward, who had filled the prescription for Boehm, testified that "retail druggists . . . used [cyanide] for medicinal purposes only."[23]

Additional Evidence Unfavorable to the Trustee

The court of appeals' decision includes additional evidence unfavorable to Ross-Lewin, suggesting that Boehm's death was in fact a suicide. There was testimony by Schayer, to which Ross-Lewin objected, that a month or six weeks before his death, Boehm asked Dr. Meuer for poison to put down a favorite dog. Dr. Meuer suggested potassium cyanide, which would result in a quick and painless death.

Earl B. Coe, Boehm's attorney, testified that when he met Boehm at Boehm's store, Coe was about to leave for Arizona. Boehm gave him a bottle of whiskey, saying "It is something to think of me on your trip."[24]

Court of Appeals' Decision

The issue that preoccupied the court of appeals was whether the jury should have been permitted to hear evidence about Boehm's conduct and statements before his death. The court noted that it was Germania's duty to prove that Boehm killed himself, and that there was a presumption against suicide. The mere fact that Boehm took cyanide was not enough to prove that he intended to kill himself, given the medical uses for that drug. The court concluded that Boehm's prior words and actions could be used against him only if they were parts of the *res gestae* — that is, parts of one continuous transaction that culminated in Boehm's ingestion of cyanide in accordance with his expressed intent to kill himself.

Surprisingly, the court concluded that under these facts, the required connection was absent. It gave two reasons: (1) the lapse of time between Boehm's statements and his ingestion of the poison; and (2) the lack of a clearly expressed intent to commit suicide. This reasoning is unexpected, given the traditional deference accorded to a jury's ability to draw inferences from the facts of a case. The court of appeals appeared to be saying that the presumption against suicide is so strong, and the evidence here so weak, that the jury should not be allowed to draw such an inference. It was the district court's duty, in fact, to exclude the evidence to prevent the inference from being drawn.

The court may have undermined its reasoning by its amateur attempt at psychoanalysis. On the issue of time lapse, for example, it opined:

> Mental agitation in the presence of financial disaster is not unusual. It is very rare to find a person who can preserve a serene countenance while his fortune is being swept away, and to assume that excited conduct or speech under the influence of temporary distraction produced by misfortune is in itself evidence of intention to commit suicide would contradict experience. As a rule, after the first shock has passed, a feeling of hope, inherent in man, asserts itself, and the impulse is towards efforts to retrieve the loss. Cases of suicide caused by the pressure of adverse circumstances are exceptional. If the language attributed to Boehm may be interpreted as an expression of an intent to commit suicide, the spoken words were completely separated from the final act by lapse of time, and, in our opinion, were no part of the res gestae.[25]

On the issue of lack of clearly expressed intent, the court opined:

> But we find nothing in the words attributed to Boehm indicative of any certain intent. His remark, upon handing the whisky to Mr. Coe, that it was something to remember him by on the trip, is absolutely without meaning, except as expressive of good fellowship. His request that Schayer would be a good friend to his wife, and his refusal to have her sent for, possibly have some significance. They might be said to point to a contemplated enforced absence from his wife, and it is possible they were associated in his mind with the idea of suicide; but they were equally consistent with an intention to abscond.[26]

The court of appeals reversed the jury's verdict and remanded for a new trial. The only saving grace, perhaps, was that a third jury would hear a great deal less evidence about Jacob Boehm's last, sad day of life.

CONCLUSION

After *Ross-Lewin*, the case disappears from the Reporters. It is not clear whether a third jury trial ever was held. Perhaps the parties threw in the towel after twelve years and settled.

We may never know what Jacob Boehm intended when he took his fatal dose of cyanide. However, anyone who has read the conflicting decisions of two different courts is likely to develop his or her own opinion on the subject.

Original printing: *The Colorado Lawyer*, July 2008. The author is grateful for the research assistance of Dan Cordova and Lynn Christian of the Colorado Supreme Court Law Library.

NOTES

1. *See* Karsner, *Silver Dollar: The Story of the Tabors* 158 (Crown Publishers, 1932). The Colorado State Capitol Building was not occupied until 1894, and its gold plating was not installed until 1908. *See* www.colorado.gov/dpa/doit/archives/cap/gold.htm. Like everything else about the Windsor, its bar was magnificent. The counter was made of Colorado pine and California redwood. Its mirror was 90 inches x 120 inches and was one of the country's largest. Three thousand silver dollars lined the barroom floor. Buchanan and Buchanan, *A Story of the Fabulous Windsor Hotel* 10 (2d ed., Hirschfield Press, 1956). Harry Haye Tammen, who styled himself the "world's best bartender," served as its head barkeep. Buchanan and Buchanan, *id.* at 17.

2. Buchanan and Buchanan, *supra* note 1 at 280-82. For a time, Horace Tabor and his wife Elizabeth McCourt, better known as "Baby Doe," lived in the Windsor Hotel's lavish bridal suite. Some sources indicate Tabor also was an investor or part owner of the Windsor. *See, e.g.,* www.babydoetabor.com/babydoedivorce.htm. He died in a much plainer four-room suite, numbered 302. Buchanan and Buchanan, *supra* note 1 at 21-26. Tabor's last words were: "This is the happiest moment of my life. I am at peace and resigned to the will of God." *Id.* at 26.

3. In their book, the Buchanans vividly capture the atmosphere inside the dying hotel after the Windsor opened its doors to the derelicts roaming Larimer Street:

> There were smells — of potatoes fried in stale grease, or cheap tobacco,
> of roach killer, of rooms with unopened windows, of disease, and of stale
> beer. There were night sounds — of a drunken quarrel, of ambulance

> sirens, of some bum sick with bootleg booze, of a lipsticked laugh, of hushed whispers, of complaining tires and gunshots, of a woman's weeping, of a man's weeping, of a cheap would-be-Tabor's boasts. Backwash city sounds.

Buchanan and Buchanan, *supra* note 1 at 30.

4. *See* "Official Misconduct: Wolfe Londoner and the Denver Mayoral Election of 1889" in this book.

5. *See* en.wikipedia.org/wiki/Tom_Horn.

6. The Windsor served as a transient hotel (or "flophouse") for many years. More than one lost soul leaped from the upper floors of the stairwell to his or her death, earning one of the staircases the name "suicide stairway." Buchanan and Buchanan, *supra* note 1 at 34.

7. *Germania Life Ins. Co. v. Ross-Lewin*, 51 P. 488 (Colo. 1897).

8. *Id.* at 489.

9. *Id.*

10. *Id.*

11. The coroner was none other than Colonel John Milton Chivington, infamous for his role in the 1864 Sand Creek Massacre. *See id.* at 490. *See also* en.wikipedia.org/wiki/John_Chivington. Interestingly, the district court was of the opinion that coroners' verdicts can be admitted in a civil proceeding like this one under some circumstances, but that this particular verdict "was impeached for irregularity in the proceeding by the evidence of Col. Chivington." *Germania Life Ins. Co., supra* note 7 at 490.

12. *Germania Life Ins. Co., supra* note 7 at 490.

13. *Id.* at 491.

14. The Supreme Court described Dr. Eskridge's qualifications as follows:

> Dr. Eskridge testified that he graduated from Jefferson Medical College, of Philadelphia, about 19 years before, and that he has been regularly and constantly engaged in the practice of his profession since that time; that he was duly licensed to practice medicine under the laws of Colorado; that toxicology was a part of the medical instruction received at college, and that he had made this branch of his profession a special study for 12 or 13 years; that he had been a lecturer and teacher in toxicology for 4 or 5 years; that he was familiar with all the authorities and had them at the time in his library; that, while he had no experience in treating a case of poisoning from cyanide of potassium, he had, in his experience,

treated many other cases, extending over a large field; that he had had nearly 100 cases of suicide or homicide from poisoning; that he had had, probably, 18 cases of arsenical poisoning; some 15 cases of opium poisoning; cases of poisoning by belladonna, by carbolic acid; one case of nitric acid poisoning; one case of veratria de veri poisoning; two cases of aconite poisoning; and one of bichloride of mercury, or corrosive sublimate, poisoning.

Id.

15. *Id.*
16. *Id.*
17. *Id.* at 492.
18. *Id.*
19. *Ross-Lewin v. Germania Life Ins. Co.*, 78 P. 305 (Colo.App. 1904).
20. The doctor's name is spelled "Muir" in the first opinion.
21. *Ross-Lewin, supra* note 19 at 306.
22. *Id.* at 307.
23. *Id.*
24. *Id.* at 306.
25. *Id.* at 308.
26. *Id.*

Death on the Kansas Pacific Railroad

A German Family's Fate

BY FRANK GIBBARD

On the evening of July 27, 1872, a passenger train owned by the Kansas Pacific Railway (KP) left Kansas City, Kansas, traveling westbound for Denver.[1] For some on board that ill-fated night train, it would be their final journey. Those passengers had traveled across the ocean, seeking the promise of a new life in America, but would only find watery death on the High Plains. Their heirs would face an entirely different sort of trip: a journey through the Colorado territorial courts.

SECOND-CLASS PASSENGERS

In 1872, Denver was part of the Colorado Territory, which was still four years away from statehood. Denver itself was only a dozen years old. The KP line to Denver was new, too. It had been completed just two years earlier, with stations that were mostly crude board-and-batten structures, scornfully referred to as "big shacks."[2]

Eight to ten of the passengers on board were riding in the second-class car. Their tickets would have been cheap, their accommodations Spartan.[3] Extended rail travel in those days often meant suffering in dirty, poorly lit, and poorly ventilated cars, with only unrefined toilet facilities.[4] A group of people comprising a family of five — a husband, his wife, and their three children — were among the passengers in the car. A witness later stated that from their clothing, appearance, and speech, they appeared to be natives of Germany. These passengers later would become the subjects of a wrongful death lawsuit.

THE TRESTLE

The KP line ran through Lincoln County, over Colorado's eastern plains.[5] About nine miles east of the tiny town of Hugo and a mile west of Mirage Station, the KP track passed over an old river basin where the Big Sandy Creek had once flowed. The basin had been dry for years. The KP had constructed a trestle approximately seventy feet long across its center. Embankments made of fill-dirt spanned the remainder, supporting the track to the east and west of the trestle.

On the east side of the trestle, the KP had made an 800-foot cut, through which the tracks approached the basin. The fill-dirt for the eastern embankment was taken from this cut. It was inferior grade fill, made of sand and clay, but it was the best available on the sandy High Plains. A witness later testified that there was no stone available for fill for 100 miles in any direction. As a result, the railroad heaped the dirt and laid the track across it.

Approximately 1,100 feet north of the trestle, a creek known as Coon Creek intersected the old Big Sandy basin. Until the accident, no one had ever seen much water flowing through Coon Creek or the basin. However, storms were not unknown in the area, and the existence of the creek beds gave evidence that water must have been present at some point. Too, the saplings growing nearby showed signs of water marks on their trunks.

On the evening before the Kansas City–Denver train passed through, a violent July rainstorm swept the plains near the head of Coon Creek. The storm was a topic of conversation at the hotel in Hugo. Not only had the guests witnessed violent thunder and lightning, but they also had noticed an unusual roaring sound.

The trestle over the Sandy Creek collapsed under the weight of the train
Katherine Haas

THE ACCIDENT

Around 1:15 a.m. on July 29, the Kansas City–Denver train passed through Mirage Station. The night was dark and cloudy. The train was traveling at about fifteen miles per hour. Its headlight allowed the engineer to see the rails for approximately 300 to 400 feet ahead.

To the engineer approaching the Sandy Creek basin, the rails across the fill-dirt east of the trestle looked intact and safe; in actuality, they were hanging by a thread. The roaring sound witnesses had heard the evening before was a flash flood that had hit Coon Creek, sending a wall of water through the basin and washing away the sandy fill-dirt beneath the rails. The rails now hung in space, unsupported, over the old river basin.[6]

The Colorado Territorial Supreme Court's opinion describes what happened when the train reached the trestle:

[W]ithout support from beneath, [the rails] yielded under the weight of the train. The engine leaped the chasm, but the baggage car fell and the second car colliding with this was broken in pieces. The water in the old channel of the Sandy was then from three to five [feet deep] and running with great violence.[7]

THE IMMIGRANT CHESTS

The next day, July 30, 1872, a man named Stockdorff appeared at a baggage room at the railway depot in Denver. He was there to collect the belongings of two German immigrants, Mr. and Mrs. John David Buger. They had both died the day before in the tragic accident on the Big Sandy Creek. Stockdorff was directed to the office of the superintendent of the KP. A clerk in the superintendent's office interrogated him to determine his authority to take the Bugers' property. He told the clerk that a Mrs. Shirmer had sent him. Satisfied, the clerk gave him some claim checks. With them, he obtained several boxes.

The boxes were made of wood banded with iron. This type of box was known at the time as an "immigrant chest." The boxes had been transported to the Denver depot the day before, along with the wrecked train and the waterlogged bodies of the dead.

Inside, Stockdorff found what he had hoped for: clothes for the Bugers' three children, who had survived the accident. There were three orphans: a girl, 8 or 9 years old; a boy aged 2 or 3; and another boy aged 16 to 18 months. Mr. and Mrs. Shirmer had taken them in after the accident.

However, there was more. The trunks also contained a trove of letters and documents. These would prove decisive in the subsequent litigation over the children's financial future.

A SUIT FOR WRONGFUL DEATH

A year later, Mr. Miller, administrator for the estate of David Buger, sat in an Arapahoe County territorial courtroom waiting for trial to commence in his wrongful death lawsuit against KP. He represented the children's interest in damages for their parents' death.

Unsurprisingly, KP had denied that it had been negligent in the railway accident. More surprising, it denied that Mr. and Mrs. Buger were deceased. Notwithstanding the children's existence, the railroad even denied that they had left any heirs. Through the course of the trial, KP would object to nearly every scrap of evidence offered to prove the identities of Mr. and Mrs. Buger, their children, and their family relationship.

In the end, however, Miller prevailed at trial. The jury awarded the Bugers' children damages of $15,000, worth nearly $300,000 today. The railroad moved for a new trial. When the district court denied its motion, it appealed to the Supreme Court of the Colorado Territory.

THE DOCUMENTS

On appeal, KP again denied that the Bugers were dead and that they had left behind any children entitled to recover damages. At trial, Miller had introduced a large quantity of evidence designed to show who the Bugers were and how they were related to each other. In its decision, the Colorado Territorial Supreme Court described this documentary evidence in detail. These documents provide a fascinating window into the lives of a late 19th Century German immigrant family.

First, there were the parents' birth certificates, which took the form of German parish registers. They revealed that John David Buger had been born on October 20, 1844. His wife, Augusta Neuschwander, had been born on March 9, 1842. They were both from "Bailiwick Brackenheim, municipality Botenheim."[8]

The land of Brackenheim lies in Germany's wine country, in southern Germany. Settlement there goes back thousands of years.[9] The tiny municipality of Botenheim appears in records as far back as the 12th Century.[10] Mr. Buger had been a shoemaker in Botenheim, at one point signing a letter addressed to his American brother-in-law — the administrator, Mr. Miller — simply as "Shoemaker Buger."[11]

Next, there were documents from the Kingdoms of Bavaria and Württemberg authorizing the Bugers' travel to America. These documents reflect the political situation in Germany at the time. In 1866, after their victory in the Austro-Prussian War, a group of German states had formed the North German Confederation. The southern kingdoms of Bavaria and Württemberg had remained independent. Then, on January 18, 1871, Germany became a united empire under a Prussian emperor, known as the Second Reich. However, as the Bugers' travel documents show, even in unified Germany, the southern German states retained some of their sovereignty and, quaint as it may seem, their existence as kingdoms.

The records also contained a "discharge from citizenship in the Kingdom of Bavaria, to the shoemaker John David Buger." The reason given was his desire to emigrate to North America. During the 1870s, more than 750,000 Germans moved to the United States, part of a massive relocation that began with the failure of the 1848 revolutions in Europe, and continued through the 1880s.[12] The KP lured immigrants to Kansas and Colorado with its offer of 6 million acres of farming and grazing lands for sale.[13] Railroads in those days were given grants of land that they could sell to help finance the cost of constructing the railroad.

Along with this was an "emigrant's pass" from the Kingdom of Würtemburg to Mr. Buger, "native of Botenheim, and resident there up to this date, from his home through Baden and Prussia by way of Bremen to North America." In the margin of this document was a physical description of Mr. Buger, along with the names of his companions, with dates of birth, including his wife and "Children, Karl David, born March 5, 1870; John David, born February 18, 1871; the illegitimate daughter of his wife, Marie Neuschwander, born February 23, 1865."[14]

Birth certificates for the children also were offered, in the form of parish registers. One of these reflected the illegitimate birth of Marie Neuschwander. Plaintiff Miller swore that his name originally also was Neuschwander, and that he had adopted the name of Miller years before.

DAVID BUGER, DECEASED

After determining that the jury had been properly instructed concerning the railroad's negligence, the Territorial Supreme Court took up KP's argument that there was no proof that David Buger had died in the accident. Although it acknowledged that there was no direct proof of death, the Court found the circumstantial evidence more than adequate. First, in the train and in the baggage car were three boxes, two of them bearing Mr. Buger's name, and marked with the name of "Botenheim," the town from which he had departed in Germany. Inside these boxes, there was clothing marked with the initials "D.B." and "A.B.," the initials of David Buger and his wife, Augusta. The boxes also contained children's clothing and the various official documents associated with the Buger family.

Evidence also showed that the family was seated together in the train; that the older boy later gave his name as Charley Buger; and that KP employees delivered the Bugers' trunks to Mr. Stockdorff when he requested them. This evidence, the Court opined, was "sufficient to warrant the jury in finding that [Mr.] Buger was numbered with the slain, and that the children with whom he had been consorting were his own."[15]

AUGUSTA BUGER, DECEASED

The Court turned next to KP's contention that insufficient proof had been offered that Augusta Buger was David Buger's wife and that she had died in the accident. In addition to the evidence about Mr. Buger, the Court noted a series of letters sent from David Buger to Miller, describing his marriage and the birth of their children. Although the envelopes had been lost, Miller testified that they bore the postmarks of Botenheim and New York.

The Court rejected any suggestion that the letters had been forged:

It cannot be said that David Buger, or any one else, deliberately set to work to prepare evidence to be used in a case which could only arise from the fact of Buger's death, growing out of an accident to a particular train on which he was to travel — such prescience as that would be unexampled in judicial history.[16]

It also rejected any argument that the "immigrant chests" would have to be produced to establish the writing found on them, reasoning that "[i]f a sign were painted on a house, it would hardly be contended that the house would have to be produced."[17] Finally, given the evidence, the Court stated it would apply a presumption that the Bugers were married rather than "living in sin."

> Their conduct being susceptible to two opposite explanations, we are bound to assume it to be moral rather than immoral. . . . We have this man and woman traveling together, surrounded with small children; their wearing apparel and bedding in the same trunks, and their initials on them. These facts certainly indicate a very intimate relation, and one that would warrant the presumption of marriage on the principle above stated.[18]

KP also argued that because Mrs. Buger might have survived Mr. Buger — if only for a moment — the action could not be maintained on behalf of the surviving children as his heirs. The Court rejected this argument as well, noting that when husband and wife die in a common accident, a presumption arises that they died simultaneously.

NEGLIGENCE

After all the wrangling about proof of the Bugers' existence and their deaths, the actual issue of KP's negligence was disposed of fairly quickly. The Court held that the railroad's conduct could support an award of damages, including punitive damages, noting that: (1) KP should have been aware of the danger of flooding; (2) KP had been warned that the material used for the embankment was liable to be washed out; and (3) after the heavy storm hit Coon Creek, railroad employees should have examined the bridge.[19] The Court also reached a surprising conclusion about evidence of KP's subsequent construction of a new bridge, with better room for passage of water, after the accident: it was admissible as an admission that the first bridge had been inadequate.[20]

THE QUESTION OF DAMAGES

The Court turned to the difficult question of how to measure the survivors' damages. It rejected a measure based on the survivor's affection for the deceased. This, it said, could only lead to embarrassing questions about how the survivor "really" felt about the person who had died.

> If [the deceased were] a confirmed drunkard, or a person of vile associations, the grief at his departure might not be so poignant. . . . If the widow had wearied of her lord, or the husband of his wife, death might be a joy instead of an anguish.[21]

On the other hand, it was difficult to establish an objective monetary value by which to measure damages.

> Human life has no market value. It will hardly do to limit the value of a man's life by his probable accumulations, for many men make none, and many have arrived at an age when they no longer attempt to make any.[22]

Nevertheless, the jury would have to "place [a] money value upon the life of a fellow-being very much as they would upon his health or reputation."[23] The jury had been instructed that it could award damages for the beneficiaries' mental suffering, so the Court reversed the damages award and remanded for further proceedings.

Justice Ebenezer T. Wells dissented from the Court's holding that beneficiaries should not be compensated for their own mental suffering in such cases. This was not surprising, for he was the very judge who had tried the case and instructed the jury in district court. Under the unusual procedure in place in territorial days, a Territorial Supreme Court justice served both on the district court Bench and on the Supreme Court; therefore, a judge often was called to exercise appellate review over his own decisions. Nevertheless, the other two judges voted to reverse on the measure-of-damages issue, and the case was re-manded. The case disappears from the reports after that, so it is uncertain how the Buger orphans fared on remand.

CONCLUSION

The *Miller* case represents a very early example of the Colorado courts wrestling with issues involving proof of facts and measure of damages. It is a reminder that the engineering marvels of humankind, however impressive, must always take into account the wild vagaries of nature.

Original printing: *The Colorado Lawyer*, July 2009. The author is grateful for the research assistance of Dan Cordova and Lynn Christian of the Colorado Supreme Court Law Library.

NOTES

1. The facts in this article are taken from two Colorado Territorial Supreme Court decisions, *Kansas Pacific Railway Co. v. Lundin*, 3 Colo. 94, 1876 WL 306 (Colo. Terr. 1876) and *Kansas Pacific Railway Co. v. Miller*, 2 Colo. 442, 1874 WL 204 (Colo. Terr. 1874).

2. Klein, *Union Pacific: The Birth of a Railroad 1862-1893* at 289 (Doubleday, 1987); Collins, *Kansas Pacific: An Illustrated History* 29 (South Platte Press, 1998).

3. For information concerning second-class rail travel during this time period on the Union Pacific, *see* Klein, *supra* note 2 at 268.

4. White, *The American Railroad Passenger Car* 400-430 (JHU Press, 1985).

5. The Kansas Pacific Railway (KP) was initially known as the Leavenworth, Pawnee & Western. Its name was later changed to Union Pacific, Eastern Division, before becoming known as the Kansas Pacific. *See id.* at 27.

6. This accident was hardly the most interesting involving flooding on the KP line. That honor probably goes to the tragic wreck of train number 51 on Kiowa Creek near Bennett, Colorado. The Kiowa Creek disaster is described in detail in Clive Cussler's book, *The Sea Hunters* 223-35 (Simon & Schuster, 1996). In that May 1878 incident, a flash flood tore apart a bridge and swept

away a locomotive and eighteen freight cars, killing the three railroad men on board the train. So violent was the flooding that the locomotive itself was carried away, lost for years, and believed to be buried somewhere along the Kiowa Creek bed. Denver's Mayor Wolfe Londoner later supposedly charged a crowbar with electricity and turned it into a magnet to search for the buried train. As the fanciful story goes, he was dragged through the creek bed by the magnet's attraction to some large buried metal object, emerging exhausted and soaked. He tried (unsuccessfully) to claim reward money. *See* Cussler at 237. The locomotive was never found. Cussler believes it was excavated early on by the railroad in a salvage operation, rebuilt, repainted, and renumbered, and then put back into service even as it was claimed as a total loss for insurance purposes — a clear case of insurance fraud. Collins suggests, however, that there are still unanswered questions about the Kiowa disaster that may cast doubt on Cussler's account:

> Would the KP have spent its precious resources to salvage a wrecked locomotive if an insurance claim had been paid? If the road's owners were trying to scam their insurer, would they have recorded the locomotive's rebuild? And could the KP have salvaged No. 51 in just one night without local residents becoming aware of the activity?

Collins, *supra* note 2 at 53.

In addition to flooding, the KP faced Indian attacks. On August 1, 1867, six track workers were killed in a skirmish with Cheyennes near what is now Victoria, Kansas. *See* Collins, *supra* note 2 at 56. Just five years earlier, a Cheyenne raiding party of approximately 100 warriors engaged a thirty-six man 10th Cavalry detachment of buffalo soldiers on the Big Sandy. Though accounts differ, it is agreed that the outnumbered African American soldiers fought valiantly, suffering seven wounded and no deaths in the action. *See* www.fort tours.com/pages/bigsandycreek.asp. For more information about Wolfe Londonder, *see* "Fear and Desire for Streetcars: Denver's Early Electric Railway Wars" and "Official Misconduct: Wolfe Londoner and the Denver Mayoral Election of 1889," both in this book.

7. *Miller, supra* note 1 at 450.

8. *Id.* at 454.

9. *See* www.brackenheim.de/3885_DEU_WWW.php.

10. *See* en.wikipedia/org/wiki/Brackenheim.

11. *Miller, supra* note 1 at 453.

12. *See, e.g.,* www.accessmylibrary.com.

13. *See* Land Department, Kansas Pacific Railway Co., *Emigrant's Guide to the Kansas Pacific Railway Lands* (Lawrence, KS, April 1871).

14. *Miller, supra* note 1 at 454. The "illegitimate daughter," though the oldest of the three children, was not given a name in the document. This may reflect a prejudice against children born out of wedlock during this time period.

15. *Id.* at 459.

16. *Id.* at 461-62.

17. *Id.* at 462.

18. *Id.* at 463.

19. *Id.* at 467-69.

20. *Id.* at 468-69.

21. *Id.* at 466.

22. *Id.*

23. *Id.*

Conservative Measures

Three Early Colorado Medical Malpractice Cases

BY FRANK GIBBARD

In recent years, concerns have been raised about the practice of "defensive medicine."[1] Fear of litigation, it is claimed, has caused doctors to conduct unnecessary tests and procedures, which has helped to drive up the cost of health care.

Three early medical malpractice cases from the Colorado courts illustrate how society may once have faced an opposite problem. In the cases discussed below, a doctor called on to provide treatment downplayed the seriousness of the patient's injury and/or prescribed conservative measures that were inadequate to treat the injury. This led to further injury and, ultimately, to malpractice litigation. These cases also serve as a time capsule, revealing something of the state of medicine in Colorado's early years.

THE CASE OF MCGRAW *v.* KERR

The patient and plaintiff in the first case, Clayton Price Kerr, was a 5-year-old boy.[2] On June 23, 1907, he fell off a horse and fractured his right arm.[3] An unnamed physician was called to the scene. The doctor determined that Clayton had only dislocated his shoulder. He "pulled

369

Medical office from the early 20th Century
Courtesy Denver Public Library, Western History Collection - #X13333

[the boy's arm] back into place," bandaged it, bound it to his body, and advised the parents to go to Denver for treatment.[4]

Dr. McGraw's Treatment

The next day, Dr. Henry R. McGraw examined Clayton in Denver. The boy's father informed Dr. McGraw that the first doctor had diagnosed the boy with a dislocated shoulder. Dr. McGraw inspected the arm visually, as well as by touching and manipulation. He stated it would be best to let Clayton get over the shock of the injury before taking any other measures. He recommended an X-ray, but stated that because X-rays were expensive, he would order only one if he later determined it to be necessary.[5]

Dr. McGraw rebandaged Clayton's arm and placed it in a sling. He re-examined the arm daily and applied electricity to the arm on several occasions.[6]

On further testing, on July 8, Dr. McGraw discovered that the boy had broken his arm. The doctor immediately ordered an X-ray (known in those days as a "skiagraph"), which verified that not only did the boy have a broken arm, but "the ends of the fractured bone were not in exact apposition; only about three-fourths of the ends butt[ed] against each other."[7] After they examined the X-rays, the X-ray specialist and Dr. McGraw informed Clayton's father that they had detected crepitus, a grating or rubbing together of the end of the bone, which proved that it had not healed. They recommended that Clayton be operated on to reduce the fracture of his humerus and, as a further step, that the bone be bound in place with a length of silver wire, if necessary.

Arrangements were made to transport the boy to a hospital, where Dr. McGraw could operate on him. However, before this could happen, the father fired Dr. McGraw.

Treatment at the County Hospital

Clayton's father took him to the county hospital, where doctors took an additional X-ray and re-examined the arm. Dr. Aubrey Williams, who treated Clayton during his time at the hospital, testified that by July 15, he had determined that the bones had actually begun to ossify. As a result, he advised against surgery. Another unnamed doctor called as a witness stated that the proper treatment would have been to place the arm in a splint or to immobilize it with a plaster cast.[8] However, the doctors agreed it would have been difficult for a doctor to make an initial determination as to whether the arm was dislocated or broken.

The Lawsuit

Clayton sued Dr. McGraw for malpractice. The arm had healed, but the bone was misshapen and the union was somewhat angular. By the time of trial, Clayton still had a lump on his arm where the bone had broken and fused unevenly. In bad weather, he favored the broken arm. Although the bone was actually stronger where it had knitted together, the contour of the shoulder was imperfect, and the arm hung in an unnatural position.

The jury awarded Clayton $800. Dr. McGraw appealed.

Appellate Decision

The Colorado Court of Appeals proved remarkably sympathetic to Dr. McGraw's position. First, it found that two of his proposed jury instructions had been improperly refused. One of the instructions would have informed the jury that "the fact that perfect or even good results were not obtained is not of itself any evidence that the physician was negligent."[9] The same instruction also would have informed the jury that:

> [I]n determining the question of whether the defendant, upon the facts in evidence, was negligent or not negligent, the condition of plaintiff's arm at the time of trial or when defendant's treatment ceased was not to be considered as evidence bearing upon that question.[10]

The court of appeals concluded that this instruction should have been given, because the evidence of a bad outcome is not in itself proof of negligence.

Second, Dr. McGraw had requested an instruction that the jury, when determining whether he had been negligent, must be guided solely by the testimony of physicians. The court of appeals was not so much interested in which physician set the standard of care. If the experts were in disagreement, the jury could pick one of the standards advocated by one of them. The important thing was that the jury be instructed that there must be some medical testimony to set the standard.[11] In earlier cases, the Colorado courts had wrestled with how to establish a standard of care in the face of widely divergent opinions provided by various schools of medicine.

Finally, the court of appeals considered an instruction that the trial court had given, and found it deficient. The trial court had instructed the jury that:

if it believed from the preponderance of the evidence that, at the time the defendant was discharged from the case, the fractured bones of plaintiff's arm had not united, and were so that they could not have at that time been brought into proper position, and that the condition of which plaintiff complains arose after that time, without fault or negligence on the part of the defendant, then the defendant is not responsible for such injury or condition, and a verdict should be in his favor.[12]

This instruction, which seemed to favor the doctor, was actually unfavorable to him, the court said, because it put the burden on him rather than on the plaintiff. The plaintiff should have been assigned the burden to show that his condition existed at the time his father discharged Dr. McGraw, and that his injury would not have been avoided if he had complied with Dr. McGraw's instructions (instead of firing him).

In addition to the instructions, the court of appeals found a basic fault with the plaintiff's theory of the case. Had Clayton's father followed Dr. McGraw's advice and permitted him to perform the surgery he proposed to knit the bones together, he might have avoided the poor result (a misshapen healing) altogether. Dr. McGraw also was not at fault for failing to use X-rays to discover the fracture earlier, because this was not part of the standard procedure for his school of medicine. At most, Dr. McGraw might be liable for the boy's pain resulting from manipulation of his arm while he mistakenly believed it was only dislocated; but this sort of pain in itself did not justify an award of $800. The court of appeals therefore reversed the judgment and remanded.

THE CASE OF *BONNET v. FOOTE*

In the course of its opinion, the court of appeals in *McGraw* distinguished an earlier case, *Bonnet v. Foote*.[13] While walking on Sixteenth Street in Denver one evening, Emma E. Foote slipped and fell on the pavement, injuring her right hip. She was helped back to her room and requested that the defendant, Dr. William M. Bonnet, be called to treat her injury.[14] Dr. Bonnet arrived within a few minutes. He found her in severe pain and told her he was afraid that she had suffered a fracture. For whatever reason, he was unable to examine her that evening.

Dr. Bonnet's Treatment

Dr. Bonnet returned the next morning and examined Foote. He felt her hip and told her she had only a severe bruise that time and rest would heal. Over the next few months, he saw her for treatment on several occasions. Although he measured her leg to ensure it was not shortening, he treated the injury as a bruise rather than a fracture.

Foote was confined to her bed for four weeks and eventually was able to walk again with crutches. Four months after her injury, she was able to travel to Santa Fe, New Mexico. She used crutches or a crutch and a cane for approximately eighteen months after her injury, and a cane alone after that. After a couple of years, her pain subsided, but her right leg was shorter than her left and not as strong as before the injury.

The Lawsuit

Approximately five years after the injury, another doctor examined Emma Foote, took an X-ray, and found that she had sustained a fracture to the neck of the femur of her right leg. Foote sued Dr. Bonnet for malpractice. At trial, the second doctor testified that this kind of fracture is difficult to detect and that surgeons have a method of determining whether the patient has suffered a fracture. This method involves having the patient lie on her back while observing whether the foot turns to one side. If the foot cannot be returned to its proper place, this is a sign of fracture or dislocation.

Foote testified that right after she was injured, as she lay on her back, her right foot lay over on the side. Dr. Bonnet observed this, and "said he did not like it, though he could not understand why it did that."[15] When he straightened it, it flopped back to the side again, and she could not use her own muscles to keep it straight.

The jury awarded Foote $1,500 for Dr. Bonnet's negligence. He appealed.

Colorado Supreme Court Decision

The Colorado Supreme Court first noted the sufficiency of the evidence to support the jury's verdict, stating "it is at once apparent from the facts that the failure of the defendant to properly diagnose and treat the injury to plaintiff's hip was inexcusable."[16] The Court explained:

> That the bone was fractured cannot be doubted. The evidence of such fracture was plain from the fact that plaintiff's foot lay over on one side, to which the attention of defendant was directed.[17]

This fact, the Court said, led inescapably to one of two conclusions:

> Either [Dr. Bonnet] did not possess that degree of learning and skill which the law requires of surgeons; or, if he did, he failed to exercise ordinary care in applying it.[18]

The Court brushed off Dr. Bonnet's argument that the testifying doctor's examination, which came five years after the fracture, was incompetent to prove his earlier alleged malpractice. The Court noted that there was other, contemporaneous evidence of failure to exercise proper care; that the later X-ray and the doctor's trial testimony tended to corroborate this evidence; and that any concerns about the time elapsed between the injury and the doctor's examination and X-ray went to the weight of the evidence, not to its competency.

The Court also rejected the doctor's argument that the shortness of Foote's leg was incompetent as evidence of malpractice, because a doctor is not a guarantor of a good medical result and must use only the degree of skill ordinarily required of members of his profession. Here, the bad result was admissible as evidence that the initial diagnosis and treatment were faulty. The Court therefore affirmed the jury verdict in favor of Foote.

THE CASE OF
JACKSON v. BURNHAM

The Colorado Court of Appeals was first organized in 1891.[19] During that year, it issued sixty published opinions.[20] Only one of these sixty cases was later reversed on review by the Colorado Supreme Court. The reversal was a medical malpractice case, *Jackson v. Burnham*.[21] Both *McGraw* and *Bonnet* cited *Jackson*, which is an important early case on the standard of care for physicians.

Dr. Burnham's Treatment

The facts of Jackson are rather disturbing. In January 1890, a Denver physician named Norman Griswold Burnham called on a young African American man named Jesse R. Jackson. He found Jackson suffering from a high fever and complaining of chest pain and looseness of the bowels. After Dr. Burnham prescribed medication for these ailments, Jackson drew the doctor's attention to his real problem: his penis.[22]

Jackson was, it would eventually be determined, suffering from a condition known as phimosis, or an adherence of the foreskin of the penis to the head of the organ, with swelling.[23] The standard treatment for this condition involves surgery to slit the foreskin and restore full circulation to the organ.[24] If circulation is not promptly restored, "strangulation" and gangrene can result.[25]

Dr. Burnham did not pursue this standard surgical treatment, however. Given his medical background, this is perhaps not too surprising. He was a homeopathic doctor who had been educated at the Cincinnati Eclectic Medical College[26] before establishing his homeopathic medicine practice in Denver in 1879.[27] Homeopathy arose in the late 18th Century as an alternative to the crude, painful, ineffectual, and dangerous allopathic (surgical) practices of that time, which included bloodletting and purging.[28] For a while, it stood on nearly equal footing with allopathic medicine, and had its own colleges and medical journals.

Homeopathy's basic principle rested on the concept that "like cures like" — that patients could be treated with substances that produced in a healthy patient the very symptoms caused by a disease. Although homeopathic medicines remain available today, as a parallel competitor to allopathic medicine, homeopathy died out in the first few decades of the 1900s.[29] In the days of the early frontier, however, it was accorded significant respect under Colorado law. For example, the State Board of Medical Examiners, which was established in 1881, included "[s]ix physicians of the regular [allopathic], two of the homeopathic, and one of the eclectic school or system of medicine."[30]

Dr. Burnham later explained that he did not operate surgically because he was concerned the organ was already infected, and that surgical treatment might simply aggravate the infection.[31] After interrogating Jackson and noting the condition of the diseased organ,[32] he prescribed antiseptics and disinfecting agents.[33] He also instructed Jackson to apply a flaxseed meal poultice to the member.[34] That, apparently, was the extent of Dr. Burnham's treatment.

Enter Doctors Rothwell, Craig, and Boice

Thirty-two to thirty-six hours after Dr. Burnham's examination of Jackson, Dr. P.D. Rothwell examined Jackson.[35] He confirmed the diagnosis of congenital phimosis. By that point, gangrene had clearly set in. Dr. Rothwell performed an operation to slit the foreskin, and dressed the wound. Noting the extent of the gangrene, he told Jackson he wanted nothing further to do with the case.[36] He called in a consultant, Dr. William B. Craig.[37]

Dr. Craig found the entire organ gangrenous. He believed this condition had resulted from the phimosis. He and Dr. Rothwell called in a third physician, surgeon John Boice. The surgeon made an incision to determine the extent of the damage. Although he found some living tissue, the gangrene had penetrated to the roots. The doctors conducted several partial amputations, but eventually it proved necessary to amputate the entire penis to save Jackson's life.

The Jury Verdict

Jackson sued Dr. Burnham in Arapahoe County District Court for medical malpractice, seeking damages of $20,000. A jury awarded him a quarter of that — $5,000.

Appellate Decision

Dr. Burnham appealed to the newly formed Colorado Court of Appeals. Before turning to his challenges to the jury instructions, the appellate court noted some facts it felt weighed in favor of Dr. Burnham. First, there was "not an atom of testimony in the entire record that satisfactorily establishes . . . that the application of the flaxseed meal poultice accelerated the gangrene."[38] Second, the court of appeals noted the high level of disagreement among the expert witnesses, with many of them vouching for Dr. Burnham's treatment.

The court of appeals then turned to the jury instructions. The first instruction it found faulty instructed the jury as follows:

> If you find from the evidence that this defendant, in the treatment of the plaintiff, omitted the ordinary or established mode of treatment, and pursued one that has proved injurious, it is of no consequence how much skill he may have. He has demonstrated a want of it in the treatment of the particular case, and is liable in damages.[39]

The court of appeals concluded that to demonstrate malpractice, a plaintiff must show, among other things, that "the great majority of medical authorities have approved the rules" for curing the disease.[40]

Although the court of appeals did not make explicit reference, it appears there was a conflict between the standard allopathic treatment involving surgery and the more conservative homeopathic methods. It would be nearly impossible to determine what treatment "the great majority of medical authorities" would recommend in such a case. The court of appeals noted general acceptance of the proposition that "a physician is not responsible if he acts in accordance with the views of his particular school."[41] It further noted that "[m]any schools among them entertain different, and almost irreconcilable, theories as to the nature and mode of treatment of diseases."[42] The court of appeals went further, noting that each patient is different in such factors as age, sex, and condition, which makes it even more difficult to generalize concerning the appropriate treatment in a given case.

The court of appeals also found fault with an instruction that if the jury determined that gangrene attacked Jackson through Dr. Burnham's negligence, or that gangrene had set in during Dr. Burnham's first visit and he failed to take the proper measures, resulting in amputation, Dr. Burnham would be liable for damages. The court rejected this instruction, because "it assumes that at the time Dr. Burnham was called, and during the time he was in attendance, gangrene had set in."[43]

The third instruction that the court of appeals found objectionable read:

> It is important to the interests of society that the profession [entrusted] with the preservation of the health and lives of the community should be held to a strict rule of accountability.[44]

The court reasoned that resolution of the malpractice case had nothing to do with the interests of society — it was purely a matter between Dr. Burnham and Jackson. In any event, society's interests lie only in having doctors act with ordinary care and skill, which the court implicitly found that Dr. Burnham had provided.

Finally, the court of appeals found fault with an instruction that said:

> [I]f writers on the treatment of phimosis or practical surgeons prescribe a mode of treatment, it is incumbent on surgeons called on to

treat such ailment to conform to the system of treatment thus established, and if they depart from it they do so at their peril.[45]

The court found this instruction objectionable because doctors are bound "only by what is universally settled in the profession."[46] The court noted that even surgical textbooks differed in their recommendations for treatment of phimosis. Therefore, there was no "guiding light" for medical treatment of the condition that Dr. Burnham had failed to follow. The court of appeals reversed for a new trial.

Colorado Supreme Court Decision

Jackson appealed to the Colorado Supreme Court, which took a very different view of the issues. Dr. Burnham had raised twenty-eight errors to the Colorado Court of Appeals, many of which it had not explicitly considered. Now, before the Supreme Court, some of these undiscussed issues resurfaced. He first challenged the jury verdict, because a hypothetical question to Jackson's expert witnesses was not limited to undisputed facts and assumed facts not in evidence. The Supreme Court noted that hypothetical questions to experts are not limited to undisputed facts. As to the second objection, the Court found evidence in the record to support each phase of the hypothetical question.

Turning to the challenged instructions, the Court stated:

[T]he instructions, taken as a whole, correctly define the nature and extent of the obligation that a physician or surgeon assumes when he accepts employment in his professional capacity.[47]

It then addressed Dr. Burnham's challenge to the district court's refusal to give an instruction that supported Dr. Burnham's use of his best judgment, even if his diagnosis was mistaken. The Supreme Court determined that this instruction was objectionable, because it would exempt the defendant from liability even if he was careless or inattentive about determining the plaintiff's true condition.

Turning to the first instruction previously addressed by the court of appeals, the Supreme Court found it acceptable in view of the issues presented in the pleadings in the case, and the testimony presented. The Court stated:

> We find abundant evidence in the record to the effect that the plaintiff was afflicted with phimosis, and that the ordinary and established practice of the profession was to treat that ailment [by slitting up the prepuce or foreskin]; and, in fact, the defendant himself testified that such was the proper treatment of that malady.[48]

The Supreme Court thus implicitly rejected the court of appeals' conclusion that there was no "settled" treatment for phimosis applicable to every case, from which Dr. Burnham's treatment could be considered deficient.

Turning to the second instruction found objectionable by the court of appeals, the Supreme Court rejected the proposition that this instruction contained any assumption of fact about when gangrene set in. Moreover, the evidence tended to show that gangrene *had* set in when Dr. Burnham was treating Jackson.

Addressing the instruction concerning the interests of society, the Supreme Court found that the instruction did not provide:

> the affirmance of any legal proposition, but is true only as a statement of a moral obligation that rests upon one who assumes to exercise the function of a profession that deals with the important matter of life and death[.][49]

However, even if the instruction highlighted an irrelevant consideration that should not have been presented to the jury, the error was not reversible. Given the remaining instructions, which correctly stated the law, any error would not have prejudiced the jury's verdict. Accordingly, the Supreme Court reversed the decision of the court of appeals, with instructions to reinstate the judgment of the trial court in favor of Jackson.

CONCLUSION

The standard of care in a medical malpractice action is measured by whether a reasonably careful physician in the defendant's area of practice would have provided the same treatment the defendant did.[50] In the early days of Colorado medicine, when there was sometimes little consensus among entire conflicting schools of medical thought about the proper diagnosis and treatment of disease, this rule may sometimes have placed a difficult burden on the medical malpractice plaintiff.

Original printing: *The Colorado Lawyer*, September 2009. The author is grateful for the research assistance of Dan Cordova and Lynn Christian of the Colorado Supreme Court Law Library.

NOTES

1. *See* www.medterms.com, type in "defensive medicine."

2. The facts are taken from *McGraw v. Kerr*, 128 P. 870 (Colo. 1912).

3. The Supreme Court's opinion may be mistaken about the boy's age. Ancestry.com identifies a "Clayton Price Kerr" born on August 16, 1900, which would make the plaintiff 6 years old at the time of his injury. *See* wc.rootsweb.ancestry.com. This entry also reveals that the boy later achieved the military rank of Major General and lived until August 13, 1977, a few days shy of his 77th birthday.

4. *McGraw, supra* note 2 at 872.

5. X-rays were still fairly new at the time, having been discovered by Wilhelm Roentgen, a Professor of Physics in Bavaria, Germany in 1895. *See* www.bl.uk./learning/artimages/bodies/xray/prnroentgen.html. In 1901, an assassin shot President William McKinley, and one of two bullets fired remained lodged in his stomach. Although an X-ray machine was available, it wasn't used due to concerns about the new technology. The bullet was not recovered, and President McKinley subsequently died of septic shock due to a bacterial infection.

6. The use of electricity was a common cure-all in those days. *See* Shikes, *Rocky Mountain Medicine: Doctors, Drugs, and Disease in Early Colorado* 220-21 (Johnson Books, 1986).

7. *McGraw, supra* note 2 at 872.

8. Apparently, there was a factual dispute involving that treatment in this case: Dr. McGraw claimed he did splint the boy's arm and the plaintiff claimed he did not.

9. *McGraw, supra* note 2 at 873.

10. *Id.*

11. *Id.* at 874.

12. *Id.*

13. *Bonnet v. Foote*, 107 P. 252 (Colo. 1910).

14. Dr. Bonnet appears to have been a colorful character. He claimed to be related to Claude François Bonnet, the one-time King of Madagascar, who on his death in 1793 supposedly left behind an estate valued at $100 million, which was an enormous sum in those days. "Vast Fortune in England for Denver Man," *Denver Times* 1 (Nov. 20, 1902). The *Denver Times* described Bonnet as follows:

> Dr. Bonnett [*sic*] is a familiar figure on the streets of Denver. He always drives about the city in a carriage with the family escutcheon painted on either side and drawn by a team of swift black horses. The physician himself has a distinguished appearance. He is tall and very large, wears a silk hat and black full beard and moustache. He always drives rapidly and attracts a large amount of attention.

15. *Bonnet, supra* note 13 at 254.

16. *Id.*

17. *Id.*

18. *Id.*

19. *See* Linz and Munger, "The Early History of the Colorado Court of Appeals," in this book.

20. This figure was derived using a Westlaw search in the CO-CS database.

21. *Burnham v. Jackson*, 28 P. 250 (Colo.App. 1891) (*Jackson I*), rev'd, 39 P. 577 (Colo. 1895) (*Jackson II*).

22. *Id.* at 252.

23. *Jackson II, supra* note 21 at 578.

24. *Id.*

25. *Id.*

26. With the emergence of the American Medical Association and the standardization of medical practices, the Eclectic Medical College declined

throughout the 1920s and 1930s before finally closing its doors in 1942. *See* www.lloydlibrary.org/archives/inventories/eclectic_medical_institute.pdf.

27. "Norman G. Burnham," in Byers, *Encyclopedia of Biography of Colorado* 400 (Century Publishing and Engraving Co., 1901).

28. *See* Steele, *Bleed, Blister, and Purge: A History of Medicine on the American Frontier* (Mountain Press Pub. Co., 2005) (discussion of various forms of medicine available in frontier times).

29. *See* Shikes, *supra* note 6 at 214-15.

30. Colo. Stat. ch. 89, § 2617 (1883).

31. *Jackson I, supra* note 21 at 252.

32. *Id.; Jackson II, supra* note 21 at 581. The opinions are full of graphic visual and tactile observations of Jackson's gangrenous organ. Dr. Burnham observed that it was "in a filthy condition, both in appearance and in odor." According to Jackson's testimony, the blighted appearance and foul odor represented more than just a hygiene problem. When he handled the organ, "[t]his gas came out, and bloodlike, and he [Dr. Burnham] saw that." Peter Vass, who made and applied the poultices, stated that the skin was no longer of natural color and the organ "seemed as though it was dead." Dr. Craig later described the head of the organ as "mummified in appearance. . . . [O]n pressure, gas came off, and the smell was simply terrible." (internal citations omitted).

33. *Id.*

34. *Jackson II, supra* note 21 at 578.

35. It appears there may have been two Dr. Rothwells involved in the case. The Supreme Court's opinion mentions both a "P.D. Rothwell" and a "William A. Rothwell." Dr. P.D. Rothwell, a pioneer physician and surgeon, lived until 1921, when he was fatally injured in a collision with a Denver streetcar. "Dr. Rothwell Hurt Fatally," *Denver Times* 3 (Dec. 2, 1921).

36. *Jackson II, supra* note 21 at 581.

37. Dr. Craig arrived in Denver in June 1882 and developed a practice revolving mostly around women's health issues and surgery. By 1891, he had developed a specialty in gynecology and abdominal surgery. Byers, *supra* note 27 at 404-05.

38. *Jackson I, supra* note 21 at 252.

39. *Id.* at 253.

40. *Id.*

41. *Id.*

42. *Id.*

43. *Id.* It is difficult to square this holding with the use of the conditional tense (the word "if") in the instruction, which does not seem to assume anything. The Colorado Supreme Court later agreed.

44. *Id.* at 253-54.

45. *Id.* at 254.

46. *Id.*

47. *Jackson II, supra* note 21 at 579.

48. *Id.* at 580.

49. *Id.* at 582.

50. *Melville v. Southward*, 791 P.2d 383 (Colo. 1990).

Sabotage and Wrongful Death
The Fountain Train Disaster

BY FRANK GIBBARD

Just after midnight on May 14, 1888, Fast Freight No. 31 (No. 31) left Pueblo, Colorado, headed north on the Atchison, Topeka and Santa Fe Railway (Santa Fe). The train's locomotive, Engine No. 565, was pulling thirteen cars and a caboose. The rear six cars and caboose of No. 31 never reached their destination that night. Instead, they became a runaway incendiary bomb. The resulting collision and explosion nearly leveled an entire town.[1]

The Santa Fe spent large sums to compensate the accident victims and their relatives for the loss of property and lives. One victim's relative, however, did not settle with the railroad and ended up in court. Mary E. Headland, the mother of Frank Shipman, a former brakeman who was found dead after the accident, filed a wrongful death suit that eventually reached the Colorado Supreme Court.

In the end, the Court ruled on Mary Headland's suit, but it never resolved the mysteries surrounding the fate of No. 31. Strange and unsettling questions remain about what happened that May night. There is evidence — never specifically discussed in the Court's opinion in *Atchison, Topeka and Santa Fe Railroad Co. v. Headland*[2] — that Frank Shipman did not die in the explosion, but was murdered before the blast occurred. In fact, it could be that his murder prompted the blast.

FRANK SHIPMAN SEEKS A FAVOR

Walter Chubbeck was the train's conductor on the night of the ill-fated trip. As he made his rounds just prior to pulling out of the station at Pueblo, he discovered a young man named Frank Shipman on the front platform of the caboose.[3] Shipman had a sad story to tell. He was twenty-six years old and disabled, with an artificial foot and leg. He planned to ride to Greenland, a small town near the railroad line between Pueblo and Denver. His brother lived there, and he hoped to find work on a farm.[4]

Shipman didn't have a ticket to ride the train; the No. 31 carried freight, not passengers. In fact, the freight it carried that night was unusually hazardous. The cars at the rear of the train included a tank car filled with 3,000 gallons of highly flammable naphtha[5] and a box car containing eighteen tons of blasting powder.[6]

Chubbeck would have been perfectly within his rights to put Shipman off the train then and there, but the young man made a play for sympathy. Shipman asked Chubbeck whether he "ever showed favors to crippled railroad men."[7] Chubbeck told him he sometimes did, but it depended on the circumstances. Shipman pulled out a letter confirming he had been a brakeman on another railroad line. After examining the letter, Chubbeck responded that he could not transport Shipman based on the letter, because it was too old. Chubbeck ordered Shipman off the train and left the caboose to go fulfill other pre-departure duties. Shipman did not get off the train; instead, he remained as a stowaway. It was a move he would later have cause to regret.

THE MEN IN THE CABOOSE

Differing accounts of the tragedy leave much of what followed shrouded in mystery. It is clear, however, that once the train was underway, Chubbeck returned to the caboose, where he found Shipman still on board. He did not have the heart to oust "a crippled railroad man" from the train to hobble along the track at night, so he let him stay.

A tanker full of naphtha and a railcar full of blasting powder spelled trouble for the town of Fountain, Colorado

Katherine Haas

Chubbeck found other men in the caboose, as well. There is significant dispute about who these men actually were. The Colorado Supreme Court identified them as "a fireman seeking employment" and "two or three men traveling with stock on the train."[8] The unemployed fireman remains a shadowy figure. Even his name is unknown. One of the stockmen, a man named Ira Pherson, later described the mysterious fireman as a heavyset man with a pockmarked face. Pherson told officials of the Santa Fe that Chubbeck collected $1.50 from the fireman in exchange for his passage on the train.[9]

Pherson and another stockman, A.C. Dodge, spent an uncomfortable few hours in the caboose. Apparently, Shipman and the fireman not only knew each other, but they also bore an old grudge they were only too happy to renew. Shipman and the fireman exchanged words first, and then came to blows. The stockmen did what they could to keep the two men separated until the train reached Colorado Springs. Once the train stopped, however, they had to leave the caboose to unload cattle. Shipman and the fireman were left alone in the caboose. At the time, they were still quarreling.

RUNAWAY TRAIN

No. 31 had stopped in Colorado Springs where the Santa Fe tracks crossed those of the Denver, Texas, and Gulf Railroad. There was a rail yard at the crossing where Chubbeck and his men needed to switch some cars from the front of the train. They detached six of the cars and the caboose from the rear of No. 31 and left them standing on the rails while they unloaded the stock cars from the front of the train into a stock chute on a stub track.

Going south from Colorado Springs, the tracks ran downhill all the way to Pueblo. Chubbeck knew it was important to set brakes to keep the detached cars from rolling away by sheer force of gravity. The conductor set air brakes on two of the cars. He ordered the train's brakeman to set the others. The brakeman, noticing that the air brakes were not holding very well, also set hand brakes on several of the cars.

Conductor Chubbeck and his men finished unloading the stock and switching the cars. The operation took approximately thirty minutes.[10] Chubbeck then began backing up the train to reconnect the six detached cars and caboose. It was at this moment that the brakeman called out that the back end of the train was gone.

At first, Chubbeck did not believe what he was hearing. He went down the darkened track to check. Sure enough, the six cars and caboose had completely disappeared.

Chubbeck knew this could only mean disaster. The brakes on the cars somehow must have come loose. The cars were rolling downhill, and they would pick up speed all the way to Pueblo. Long before they reached that town, however, they either would jump the tracks or would collide with an oncoming train.

THE COLLISION

Chubbeck ran to the Colorado Springs depot to telegraph a warning to Fountain, the next stop, twelve miles down the line. The night operator was unable to reach Fountain.[11] Chubbeck then fired up Engine No. 565 and sped down the track, hoping to somehow overtake the runaway cars. He had traveled only a couple miles south of Colorado Springs when he saw the sky illuminated by fire. He was too late.

Earlier, at 1:30 a.m., passenger train No. 7 had left Pueblo carrying thirty-four passengers.[12] The No. 7 had been traveling north on the same track that carried the cars hurtling south from the Colorado Springs yard. Ordinarily, there was no danger of collision, because the No. 31 freight would lay over on a side-track in Colorado Springs, allowing No. 7 to pass and proceed to Denver.[13] This was no ordinary night.

At 2:41 a.m., the No. 7 stopped in Fountain just north of the station to take on water.[14] A short time later, its engineer heard a loud noise and saw a horrifying sight — the caboose and cars from No. 31 heading straight for his train. They were flying south, unmanned, down the track.

The engineer leapt from the train just before the two trains collided. The collision was catastrophic. It flung cars off the rails and blasted the passenger train backward several yards. Worst of all, the car full of naphtha ruptured, dousing the ground and the railroad platform with 3,000 gallons of flammable liquid.

FIRE AND EXPLOSION

The naphtha quickly caught fire, leading to a hellish scene of a burning station and fiery train wreckage, the flames filling the night sky. Citizens of Fountain left their homes to peer at the disaster. Train crews, working frantically, managed to detach the passenger cars from No. 7 and to push them far down the track to safety. Their work was heroic. Though many of the passengers were injured, none died from the collision or the fire.

The trainmen organized a bucket brigade, which the Fountain residents were quick to join. A courageous man named C.F. Smith, manager of a lumber company, climbed on top of the flaming depot and dumped buckets of water on its roof and walls.[15]

Even if those working to control the flaming naphtha had succeeded, the fire was only one of the horrors that awaited the town of Fountain; there were eighteen tons of explosive powder to contend with. J.C. Denny, the Santa Fe's agent in Fountain, telegraphed Pueblo to find out if the car from No. 31's wreckage marked "powder" really contained blasting powder. When informed that it did, he ran out of the depot yelling, "Powder, run for your lives!"[16] Denny's warning probably saved quite a few souls who fled the scene, because just minutes after he gave it, the flames reached the powder car. As Dr. Lester L. Williams later described it in his account of the tragedy:

> [T]he color of the flames changed from gold to silver, then with a tremendous flash and a shattering, earth-shaking blast it exploded. A great flame shot upward. For many miles it could be seen coming up like the flash of a volcano fire.[17]

The blast hurled shattered steel in all directions. C.F. Smith, who continued to work on the roof trying to put out the fire, was killed when a large piece of shrapnel caught him in the back, knocking him from the roof. Before he died, he assured the men who found him on the ground, "Boys, I am not a coward."[18] Doubtless they knew it already.

Two other people died from the blast, one of them a woman struck by a piece of iron that penetrated her skull while she stood 500 feet from the explosion site.[19] Dozens of people were injured, some of them seriously. The blast left an enormous crater in the ground, demolished several buildings, and damaged nearly every other structure in town.

THE FATE OF FRANK SHIPMAN

Frank Shipman's crumpled body was found by the tracks, burned almost beyond recognition.[20] With no known friends or relatives, he was hastily buried in the potter's field at Evergreen Cemetery.[21] Later, relatives came and exhumed the body to take it to Greenland for burial.

In the meantime, prior to the exhumation, a coroner's inquest had been held. The stockmen Pherson and Dodge had related their story at the inquest about Shipman's fight with the unnamed fireman. This drew the interest of railroad investigators, who asked to examine Shipman's body before it was re-buried. The examination revealed that Shipman's skull had been fractured by a blow that appeared to have resulted from a blunt impact rather than debris hurled by the explosion.[22]

The investigators developed a theory. They believed the unknown fireman in the caboose with Shipman had killed Shipman during their quarrel. Wishing to conceal the murder, he released the brakes on the six cars as they stood on the track, knowing they would roll downhill and be destroyed. The railroad hired detectives to track down the fireman, but they never found him.[23] No one was ever prosecuted for Shipman's murder — if it was a murder.

THE LAWSUIT

Shipman's mother sued the railroad, alleging a more prosaic theory of recovery: negligence. A jury awarded her $3,500 on her claim that the railroad "had assumed toward the deceased [Shipman] the duties and obligations due from a common carrier to a passenger."[24] Mary Headland relied on a statute establishing a right of recovery for wrongful death when

1) any person shall die from any injury resulting from or occasioned by the negligence, unskillfulness, or criminal intent of any officer, agent, servant, or employe[e] whilst running, conducting, or managing any locomotive, car, or train of cars [or]

2) [a passenger died on the railroad] from any injury resulting from or occasioned by any defect or insufficiency in any railroad, or any part thereof, or in any locomotive or car[.][25]

The railroad appealed.

The Supreme Court ruled out an action under the first section of the statute, which Headland had not relied on at trial. The Court determined that there was no evidence of negligence by employees of the railroad. The Court stated:

> The uncontradicted evidence shows that the brakes upon the cars left upon the track were properly set, and it is conclusively shown that if the machinery of the road had been in good order and condition the brakes would have been sufficient to have held the cars for many hours.[26]

Also, the railroad was not required to leave a brakeman in charge of the cars, given that the train carried only freight, not passengers.

The second section of the statute posed a more significant problem, because there was some evidence to support the jury's verdict based on "any defect or insufficiency in any railroad ... or in any locomotive or car." Specifically, the evidence at trial showed that there might have been a defect in the air brakes. This being the case, the Court was compelled to consider the issue of whether Shipman could be considered a passenger of Fast Freight No. 31, which was a requirement for Headland's recovery under the statute.

The Court held that Shipman could not be considered a passenger of No. 31. The Court first took judicial notice of the general division in the railroad business between freight and passenger traffic. Freight trains generally do not carry passengers. Even though they have a caboose where passengers can ride, because "such vehicles are necessary for the accommodation of the employees of the company, [they] are typically used for this purpose only."[27] Moreover, Chubbeck had specifically refused to carry Shipman on the train.

The fact that Chubbeck did not eject Shipman from the train when he discovered his presence did not convert Shipman's status to that of a passenger. Chubbeck had merely taken pity on a disabled man. Both the stockmen and the fireman who rode in the caboose had other reasons for being there; their presence did not indicate that the railroad was engaged in passenger traffic on No. 31. Finally, the Court cited a long line of cases that held that persons present on freight trains generally are not considered passengers. The Court concluded that because Shipman was not a passenger, the judgment in favor of his mother must be reversed.

CONCLUSION

The Colorado Supreme Court's opinion provides a classic example of a court stating unnecessary background facts that implicitly bolster its result, albeit on a theory it did not adopt. The basis for the Court's opinion — that Shipman was not a passenger on the train — did not depend on who released the air brakes or why. Nevertheless, the Court alluded to the fireman's role in the tragedy. Its factual recitation ends with this intriguing language:

> What became of the fireman does not appear. He was not seen by any witness after the separation of the cars at the crossing near Colorado Springs, and a diligent search failed to disclose any trace of him after that time. The theory of the defense was that in a moment of passion he loosened the brakes, and fled.[28]

It could be argued that the fireman's culpability for the disaster was at least tangentially relevant to the Court's other conclusion — that the brakes were properly set and the railroad's employees therefore were not negligent under the first subsection of the statute. Given the jury's verdict in favor of Mrs. Headland, however, the Court never drew the conclusion that the fireman had released the brakes and caused the tragedy. Instead, it just stated the facts and left the fireman's nefarious role within the realm of possibility. No one was ever prosecuted for the disaster, and that is how the story of the Fountain train disaster ends.

Original printing: *The Colorado Lawyer*, November 2010. The author is grateful for the research assistance of Dan Cordova and Lynn Christian of the Colorado Supreme Court Law Library.

NOTES

1. The explosion, known as "The Blast," remains a legendary historical event in the city of Fountain. Nearly 125 years later, Fountain residents commemorate The Blast every July with a street dance held at Fountain's City Hall Plaza. *See* en.wikipedia.org/wiki/Fountain,_Colorado.

2. The facts involving Shipman are taken from the Colorado Supreme Court's opinion in *Atchison, Topeka and Santa Fe Railroad Co. v. Headland*, 33 P. 185 (Colo. 1893).

3. The Court's opinion does not supply a first name for Shipman, but several other sources identify him as Frank Shipman. *See, e.g.*, Lane and Gregg, *The Encyclopedia of Mass Murder* 126 (Carroll and Graf, 2004).

4. Greenland still exists as an unincorporated community in Douglas County. It is served by the U.S. Post Office in Larkspur. *See* en.wikipedia.org/wiki/Greenland,_Colorado.

5. *See* en.wikipedia.org/wiki/Naphtha.

6. Williams, "Disaster in Fountain — 1888," *Denver Westerners Monthly Roundup* 4 (March 1965).

7. *Headland, supra* note 2 at 185.

8. *Id.* At a coroner's inquest, Chubbeck told a different story, saying that instead of the fireman, "he thought a bum had boarded the train in Fountain [and] that he had put the tramp off when they arrived in Colorado Springs." Williams, *supra* note 6 at 11. Some accounts mention a group of vagrants instead of stockmen on board. Finally, to further confuse matters, the Supreme Court's account has Chubbeck meeting the mysterious fireman near the front of the train and sending him to the caboose to get him out of the way of the brakeman. *See Headland, supra* note 2 at 185.

9. Williams, *supra* note 6 at 14.

10. *Id.* at 4.

11. *Id.*

12. *See id.*

13. "Horrible Holocaust," *Rocky Mountain News* 1 (May 15, 1888).

14. *Id.*

15. Williams, *supra* note 6 at 6.

16. This was the milder exclamation quoted in the *Rocky Mountain News, supra* note 13 at 2. Another account has Denny yelling, "Look out! The last car is filled with powder. Run, for God's sake!" Williams, *supra* note 6 at 6.

17. Williams, *supra* note 6 at 6. Dr. Williams, who wrote a detailed and colorful article on the blast in 1965, was a well-known historian of the Colorado Springs Fire Department. *See* http://fire-museum.netfirms.com/page5.html.

18. Williams, *supra* note 6 at 7. The *Rocky Mountain News* account has Smith poignantly asking, "I am not a coward, am I?" *Rocky Mountain News, supra* note 13 at 2.

19. *Id.* at 8.

20. *Id.* at 12.

21. *Id.* at 14.

22. *Id.*

23. *Id.* at 14-15. Dr. Williams reported that an investigator unconnected to the investigation located the fireman briefly in Glenwood Springs, but he had departed before the railroad detectives could arrive to detain him.

24. *Headland, supra* note 2 at 185.

25. *Id.* at 186, *quoting* 1 Mills' Ann. Colo. Stat. Ch. 37, § 1508 (1891).

26. *Headland, supra* note 2 at 187.

27. *Id.*

28. *Id.* at 185.

XI

THE BUSINESS
OF NEWS

INTRODUCTION

Today's newspaper business, with its color features, satellite feeds, and Internet presence, bears little resemblance to the days when aspiring publishers hauled their wooden presses over the plains and set up shop in cramped quarters to print inked broadsheets by hand. Early Colorado newspapers differed both in style and substance from the dailies mass-produced by today's corporate media giants. Whereas newspapers today at least make some pretense of fair and balanced reporting, vintage papers were often blatantly partisan and made little distinction between pure news and editorializing. More than once in America's early days, a paper's outspoken political stance caused its press to be burned by an angry mob or tossed into a river. Sometimes the publisher was tossed in with it.

There were no wire services on the Western frontier, so city papers relied for filler on witty sayings, maxims, jokes, and poetry. They also printed stories of local interest of the sort that would not be considered newsworthy in a large metropolitan paper today. Sometimes these "lost dog" stories betray an excess of Victorian sentimentality. Other times, as in the stories from the 1890s papers in Wisconsin collected by Michael Lesy in his book *Wisconsin Death Trip*, they are disturbing or even downright weird.

The maxim "if it bleeds, it leads" was as true in the 19th Century as it is today. Murder, fires, train wrecks, catastrophes, all got front-page space in Colorado's early dailies. Another continuity between today's papers and those of yesteryear lies in the ubiquity of advertisements, even if ads for patent medicines have nowadays given way to those for medical marijuana. If subscription fees and advertisements did not cover their budgets, newspaper publishers in the frontier days sometimes also made money printing legal notices or session laws.

Early papers contained no color photographs. They contained no black and white photographs, either. Instead, they relied on woodcuts to illustrate their stories. In the beginning, these illustrations were few and far between, except when advertisers were willing to pay for them to illustrate ads. Most of the paper consisted of printed words in narrow columns set in a font much smaller than those in general use today. Nineteenth Century America, particularly toward the end of the century, was a highly literate culture with a much greater attention span than one finds in today's Internet age. Wordy newspapers, like wordy novels, were the order of the day.

The *Rocky Mountain News* produced its first edition on April 23, 1859. This first daily edition was rushed into print as part of a competition with a rival paper, the *Cherry Creek Pioneer*. The competition reflected the larger rivalry between the City of Auraria, where the *Rocky Mountain News* was located, and the City of Denver, where the *Pioneer* printed its first and only edition. The *News* won the competition, reportedly delivering an edition twenty minutes in advance of the *Pioneer*, which folded and sold its printing press to the *News*. Denver, of course, later absorbed Auraria and the *News* became a Denver staple.

William N. Byers, the *News*'s first publisher, relied on a second-hand press known as a Washington Hand Press. The "Imperial" model he used produced a folio consisting of two six-column pages measuring 13¾ inches by 19 inches. The press could only produce one folio page at a time. The press had to be inked with a hand roller and then the hand-set type was impressed onto a single page. The work was messy, laborious, and time-consuming. Nevertheless, Byers kept the Imperial press in service until it was washed away in the great Denver flood of 1864.

Although the *News* faced competition from several rival papers over the years such as the *Denver Republican* and the *Denver Daily Times*, its great nemesis, *The Denver Post*, did not come into being until more than three decades after the *News* began publication. The first issue of the *Post* appeared on April 8, 1892, the same year Colorado elected its Populist governor, Davis Hanson Waite. The two events are not unrelated; the *Post*'s origin was politically motivated. Traditional Democrats, feeling abandoned by the Populist faction of their party, started the *Post* as a paper that would reflect their views. Few realized at the time that the *Post* would become the great rival of the *News*, waging circulation wars that lasted for decades and ultimately forcing the *News* out of business when its last issue appeared on February 27, 2009, just shy of what would have been its 150th Anniversary.

FOR FURTHER READING

Michael Madigan, *Heroes, Villains, Dames & Disasters: 150 Years of Front-Page Stories from the* Rocky Mountain News (Denver, CO: Madideas LLC 2009).

David Dary, *Red Blood & Black Ink: Journalism in the Old West* (New York, NY: Alfred A. Knopf 1998).

William H. Hornby, *Voice of Empire: A Centennial Sketch of* The Denver Post (Denver, CO: Colo. Historical Society 1992).

Bill Hosokawa, *Thunder in the Rockies: The Incredible* Denver Post (New York, NY: William Morrow 1976).

Michael Lesy, *Wisconsin Death Trip* (New York, NY: Doubleday 1973).

Robert L. Perkin, *The First Hundred Years: An Informal Sketch of Denver and the* Rocky Mountain News (Garden City, NY: Doubleday 1959).

Libel, Contempt, and the Republican Publishing Company

BY FRANK GIBBARD

In 1878, W.A.H. Loveland purchased the *Rocky Mountain News* and turned it into a "Democratic newspaper."[1] Shortly thereafter, the owners of Denver's other Democrat-affiliated newspaper, the *Colorado Democrat*, decided to sell. A group of ardent Republicans purchased the *Colorado Democrat*, discontinued its publication, incorporated as the Republican Publishing Company (RPC) in 1879, and began publishing a daily paper called the *Denver Republican* (*Republican*).[2] The RPC went on to publish a number of other Colorado newspapers, as well.

Over the next two decades, the RPC was the subject of a remarkable string of libel verdicts and contempt citations. The *Republican*'s sensationalistic, opinionated, and sometimes scurrilous articles offended private parties and public officials alike. Of the dozen or so Colorado appellate libel decisions involving newspaper publications prior to 1900, the RPC was involved in half.[3] No other Colorado newspaper publisher created nearly as much libel law.[4]

It appears the RPC "pushed the envelope" even by relatively lax 19th Century journalistic standards.[5] Three 19th Century cases will provide a flavor of the RPC newspaper's reporting style and demonstrate how it fared in the courts.[6]

THE CASE OF *MINER*

The RPC makes its first appearance in the Colorado Reports as a defendant in a libel action brought by Liza Miner. The case of *Republican Publishing Co. v. Miner*[7] arose from a June 21, 1882 story in the *Denver Republican*, accusing Miner of a horrific crime.[8]

An Allegation of Poisoning

The headline screamed: "A FIENDISH ACT. An Attempt at Murder by the Poisoning of the Family of J.T. Potter."[9] According to the article, eight members of the James T. Potter family, who lived on Lawrence Street in Denver, had been poisoned with arsenic. The article described the awful symptoms suffered by the victims and the heroic progress in treating them made by Dr. McBeth, the family physician, who made the diagnosis of arsenic poisoning. The reporter expressed hope that the victims would recover. The article also opined that if the facts could be "confirmed judicially," they indicated "the presence of a dangerous member of the community, whose apprehension and confinement should be at once directed by the authorities."[10]

The "New Lucrezia Borgia"

The *Republican* did not spare its readers a conjecture about who this "dangerous member of the community" might be. Its reporter, "search[ing] for the author of this deplorable state of affairs," was directed to a woman in the neighborhood, "known under the historic pseudonym of 'Lucretia [*sic*] Borgia.'"[11] This fiendish woman was, however, "more familiar to her neighbors and officers of the law as Liza Miner."[12]

The ensuing description of Liza Miner seemed calculated to make the reader shudder with horror. After failing in attempts to kill herself on several occasions, the article noted that Miner had satisfied her "craving for death" by poisoning household pets, chickens, and even a neighborhood cow.[13] According to one of her neighbors, she started a fire in her own rooming house to try to get rid of tenants who refused to leave.

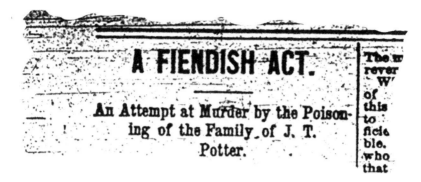

A FIENDISH ACT.

An Attempt at Murder by the Poisoning of the Family of J. T. Potter.

Libelous headline from *The Denver Republican*, June 21, 1882
Courtesy Denver Public Library

She reportedly later told another neighbor named Mrs. Nichols that "it was her intention to obtain possession of the rooms, even if she was obligated to do so at the sacrifice of life."[14]

Her "neighbors speak of her as one who has been guilty of eccentricities that can be accounted for on no other hypothesis than insanity."[15] Although the reporter never actually met Miner, he was not averse to adding insult to injury by deriding her physical appearance: "[Lucrezia] Borgia of the fourteenth century [*sic*] is represented as having been beautiful as the phantom of a dream, tall and commanding, with a form of matchless symmetry. The modern Borgia is diametrically the [opposite] in nearly every instance."[16]

Near its end, the article made a desultory attempt at fair and balanced reporting, noting that "[i]t may be anything or nothing, [Miner's] alleged complicity."[17] However, it immediately returned to vituperation, stating "the one thing certain about it all is[ ] that Mr. Potter's family [has] been poisoned. And it seems to be the duty of the officers to seek out and punish the guilty party or parties."[18]

A Retraction

Two days later, the *Republican* published an article with a very different tone:

MRS. MINER UNJUSTLY ACCUSED. At the time of the poisoning in the Potter family, on upper Larimer street, it was generally circulated that a Mrs. Liza Miner, a neighbor of the Potters, was implicated in the administering of the poison. It now transpires that the sickness of the Potter family was caused by eating a poor article of ice-cream, and of course Mrs. Miner is exonerated from all connection with what was supposed to be an attempt at murder."[19]

Remarkably, this second article did not apologize for the *Republican*'s rush to blame Miner for attempted murder. Instead, it blamed her neighbors. The paper declared that "the parties who were so assiduous in connecting her name with this affair owe the lady the most abject apology," because they had "embraced the Potter poisoning case as an opportunity to vilify the name of their enemy."[20]

The *Republican* then laid it on thicker. With a roll of the press, Miner's whole character was transformed. Rather than a hideous and insane misanthrope, she now became a woman who "comes from one of the best families," and whose "friends are extremely glad to have the outcome as it is."[21]

First Decision: Colorado Supreme Court

Notwithstanding the retraction, Miner sued the RPC for libel. The subsequent trial centered on whether a reader of the article could reasonably have concluded that it accused Miner of attempted murder. A jury found that such a reader could have concluded as much, and it awarded her $3,000.

The Colorado Supreme Court reversed and remanded to the trial court. The trial court had improperly permitted the jury to hear opinion testimony from witnesses that the article charged Miner with attempted murder by poisoning. This was improper, the Court held, because these witnesses neither had "superior knowledge" of what the article meant, nor was it shown that the jury required expert testimony to determine the article's meaning.[22]

Second Decision: Colorado Court of Appeals

On remand, judgment was again entered for Miner. The RPC again appealed, now to the Colorado Court of Appeals, this time arguing that the case should have been dismissed, because the article did not actually charge Miner with committing a crime. In an 1893 decision, the Colorado Court of Appeals disagreed, stating, "There is no direct charge, but there is insinuation, which may be equally injurious."[23] Accordingly, it upheld the judgment against the RPC.

THE CASE OF COOPER

While the *Miner* case was working its way through the courts, the RPC became embroiled in another legal proceeding — *Cooper v. People ex rel. Wyatt*.[24] This case involved an Arapahoe County judge. The stakes in this case were political rather than merely personal.

Wyatt's Habeas Petition

John J. Wyatt was imprisoned for contempt in connection with the alleged theft of government property from the state assembly. He prepared a petition for a writ of habeas corpus and attempted to get it heard by two judges, both of whom said they were too busy to consider it. Finally, Judge T.B. Stuart agreed to hear the petition. As part of the habeas proceeding, Judge Stuart released Wyatt on bond.

Judge Stuart Criticized

An article appeared in the next day's Republican. The title read: "STUART WAS THE TOOL."[25] Deploring the court's exercise of a "bail-stretching power," the article charged that Judge Stuart had been willing to "step outside . . . precedent" on the basis of a "gauzy fiction."[26] It alleged that "Johnny got out of jail" due to Judge Stuart's "unwarranted interference" with normal procedures.[27]

The article went from bad to worse. It included interviews with several people who denounced Judge Stuart's actions. Characterizing his grant of bail as "a judicial outrage" the article deemed that the judge had "dug his official grave both wide and deep."[28] "No wonder the natural sense of justice of men often prompts them to take the law into their own hands," the paper argued, when "the courts cannot be depended on to insure the administration of justice."[29] The writer went on to insinuate that Judge Stuart had been unduly influenced by "the supposed political pull of the gang of which Johnny Wyatt is such a prominent member."[30]

Judge Stuart Responds

Judge Stuart appointed two attorneys to investigate whether the *Republican* should be held in contempt for its coverage of his actions. The *Republican* responded defiantly. The new article declared that "we not only do not take back a word we have already said in this matter, but repeat it with all emphasis."[31] It then reported, incorrectly, that the other two judges who had been too busy to determine Wyatt's *habeas* petition "refused" to enter the writ, implying that they had found it meritless. The *Republican* also published a large cartoon entitled "The Tug of War — The People Against the Gang," showing a rope-pulling contest with Wyatt at the center. Judge Stuart and members of Wyatt's "gang" are shown pulling from one side, while "citizens" pull from the other end of the rope.[32]

Colorado Supreme Court Decision

Judge Stuart held the *Republican*'s manager and its editor in contempt for the coverage, fining them $300 each. They appealed to the Colorado Supreme Court. The Court held that a judge could punish a newspaper for contemptuous articles, notwithstanding the free speech and free press provisions of the Colorado Constitution, and notwithstanding the fact that the articles were published outside the judge's presence. The press is not permitted to "use language in reference to a pending cause calculated to intimidate or unduly influence and control judicial action."[33] Accordingly, the Supreme Court upheld the judgment of contempt.

THE CASE OF CONROY

The last reported pre-1900 libel case involving RPC — *Republican Publishing Co. v. Conroy*[34]— dates from 1894. The *Republican* reported on a crime using such strongly worded editorial language that it was sued for libel. The offending article stated as follows:

> In the Proper Place. John Conroy Jailed for Making Assaults on Little Girls. John Conroy was yesterday arrested by Detectives Ingersoll and Ustick for assault and battery. Conroy is one of the mean, low-lived counterfeits on manhood who make a practice of enticing little girls from their homes, and then attempting assault. Two children, living at 935 and 945 Seventh Avenue, on Tuesday, were decoyed by Conroy. He did not succeed in his dastardly purpose, being driven from it by the cries of the girls. Yesterday Conroy was identified by the girls' mothers, and his arrest followed.[35]

A jury awarded Conroy $1,500 for libel. The Colorado Court of Appeals found the libel actionable but reversed the judgment in favor of Conroy.

The newspaper was free to report Conroy's arrest and the charge, the court said, but the article's author went further than simple reporting when "he proceeded upon his own responsibility to brand the plaintiff with an opprobrious epithet, and to assert him guilty of the most disgraceful and infamous of offenses."[36] If these editorializing statements were false, they were actionable and not privileged.

Reversal was necessary, however, for another reason. The district court had instructed the jury that it could award punitive damages, without requiring a showing of express malice. Although malice could be implied from the fact of publication, resulting in an award of compensatory damages, an award of punitive damages required a showing of "circumstances of fraud, malice, or insult, or a wanton and reckless disregard of the injured party's rights and feelings."[37] The judgment was reversed so that the jury could be properly instructed concerning the requirements of a punitive damage award.

FATE OF THE DENVER REPUBLICAN

The *Republican* continued publication until 1913. In October 1913, it was consolidated with the *Rocky Mountain News.*[38]

The same year the *Republican* ceased independent publication, the Colorado Supreme Court decided yet another libel case against the RPC, *Burns v. Republican Publishing Co.*[39] In that case, the *Republican* had charged the plaintiff with bribery. The plaintiff alleged that the charge was false. The RPC argued that the language of the statement was not actionable *per se*, because it did not charge a crime under Iowa law, where the bribery purportedly took place. The Colorado Supreme Court, relying on an earlier case also involving the RPC, reminded the publisher that "[a] false writing published of another of a character which manifestly tends to charge him with the commission of an act which will make him the subject of odium is libelous per se."[40] Accordingly, it reversed the district court's demurrer against the plaintiff.

A LEGACY OF LIBEL

While it lasted, the *Republican* provided a strongly opinionated voice in Denver's journalistic scene. It was a voice, however, that sometimes got its publisher in serious trouble. On the positive side, the paper's activities certainly did contribute to the development of early libel law in Colorado.

Original printing: *The Colorado Lawyer*, September 2008. The author is grateful for the research assistance of Dan Cordova and Lynn Christian of the Colorado Supreme Court Law Library.

NOTES

1. *See* Walbert, "Reading newspapers: Editorial and opinion pieces," available at www.learnnc.org/lp/editions/thinking-guide-newsopinion/4184.

Historically, some newspapers have had a particular editorial bent, leaning in one political direction or another. In some larger communities, there might be two or more newspapers, each with a strong affiliation with a particular political party or set of political ideals. Readers could then choose the newspaper that they wished to read based on their own interests.

2. Stone, *History of Colorado* 791 (S.J. Clarke, 1918). *See also* "Reconstructing the Republican," *Rocky Mountain News* 8 (July 30, 1899).

3. A Westlaw search uncovered six pre-1900 libel and/or contemptuous libel decisions involving the Republican Publishing Company: *Republican Pub. Co. v. Conroy*, 38 P. 423 (1894); *Republican Pub. Co. v. Miner* (*Miner I*), 34 P. 485 (Colo.App. 1893); *People ex rel. Connor v. Stapleton*, 33 P. 167 (1893); *Republican Pub. Co. v. Mosman*, 24 P. 1051 (Colo. 1890); *Cooper v. People ex rel. Wyatt*, 22 P. 790 (Colo. 1899); and *Republican Pub. Co. v. Miner* (*Miner II*), 20 P. 345 (Colo. 1888). This represents half of the twelve libel cases involving newspapers from this period. The other six are detailed in note 4, *infra*.

4. The other six pre-1900 cases involved the following papers: *Hazy v. Woitke*, 48 P. 1048 (Colo. 1897) (*Durango Weekly Tribune*); *Bloom v. People*, 48 P. 519 (Colo. 1897) (publication name unspecified); *Craig v. Pueblo Press Pub. Co.*, 37 P. 945 (Colo. 1894) (Pueblo Press Publishing Co.); *McKenzie v. Denver Times Pub. Co.*, 34 P. 577 (Colo.App. 1893) (Denver Times Publishing Co.); *Downing v. Brown*, 3 Colo. 571 (Colo. 1877) (*Denver Tribune*); and *Byers v. Martin*, 2 Colo. 605 (Colo.Terr. 1875) (*Rocky Mountain News*).

5. Newspapers of this era often focused on individual foibles, private eccentricities, personal tragedies, and minor criminal acts. Many articles described (and sometimes offered gushing, moralistic commentary on) happenings that today either would not be considered newsworthy or would at best be relegated to a brief mention in the police blotter. At the other end of the spectrum, a well-known abstract of very grim newspaper articles from this period contains disturbing tales of arson, murder, vandalism, disease, poverty, insanity, death, and suicide, all recounted in a matter-of-fact tone. *See* Lesy, *Wisconsin Death Trip* (Doubleday, 1973).

6. The researcher can locate a number of post-1900 decisions by running the following Westlaw query in the CO-CS database: "Republican Publishing" & date(after 1900).

7. *Miner II, supra* note 3.

8. *Id.* The facts, including the text of the newspaper articles involved, are taken from *Miner II*. In its decision, the Colorado Supreme Court incorrectly reported the newspaper's name as the "Daily Republican." *See id.* at 348.

9. *The Denver Republican* (June 21, 1882).

10. *Miner II, supra* note 3.

11. *Id.* at 347. Lucrezia Borgia (1480–1519) was a member of a powerful and ruthless Italian Renaissance family associated with political corruption, assassination, and sexual misconduct, as well as patronage of the arts. She is rumored to have poisoned her enemies and her name has become synonymous with feminine evil. *See* en.wikipedia.org/wiki/Lucrezia_Borgia. At least one biographer, however, has attempted to rehabilitate her reputation, portraying her as a romantic, intelligent, and highly cultured woman who was manipulated by a family of ambitious and dynastically-oriented men. *See* Bellonci, *Lucrezia Borgia* (London: Phoenix Press, 2003).

12. *Miner II, supra* note 3 at 347.

13. *Id.*

14. *Id.*

15. *Id.*

16. *Id.*

17. *Id.* at 347-48.

18. *Id.* at 348.

19. *Id.* at 349.

20. *Id.*

21. *Id.*

22. *Id.*

23. *Miner I, supra* note 3 at 488.

24. *Cooper, supra* note 3.

25. *Id.* at 791.

26. *Id.* at 791-92.

27. *Id.* at 791.

28. *Id.* at 792.

29. *Id.*

30. *Id.* at 792-93.

31. *Id.* at 793.

32. "The Tug of War — The People Against the Gang" (editorial cartoon), *Denver Republican* 1 (July 14, 1889).

33. *Cooper, supra* note 3 at 799.

34. *Conroy, supra* note 3.

35. *Id.* at 424.

36. *Id.*

37. *Id.* at 425.

38. "Buys Denver Republican: John C. Shaffer to Consolidate it with the Times and News," *The New York Times* 1 (Oct. 20, 1913).

39. *Burns v. Republican Pub. Co.*, 128 P. 1122 (Colo. 1913).

40. *Id.* at 1123, *citing Mosman, supra* note 3.

XII

DISORDER
IN THE COURTS

The Long, Strange Flight of George Irving Norman, Jr.

BY FRANK GIBBARD

George Norman's name may be unfamiliar to the general public, but he will live forever in the annals of tax-related legal history. He was indirectly responsible for a key case limiting the power of the Internal Revenue Service (IRS): *G.M. Leasing Co. v. United States.*[1] However, that tax case, as important as it was, was just one small aspect of the larger-than-life story of a man who brought rock-and-roll to Salt Lake City, amassed a fortune estimated at $50 million,[2] was sentenced to federal prison for embezzlement, and remained a fugitive from law enforcement for twenty-three years before his recapture in 1996 made news all over the world.[3]

AN ORANGE PONTIAC LEMANS

On March 13, 1973, Utah attorney Orrin G. Hatch and his client pulled up to the Denver law office of James Morrato.[4] Hatch, the future U.S. Senator from Utah and chairman of the Senate Judiciary Committee, was at that time a high-powered defense attorney. The federal marshals had agreed to give his client, George Irving Norman, Jr., time to take care of some last-minute legal business before Norman began serving a two-year sentence for bank fraud.

Morrato, Norman's Colorado attorney, had loaned Norman the car he and Hatch were sitting in — an orange Pontiac LeMans convertible. The colorful automobile suited Norman well. He was known for his lavish lifestyle, his million-dollar mansion in Salt Lake City, and his Hollywood friends.[5] Some even thought Norman had the good looks of a movie star.

Norman epitomized Utah's burgeoning commercial empire more than he represented the state's austere Mormon origins. Since his arrival in Salt Lake City from Los Angeles, he'd founded a national chain of health clubs and brought rock-and-roll music to the area through one of twenty radio stations he owned in the Rocky Mountain region.

Religion, money, and glamour followed Norman all his life. He was born in 1930 in Chicago to not one but two reverends: Rev. George Irving Norman, Sr. and Rev. Olga Marie Isoz-Norman. He attended Clemson University and the Chicago Conservatory of Music, graduating with a master's degree in 1953. In addition to his considerable entrepreneurial talents, he was later known for composing gospel hymns.

Norman was best known for his phenomenal ability to make money. Rumor had it that he began amassing his considerable fortune by selling bomb shelters at the height of the Cold War nuclear panic. He later engaged in "radio and television broadcasting, real estate development, mortgage banking, oil and gas exploration, broad market investment, marine product development,"[6] and, apparently, fraud.

A TWO-YEAR SENTENCE

Norman's circumstances that March day in 1973 were anything but glamorous. He recently had been convicted in federal court of "aiding and abetting misapplication of moneys of a statutorily defined insured bank,"[7] which netted him the two-year sentence in federal prison. The bank in question was the Rocky Mountain Bank in Lakewood, Colorado. The government charged that Norman had secured borrowers to apply for loans, and then obtained the loan proceeds and used them for his own business ventures.

The story in the November 24, 1996, edition of *The Denver Post*
Courtesy *The Denver Post*/Denver Public Library

Some of the bank's officers and directors had allegedly engaged in similar illegal transactions, and although he was neither an officer nor a director of the bank, Norman was charged with them as an aider and abettor. In an odd twist, the government asserted that some of the conspirators tried to move loans off the bank's books by swapping them for ownership of the Denver Revival Tabernacle, an establishment owned by conspirators Donald and Delmar Cooper.[8] The Tabernacle was grossly overvalued in the transaction, resulting in a large loss to the bank.

The Tenth Circuit upheld Norman's conviction,[9] and the U.S. Supreme Court denied him a writ of *certiorari*.[10] Notwithstanding these prior losses on appeal, Orrin Hatch was surprisingly upbeat on that day in March 1973. That morning, he had asked the sentencing judge to grant Norman a new trial, citing a case on point that he had discovered during an all-night research session. The judge seemed "shaken" by his argument, Hatch would later recall, and he was confident that he could win on appeal.[11]

For now, though, Norman would have to report to prison and begin serving his sentence. Hatch exited the vehicle and went inside Morrato's office to get some paperwork. When he came back outside, Norman and the LeMans were gone.

A 1968 CADILLAC DEVILLE

Soon after he disappeared with the LeMans, Norman phoned an old friend, Colorado Supreme Court Justice Edward Day. He told Day that he was attempting to obtain a stay of his sentence from the U.S. Supreme Court and needed to borrow Day's car to take care of some legal business. He did not, of course, tell the judge that he was a fugitive from justice who had already driven away with another lawyer's car.

They met in person, and Day gave Norman the keys to his 1968 Cadillac DeVille. He stayed up until two in the morning, waiting for Norman to return with the car, but neither Norman nor the car returned. A month later, Day received a note with the keys in the mail. The Cadillac was found in Idaho; however, Norman had vanished — and he would remain missing for the next twenty-three years.

ENTER THE INTERNAL REVENUE SERVICE

In addition to his troubles with the Rocky Mountain Bank, Norman and his wife had experienced certain difficulties with their 1970 federal income tax return.[12] After obtaining four extensions, they filed a 1040 form "on which, apart from their names, address, social security numbers, occupations, and dependents, they indicated only that their tax for that year '[e]stimated,' was $280,000."[13] That was the precise amount they sent in with the return.

The IRS was not terribly thrilled about receiving a tax return containing no information about income or deductions; but at least Norman had paid some taxes for 1970. In 1971, after obtaining numerous filing extensions, he avoided filing a return altogether. Instead, he sent the IRS a check for $405,125, which promptly bounced.

After the Tenth Circuit affirmed his conviction for bank fraud, the IRS assigned Agent Phillip J. Clayton to Norman's tax case. Agent Clayton took a no-nonsense approach to the delinquency. On March 19, 1973, six days after Norman's disappearance, IRS agents sat down with Norman's brokerage statements and calculated that he owed the government nearly $1 million. Because Norman had fled from justice, the IRS issued a jeopardy assessment, which allowed them to begin immediate collection efforts.

On March 20, 1973, revenue agents showed up at Norman's address, demanding payment. Mrs. Norman met them at the door. After they explained the jeopardy assessment to her, she told them to get in touch with her lawyer. The agents then filed notice of tax liens with the Salt Lake County Recorder's Office and levied on one of Norman's bank accounts; however, their best bet to collect the debt was parked in Norman's driveway.

The agents later described the cars parked at the Norman residence as "show" or "collector" cars.[14] How curious, then, that all of them were registered not to Norman, but to a Utah corporation called "G.M. Leasing Corp.," whose principal business activity was described as "leasing Luxury Automobiles, Boats, etc."[15] The agents did not think the automobiles they had seen were the kind of cars typically used in a leasing business. Moreover, G.M. Leasing had some interesting business practices. The report of the Utah Department of Employment Security listed the average number of employees in G.M. Leasing's business at "zero" and noted that the company had paid no wages during its existence.[16]

TWO ROLLS, THREE STUTZES, AND A JAGUAR

After consulting with IRS Regional Counsel, the agents concluded that Norman was using G.M. Leasing to hide his personal assets. They decided to seize the cars titled in the corporate name to help satisfy Norman's tax liability. Acting without a warrant, on March 21, 1973, agents seized a number of these cars — and what fine cars they were! The autos seized included "a 1972 Stutz, a Rolls Royce Phantom V, a 1930 Rolls Royce Phantom I, two 1971 Stutzes, and a Jaguar."[17] The agents courteously left Mrs. Norman a Chevrolet and a station wagon for the family to use.

Continuing their aggressive collection efforts, the IRS agents headed to the offices of G.M. Leasing, with a plan to levy on any property subject to seizure, including the office building itself, if necessary. When they arrived, they found that the premises consisted of a cottage and a garage. By the time a supervisor named Bert Applegate arrived, a locksmith already had removed the lock from the garage door and the lock on the cottage's rear door.

Inside the garage they found another Stutz automobile. When Applegate entered the cottage, however, he noticed that it looked more like a residence than a business. For one thing, there was a kitchen. Applegate halted the seizure and the agents left the cottage without taking anything. They replaced the lock.

Before the agents left the premises, Norman's son, George I. Norman III, age 19, arrived at the cottage. He told them he was living there, "as security," and that the Stutz belonged to the corporation, not to Norman.[18] The agents refrained from seizing the Stutz. Within the next two days, however, several events occurred that caused them to rethink their restraint. First, they received information from one of Norman's contractors that the cottage was a business and not a residence. Second, they noticed there was activity at the cottage at night: the lights were on, boxes were being moved, and the Stutz disappeared from the garage.

The agents had had enough. On March 23, acting without a warrant, they re-entered the cottage, again using a locksmith, but this time bringing along a moving van, into which the cottage's remaining contents were loaded. They later returned the corporate records, but not before photocopying them.

G.M. Leasing subsequently sued the IRS, seeking return of the automobiles; suppression of all information obtained during the search and seizure; and damages from the agents. George Norman III joined in the suit. The plaintiffs won in federal district court in Utah, but the Tenth Circuit mostly reversed this judgment. On *certiorari* review, the

U.S. Supreme Court addressed a narrow issue: whether the warrantless seizures violated the Fourth Amendment.

The Supreme Court ruled that seizure of the cars was not unconstitutional, because it "took place on public streets, parking lots, or other open places, and did not involve any invasion of privacy."[19] The warrantless seizure of books and records from an office/residence, however, was another matter. The IRS did not take the position that business premises are not protected by the Fourth Amendment; clearly, they are. Instead, it argued that when it is enforcing the tax laws, the Fourth Amendment warrant requirement simply does not apply.

The stakes in this case were now huge. If the IRS had unchecked authority to enter any premises at any time to enforce the tax laws, without obtaining a warrant, it would open a gigantic loophole in the Fourth Amendment's protection against unreasonable searches and seizures. The Supreme Court rejected the government's argument. Noting that the Fourth Amendment was enacted against the backdrop of oppressive taxation by British authorities, the Court dismissed any claims of special exemption from the warrant requirement connected with the business of collecting taxes. The Court concluded that "the warrantless entry into [G.M. Leasing's] office was in violation of the Fourth Amendment."[20]

NORMAN'S LIFE ON THE LAM

While these weighty constitutional issues were being debated in the federal courts, George Norman, Jr. apparently was enjoying his life as a fugitive. He evaded capture "by relying on aliases, paying bills in cash and operating out of rented mailboxes and a mobile home."[21] However, his lifestyle was anything but a furtive one, and he did not lead an impoverished sort of existence. He traveled from country club to country club, living it up, surrounded by "tennis courts, swimming pools, card rooms and golf courses."[22] Along the way, he acquired a new wife, thirty years his junior, who apparently knew of his fugitive status and married him anyway. He played tennis; she won club championships in golf. Toward evening, Norman would relax with a drink and sell penny stocks to his fellow club members. He used the names and social security numbers of family members to help him hide from authorities. During his years on the lam, he evidently accumulated the bulk of his large fortune, later estimated at $50 million.

There were some close calls over the years. Once, in 1984, federal marshals learned that he was living with his new wife's family in Tampa, Florida, and paid them a visit. Norman was on his way home when he spotted a police vehicle in front of the house. He made a quick U-turn, and disappeared.

Another time, agents tracked him to San Diego, California, where he had been playing tennis at a country club. Before they could close in, he disappeared again. He and his wife traveled incessantly in their luxury motor home — a $180,000 Monaco Dynasty — regularly crisscrossing the United States.

ENTER MARSHAL MARTIN

In November 1995, Norman's thick police file landed on the desk of Senior U.S. Deputy Marshal Randy Martin. The fugitive case against Norman had not been actively pursued in five years. Norman's story, involving such large sums of money and his disappearance for so many years, intrigued Martin. He began investigating old leads in the case, checking for use of aliases. He found that Norman was constantly on the move and always seemed to stay one step ahead of his pursuers.

When Martin was detailed to the investigation of the Oklahoma City bombing case in October 1996, he took the case file with him and kept looking for Norman. In the spring of 1996, he'd had a break: Social Security employees had noticed some new activity on numbers belonging to Norman's grandparents, who had died years ago. After contacting several marshals in various Southern states, he narrowed his search to Tennessee. Then, he had a brainstorm.

Norman had always stayed in fancy hotels that charged in the neighborhood of $1,200 per night. There was the possibility, though, that if he thought he was being pursued, he might have changed his behavior pattern. Martin tried something new. He began sending agents with Norman's photo to lower-cost motels.

A GREEN LINCOLN CONTINENTAL

In late November 1996, agents cornered Norman in a parking lot of a Comfort Suites hotel in Knoxville, Tennessee. He'd brought his motor home to Knoxville to get it repaired. Behind the motor home, he and his wife had towed "a matching green, late model Lincoln Continental adorned with a disarming bumper sticker: 'Prayer Changes Things.'"[23] Norman surrendered peacefully. He knew it was the end of the road.

The press had a field day while Norman was being transported back to Denver to begin serving his sentence. Norman, who was 66 years old, ended up serving the two-year sentence he should have begun in 1973. He was not charged with auto theft of the LeMans or the Cadillac; nor, apparently, did he serve time for escape.

After his release from prison, George Norman lived a relatively anonymous life until March 18, 2006, when he died at age 75. His story lives on as a colorful tale and in the reaffirmation of Fourth Amendment freedoms on which we all depend.

Original printing: *The Colorado Lawyer*, May 2009. The author is grateful for the research assistance of Dan Cordova and Lynn Christian of the Colorado Supreme Court Law Library.

NOTES

1. *G.M. Leasing Corp. v. United States*, 429 U.S. 338 (1977).

2. Norman's lawyer, John Eldridge, denied that Norman's fortune was anywhere near $50 million. "Aliases Kept Norman One Step Head of Law," *Colorado Springs Gazette* A6 (Nov. 26, 1996).

3. In addition to sources specifically cited in this article, background information concerning the life of George Norman and the events described is

derived from a number of contemporaneous newspaper articles that appeared in *The Denver Post*, the *Colorado Springs Gazette*, the *Rocky Mountain News*, the *Deseret News*, the *Commercial Appeal* (Memphis, Tennessee), and *The New York Times*. Readers interested in specific citations to the articles used may contact the author.

4. Some sources state that these events occurred on March 12, 1973; others give a date of March 23, 1973.

5. *The New York Times* later reported that Norman "played golf with Bob Hope, gambled in Las Vegas with Chuck Connors and played host to the likes of Lucille Ball" at his mansion in Salt Lake City. "Fugitive Financier, on the Lam Since 1973, Has a Court Date Today in Denver," *The New York Times* (Dec. 6, 1996).

6. Obituary: George Irving Norman, Jr., *Deseret News* (March 27, 2006), available at archive.deseretnews.com/archive/1049282/Obituary-George-Irving-Norman-Jr.html.

7. *United States v. Cooper*, 464 F.2d 648, 649-50 (10th Cir. 1972). See 18 U.S.C. § 656 (1948).

8. Denver Revival Tabernacle was founded by charismatic evangelist and healer Kathryn Kuhlman in 1935. *See* www.whiskeyfoxtrot.com/articles/revival/denver/kuhlman.htm. The Tabernacle was housed in a building located at 9th and Acoma streets in Denver.

9. *Cooper, supra* note 7 at 652-57.

10. *Norman v. United States*, 409 U.S. 1107 (1973).

11. "Lawyer Hatch Says Swindler Didn't Listen," *Deseret News* B1 (Dec. 25, 1996).

12. The facts of the tax case are taken from *G.M. Leasing Corp., supra* note 1.

13. *Id.* at 341.

14. *Id.* at 343.

15. *Id.*

16. *Id.*

17. *Id.* at 344.

18. *Id.* at 345.

19. *Id.* at 351.

20. *Id.* at 359.

21. "Fugitive Financier," *supra* note 5.

22. *Id.*

23. *Id.*

Early Colorado Justice and
the Straying Jury

BY FRANK GIBBARD

Common law jurisdictions pay considerable reverence to the concept of trial by jury. This being the case, it is interesting to notice that courts have not always treated jurors with much respect. In earlier centuries, they may have been hurried into reaching a verdict, or punished (by the notorious "Star Chamber," for example) for reaching the "wrong" verdict.[1] Deprived during their deliberations of civilized comforts and even of the necessities of life, it is probable that many jurors experienced jury service more as a trying discomfort than as an uplifting exercise in citizenship.

THE CASE OF WILLIAM PENN

One well-known example of juror mistreatment is the case of William Penn. In late 17th Century London, Penn, a Quaker leader, was arrested for seditious assembly after he preached a sermon unsanctioned by the Church of England. For this "crime," he faced the death penalty. An English judge of the Old Bailey ordered the jurors assigned to his trial confined in a room without food, water, heat, tobacco, or toilet facilities until they reached the "correct" verdict: guilty. Despite increasingly filthy conditions, the jury somehow held out for days. Although it faced tremendous pressure from the presiding judge, the jury refused to convict Penn, and ultimately acquitted him. The furious judge fined the jurors, and when they refused to pay the fine, he sent them to prison for contempt of court. After spending months in jail, they were released when an English appellate court finally issued a writ of *habeas corpus*.[2]

William Penn's case was instrumental in establishing the right of a jury to reach a just and independent verdict.[3] However, the jurors in the Penn case were not treated much worse than other English juries that served after them. In the *Commentaries on the Laws of England*, Sir William Blackstone affirms that jurors were routinely "kept without meat, drink, fire, or candle, unless by permission of the judge, until they were all unanimously agreed."[4] Worse, if the jurors "did not agree in their verdict before the judges [were] about to leave the town . . . the judges [were] not bound to wait for them, but [could] carry them around the circuit from town to town in a cart."[5]

HARSH CONDITIONS CONTINUE FOR JURORS

William Penn later left England to found a colony that became the state of Pennsylvania, part of the new American experiment in tolerance and freedom. However, two centuries later, the treatment of jurors still had not much improved in some American jurisdictions. Jurors often were kept in very uncomfortable conditions, deprived of food, detained behind locked doors, and even required to sleep on the floor.[6] As late as 1891, the Colorado statutes affirmatively prescribed the following rather Spartan environment for jurors during their deliberations in criminal cases:

> When the jury shall retire to consider their verdict in any criminal case, a constable or other officer shall be sworn or affirmed to attend the jury to some private and convenient place, and to the best of his ability keep them together without meat or drink, water excepted, unless by leave of the court, until they shall have agreed upon a verdict[.][7]

Bailiffs were charged with enforcing these restrictions, under penalty of fine or imprisonment, and under oath.[8] However, these rather puritanical prescriptions of Colorado law, as well as their more general duty to help keep jurors sober during trial, sometimes were dishonored by lax or careless bailiffs. Those charged with securing the jury sometimes allowed jurors to eat, drink, and make merry inappropriately during both the trial and their deliberations, as well as to wander off from the assigned jury room.

COLORADO'S STRAYING JURORS

Colorado appellate judges often were asked to decide whether a verdict reached by such dissipated jurors could be upheld. Challenges to verdicts on this basis achieved mixed results, usually based on a judicial determination of how far the jurors had strayed from sobriety. The Colorado cases discussed below arose prior to the close of the 19th Century. They illustrate how the courts handled the problem of jurors who strayed from their duties during trial and deliberations.

Tippling Jurors and a Night at the Theater — Jones v. People (1882)

In this early case, the defendant was tried and convicted for murder after he stabbed his roommate to death following a quarrel over a pair of boots.[9] He raised many issues on appeal, one of which related to "the misconduct of the jury in the use of intoxicating liquors."[10] He presented affidavits to the trial court, stating that during the trial, "the jurors, or some of them, at their own expense, procured and had sent to their room about two quarts of whiskey, of which several of the jurors drank, but no considerable quantity was drunk by any one."[11] Several of the jurors, in fact, had become "accustomed to taking a dram every morning" during the trial.[12] However, the jurors and the bailiffs testified that in spite of this inclination to imbibe, "every juror on the panel was perfectly sober at all times during the trial."[13]

The Colorado Supreme Court, after reviewing Blackstone's *Commentaries* and cases from other American jurisdictions concerning tippling jurors, adopted the rule stated in Francis Wharton's *A Treatise on Criminal Law*:

> The verdict will not be set aside on account of the misconduct or irregularity of a jury, even in a capital case, unless it be such as might affect their impartiality or disqualify them from the proper exercise of their functions.[14]

The Court rejected a *per se* rule that would require invalidating a verdict every time a juror used intoxicating liquor during the proceedings. The key was whether the drinking was so severe as to have affected the verdict. Here, the Court determined, it was not.

The other jury misconduct issue in *Jones* may seem strange to us today, but it actually is a recurrent one in Colorado cases from this period. The defendant complained that in addition to drinking whiskey during his trial,

> on the evening of the day they were impaneled, the entire jury, in charge of a sworn officer of the court, attended a theatrical play at a hall or opera house in Georgetown, where the court was sitting.[15]

There, "they occupied seats specially engaged for them, in a body" and did not interact with the rest of the audience.[16] This was done by consent of the judge, to provide recreation for the jurors. The Court remarked dryly:

> The record is silent as to the literary or moral character of the play, whether tragic, comic or sentimental, but we think it entitled to a presumption favorable, rather than unfavorable, to its quality.[17]

The Colorado Supreme Court was unimpressed by the claim of error. It concluded that although "such a relaxation, as a rule, is not to be countenanced," it could not say "that it was misconduct, or conduct by which the prisoner was in any way prejudiced."[18] Therefore, the verdict would stand.

Prejudicial Misconduct – May v. People (1885)

The defendant was drinking in a saloon in Georgetown at midnight, when a policeman passed by and told the barkeep to close up shop for the night. The barkeep told the defendant he would have to leave. The defendant refused, saying he wouldn't go until he "damned pleased."[19] The barkeep responded by manhandling the defendant out and into the street, where the defendant was either pushed or tripped and fell to the ground. The barkeep then turned and began walking back toward the saloon. The enraged defendant drew a jackknife and stabbed the bartender in the heart, killing him. A jury convicted him of second-degree murder.

An affiant later swore that during the defendant's trial, he saw two of the jurors enter the barroom at a fancy hotel known as the Barton House in Georgetown,[20] where they drank at the bar and bought a bottle of beer. The trial court took testimony from various witnesses, who generally confirmed the story given in the affidavit. Following the rule established in the *Jones* case, however, the Colorado Supreme Court held that the alleged misconduct was not sufficiently serious to have prejudiced the defendant or to require reversal.

Upright, Scrupulous, and Impartial – Repath v. Walker (1889)

Repath was a civil case in which the jury rendered a verdict for the plaintiffs in the amount of $106.95.[21] During the time they were supposed to have been deliberating, the jurors were seen on the streets of Lake City; one of them appeared to be intoxicated. The town marshal of Lake City confirmed this, signing an affidavit stating that the jurors had been permitted to wander the town streets and that one of the jurors had been drunk. To make matters worse, the judge who sat on the case and who heard the defendant's motion for a new trial allegedly had been intoxicated, as well.

The Colorado Supreme Court drew the line at such boozy misconduct. It thundered:

It would be better to submit questions in dispute to the arbitration of chance than to the decision of a tribunal which is not thoroughly upright and scrupulously fair as between litigants[.][22]

It went on to ask, rhetorically:

Can it be said that an upright judge, a scrupulously fair man, one who appreciates the dignity of his office, can impartially determine the interests of litigants, and fairly administer the law, when in a state of intoxication?[23]

Concluding such conduct was "reprehensible" and even "criminal," the Court reversed the jury's verdict "owing to the misconduct of the juror as well as of the judge."[24]

Unsubstantiated Misconduct — Heller v. People (1895)

David Heller was convicted of embezzlement of a promissory note. The Colorado Court of Appeals affirmed his conviction.[25] He appealed to the Colorado Supreme Court, raising no fewer than seventy issues. Addressing issues of juror and bailiff misconduct barely addressed by the court of appeals, the Supreme Court reversed.[26]

The misconduct of both jurors and bailiffs in *Heller* was particularly egregious. An affidavit from one of the jurors, filed in support of the defendant's motion for a new trial, asserted that the bailiffs not only permitted the jury to drink throughout the proceedings, but also had engaged in a campaign of vilifying the defendant and his attorney to the jurors. The affidavit alleged:

[A]fter the jury was sworn and impaneled . . . and on several occasions, bottles of whisky were brought into the jury room, and drank by the jury; and on one occasion every juror partook of said whisky. That on one occasion a juror remarked to the colored bailiff in charge of said jury, "How would it do to send down a pitcher or a jug for whisky?" to which the said bailiff replied: "That is your own business. . . ." That said jury was fed at Mrs. Given's restaurant . . . during their entire service, and frequently, when so at meals, the jurors would separate and go into the bar opening out of the dining room, and drink alcoholic drinks. That on one occasion, . . . Mr. Stone, the bailiff in charge of the jury, remarked: "Gentlemen, don't Taylor make you sick? Just wait until he gets started. He will whine and cry around, and can't present a case. He has no ability as a lawyer. He reads in a monotone. That old fellow Heller has no case." That "he has been tried twice, and found guilty. . . . Just wait, when Ward gets up; he can present a case like an attorney, and you can see through it." . . . That the conduct of the said bailiff Stone and the said colored bailiff became so notorious and offensive in making remarks and statements and interfering with the deliberations of the jury while said case was in progress, in order to prejudice the minds of the jury in such frequency. . . . That said colored bailiff, becoming aware of affiant's intention of reporting said matters and things to the court, interfered, and tried to raise a prejudice between the members of the jury. . . .[27]

The Court described the misconduct of the bailiffs as "a matter that we cannot overlook."[28] The facts surrounding much of the misconduct were essentially unchallenged. Interestingly, however, the juror's affidavit could not be used to substantiate misconduct by other jurors. The Court noted that "it is well settled that such affidavits cannot be received for the purpose of showing misconduct on the part of the jury."[29] Given the conflicting evidence on the underlying charge, the bailiffs' misconduct, improper arguments by the district attorney, and other errors, the jury's verdict could not stand.

Evidence of Prejudice Lacking – Chesnut v. People (1895)

Robert Chesnut was charged with cattle rustling in Larimer County.[30] On appeal, he raised numerous errors, including jury and bailiff misconduct.

He complained that after the evidence was presented and the judge instructed the jury, one of the jurors left the others at dinnertime to go back to the courthouse by himself to "answer the call of nature."[31] The bailiff caught up with that juror, let him go "to the water closet," and then took him back to the jury room, where he locked him in and went back to retrieve the other jurors.[32] Then, the next morning, the bailiff took all the jurors to the post office to get their mail. Three hours later, the jury rendered their verdict, finding Chesnut guilty as charged.

The Colorado Supreme Court affirmed the conviction. Although it found the bailiff's and jury's conduct "an irregularity" and even "reprehensible," the Court found no evidence that the defendant had been prejudiced by it.[33]

Drinking With the Witness – Outcalt v. Johnston (1897)

This was an action on a promissory note executed by the defendant in favor of the plaintiff.[34] The defendant lost, and asserted numerous issues on appeal. Among his claims was that one of the plaintiff's witnesses had invited two of the jurors to go drinking with him at a bar during a recess in the proceedings, and that the jurors had in fact imbibed with the witness. The charge was supported with affidavits from two witnesses. One of the witnesses, however, partially recanted or explained his testimony in a subsequent affidavit. He said he did not actually see the witness buy any liquor for the jurors. As for the witness and the jurors, they affirmatively denied that the alleged incident had occurred at all. The Colorado Court of Appeals found this enough to rebut the charge of misconduct and ruled that the district court did not err in denying the defendant a new trial. The court stated:

> The great weight of the testimony being against the truth of the charge of misconduct, and there being nothing in the record from which the court could infer that the defendant was in the slightest degree prejudiced by the conduct of the jurors.[35]

Judicial Proceeding in Burlesque –
Moore v. People (1899)

The defendant was charged with murder and convicted of voluntary manslaughter after he shot a man following an altercation at a bar.[36] As in Jones, the claim of error involved the bailiffs taking the jury, with the court's permission, to attend a theatrical performance. The Court in Jones presumed the performance harmless in the absence of evidence concerning its content. In this case, however, there was disturbing evidence that the performance might not have been so harmless. The Colorado Supreme Court described the show as follows:

> [T]he entertainment so attended was a burlesque representation of judicial proceedings; . . . among the incidents introduced was one in which it was represented that a prisoner charged with stealing a jug of whisky was brought to the bar for trial, and the judge and court officers became intoxicated by drinking the stolen whisky; that, in short, the performance was a satire upon the judiciary and judicial proceedings.[37]

The Court noted that although "the practice of allowing juries impaneled in important criminal cases to attend public entertainments should not be permitted," in this case, there had been no showing of prejudice.[38] It may have helped that six of the jurors filed affidavits stating that the performance had no influence on their verdict. The Court affirmed the defendant's conviction.

CONCLUSION

In the late 1800s, Colorado law specifically prescribed a strictly cloistered environment for deliberating jurors in criminal cases, and seems to have anticipated that jurors would remain focused on their duties and remain sober throughout all trial proceedings. The reality did not always fit this high-minded prescription. Jurors, with or without court permission, allegedly brought liquor into jury rooms, went out on the town to bars and saloons, drank with witnesses in the case, went to the post office to get their mail, answered the call of nature without leave, and even attended theatrical performances. This sort of misconduct was rarely enough to overturn a verdict in and of itself; however, when coupled with other errors, it might serve to tip the scale in favor of reversal.

Original printing: *The Colorado Lawyer*, January 2010. The author is grateful for the research assistance of Dan Cordova and Lynn Christian of the Colorado Supreme Court Law Library.

NOTES

1. *See* Rembar, *The Law of the Land: The Evolution of Our Legal System* 361 (Simon and Schuster, 1980)

2. Clarkson, *Memoires of the Public and Private Life of William Penn; Who Settled the State of Pennsylvania and Founded the City of Philadelphia* 32-38 (Samuel E. Stevens, 1827). *See also generally* Chapman, "Punishment by the People: Rethinking the Jury's Political Role in Assigning Punitive Damages," 56 *Duke L.J.* 1119, 1124 (2007), available at www.law.duke.edu/journals/dlj/articles/DLJ56P1119.htm.

3. The appellate case that led to acquittal of the jurors and essentially ended the practice of punishing juries in the absence of corruption for reaching a "wrong" verdict is known as *Bushel's Case*, named after one of the incarcerated jurors. *See* Rembar, *supra* note 1 at 361.

4. Blackstone, *Commentaries on the Laws of England in Four Books*, Book III at 375 (Clarendon Press, 1765–69).

5. *Id.*

6. *See generally* King, "Juror Delinquency in Criminal Trials in America, 1796–1996," 94 *Mich. L.Rev.* 2673, 2678-79 (Aug. 1996), available at www.questia.com, type in "Juror Delinquency."

7. Colo. Gen. L. at 323 § 822 (1877). *See also* Mills, Ann. Stat., Ch. 36, § 1469 (1891).

8. Colo. Gen. L. at 323 § 823 (1877).

9. *Jones v. People*, 6 Colo. 452 (Colo. 1882).

10. *Id.* at 459.

11. *Id.* at 460.

12. *Id.* Officially, a dram is equivalent to 1/16 of an ounce, but here the word probably is used in its figurative sense, meaning "a small portion of something to drink." *Webster's New Collegiate Dictionary* 345 (1975).

13. *Jones, supra* note 9 at 460.

14. *Id.* at 462, quoting Wharton, A Treatise on Criminal Law, § 3111. See Torcia, Wharton's Criminal Law (Thomson West, 2009).

15. *Jones, supra* note 9 at 463.

16. *Id.*

17. *Id.* at 464.

18. *Id.*

19. *May v. People*, 6 P. 816 (Colo. 1885).

20. The Barton House was a delightful early Colorado hotel, outfitted for the luxury and comfort of its well-paying guests. A newspaper of the time described the hotel after an 1877 renovation as follows:

> The office has been remodeled, and a check-room for coats and packages, and a wash room, marble-finished, added. A gentlemen's parlor is entered from the office, with an outlook upon Taos and Burrell streets. This is 12 by 16 feet; finished with walnut and curled maple, upholstered with elegant writing desk, walnut-and-leather chairs, Brussels carpet and Venetian blinds. The ladies' parlor, 16 by 24 feet, will be heated by coal grate, is newly papered, and will be furnished with elegant carpet, chairs, sofa, center table, piano, marble mantle and pier-glass. The Billiard Room, 19 by 41 feet, is resplendent with its new paint and elegant bar. The dining room will lose its yellow tinted walls and be clad in cheerful French gray. The laundry will be made larger and prepared to do the entire work in this line for the guests of the house. The lower story of the Hotel has been refloored with hard maple in 2 ½ inch strips. On the second floor three new rooms have been added; a suite of parlor and two rooms prepared for guests with families; all the rooms have been repainted and kalsomined in light and cheerful tints; a bath room with hot and cold water has been added; and two water-closets have been put in for the accommodation of lady guests.

Colorado Miner 3 (May 26, 1877).

21. *Repath v. Walker*, 21 P. 917 (Colo. 1889).

22. *Id.* at 918.

23. *Id.*

24. *Id.*

25. *Heller v. People*, 31 P. 773 (Colo.App. 1892).

26. *Heller v. People*, 43 P. 124 (Colo. 1895).

27. *Id.* at 124.

28. *Id.* at 126.

29. *Id.*

30. *Chesnut v. People*, 42 P. 656 (Colo. 1895).

31. *Id.* at 660.

32. *Id.*

33. *Id.*

34. *Outcalt v. Johnston*, 49 P. 1058 (Colo.App. 1897).

35. *Id.* at 1060.

36. *Moore v. People*, 57 P. 857 (Colo. 1899).

37. *Id.* at 859.

38. *Id.*

Modern-Day Minutemen

The Colorado Bar and Legal Reform in Cold War Colorado

BY TOM I. ROMERO, II

The year 1958 was noteworthy for all of Colorado. Exactly 100 years since American prospectors discovered gold on the banks of the Platte River, the centennial celebration of the "Rush to the Rockies" served to show how modern and progressive the state had become. Most important, the state emerged as an essential player in the worldwide struggle against communism. In 1949, the federal government designated Denver as the alternative capital to Washington, D.C. in the event of a nuclear war. By the 1950s, the state soon housed a high-level nuclear weapons facility, the North American Aerospace Defense Command ("NORAD"), the Air Force Academy, and a plethora of defense-related industries spanning the I-25 corridor. Consequently, Coloradans boasted with pride their position as a symbol of all that was right and good with American-style growth and democracy.

Beneath such Cold War rhetoric, however, social and institutional fissures threatened to undermine the state's ability to live up to its democratic promise. As early as 1946, a committee of the Colorado Bar Association ("CBA") studied the Colorado court system. In the committee report, the CBA noted shortcomings in every level of the state's judicial administration. The report detailed one comic instance where the committee discovered "one senile District Judge, in an automobile personal injury case where the injured plaintiff was alive and in court, gave first degree murder instructions to the jury."[1] In subsequent reports, the CBA gave vivid accounts about significant weaknesses in Colorado's legal regime, including the overwhelming case dockets of many judges, poorly represented defendants, and unequal administration of state and municipal laws. Such judicial problems documented by the Colorado Bar in the 1940s and 1950s exposed widespread threats to the sanctity of due process, equality, and fairness in judicial proceedings in the state. Without reform, the CBA reports suggested that the judicial system would be incapable of safeguarding the liberties of the state's rapidly growing and increasingly urban citizenry.

Despite these findings, Colorado's legal system remained fundamentally unchanged throughout the 1950s and early 1960s. As Colorado Supreme Court Justice and later U.S. District Judge William Doyle declared, it was a "frontier" system ill-suited to the demands of modern society.[2] Not surprisingly, members of the Colorado Bar increasingly made public their grievances with the state's legal system. In an unsigned editorial in the official publication of the Denver Bar, one lawyer made the following challenge:

> Paul Revere—yes, many Paul Reveres—are riding today, warning the countryside that the enemies who seek to destroy the supremacy of law and the rule of the people—have landed. . . . The minute men who should be hearing Paul and putting on the battle dress are the members of the bar—in whose hands . . . have been the task of writing and interpreting laws, of forming government, and of protecting the sacred rights of the people. Are our lawyer minute men of this day hearing the call to arms, putting on their battle garbs and rushing to the defense of democracy, or are they sitting in their law offices collecting five dollar fees while Paul Revere rides by unheeded?[3]

It would take more than a decade after this was written to overcome the inertia and antipathy that existed among Colorado lawyers and jurists for legal reform. By the middle of the 1960s, however, constitu-

Judge William E. Doyle, a
supporter of updating Colorado's
legal system
Greg Hobbs Collection

tional and institutional changes were made with the encouragement of
the Colorado Bar. These included the passage of Amendment 1 in 1962
and Amendment 3 in 1966, which repealed Articles VI and XIV, § 11,
of the Colorado Constitution and replaced them with a completely re-
worked Article VI to the state constitution. In addition to eliminating
the Justice of the Peace system, the amendments restructured the jurisdictional boundaries of Colorado's courts, provided more qualified
judges, and implemented a system of merit selection for judges in the
state. These changes compelled the American Judicature Society to
praise Colorado for leading the nation in progressive and meaningful
judicial reform. Although a long and protracted struggle, Colorado's
judicial "minutemen" fortified institutional weaknesses that threatened
democracy, liberty, and due process in the state's legal regime.

Original printing: *The Colorado Lawyer*, March 2003. The many challenges and problems existing in Colorado's Cold War legal regime are heavily documented in post-World War II issues of *Dicta* and the *Rocky Mountain Law Review*. Noteworthy is Albert C. Jacobs, "The Function of Courts in Maintaining Constitutional Government and Individual Freedom 29 *Dicta* 341 (Sept. 1952). In addition, many of the problems threatening judicial administration in the state are assessed in transcripts of the proceedings of "Judicial Organization for Colorado" (Colorado Bar Association, Dec. 16–17, 1960), located at the University of Colorado Law Library. Finally, the papers of Judge William Doyle, housed in the archives at the Auraria Campus Library, provide compelling evidence of the deep divisions slowing legal reform in the state.

NOTES

1. *See* Van Cise, "The Colorado Judicial System — Can It and Should It Be Improved?" 22 *Rocky Mountain L.Rev.* 142, 145 (Feb 1950).

2. *See* Doyle, "Colorado's Program to Improve Court Administration," 38 *Dicta* 1, 9 (Jan.–Feb. 1961).

3. "Paul Revere Rides Again — Who Hears Him This Time?" 24 *Dicta* (Aug. 1947), at 165.

Rock and Roll's T.R.O.
The Family Dog and Detective Gray

BY JEFFREY P. KELSON

In September 1967, a cultural outpost of hippies, rock and roll, and the San Francisco "Summer of Love"[1] came to Denver. The outpost was a music hall called the Family Dog, located on West Evans Avenue.[2] Hippies, rock and roll, and drug use raised widespread controversy in 1967. The Family Dog quickly faced conflict with the Denver Police because it was owned and operated by San Francisco hippies, it was a popular venue for live rock and roll performances, and it was associated with drug use. By late October 1967, this conflict had ripened into litigation against the Denver Police, including Denver Police Detective John Gray. This is the story behind the Family Dog's temporary restraining order against Detective John Gray, a detective who was said to "strike fear into the very heart[] of every Hippie in Denver."[3]

A NEW VENUE FOR HIPPIE ROCK AND ROLL IN DENVER

In the summer of 1967, Barry Fey,[4] then a nascent concert-promoter in Denver, flew to San Francisco to meet with music promoter Chet Helms.[5] Fey took Helms a tape of a local band called the Eighth Penny Matter.

Helms and his partner, Robert Cohen, owned and operated Family Dog Productions in the Haight-Ashbury district of San Francisco. Family

Dog Productions was a decidedly hippie enterprise that produced concerts at the Avalon Ballroom and the Fillmore Auditorium in San Francisco, published posters for such events, and promoted a variety of other music events.[6] Fey met with Helms, toured the Haight-Ashbury district, and went to a show at the Avalon Ballroom with Helms and Cohen. Fey recalled being "charmed" by the happiness of the music and the Family Dog scene in San Francisco.[7]

Shortly after he returned to Denver, Fey learned that space for a music hall might be available in a building on West Evans Avenue that was co-owned by Denver lawyer Francis Salazar and his wife, Patricia.[8] Fey contacted Helms and Cohen in San Francisco to suggest a Family Dog outlet in Denver.[9] Helms and Cohen responded immediately and enthusiastically.[10]

Tour Stop for Big-Named Bands

The Family Dog opened in Denver on September 8, 1967, in the building owned by Salazar. The opening attractions were two of the biggest San Francisco rock groups of the time, Big Brother & the Holding Company and Blue Cheer, with Denver's own the Eighth Penny Matter as an opening act.[11] By this time, Helms had recruited his friend Janis Joplin to be the lead singer for Big Brother and the Holding Company.

The Family Dog was an immediate sensation in Denver. By the end of 1967, the Family Dog had hosted such renowned bands and performers as Quicksilver Messenger Service, the Grateful Dead, Captain Beefheart, The Doors, Buffalo Springfield, Van Morrison, Canned Heat, Jefferson Airplane, and many others. Each performance included a light show produced by the Diogenes Lantern Works. As described in a newspaper write-up, huge screens on three two-story high walls "were used for magnified moving shots of all shapes and colors. The movements on some screens looked like oil under a microscope."[12]

Lee Brenkman, a sound mixer at the Family Dog, said in a recent telephone interview that the music at the Family Dog typically was "brutally loud, and acoustically (the building) was horrid."[13] Brenkman

The former Family Dog music hall on West Evans Avenue in Denver, now the home of P.T.'s Show Club
Katherine Haas

remembers that the opening-night bands were so loud that a police officer on the scene took two .38 caliber bullets from his belt and put one in each ear for sound protection.[14] Writing for *The Denver Post* about a show headlined by Jefferson Airplane, Virginia Culver reported that the bands were "unbelievably loud" and the "changing lights, constant motion and deafening sounds added up to a headache."[15] However, loud music and light shows were popular with many young people, and the Family Dog's music and light shows drew crowds of willing attendees, most of whom fondly recall the shows they saw at the Family Dog.[16]

HIPPIES, THE DENVER POLICE, AND DETECTIVE GRAY

In 1967, a Denver Police Department publicity sheet described Denver Detective John Gray as "the foremost authority, in Colorado, on the Hippie population in Denver and surrounding counties. . . . His name or his presence, strike fear into the very heart[] of every Hippie in Denver."[17] As Gray tells it, by 1967, the hippie movement had "hit Denver hard." He was keeping his eyes on the hippie movement, because Denver had become a "haven for hippies and runaways."[18] Gray focused heavily on drug use by hippies.[19]

Denver's Curfew Ordinance

From Gray's perspective, the hippie enterprise at the Family Dog raised an additional concern — the young age of many Family Dog patrons. Liquor was not served at the Family Dog, so the venue was open to all ages.[20] Denver had a curfew ordinance that prohibited any child under the age of 18 from being on the streets or in any establishment open to the public between the hours of 10:30 p.m. and 5:00 a.m., except for lawful employment, reasonable necessity, or when accompanied by a parent.[21] The curfew was extended to 11:30 p.m. on Friday and Saturday nights.[22] Gray says he often made sure to go to the Family Dog around closing time to enforce the curfew against juveniles.[23] Gray also said "there was lots of crime and dope at the Family Dog," so it got a great deal of police attention.[24]

Law Enforcement Versus Police Harassment

What Gray saw as proper and objective law enforcement, Family Dog management and patrons saw as unfair police harassment that was driven by Gray's disdain for hippies. "Detective Gray was way over the line," commented Leslie Haseman in a recent telephone interview. Haseman worked as the office manager at the Family Dog from the day it opened until the day it closed.[25] Gray would "slam kids against the wall, ask for their ID, and harass them," Haseman said.[26]

Marc Arno, who operated the Family Dog light shows, says the police would wait outside the Family Dog and confront young people as they approached Arno to enter the club. Police officers would "throw them up against the wall" and say "you look like you're on drugs. Does your mother know where you are?"[27] Arno says the police sometimes would follow young patrons home from the Family Dog and confront them outside their homes.[28]

Several Family Dog employees remember a number of occasions when the Denver Police parked several marked police cars near the Family Dog, with their emergency lights spinning, as showtime approached.[29] This tactic, Haseman said, effectively dissuaded many patrons from going to the Family Dog.[30] Arno recalls that parents sometimes would drop off their kids in front of the Family Dog shortly before showtime. Arno believes the apparent police activity in front of the Family Dog caused some parents to keep their children from attending shows there.[31]

Barry Fey recalled that palpable tension existed between Family Dog management and the Denver Police almost immediately after the club opened.[32] The police didn't like the Family Dog, and many employees of the Family Dog did not like the ubiquitous police. The San Francisco people were coming to Denver "to make their magic" at the Family Dog and they did not want to work with the police.[33]

Brenkman, sound mixer at the Family Dog, said the Denver Police regarded the Family Dog as "San Francisco lunatics" who wanted to transplant their culture to Denver. This transplant of hippie culture was a "clear and present danger" in the minds of the police,[34] and that perceived danger fostered an "us against them" mentality, said Brenkman.[35]

Give and Take

In Leslie Haseman's view, the Family Dog people from San Francisco had an "abrupt and arrogant attitude" toward the police.[36] Fey recalled that Anthony Guillory, the on-site manager of the Family Dog, was particularly arrogant and confrontational with the police.[37] Brenkman's recollection was similar — that Guillory was confrontational with everyone, and that he "didn't like cops."[38] Guillory was not a diplomat like Chet Helms, according to Brenkman.[39]

The police matched this bluster. A 1967 Denver Police publicity sheet, which included an extensive profile of Detective Gray, described hippies as "long-haired, vagrant, anti-social, psychopathic, dangerous drug users, who refer to themselves as a 'hippie sub culture.'"[40] Hippies, the publicity sheet said, "do not believe in any form of productive activity"; they have a "distaste for money and material wealth"; and they are "responsible for hundreds of crimes in the Capitol area of Denver."[41] Gray expressed a hope that Denver's hippies would return to "the HIPPIE CAPITOL of USA — The Haight-Ashbury' area of San Francisco, California."[42] Of course, the Haight-Ashbury district was home to the owners of the Family Dog.

LITIGATION IN THE MAKING

After The Doors played the Family Dog on September 30, 1967, Fey says he had "a bad feeling" about the rising tension between the Denver Police and the Family Dog.[43] Buffalo Springfield and the Eighth Penny Matter played at the Family Dog the next weekend, and Fey's bad feeling became a reality. On Saturday night, October 7, 1967, the Denver Police conducted what Barry Fey calls a "raid" on the Family Dog.[44] The police cordoned off the parking lot and searched Family Dog patrons.[45] Denver police, Fey says, intimidated young people who were there to see the show. On this and many other occasions, they even went into the bathrooms of the Family Dog to confront patrons.[46]

After the October 7 show, the Family Dog adopted a policy of having an employee follow any police officer who entered the club.[47] Some at the Family Dog thought this strategy was effective because it unnerved the police a bit.[48] Detective Gray recalled that sometimes the house lights would be turned on when he entered the Family Dog, and someone would announce to the crowd: "Detective Gray is here!" Gray also remembered sometimes being followed by Family Dog employees when he was in the club.[49]

According to Barry Fey, by mid-October 1967, attorney Francis Salazar had become "incensed" with what he considered police harassment of the Family Dog.[50] Salazar decided to seek a restraining order against the police.

FAMILY DOG PRODUCTIONS
VERSUS DETECTIVE JOHN GRAY

On October 20, 1967, Francis Salazar filed a complaint in Denver District Court on behalf of Family Dog management, naming Anthony Guillory, Chester Helms, Robert Cohen, and Family Dog Enterprises as plaintiffs.[51] The Family Dog named the City and County of Denver, the Denver Chief of Police, and the Denver Manager of Safety as defendants; however, Detective Gray was the key defendant.

Plaintiffs' Allegations

The plaintiffs alleged that Detective Gray had stated publicly "that he will run the hippies out of town." They claimed that Gray used his police authority to carry out his "vendetta and threat that he will run the 'hippies' out of town."[52] The plaintiffs also alleged that:

a large percentage or portion of the patrons and customers of the FAMILY DOG belong to an unorganized social class, which is not accurately definable, but which has been commonly called "hippies." Being a "hippie" or a member of the group or class of persons known as "hippies" is not illegal or unlawful.[53]

The plaintiffs alleged that on October 7, 1967, during the Buffalo Springfield show, Gray entered the Family Dog uninvited and, without any legal justification or excuse, proceeded to accost patrons and customers on the premises for the purpose of intimidating them into leaving the premises and withdrawing their business and patronage from the plaintiffs.[54]

According to the complaint, Gray told Family Dog manager Anthony Guillory that "the patrons do not belong in this establishment, and [ ] the least number of places of this sort that are in operation, the more the kids would stay home."[55]

The complaint also included a description of Gray's alleged actions the following weekend, on October 14, 1967, when Van Morrison and the Daily Flash were playing at the Family Dog. The plaintiffs alleged that Gray "again proceeded to harass, intimidate, and accost the patrons and customers [in the Family Dog] and, said defendant did, in fact, arrest several patrons who were proceeding home," for violating the Denver curfew ordinance.[56] These arrests, the plaintiffs claimed, "were for the single and only purpose of causing persons to avoid frequenting the business premises commonly known as the FAMILY DOG."[57]

Selective Enforcement: The complaint stated that the Denver curfew ordinance "has never been enforced and is impossible, as a practical matter, to enforce." The attempt to enforce the ordinance "only against the FAMILY DOG and its patrons" denied the plaintiffs equal protection of the law.[58] The alleged purpose of Gray's selective enforcement was to cause Family Dog patrons to "boycott and avoid doing business with the Plaintiffs, and thereby . . . to cause said business to fail," which amounted to a deprivation of property without due process of law.[59] The Family Dog plaintiffs claimed that the Denver curfew ordinance was unconstitutional because it denied the plaintiffs due process of law and equal protection of the law.[60]

ROCK AND ROLL'S T.R.O.

The Family Dog sought a restraining order prohibiting the entire Denver Police Department from entering or visiting the Family Dog "without good cause," and from entering the Family Dog "for the purpose of intimidating and harassing the patrons and customers" of the Family Dog, or for the purpose of enforcing the Denver curfew ordinance.[61] The complaint did not include a claim for damages. Judge John Brooks of the Denver District Court held a hearing on the Family Dog's request for a temporary restraining order (T.R.O.) on the same day the complaint was filed, Friday, October 20, 1967. The newspaper report stated:

> Earring wearing Anthony Guillory, cabaret manager, Friday testified Gray is harassing Family Dog patrons. . . . Guillory and long-haired Chester Helms, co-owner of the establishment, said Gray makes a habit of searching teenagers frequenting the cabaret for narcotics.[62]

Before the close of business, Judge Brooks signed a T.R.O. against Detective Gray.[63] In the key orders paragraph of the proposed order, Judge Brooks crossed out the name of every defendant, except that of Detective Gray.[64] Judge Brooks's T.R.O. prohibited Gray from "entering upon or visiting" the Family Dog "until further order of this Court."[65]

Hippies Pack Hearing

Typically, a T.R.O. becomes more than temporary when it ripens into a preliminary injunction.[66] A hearing on the Family Dog's motion for a preliminary injunction began on November 3, 1967, in Courtroom 7 of the Denver City and County Building.[67] "More than 100 hippies — wearing bells, beards and beads — packed the courtroom of Dist. Judge John Brooks Friday for a hearing" on the question of whether Detective Gray would be allowed to re-enter the Family Dog.[68] Many years later, Judge Brooks recalled telling his bailiff, Sylvester Byers, to open the windows in the courtroom for the Family Dog hearing. This was necessary, Judge Brooks said, because the large crowd of Family Dog patrons in the courtroom carried a strong body odor.[69] Brooks also ordered Byers to "bar blue-jean clad girls" from the courtroom.[70] Byers said this was troublesome because "I don't know the girls from the fellows."[71]

Arguments at the Hearing

At the hearing, lawyer Francis Salazar repeated the claim that Gray was behind a "concentrated effort" by police to "'run out of town people they consider hippies' and to put the Family Dog out of business."[72] Salazar argued that Gray was "guilty of unequal treatment in his attempt to 'set himself up as a tin god to destroy hippies.'"[73]

Representing Detective Gray, Assistant City Attorney James Snyder argued that the plaintiffs were attempting to make the Family Dog "a sanctuary for curfew violators" by keeping the police away from the Family Dog.[74] Snyder argued also that Judge Brooks did not have the authority to enjoin a police officer from enforcing the law.[75]

CASE DISMISSED

On Tuesday, November 7, 1967, Judge Brooks lifted the temporary restraining order against Gray and dismissed the Family Dog's case. "Judge Brooks ruled that an injunction against a police officer enforcing the law is improper, even though the constitutionality of the law is being challenged."[76] Judge Brooks told Salazar that the constitutionality of the curfew ordinance "is a question that should be resolved, but that an inappropriate method for challenging it had been chosen."[77] Judge Brooks also ruled that "Salazar's contention that Gray's presence in the

Family Dog was ruining his client's business was not one that could be decided by a court of equity."[78] Judge Brooks said, "Salazar should have asked for damages along with the injunction. Had damages been sought . . . the injunction then might properly have been issued."[79]

After Judge Brooks dismissed the Family Dog's case in state court, two civil cases concerning the alleged police harassment of the Family Dog and its patrons were filed in the U.S. District Court for the District of Colorado (*see* accompanying article, "The Family Dog in Federal Court," on page 460). Neither case led to a ruling in favor of the Family Dog or its patrons.

WHITHER THE FAMILY DOG?

Promoter Barry Fey recalls celebrating when Judge Brooks issued the restraining order against Detective Gray, but Fey later concluded that this victory really was a defeat for the Family Dog. With the publicity surrounding the restraining order, and the other write-ups in the press about the Family Dog's problems with the police, Fey thinks parents began to say "if cops can't go there, my kids ain't going there."[80] This perception, Fey says, was the beginning of the end of the Denver Family Dog.[81] The spread of this perception, Lee Brenkman says, coincided with a drop in attendance at many Family Dog shows.[82]

Further, the restraining order against Detective Gray did not stop him from causing bad press for the Family Dog. On October 21, 1967, one day after the restraining order was issued, Gray and other detectives arrested on marijuana charges all five members of the band Canned Heat at their motel, just prior to their scheduled Saturday night performance at the Family Dog.[83] Both Denver newspapers ran articles about the arrest, including large photos of the members of Canned Heat standing in court with their lawyer, Francis Salazar.[84]

"[E]ffectively, the Family Dog was dead" by the end of 1967, Fey said.[85] Three shows were booked in January 1968, and two more in February. Chet Helms, Robert Cohen, and their Family Dog Productions withdrew as the financiers and operators of the Denver Family Dog in mid-February 1968.[86] The last show at the Denver Family Dog, under the auspices of Family Dog Productions, was a private show by American Standard, featuring guitarist Tommy Bolin, which included a late-night guest appearance by Jimi Hendrix.[87] Barry Fey then operated the club as "The Dog" until June 1968.[88] The last show at The Dog, like the first show at the Family Dog, included Big Brother and the Holding Company, with Janis Joplin.[89]

Of course, the music didn't die with the Family Dog. Barry Fey quickly achieved national prominence as a promoter of rock concerts, routinely booking shows much larger than anything the Family Dog could have handled.

Leslie Haseman worked at the Family Dog from its beginning to its end and worked with Barry Fey for many years after the Family Dog closed. In Haseman's estimation, Barry Fey maintained an effective working relationship with the Denver Police throughout his post-Family Dog career, and Fey's ability to maintain this relationship was one of the keys to his long-term success.[90] During her interview, Haseman recalled being surprised to see police officers she remembered from the Family Dog working, off-duty, as part of the security team for the Rolling Stones when Fey brought that band to Denver in 1973.[91] Detective Gray was not one of those officers, but it was clear that something significant had changed in the relationship between live rock and roll and the Denver Police.

Original printing: *The Colorado Lawyer*, May 2007. The author thanks attorney Robert L. Pitler and Hon. Larry Bohning, Denver County Court Judge, for their assistance in contacting the key players in the Family Dog saga.

NOTES

1. *See* http://en.wikipedia.org/wiki/Summer_of_love:

> The Summer of Love refers to the summer of 1967, and particularly to the Haight-Ashbury district of San Francisco, [California,] where thousands of young people from all over the world loosely and freely united for a new social experience. As a result, the hippie counterculture movement came into public awareness.

2. The building that housed the Denver Family Dog still stands at 1601 W. Evans Ave. For many years it has been home to PTs Show Club.

3. Complaint, Exhibit A, *Guillory v. City & County of Denver*, No. C02809 (D.Colo. filed Oct. 20, 1967).

4. Barry Fey later dominated concert promotion in Denver, operating Feyline Productions and Fey Concerts.

5. Interview with Barry Fey, concert promoter, in Greenwood Village, Colorado (Feb. 14, 2007).

6. Information available online at http://en.wikipedia.org/wiki/Chet_Helms.

7. Telephone interview with Barry Fey, concert promoter, in Greenwood Village, Colorado (March 3, 2007).

8. Fey, *supra* note 5. Newspaper reports indicate that Francis Salazar's wife, Patricia, owned the building. Browne, "'Family Dog' Off Limits to Anti-Hippie Detective," *Rocky Mountain News* (Oct. 21, 1967) at 24; Browne, "Hippies Pack Court as Hearing Continues," *Rocky Mountain News* (Nov. 4, 1967) at 8.

9. Fey, *supra* note 5.

10. *Id.*

11. Hanna, "Our Nightlife," *Rocky Mountain News* (Sept. 8, 1967) at 80.

12. Culver, "Big Night at Family Dog Not Quite Out of This World," *The Denver Post* (Nov. 10, 1967) at D41.

13. Telephone interview with Lee Brenkman, former sound mixer, the Denver Family Dog, in San Francisco, California (Feb. 23, 2007).

14. *Id.*

15. Hanna, *supra* note 11.

16. *Id.*; telephone interview with Norm Ruggles, Family Dog patron, in Denver, Colorado (Feb. 15, 2007) ("The Doors were loud, but not that loud."); telephone interview with Judy Perry, Family Dog patron, in Denver, Colorado (Feb. 27, 2007).

17. *Guillory, supra* note 3.

18. Telephone interview with John Gray, retired Denver Police Detective, in Kerrville, Texas (Feb. 26, 2007). John Gray was a Denver Police Officer for thirty-eight years, beginning in 1961.

19. *Guillory, supra* note 3.

20. Hanna, *supra* note 11.

21. Sec. 813.1, RMC, Denver, Colorado (Ord. 191, Series 1964).

22. *Id.*

23. Gray, *supra* note 18.

24. *Id.*

25. Telephone interview with Leslie Haseman, Family Dog employee, in Denver, Colorado (Feb. 19, 2007).

26. *Id.*

27. Telephone interview with Marc Arno, Family Dog lighting technician, in Marietta, Georgia (Feb. 19, 2007). In a telephone conversation on March 27, 2007, Arno said that the police officers who confronted patrons typically were plain-clothed officers, although uniformed officers often were present outside the Family Dog. Leslie Haseman also recalled that the officers who confronted patrons typically were plain-clothed officers, and that uniformed officers often were present at the Family Dog (including off-duty officers working security at the establishment). Telephone conversation with Leslie Haseman, Family Dog employee, in Denver, Colorado (March 26, 2007).

28. *Id.*

29. Haseman, *supra* note 25; Arno, *supra* note 27; Fey, *supra* note 5; Brenkman, *supra* note 13. Detective Gray said he did not recall any such incidents, Gray, *supra* note 18.

30. Haseman, *supra* note 25.

31. Arno, *supra* note 27.

32. Fey, *supra* note 5.

33. *Id.*

34. Brenkman, *supra* note 13.

35. *Id.*

36. Haseman, *supra* note 25.

37. Fey, *supra* note 5.

38. Brenkman, *supra* note 13.

39. *Id.*

40. *Guillory, supra* note 3.

41. *Id.*

42. *Id.* (capitalization in original).

43. Fey, *supra* note 5.

44. *Id.*; *Guillory, supra* note 3.

45. Fey, *supra* note 5.

46. "Backstage With Barry Fey," KRFX-FM radio broadcast (April 5, 1998).

47. Interview with Robert L. Pitler, Esq., an associate of Francis Salazar from 1966 to 1968, in Denver, Colorado (Nov. 29, 2006); Fey, *supra* note 5; Haseman, *supra* note 25.

48. Pitler, *supra* note 47.

49. Gray, *supra* note 18.

50. Fey, *supra* note 5.

51. *Guillory, supra* note 3.

52. *Id.* at 2.

53. *Id.* (capitalization in original).

54. *Id.* at 3.

55. *Id.*

56. *Id.* at 4.

57. *Id.* (capitalization in original).

58. *Id.* at 5 (capitalization in original).

59. *Id.*; Gray, *supra* note 18 (Detective Gray said he enforced the curfew ordinance at places other than the Family Dog).

60. *Guillory, supra* note 3 at 5.

61. *Id.* at 7.

62. Browne, *supra* note 8 at 24.

63. Temporary Restraining Order, *Guillory v. Denver* (D.Colo., filed Oct. 20, 1967).

64. *Id.* at 3.

65. *Id.* at 3-4.

66. C.R.C.P. 65.

67. Pitler, *supra* note 47.

68. Browne, "Hippies Pack Court as Hearing Continues," *Rocky Mountain News* (Nov. 4, 1967) at 8.

69. Interview with Hon. Larry Bohning, Denver County Court Judge, in Denver (Feb. 8, 2007) (reporting conversation between Dist. Ct. Judge John Brooks and Judge Bohning, which took place sometime in the 1980s).

70. Browne, *supra* note 68.

71. *Id.*

72. *Id.*

73. "Family Dog Battle in 2nd Day at Court," *The Denver Post* (Nov. 6, 1967) at A2.

74. *Id.*

75. Kokish, "Ban Removed At Family Dog," *The Denver Post* (Nov. 7, 1967) at A2.

76. *Id.* (The court file in *Guillory, supra* note 63, does not contain a written order lifting the temporary restraining order and dismissing the case.)

77. Kokish, *supra* note 75.

78. *Id.*

79. *Id.*

80. "Backstage With Barry Fey," KRFX-FM radio broadcast (April 12, 1998).

81. Fey, *supra* note 5; "Backstage With Barry Fey," *supra* note 80. Others say there were additional factors that contributed to the Family Dog's demise: interview with Salazar, Family Dog attorney, in Englewood, Colorado (Jan. 15, 2007) ("Bands became expensive and went elsewhere."); Brenkman, *supra* note 13 ("Chet Helms was a great promoter, but not talented at business."); Pitler, *supra* note 47 ("Police had an effect, but shows also became repetitious."); Arno, *supra* note 27 ("Helms's IOUs and booking decisions").

82. Brenkman, *supra* note 13.

83. "5 in Band Deny Marijuana Charge," *The Denver Post* (Oct. 25, 1967) at E60. The marijuana possession and conspiracy charges against the members of Canned Heat later were dismissed because the District Attorney did not endorse any witnesses for their preliminary hearing. Pitler, *supra* note 47. The Canned Heat song "My Crime" chronicles their arrest in Denver. "Backstage With Barry Fey," *supra* note 80.

84. "5 in Band Deny Marijuana Charge," *supra* note 83; "Plea of Innocent Entered by Band," *Rocky Mountain News* (Oct. 25, 1967) at 97.

85. "Backstage With Barry Fey," *supra* note 80.

86. Fey, *supra* note 5.

87. Leslie Haseman says this show was not open to the public, but was a private event for those connected with the Denver Family Dog. Haseman, *supra* note 25.

88. Fey, *supra* note 5. The 1968 shows at the Family Dog and "The Dog" included Leopold Fuchs, The Fugs, Blue Cheer, The Siegal Schwall Blues Band, Climax, Cream, Canned Heat, Frank Zappa and the Mothers of Invention, The Byrds and, finally, Big Brother and the Holding Company, with Janis Joplin.

89. Fey, *supra* note 5.

90. Haseman, *supra* note 25.

91. *Id.*

THE FAMILY DOG IN FEDERAL COURT

On November 15, 1967, Family Dog management filed a case in the U.S. District Court in Denver, naming Detective Gray and other Denver Police officers as defendants.[1] This complaint contained several colorful descriptions of how Gray and the other Denver Police defendants allegedly required Family Dog patrons to "place their hands above their heads or against the wall" to be searched without cause, and how the policy allegedly parked as many as five "marked police cars, some with red lights flashing, immediately in front of" the Family Dog "for the sole purpose of intimidating prospective customers. . . ."[2] According to the complaint, Gray told Family Dog customers "you go home or I'm going to arrest you, this is not a place for you to be."[3]

In January 1969, almost a year after Helms and Cohen had withdrawn as the financiers and operators of the Denver Family Dog, attorneys Francis Salazar and Robert Pitler moved to withdraw as the plaintiffs' lawyers in the Family Dog's federal case. Salazar and Pitler reported that they were unable to contact their clients, Helms, Cohen, and Guillory.[4] The motion to withdraw was denied, and the case was called for trial on April 21, 1969. The plaintiffs were not present, and Judge William E. Doyle ordered that the case "shall be dismissed upon motion" if the plaintiffs did not seek to reset the trial within six months.[5] The court's file bears no indication of any further activity in this case.[6]

On November 28, 1967, Brian Kreizenbeck filed a complaint in the U.S. District Court in Denver, naming Denver Police officers John Gray and Charles J. Kennedy as defendants. Kreizenbeck alleged that Kennedy and Gray had arrested Kreizenbeck while he was at the Family Dog on November 18, 1967.[7] Kreizenbeck alleged that said arrest was without probable cause and done for the sole and only purpose of harassing (*sic*) and intimidating this Plaintiff because of his so-called association with the class of persons called "hippies."[8]

Kreizenbeck claimed the defendants had deprived him of equal protection of the law and his right to "equal privileges and immunities under the laws. . . ."[9]

Kreizenbeck's case was tried to a jury, beginning on July 31, 1968, with Chief Judge Alfred A. Arraj presiding. Robert L. Pitler, Francis Salazar's associate, represented Kreizenbeck at trial, and Daniel S. Hoffman represented Gray and Kennedy. The jury returned a verdict for the defendants on August 1, 1968.[10]

Notes

1. Complaint, *Guillory v. Gray*, No. 67-C-546 (D.Colo. filed Nov. 15, 1967).

2. *Id.* at 7-8.

3. *Id.* at 7.

4. Motion to Withdraw, *Guillory v. Gray*, No. 67-C-546 (D.Colo. filed Jan. 24, 1969).

5. Order, *Guillory v. Gray*, No. 67-C-546 (D.Colo. filed April 25, 1969).

6. *Id.*

7. *Kreizenbeck v. Gray*, No. 67-C-573 (D.Colo. filed Nov. 28, 1967).

8. Amended Complaint at 2, *Kreizenbeck v. Gray*, No. 67-C-573 (D.Colo. filed April 11, 1968).

9. *Id.* at 5.

10. Verdict, *Kreizenbeck v. Gray*, No. 67-C-573 (D.Colo. filed Aug. 1, 1968).